THE GENIUS OF WEDGWOOD

The GENIUS of WEDGWOOD

Edited by Hilary Young

The Genius of Wedgwood is supported by Wedgwood
who wish to thank Fitzwilton PLC and Cazenove & Co for
their generous contributions.

VICTORIA & ALBERT MUSEUM

All ceramics in the exhibition are attributed to Josiah Wedgwood or the Wedgwood & Bentley partnership unless stated otherwise

Height of exhibits is given before width

Wherever possible quotations taken from 18th-century documents follow the orthography and spelling of the original. Unless indicated otherwise all quotations from Wedgwood manuscripts are taken from those owned by the Trustees of the Wedgwood Museum and on deposit at the University of Keele, or preserved at the Wedgwood Museum, Barlaston. In accordance with current practice the modern shortened spelling Basalt has been used in place of Basaltes, the form used by Wedgwood himself, except where this occurs in quotations.

Abbreviations
b.   born
d.   died
LHP Leith Hill Place Collection
Lit   literature (works cited in Bibliography)
MS   manuscript
MSS manuscripts
Ref   manuscript references

First published in 1995 by the Victoria and Albert Museum, London

The Victoria and Albert Museum,
South Kensington,
London SW7 2RL

ISBN: 1 85177 159 X

A catalogue record for this book is available from the British Library

Designed by Bernard Higton
Typeset by Nene Phototypesetters Ltd
Printed and bound in England by Butler and Tanner

CONTENTS

Lenders to the Exhibition

We are grateful to the following institutions, trustees and individuals
who have generously lent objects to the Exhibition:

State Hermitage Museum, St Petersburg

Trustees of the British Library
Trustees of the British Museum
His Grace the Duke of Buccleuch
E. L. Buckman
London Borough of Camden (Local Studies & Archives Centre)
Christie, Manson & Woods Ltd.
William Drummond
Peter J. Greenhalgh
Guildhall Library, City of London
Harris Museum and Art Gallery, Preston
Holburne Museum and Craft Centre, Bath
Manchester City Art Galleries
Manchester Public Libraries (Local Studies Unit)
Trustees of the National Museums and Galleries on Merseyside
His Grace the Duke of Northumberland
Nottingham City Museums
Robin Reilly
Royal Academy of Arts
Russell-Cotes Art Gallery and Museum, Bournemouth
Shugborough Park, National Trust and Staffordshire County Council
The Society of Antiquaries of London
R. M. Stevenson
Stoke-on-Trent City Museum and Art Gallery
University of Manchester (The Tabley House Collection)
Trustees of the Victoria and Albert Museum
Sir Martin Wedgwood, Bt.
Trustees of the Wedgwood Museum, Barlaston
Trustees of the William Salt Library, Stafford

FOREWORD

The Victoria and Albert Museum was founded as a direct consequence of Prince Albert's Royal Commission for the Exhibition of 1851, one of whose principal objectives was 'to extend the influence of Science and Art upon Productive Industry'. So it is no coincidence that the Museum's small original collections of more than a hundred years ago included Wedgwood pottery.

In founding the industrial dynasty that bears his name, Josiah Wedgwood harnessed the burgeoning scientific knowledge of his age (including the results of his own experiments) to the acute perception of the role design and art could play in commercial manufacturing. On the bicentenary of his death, *The Genius of Wedgwood* pays tribute to the brilliance of his pioneering and enduring achievement.

Financed principally by Wedgwood, the exhibition results from an alliance between the V&A and the Wedgwood Museum at Barlaston, and from an indispensable collaboration with the State Hermitage Museum, St Petersburg, to whose Director Dr Mikhail Piotrovskii we extend our gratitude.

Elizabeth Esteve-Coll
Director, Victoria and Albert Museum

A. J. F. O'Reilly
Chairman, Waterford Wedgwood plc

ACKNOWLEDGEMENTS

Our aim in putting together the first six sections of this exhibition has been to celebrate some of the most significant technical, aesthetic and entrepreneurial achievements of Josiah Wedgwood, and to present something of the world in which he moved and the context in which these achievements were realized. The seventh and final section of the exhibition is devoted to the Frog Service. Made for Catherine the Great in 1773–74, and celebrated at that time, this Service is today virtually unknown in the west; yet it was perhaps Wedgwood's most important commission and – in view of the scope, ambition and quality of its landscape decoration – was certainly among his greatest achievements.

Our warm thanks are extended to Lydia Liackhova, Curator of West European Porcelain at the State Hermitage Museum – not only for her essay on the history of the Frog Service in Russia, but also for her assistance in St Petersburg, and for her generosity in making available her cataloguing. We owe an enormous debt of gratitude to Michael Raeburn, Guest Curator of the Frog Service displays, for taking on the gargantuan task of selecting and cataloguing these loans, and for sharing with us his researches into this extraordinary commission. Malcolm Baker selected and catalogued the exhibits in the section entitled 'Business & amusement hand in hand', and the remaining entries were prepared by ourselves with assistance from Wedgwood Museum's Information Officer, Lynn Miller. Robin Reilly contributed a biographical profile of Josiah Wedgwood, and made valuable comments on the content and shape of the exhibition at an early stage.

The photographs of the Frog Service were taken in St Petersburg by Vladimir Terebenin and Leonard Kheifets, working with Ken Jackson of the V&A Museum; and photographs of both V&A Museum and Wedgwood Museum items were specially taken for the catalogue by Christine Smith, Philip Spruyt de Bay, James Stevenson and Ian Thomas of the V&A's photographic studio.

The exhibition was created under the guidance and direction of John Hambley, and was designed by Paul May of M&M Design with lighting by Mark Sutton-Vane. The administrative arrangements were carried out by Linda Lloyd Jones, Head of Exhibitions at the V&A, assisted by Juliette Foy – who supervised the installation of the exhibits – and Susanne Bretherton.

We would like to extend our thanks to the following curators and scholars who made their collections or researches available to us, or who eased the path with securing and cataloguing loans: David Alexander, Marjorie Carnie, Peter Cannon-Brookes, Martin Chaplin, Catherine Coldcutt, James Collett-White, Aileen Dawson, William Drummond, Ann Eatwell, Madeline Edmead, David Ekserdjian, Julia Elton, Robin Emmerson, Heather Farrar, Dr Ian Fraser, Edward S. Harwood, Miranda Hunter, Sharon Gater, Charlotte Grant, Richard Gray, Paul Greenhalgh, Antony Griffiths, Kate Hannah, John Harris, Ralph Hyde, Alison Kelly, Pat Latham, the Lady Lucas of Dingwall, Marilyn McCully, Elizabeth Miller, Edward Morris, Kathy Niblett, Andrew Nurnberg, Bernard Nurse, Vicky Oakley, Margaret Rose, Nicholas Savage, Colin Shrimpton, Janet Skidmore, John Styles, David Taylor, Julie Taylor, Marjorie Trusted, Mme Nina Vernova, L. N. Voronikhina, Oliver Watson, Sir Martin and Lady Wedgwood, Sir David Wilson, Pamela Wood, and Martin Phillips, Special Collections, Keele University. Especial thanks are extended to the Trustees of the Wedgwood Museum, and its chairman Sir Arthur Bryan, for agreeing to lend a significant part of the collection housed at Wedgwood, Barlaston.

A deep debt of gratitude is owed to Dr Mikhail Piotrovskii, Director of the State Hermitage Museum, St Petersburg, without whose cooperation this exhibition would not have been possible.

The occasion of the bicentenary of the death of Josiah Wedgwood gave inspiration to the exhibition, but it would not have come to fruition had it not been for the generous support of its sponsors.

Hilary Young,
Research Department, Victoria and Albert Museum
Gaye Blake Roberts,
Curator, The Wedgwood Museum, Barlaston

INTRODUCTION

From the Potteries to St Petersburg: Wedgwood and the Making and Selling of Ceramics

The remarkable success of Josiah Wedgwood as a potter and entrepreneur can be attributed to a unique combination of personal qualities. First, he had a rare grasp of the chemistry and physics of the potter's craft, and this, coupled with his passion for experiment, led him to improve or invent a number of ceramic bodies and glazes, most notably Jasper, Black Basalt and Queen's Ware. Secondly, he was sensitive to the shifts in fashions and taste taking place in his time – particularly during the 1760s and 1770s – and he responded by introducing new designs and materials, the excellence of which put him beyond the reach of his competitors. Finally, he possessed exceptional entrepreneurial skills and had the vision and daring to promote his wares in a bold and, at times, innovative manner. A self-taught man and polymath of colossal energy and ambition, Josiah Wedgwood has been claimed equally as a champion of Neo-classical taste and as pioneer potter, industrialist and marketeer.

Arguably, a man of Wedgwood's talents would have succeeded in whichever era he was born, but it is certainly true that he was very fortunate in entering the Staffordshire pottery business in the 1740s. During the four decades spanning the years 1720 to 1760 the pottery trade there underwent rapid growth and complete transformation; and the materials and processes that had been developed over the years were fully established and ripe for exploitation and perfection. Staffordshire ceramics made before about 1720 were predominantly coarse,

manufactured by small-scale pot-works and aimed at local and country markets. By about 1760 the picture had entirely changed: there was twice the number of people engaged in the trade, which had grown in complexity, with much specialization and division of labour. The wares were finely potted and were increasingly aimed at new markets of consumers, to which the Potteries were connected by a recently developed network of trade links and communications.

Access to raw materials, especially fuel and clay, were the main determinants for the siting of pot-works during the 17th century. The area of North Staffordshire known today as the Potteries is situated above coal measures, and local clays are abundant but predominantly coarse, firing to a range of reddish-browns and yellows. During the first half of the 18th century Staffordshire potters increasingly used white-firing clays imported from the south-west of England in preference to local clays. When these were mixed with ground flints the result was a white-bodied ceramic material, one that could be potted very thinly, fired at high temperatures and glazed with salt thrown into the kiln. The resultant material, known today as salt-glazed stoneware, was one of the principal products of the Staffordshire Potteries during the years of Wedgwood's apprenticeship. The same combination of ground flint and white-firing clays formed the basis of the recipe for the low-fired material known as cream-coloured earthenware, or creamware, which had been developed by 1743 (Cat. A9), but not perfected until the 1760s. At the same time a number of techniques for reproducing shapes and ornament entered into widespread use. These included slip-casting and press-moulding as a means of repeating pottery shapes and lathe-turning, 'sprigging' and stamping as a means of finishing and ornamenting them (Cat. A4–7). In addition, towards the middle of the century, new clear and coloured glazes were introduced; and by 1752 transfer-printing had been invented, making it possible to print pottery with engraved decoration in the latest styles at very low cost (Cat. A8).

Thus by the middle of the century considerable refinements had been made in both the materials used and the techniques for working and ornamenting them. No doubt the high regard that porcelain was accorded, and the profits to be made from a product that could compete with it in whiteness of body and quality of finish, were the spur to many of these improvements. Refinements in materials and techniques were complemented by advances in design – so much so that by the 1750s and 1760s patterns of considerable sophistication were being produced. The *trompe l'oeil* and chinoiserie tewares (Cat. B3–7), and the transfer-printed creamwares (Cat. D58), all echo designs current in English porcelain. But the pottery of Staffordshire was far cheaper to produce than the unstable and unpredictable soft-paste body of the English porcelain factories; and this pottery was aimed at new and expanding markets of consumers – those who wanted to enjoy wares with a flavour of metropolitan styles but who could not yet aspire to buy china.

These people were among the constituents of what Wedgwood called the 'Middling class',[1] a huge swathe, or middle range, of the market that is probably best defined only in terms of what it excluded – the 'Great People' on the one hand and those at the opposite extreme of the spectrum of wealth on the other. Increasing real incomes and falling prices[2] resulted in significant sections of this heterogeneous group having more money to spend on

Pl. 1 (Cat. A9) Creamware teapot, possibly by Enoch Booth, about 1745. One of the earliest surviving Staffordshire creamwares.

such small luxuries as pottery. Widening markets for finely potted tablewares went hand-in-hand with that for hot beverages, especially tea, the consumption of which rose dramatically during the course of the 18th century. Increased tea consumption was a great stimulus to the Staffordshire pottery trade, and teawares dominated production during the first half of the century.

Throughout the 18th century Staffordshire potters sought wider markets for their wares. By the 1730s they had broken beyond the confines of local and regional purchasers, and, as transport conditions improved, their products increasingly found nationwide outlets in the towns and cities of Britain. An event of cardinal importance was the opening of the River Weaver to navigation in 1733.[3] This linked the Potteries to the port of Liverpool, greatly reducing the amount of overland carriage by packhorse. It was also the route by which much of the white clays and other imported raw materials were brought into Staffordshire, the widespread adoption of white-firing clays and ground flint being datable to precisely this period. In addition, turnpike roads were being opened, supported by the potters (including Thomas Whieldon,[4] Wedgwood's partner, 1754–9), much as Josiah Wedgwood was to promote them during the 1760s.

Improved transport was the precondition for the development of a country-wide sales network, which was largely in place by the 1750s. Already by the middle of the decade most of the wares of John Wedgwood, Josiah's cousin, were being sold to dealers in London.[5] The importance of the capital was two-fold. First, London's size made it the single most important market, since it housed about 11 percent of the population of mid-18th century England, and one in six of adults lived or worked there at some stage in their lives.[6] Secondly, it was the distribution centre, as middlemen elsewhere in the country tended to buy their stock from London china and pottery dealers rather than direct from the makers. These London 'Chinamen' are believed to have been innovative in developing techniques for selling their stock, and their shops are reported to have been fashionable resorts of the genteel, but little is known about the manner in which they displayed and sold their goods (Pl. 3).[7]

The picture that has been pieced together of the Staffordshire pottery business by the years around 1760 is one of complexity at every stage of making and selling, with much specialization and division of labour. Production now required many separate processes: wedging,

Pl. 2 (Cat. B3) Teapot. Probably made by Josiah Wedgwood or Thomas Whieldon, early 1760s.

Pl. 3 Trade card of John Dobson, London china and earthenware merchant, probably 1750s–1760s.

slip-preparing, throwing, block-making, saggar-making, glaze-dipping, polishing, engraving, turning, packing and so on, many stages of which needed separate workroom spaces and a trained labour force. As manufacturing became more complex – requiring an increasing number of stages and workrooms and more complex tools and machinery – circumstances increasingly favoured larger concerns. From the evidence of kiln-site excavations it is known that potters tended to specialize in certain product types, but that they often manufactured more than one type of material. Such specialization encouraged the practice of subcontracting orders from one potter to another, and this trade was not confined to the exchange of finished and glazed wares: biscuit-fired pottery and moulds was also traded in this way. Specialization extended outside the factory, this tightly-knit community of potters being served by a network of ancillary trades, including flint grinders and the merchants who shipped the finished and crated goods to coastal ports.

Much of what is now known about the Staffordshire pottery business in the years of Wedgwood's apprenticeship has been painstakingly pieced together by a handful of researchers[8] using documentary sources such as wills, inventories and shipping registers. Records such as these tend to be scattered between archives; their evidence requires careful sifting and analysis before even the sketchiest of pictures emerges, and the individuals whose names are recorded have but the most shadowy of presences. For Josiah Wedgwood, on the other hand, exactly the opposite is true, thanks to the remarkable survival of a wealth of archival material – including over 1,200 letters written to Thomas Bentley during the 18

years of their friendship and partnership: we have an astonishingly rich picture of both the man and his achievements. And in the absence of a fully fleshed-out account of his competitors there is a very real temptation to assume that he was a pioneer in all he did, and that where he led others necessarily followed.

An example here is his use of division of labour, which was already well-established in the pottery business by the 1760s.[9] What Wedgwood did was to develop it much further, making it the principle central to his factory management. Similarly, in opening his London showrooms and energetically marketing his goods he was probably adopting some of the sales strategies of his competitors in the market for luxury goods.[10] If so, this would be entirely consistent with his overall sales strategy, for he aimed above all at capturing the fashionable market (while not relinquishing his grip on the larger one of the 'Middling class'), his stated intention being to 'begin at the <u>Head</u> first, & then proceed to the inferior members'.[11] The upper reaches of the market had hitherto been denied the Staffordshire potters, these being the preserve of porcelain factories, notably Chelsea and Derby. It was one of Wedgwood's great successes that he achieved for his ornamental wares a status higher than that of porcelain; the Derby pieces that follow patterns introduced by Wedgwood tacitly acknowledge this fact (Cat. D39–40).

Just as there is little material on which to base a sound judgement of the sale and marketing practices of Wedgwood's competitors, so there is little conclusive proof of Thomas Bentley's contribution in the promotion of their wares. Very few of Bentley's letters to Wedgwood survive, but we can infer from Josiah's own that his partner's influence in this sphere was considerable. Furthermore, unlike Wedgwood, Bentley had a sound Classical education, and he possessed a polished social manner, enabling him to move at ease among the highest social levels. Through taste, education and contacts – and by virtue of being based in London during the years of their partnership – Bentley was able to keep Wedgwood well informed of changes in metropolitan fashions. He was probably instrumental in steering Wedgwood towards the use of Classical prototypes during the late 1760s. The fashion for these had already been taken up in architecture and interior design, but it had not yet affected the design of pottery; Wedgwood's adoption and promotion of the 'antique style' was absolutely fundamental to the fashionable success of his wares.

It may seem strange that so many of Wedgwood's productions are close copies of, or adaptations from works in other materials; but 18th-century opinions on creativity and design are very different from those held today. Wedgwood, like his keen rival Matthew Boulton (and his friend Sir Joshua Reynolds), aimed at emulation and quotation from the most admired sources and the creation of 'new combinations of old ornaments';[12] probably he found no particular virtue in originality in design as such. It should be remembered, too, that the remains of Classical antiquity were the subject of a passionate admiration, the strength of which is difficult to appreciate today.

The revival of Classical prototypes and the emergence of Neo-classical styles of decoration are often attributed to the excitement over excavations at Pompeii and Herculaneum and to the impact of the Grand Tour. Recently, however, it has been argued that their popularity lay in their fusion of modernity with Classicism, a combination that allowed the middle and upper classes to feel at ease with the march of progress.[13] Certainly, it is one of the paradoxes of the age that the increasingly industrialized society of the 1770s and 1780s should have been obsessed with the culture of Classical antiquity and should have sought to express its ideals of progress in the imagery of Classical art. Wedgwood's wares – made at a showcase modern factory and formed in the image of the Classical past – exemplify this fusion. A strand or trace of this filters through into the landscape decoration of Wedgwood's celebrated Frog Service, where industrial scenes are included in an iconographic programme that presents an ideal of 18th-century Britain as a land of liberty, opportunity and democracy – as a reincarnation of ancient Rome.[14] A selection from the Service forms the centrepiece to this exhibition, and its commission and the meanings of its landscapes are discussed in detail in Chapter 5.

Shifts in the taste of the fashionable élite gave Wedgwood a new focus for his constant experimentation with ceramic bodies and glazes. In order to emulate the Greek pottery that was then the subject of renewed attention, he developed the Black Basalt body; and his Jasper stoneware was intended from the start to harmonize with the interior decoration of such leading architects as Robert Adam, James Wyatt and Sir William Chambers. Not only did he develop new materials to meet the requirements of the fashionable world, but in order to satisfy it he also introduced a number of products that were new to English pottery – vases, plaques, tablets, seals, and cameos among them. Some were used in ways that were virtually unprecedented in English pottery, being cabinet and collectors' pieces aimed at the connoisseur; analogous to gems and small-scale sculpture, these were intended to be viewed and appreciated as art, much as the viewing of the landscape decoration of the Frog Service was probably informed by familiarity with topographical prints.

The manufacture of vases – which was one of the principal foundations for his fashionable reputation – was another significant innovation; they were the first to be

*Pl. 4 (Cat. B49) Jasper portrait medallion of the sculptor
John Flaxman junior, about 1790–5.*

made in pottery in England.[15] Like his medallions and
tablets they would have been bought and sold entirely
on the strength of their appearance and associations, few
having any function beyond ornament. In this they were
typical of much of Wedgwood's work, particularly in
Jasper and Basalt. He seems to have realized early on the
importance of design and of associations in selling
goods; and he was constantly seeking fresh patterns to
adapt and copy, most actively during the years of 'Vase
madness' around 1770, when the vase was taken up as a
leitmotif of the revived Classical styles[16] (Pl. 9).

By August of 1770, when the 'madness' was at its
height, Wedgwood and Bentley had already assembled
an impressive collection of source books on antiquities
(which, most tellingly, were augmented by volumes of
the *British and Irish Peerage* listing the constituents of
one of their principal markets for these pieces).[17] And by
the middle of the decade they were able to draw on a
pool of extremely talented modellers for their portraits
and sculptural ornament, John Flaxman and John Bacon
among them (Cat. B49). But in addition, Wedgwood enlisted the help of the nobility, antiquaries and architects
in his quest for designs and models: Sir William Hamilton, Sir Roger Newdigate, Sir Watkin Williams Wynn,

the Dukes of Bedford and Marlborough and Lords Lansdowne and Bessborough – to name only those that feature in the present exhibition – were among those who
gave him privileged access their collections; and the architects they employed – Adam, Wyatt, 'Athenian' Stuart and Chambers – were similarly targeted for their
support, most effectively so with Chambers (Cat. C25).

In pursuing fresh design sources at this high social
level, Wedgwood sought not only the designs and patterns themselves but also the active encouragement and
support of the leaders of fashion – the 'legislators of
taste' – being well aware that excellence of design and
materials was not enough to capture the exclusive
market he aimed at. '<u>Fashion</u>,' he wrote to Bentley in
1779, 'is infinitely superior to <u>merit</u> … and it is plain
from a thousand instances if you have a favourite child
you wish the public to fondle and take notice of, you have
only to make choice of proper sponcers'.[18] From
sponsorship at such levels many benefits would flow,
including and above all greatly increased profits.

*Pl. 5 (Cat. C4) Portrait medallion of Sir William Hamilton,
about 1772.*

Pl. 6 (Cat. C 25) Presentation drawing of a griffin candlestick. John Yenn after Sir William Chambers, undated.

Pl. 7 Advertisement for Wedgwood's Queen's Ware. Undated newspaper cutting, about 1771–4.

At the highest rung of the social ladder was the royal family, headed by King George III and Queen Charlotte. Wedgwood's first royal order came in 1765, when he made a creamware tea service with green flowers on a gold ground for the Queen. The commission had first been placed with another potter, who turned it down because of technical difficulties in applying a solid ground of gilding in the specified manner. When the order was passed on to Wedgwood he seized the opportunity, realizing at once its enormous advertising value. Having completed the tea-set he followed it up with a crate of 'patterns' offered as a gift; from June 1766 he was advertising his position as Potter to the Queen, and by the following year he had renamed his creamware 'Queen's Ware' (Pl. 7).

That the royal commission for a creamware service should have been made at all indicates the high regard in which the pottery was already held by that date. Creamware's rise in status to the point where it was a fit material for royalty is often attributed to Wedgwood's efforts alone. The fact that the commission was first offered elsewhere shows that this cannot have been the case, but is certainly true that Wedgwood's subsequent promotion of his own products earned the material a widespread fashionable status. His appreciation of the importance of noble patronage in this achievement is clear in a letter written to Bentley in 1767:

The demand for this s^d. Creamcolour, Alias, Queens-ware, … still increases. It is really amazing how rapidly the use of it has spread allmost over the whole Globe, & how universally it is liked – How much of this general use, & estimation, is owing to the mode of its introduction – & how much to its real utility & beauty? are questions in which we may be a good deal interested for the governm^t. of our future Conduct …. For instance, if a Royal, or noble introduction be as necessary to the sale of an Article of Luxury, as real Elegance & beauty, then the Manufacturer, if he consults his own inter^t. will bestow as much pains, & expence too, in gaining the former of these advantages, as he wo^d. in bestowing the latter.[19]

In his pursuit of 'noble introductions' Wedgwood targeted two overlapping social groups within the tightly knit world of 18th-century patronage and art and design, knowing that where the leaders went others would follow. In addition to his contacts with architects, antiquaries and connoisseurs, he courted the nobility, making gifts to them of his wares and naming particular lines in their honour. He indulged them by agreeing to make costly 'uniques', that is one-off commissions, which were undertaken at a loss largely for the publicity and goodwill that would accrue. Queen Charlotte's gold and green tea service was the earliest of these, but the most celebrated was the 'Frog Service' made for Catherine the Great in 1773–4.

The Frog Service (so called because each piece bears a frog crest in allusion to the location of the Russian palace for which it was made) was a vast, 952-piece creamware dinner and dessert service painted with views of British antiquities, landscapes and parks and gardens. This appears to have been the first use of named topographical views on ceramics, a form of decoration later taken up at Derby and elsewhere. Wedgwood and Bent-

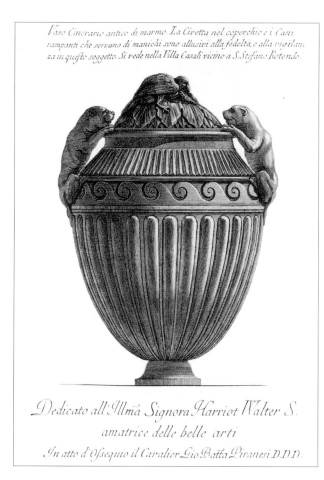

display in a socially exclusive London exhibition, would do much to consolidate their home market. Writing to Bentley in November 1773, Wedgwood argued that the London showing would:

> fully complete our notoriety to the whole Island & help us greatly, no doubt, in the sale of our goods, both usefull and ornamental – It w^d. confirm the consequence we have attain'd, & increase it, by shewing that we are employ'd in a much higher scale than other Manufacturers. We should show that we have paid many comp^ts. to our Friends & Customers, & thereby rivet them the more firmly to our interests …[21]

Admission to the exhibition during June 1744 was by ticket only, the nobility and gentry being invited to apply for these at Wedgwood's warehouse: it is indicative of the

Left: Plate 8 Vase by Giovanni Battista Piranesi. Etching from 'Vasi, candelabri, cippi...', published 1778.
Below: Plate 9 (Cat. C14) Agate ware vase, the design probably after a print by G.B.Piranesi or J.C.R.de Saint Non, probably 1770s.

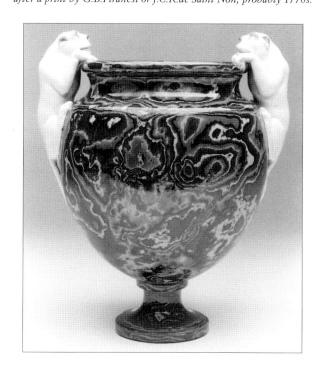

ley undertook the commission with little expectation of any real financial profit and indeed at considerable risk of non-payment.[20] They realized from the outset that the painting would be very costly, that obtaining a sufficient number of views to copy would be extremely difficult (as would be finding enamellers who were sufficiently skilled to be entrusted with the work) and that this decoration could only be carried out to the detriment of other work in the London Decorating Studio. Nevertheless, they saw that given the size of the Service and the fame of the patron the advertising value of the commission would be enough to offset these considerations. As work on the Service progressed they came to appreciate that the interest of the landscape views, and its

Pl. 10 (Cat. C31) Jasper portrait medallion of the architect James 'Athenian' Stuart, about 1785.

high standing of his wares, and of his fashionable reputation, that he could make such a stipulation.

Just as he courted the connoisseurs and fashionable élite knowing that others would be led by their example, so he also reckoned that the people of the 'Middling class' would or could be persuaded to do likewise. As he and the architect James Stuart concluded there were those who would:

> of themselves choose shewy, rich and gawdy things, but who wo^d. be over ruled by their betters in the choice of their ornaments as well as [in] other matters; who wo^d. do as their architects, or whoever they depended upon in matters of taste directed them ...[22]

From his position as a manufacturer of fashionable goods Wedgwood saw social emulation and the emulative spending it encouraged as powerful determinants on the size and shape of the market. In holding such views he was not alone. Satirical columns in the press graphically convey the power that wealth and luxuries brought in a society not bound by inflexible ranking.

The people of the 'Middling class' may perhaps not have bought Wedgwood's ornamental pieces, but they certainly bought his less costly creamwares. It was long thought that these enjoyed large sales because a number of factors – including division of labour, the logical layout of the factory at Etruria, the use of steam power and Wedgwood's managerial discipline – ensured that they were cheaper than those of his competitors. In fact, the reverse was true: Wedgwood charged what the market would bear, keeping his prices consistently higher than others'. He did this partly in order to maintain quality,

arguing that 'low prices must beget a low quality in the manufacture, which will beget neglect, & disuse ...',[23] and also in order to cover the exceptionally high costs of his experiments, investments and showrooms. But in addition the high prices he charged commanded respect for his products, as is clear from a letter of 1772, when overproduction of vases had brought about a crisis in the finances of the partnership:

> The great people have had their Vases in their palaces long enough for them to be seen and admir'd by the Middling Class of People, which class we know are vastly, and I had almost said infinitely, superior in numbers to the great, & though a great price was I believe at first necessary to make the Vases esteemed Ornaments for Palaces that reason no longer exists. Their character is established, & the middling People would probably buy quantities of them at a reduced price.[24]

Here Wedgwood was proposing to reduce the prices of his prestigious ornamental pieces. With his creamwares, on the other hand he managed to combine high prices with wide sales. He was able to do so not only because of the technical and aesthetic excellence of his Queen's Ware, and the prestige of its royal patronage, but by forcing these advantages home through promotion and advertisement. Like such competitors as Duesbury of Derby, Turner & Abbott and the Worcester porcelain factory he advertised his royal appointments, showrooms, factory and wares. He advertised widely in the London and provincial newspapers, especially after 1771, and he contrived for 'puffing' articles extolling the virtues of his wares to be placed in the press. In 1773 he considered advertising his trademark, the practice of marking his wares having been intro-duced at Etruria in 1771. In 1774 he published a Queen's Ware catalogue (the first catalogue of ornamental wares was issued in the previous year) and in 1777 introduced travelling salesmen equipped with cases of samples.[25] Other promotions aimed at the provinces included (from 1771[26]) free carriage anywhere in the country, making good any breakages suffered in transit and money back on goods sent to customers found not 'agreeable to their wishes', the last of these anticipating the 'satisfaction guarantee' policy usually said to have been introduced nearly a century later by John Wanna-maker in America.[27]

But it was in the capital that reputations were made and that fashions were set, as was repeatedly acknowl-edged in provincial newspaper advertisements. Here Wedgwood centred his promotional activities on his showrooms. In May 1767 he set out his requirements in a letter to Bentley. He wanted a

<u>large</u> Room … not to shew or have a large stock of Ware in Town, but to enable me shew various Table & desert services … in order to <u>do the needfull</u> with the Ladys in the neatest, genteelest and best method. The same, or indeed a much greater variety of setts of Vases should. decorate the Walls, and both these articles may, every few days, be so alter'd, revers'd, & trans-form'd as to render the whole a new scene, even to the same company, every time they shall bring their friends to visit us. I need not tell you the many good effects this must produce, when business & amuse-ment can be made to go hand in hand.[28]

Pl. 11 (Cat. B24) Queen's Ware bowl and stand, about 1790–5.

Wedgwood's satisfied aside on the combination of business and pleasure is highly revealing of contemporary attitudes to shopping. It has long been assumed that 18th-century shops were dark and unappealing, that goods were by and large sold on their own merits, with very little promotion from the shopkeepers, and that there was no attempt on the part of retailers to turn shop-going into a pleasant or convenient experience.[29] Recent research has shown these assumptions to be unfounded. Rather, as a result of a combination of factors – including improvements in street lighting and pavementing, and increased emphasis on shop design and presentation of goods,[30] but above all fuelled by a pattern of consumption that by the 1770s was considered by contemporaries to be manic and addictive[31] – shopping and shop-going were enjoyed by the wealthy as fashionable leisure pursuits throughout the 18th century. In opening well-appointed rooms in a fashionable quarter, and in paying great attention to the display of his goods, Wedgwood was capitalizing on this trend, just as he capitalized, with his shows of the Frog Service and Portland Vase, on the closely related and contemporaneous vogue for exhibition-viewing.

While London dominated the home market, by the mid-1760s Wedgwood's pottery was already being sold abroad, much of the trade being handled at this date by Bentley & Boardman, Thomas Bentley's Liverpool shipping partnership. Wedgwood was probably not exceptional in this: records for his contemporaries are scarce, but both John Wedgwood and John Baddeley of Shelton were certainly selling wares for export during the 1750s. Wedgwood rapidly built up an enormous export trade, so much so that by the 1780s foreign sales are estimated to account for 80 percent of his production,[32] and by 1793–5 he had agents acting on his behalf in Amsterdam, Antwerp, St Petersburg, Italy, the German states and principalities and elsewhere.[33]

A number of Wedgwood's overseas sales and market-ing strategies echoed those at home. He followed, insofar as he could, the policy of starting at the head and 'proceeding to the inferior members', contriving for 'proper and noble introductions' by enlisting the support of ambassadors as envoys and proselytizers, a tactic that was most successful with Lord and Lady Cathcart in St Petersburg. But he also indulged in bold export drives and campaigns, such that of 1771, in which he proposed to send a thousand parcels containing £20,000 worth of goods to Europe.[34] A considerable amount of the pottery exported was specially designed or tailored for individual foreign markets, most obviously the portraits and busts of foreign monarchs and notables, but also Queen's Ware transfer-printed with Rococo ornament that would have been considered outmoded in London but which was still in vogue in the Netherlands and elsewhere. Although the structure of this trade has been mapped out, its growth and organization is one of the most complex and least published aspects of his business. The Dutch trade has been fully documented, and now much light has been cast on the exports to Russia, but a fully detailed picture awaits further research.[35]

There are, however, more compelling tasks. Wedgwood's letters tell us much about the man and his products and his business empire and entrepreneurial techniques. The insight that they have provided has been instrumental in provoking a reassessment of 18th-century commercial activity and the recognition that consumerism was a fact of 18th-century life.[36] But they cast little light on the constituents of these consumer markets, and still less on the meanings that the products they bought once held. Objects such as the bowl in Pl. 11 must have signified something to their first owners and carried meanings that elude us today. Unless these can be drawn out, they will remain beautiful but mute.

Hilary Young

CATALOGUE
A
The State of the Art

In the four decades spanning 1720 to 1760 there was a complete transformation of the Staffordshire pottery trade. During this period a number of new clay bodies and techniques of making and decorating pottery were developed and introduced, improvements which formed the foundations for Josiah Wedgwood's experiments and innovations. As the wares became more sophisticated, Staffordshire pottery was increasingly able to compete with porcelain both in quality and design. Teaware accounts for much of the pottery of this period because of the great stimulus provided by the increased consumption of hot beverages.

A1 Tea-bowl

Staffordshire
Slip-cast white salt-glazed stoneware, with *sgraffito* (scratched) decoration picked out with underglaze cobalt blue
About 1745
Height: 3.9 cm

The cup was slip-cast in a plaster mould made from the block mould Cat. A2. Slip-casting is a method of making complex hollow shapes in a mould. A clay slip (a suspension of clay particles in water) is poured into a concave plaster mould. The water is then allowed to evaporate, and the process repeated until the clay adhering to the mould is judged sufficiently thick to form the vessel. As the clay dries it shrinks, facilitating removal, which takes place when the clay has dried to a 'leather-hard' state. Slip-casting probably entered widespread use in Staffordshire during the 1740s. It was much employed by Wedgwood and his

contemporaries for forming shapes that could not be thrown on a wheel, and it remains one of the basic ceramic-forming techniques in use today.

Victoria & Albert Museum. Jermyn Street Collection (2215-1901)

A2 Block mould for a tea-bowl

Staffordshire
Salt-glazed stoneware
About 1745
Height: 4.7 cm

Block moulds are convex 'master' moulds, which are used to make the concave plaster moulds in which hollow wares such as cups, bowls and teapots are cast. This block mould was used for making the tea-bowl Cat. A1.

Victoria & Albert Museum (3098-1852)

A3 Pickle-tray

Staffordshire
White salt-glazed stoneware
Probably about 1745–50
Length: 16.6 cm

Salt-glazed stoneware was one of the main products of the Staffordshire Potteries during the years of Wedgwood's apprenticeship – completed in 1749 – and his partnerships of the 1750s. The mixture of calcined flints and white-firing clays from Devon used in this white stoneware was substantially the same as that later used for making creamware (the ceramic body that superseded it during the 1770s), the principal difference being that creamware was fired at a much lower temperature.

Ground flint, which was introduced before about 1720, was added to increase strength and to whiten the clay body.

Victoria & Albert Museum. Jermyn Street Collection. Formerly in the Enoch Wood Collection (2224-1901)

A4 Two-part mould for a pickle-tray

Inner mould of engraved brass, with lead core; iron outer mould
Probably about 1745–50
Length of outer mould: 20.6 cm

The pickle-tray Cat. A3 was made in this mould. The use of such paired concave and convex moulds is limited to shapes that can easily be removed from them. Their use was widespread in the Staffordshire Potteries by the 1740s.

Victoria & Albert Museum. Jermyn Street Collection. Formerly in the Enoch Wood Collection (2225&A-1901)

A5 Teapot and cover

Staffordshire
Red earthenware, with applied reliefs in white clay, lead-glazed, and with later metal mounts
Mid-18th century
Height: 13.6 cm

The ornament in relief decoration was produced using an engraved metal stamp similar to Cat. A6. White clay was pressed into the engraving of the stamp, and this was then applied to the surface of the teapot.

Victoria & Albert Museum. Given by Lady Charlotte Schreiber (Schr. II 244&A)

A6 Stamp for decorating pottery

Engraved brass
About 1750
Length: 5 cm

See Cat. A5.

Trustees of the Wedgwood Museum, Barlaston, Staffordshire (No.59)

A7 Teapot and cover

Staffordshire
Earthenware, with 'sprigged' decoration under a lead glaze stained with pigments
About 1760
Height: 9.1 cm

'Sprigging' is a technique in which low-relief ornament is formed in a hollow plaster mould and then applied to the 'leather-hard' surface of a pot, a clay slip being used to join the two together. It was used for the relief decoration on much of Wedgwood's Jasper and Basalt wares. Teapots similar to this one have been attributed to Thomas Whieldon, Wedgwood's partner between 1754 and 1759.

Victoria & Albert Museum (C.47-1938)
Lit: Towner 1978 pl. 7A

A8 Tile with a design of shepherd lovers with a dog

Printed by John Sadler (1720–89) at Liverpool
Tin-glazed earthenware, transfer-printed over-glaze in black
Lettered: 'J. Sadler. Liverpl.'
1758–61
12.7 × 12.7 cm

Transfer-printing is a method of reproducing designs on ceramics that allowed highly sophisticated decoration at very low cost per unit. A design was engraved in reverse on a copperplate or wood-block and then printed on to a sheet of treated paper or – as has been suggested, but not finally settled – on to a layer (or 'bat') of solidified glue. This impression was then laid face down on the surface of the ceramic, to which the design was transferred, and then subsequently fixed by firing in a kiln.

Transfer-printing was invented in 1751 by John Brooks, a mezzotint engraver, and it was probably independently discovered by John Sadler of Liverpool, who applied to patent the technique in 1756. From 1762 Sadler and his partner, Guy Green (d.1799), entered into an exclusive agreement with Wedgwood to print his creamwares. Sadler retired in 1770, but the arrangement was continued until the 1790s by Green alone. The design here is taken from a drawing book published by John Bowles in 1756-7. Tin-glazed earthenware, the material of which this tile was made, was widely used for domestic tableware until the 1770s, when it was superseded by Staffordshire creamware.

Victoria & Albert Museum. Given by R. J. Charleston (C.137-1981)
Lit: Compare Ray 1973 no. B 3-2

A9 Teapot *(Pl. 1)*

Possibly by Enoch Booth (d.1773), Tunstall, Staffordshire
Cream- or buff-coloured earthenware, painted with underglaze blue and powdered manganese, under a greenish lead glaze
About 1745
Height: 10.7 cm

One of a small group of very early cream-coloured earthenwares, one of which is dated 1743 and initialled 'EB', possibly for Enoch Booth. Booth was a leading Staffordshire potter of his day, and he is traditionally but probably erroneously held to have introduced liquid lead glazes – in place of the traditional and more toxic powdered lead glazes – into the Stafford-shire pottery industry. This innovation was widely taken up at the same time as the practice of firing pottery in two stages: in the first the clay was fired to a porous 'biscuit' state, and then the glaze was applied and fired subsequently at a lower temperature. This separation into two stages allowed for greater specialization and sub-division of labour among the potters, greater control over their products, and for the development of a richer variety of glaze colours and effects.

Victoria & Albert Museum (C.66&A-1989)
Lit: Towner 1978 p. 23; Barker 1991 p. 16

A10 Teapot and cover

Staffordshire
Solid agate ware, the body press-moulded in the form of a shell, with a lead glaze; later metal mount
Mid-18th century
Height: 14.6 cm

Pottery in imitation of agate and other hardstones can be made by 'wedging' coloured clays together or by blending coloured slips together on the surface. The former type is known as 'solid agate' and the latter as 'surface agate'. Writing in the introduction to his 'Experiment Book' about his 'suite of Experiments begun … in 1759' Wedgwood noted: 'I had already made an imitation of Agate; which was esteemed beautiful & a considerable improvement; but people were surfeited with wares of these various colours …'. However, he revived the techniques during the years around 1770 for the decoration of his variegated and white terracotta stoneware vases.

Victoria & Albert Museum (3200-1853)
Ref: Wedgwood MS E.29-19121, see Reilly 1989 I p. 32

A11 Teapot and cover

Staffordshire
Solid agate ware, the body press-moulded in the form of a shell, with a lead glaze
Mid-18th century
Height: 13.1 cm

Victoria & Albert Museum. Part of the Arthur James Collection bequeathed by his wife (C.73&A-1948)

A12 Teapot and cover

Probably Staffordshire
Red stoneware, with stamped decoration
and later metal mounts
Mid-18th century
Height: 7.3 cm

Unglazed red stoneware had been made in
Staffordshire in emulation of imported
Chinese redware teapots from the end of
the 17th century (Cat. A13). Wedgwood's
refinement of the stoneware body was
developed during the early 1770s and was
named *Rosso Antico* in 1776. Wedgwood
did not regard the body highly himself,
considering it vulgarized by association
with Staffordshire red stoneware teapots, a
common product of the Potteries during
the third quarter of the 18th century.

Victoria & Albert Museum. Given by Lt.-Col.
K. Dingwall, DSO through the National Art-
Collections Fund (C.423-1923)

A 7

A13 Mug

Made by John and David Elers (active
1688–1710), Bradwell Wood, Staffordshire
Red stoneware, slip-cast and lathe-turned,
with applied decoration and silver rim
About 1690–98
Height: 8.8 cm

Lathe-turning, in which 'leather-hard'
pottery is finished on a lathe, was
extensively employed by Wedgwood, most
notably for the sophisticated development
of the technique known as engine-turning,
in which the cutting of the machine is
guided by cams. Lathe-turning was
introduced into Staffordshire by the Dutch
potters David and John Phillip Elers. Their
work was known to Wedgwood, who wrote
in July 1777 of their 'improvement' in
'refining our common red clay, by sifting, &
making it into Tea & Coffee ware in
imitation of the Chinese Red Porcelaine, by
casting it in plaister moulds, & turning it on
the outside upon Lathes & ornamenting it
with the Tea Branch in relief, in imitation of
the Chinese manner of ornamenting this
ware'. In 1777 Wedgwood issued a portrait
medallion of John Phillip Elers at the
request of the latter's son, Paul. Their mugs
are exceptionally finely potted compared to
other work from Staffordshire of this date.

Victoria & Albert Museum (C.15-1931)
Lit and refs: Wedgwood MS E.25-18772, see Reilly
1989 I p. 508 and pl. 826

A 13

The Pursuit of Perfection

Wedgwood's great reputation as a potter is founded first and foremost on the several ceramic bodies that he perfected or invented, notably Queen's Ware, Black Basalt and Jasper. The work that immediately preceded these developments, however – made near the start of his career in partnership with Thomas Whieldon between 1754 and 1759 and at his own works during the early 1760s – was notable for its innovations in glaze colours and effects.

EARLY WARES WITH COLOURED GLAZES

B1 Teapot and cover

Probably made by Thomas Whieldon or the Whieldon-Wedgwood partnership
Cream-coloured earthenware, with applied moulded decoration, under a lead glaze mottled with grey, green and yellow
Unmarked
Probably 1750s
Height: 11.6 cm

The applied Tudor rose decoration has been found on fragments excavated on the site of Thomas Whieldon's works at Fenton Vivian, near Stoke-on-Trent.

Victoria & Albert Museum. Wallace Elliot Bequest (C.94&A-1938)
Lit: Towner 1978 p. 28 and pl. A

B2 Teapot and cream jug

Probably made by Josiah Wedgwood
Cream-coloured earthenware, with stamped and applied reliefs, under a green lead glaze, and with traces of gilding

Marks: the milk jug incised 'Joseph', and with other inscriptions illegible under the glaze
About 1760
Height of teapot: 13.4 cm; height of jug: 12.7 cm

One of Wedgwood's principal achievements during his partnership with Thomas Whieldon at Fenton is thought to have been his development of a rich and clear and deep green lead glaze. An entry dated 23 March 1759 in Wedgwood's 'Experiment Book' reads: 'A Green Glaze to be laid on common white (or Cream color) Biscuit ware. Very good ...'. Wedgwood continued to manufacture green-glazed wares during the early and mid-1760s, particularly for export to the West Indies. By 1774, however, he had come to disdain the styles of Staffordshire pottery of the mid-18th century, commenting that 'the Agate, the Green and other colour'd Glazes have <u>had</u> <u>their</u> day, & done pretty well, & are certain of a resurrection soon, for there are, & ever will be a numerous class of People, to purchase <u>Shewy</u> & <u>cheap</u> things'.

Victoria & Albert Museum. Given by J. H. Fitzhenry, Esq. (891&A, 892-1905)
Lit and refs: Wedgwood MSS 26-19115 and E25-18521, see Reilly 1989 I p. 180; Honey 1948 pl. 11; Towner 1963 pl. 170; Towner 1978 pl. 8A

B3 Teapot and cover *(Pl. 2)*

Probably made by Josiah Wedgwood or Thomas Whieldon from a block mould by William Greatbatch (b. about 1735–d. 1813)
Cream-coloured earthenware, with moulded chinoiserie decoration, under a lead glaze stained yellow, green and brown
Unmarked
Probably early 1760s
Height: 13.4 cm

The moulded design with its elegant chinoiserie figures and scrollwork shows a sophisticated use of fashionable metropolitan Rococo, or *genre pittoresque* styles. The design and modelling of the block mould for this teapot has been attributed to William Greatbatch.

Victoria & Albert Museum. Arthur Hurst Bequest (C.20&A-1940)
Lit: Reilly 1989 I pl. 148

B4 Hexagonal teapot and cover

Probably made by Josiah Wedgwood or Thomas Whieldon from a block mould by William Greatbatch (b. about 1735–d. 1813)
Cream-coloured earthenware, with moulded chinoiserie decoration under a lead glaze stained with green, yellow, grey and manganese brown

B 4

Unmarked
Early 1760s
Height: 12.9 cm

A number of variations on this pattern exist, and it is clear from this, and from the evidence of excavated sherds, that the design was made by several potters. The block moulds of the finest examples have traditionally been attributed to William Greatbatch. The form of the spout here suggests that the teapot was probably made by Wedgwood or Whieldon.

Victoria & Albert Museum (C.201&A-1926)
Lit: Honey 1948 pl. 2; Towner 1963 pl. 176a;
Towner 1978 pl. 9A

B5 Slop basin

Staffordshire
Cream-coloured earthenware, the exterior with pineapple ornament moulded in relief, under a clear lead glaze stained green and orange-yellow
Unmarked
Probably early 1760s
Diameter: 14.5 cm

Creamware shapes in the form of fruit and vegetables follow a fashion already well established at such English porcelain factories as Longton Hall and Chelsea and a taste ultimately traceable to Meissen porcelain of the 1740s.

Victoria & Albert Museum. Jermyn Street Collection (2273-1901)

B6 Tea canister and cover

Probably made by Josiah Wedgwood or Thomas Whieldon
Cream-coloured earthenware, with pineapple ornament moulded in relief under a lead glaze stained with green and orange-yellow
Unmarked
Probably early 1760s
Height: 11.5 cm

The relationships between Josiah Wedgwood, Thomas Whieldon (Josiah Wedgwood's partner 1754–9) and the

B 8
B 9

blockcutter and potter William Greatbatch (who is believed to have been apprenticed to Whieldon) are extremely complex. Wedgwood may have continued to fire wares at Whieldon's works after he set up independently, and Greatbatch probably supplied both potters with block moulds. Greatbatch had established his own pot-works by 1762, and he is recorded as having supplied Wedgwood with both glazed and unglazed wares between that year and 1765. Among the orders for 1764 were two crates of pineapple ware.

Victoria & Albert Museum. Given by Lady Charlotte Schreiber (Schr.II.295)
Lit: Reilly 1989 I pl. 129; Barker 1991 passim

B7 Teapot and cover

Possibly by Josiah Wedgwood
Cream-coloured earthenware, with pineapple ornament moulded in relief under a lead glaze stained with green and orange-yellow

Unmarked
Early 1760s
Height: 12 cm

The shapes of the spout and handle have been associated with Josiah Wedgwood's production. For a similar spout see block mould Cat. B9.

Victoria & Albert Museum. Given by Lady Charlotte Schreiber (Schr.II.294)
Lit: Honey 1948 pl. 8; Towner 1963 pl. 174b

B8 Block mould for a cauliflower teapot

Attributed to William Greatbatch (b. about 1735–d. 1813)
White salt-glazed stoneware
Unmarked
About 1760
Height: 13 cm; width: 13.6 cm

William Greatbatch is thought to have been apprenticed to Thomas Whieldon and therefore probably knew Josiah Wedgwood before both men established their

independent works in 1759. Greatbatch opened his works at Lower Lane, Fenton, and had a special agreement to produce biscuit wares for Wedgwood's new Ivy House Works. From the surviving manuscripts for 1762 to 1764 it is very clear that Greatbatch was making certain shapes for Wedgwood alone. Cauliflower wares were among the most popular objects produced by Staffordshire potters in the mid-18th century. A manuscript dated 21 September 1763 indicates the range available: '12 Setts Colly flower ware viz 1 coffee pot, 1 stand to it, 1 Teapot and stand, 1 Milk Pot, 1 Sugar Dish, 1 Slop Bason, 1 Spoon Boat, 6 Cho. and 6 saucers, 6 Teacups and 6 sau. 6 coffes and 6 saucers. 1 Tea cannister.'

Trustees of the Wedgwood Museum, Barlaston, Staffordshire (No.9)
Lit and refs: Wedgwood MS cited in Towner 1963 p. 186; Reilly 1989 I pl. 131; Barker 1991 p. 91

B9 Two block moulds for teapot spouts

Attributed to William Greatbatch (b. about 1735–d. 1813)
White salt-glazed stoneware, modelled with a pattern of overlapping leaves
Unmarked
About 1765
Length: 15 cm and 11 cm

See Cat. B7 and B8.

Trustees of the Wedgwood Museum, Barlaston, Staffordshire (No.31 and 1994)
Lit: Barker 1991 pp. 174–5

B10 Tea canister

Attributed to Josiah Wedgwood
Cream-coloured earthenware, moulded in relief with cauliflower ornament under a clear lead glaze partly stained green
Mark: the base inscribed 'JW'
Early 1760s
Height: 10 cm

The initials 'JW' incised on the base have been identified by Donald Towner as being in Josiah Wedgwood's hand. The popularity of cauliflower ware declined towards the end of the 1760s, and Wedgwood sold some of his 'Coly Flowr' block moulds to John

B 10

Baddeley of Shelton in 1766, probably on the understanding that Baddeley would make any orders that Wedgwood continued to receive.

Victoria & Albert Museum. Arthur Hurst Bequest (C.16-1940)
Lit: Towner 1963 pl. 173; Reilly 1989 I pp. 179–80

B11 Plate

Staffordshire
Cream-coloured earthenware, moulded in relief with cauliflower ornament under a clear lead glaze partly stained green
Unmarked
Probably 1760s
Diameter: 19.8 cm

Victoria & Albert Museum. Arthur Hurst Bequest (C.23-1940)

B12 Cream-jug

Staffordshire
Cream-coloured earthenware, moulded in relief with cauliflower ornament under a clear lead glaze partly stained green
Unmarked
Probably 1760s
Height: 9.3 cm

Victoria & Albert Museum. Joicey Bequest (C.1242-1919)

CREAM-COLOURED EARTHENWARE (OR CREAMWARE)

Cream-coloured earthenware was first produced in Staffordshire some time between 1730 and 1740, and early documentary pieces, dated 1743 and possibly manufactured by Enoch Booth, are now in the collections of the British Museum and the City Museum and Art Gallery, Stoke-on-Trent. The principal ingredients were white-firing clay and ground flint, the flint being used to increase the whiteness and strength of the composition. The result was a durable body, varying in tone from buff to a deep cream colour, which required the application of a clear lead glaze and a second firing to make it impervious to liquids. Production of cream-coloured earthenware (or creamware) spread rapidly from Staffordshire to other parts of England and Continental Europe.

Wedgwood worked on the foundations laid by other potters, carrying out an enormous number of trials to perfect the cream-coloured earthenware body. He commenced work whilst still in partnership with Thomas Whieldon in Fenton, although his first really successful creamware was produced at his Ivy House Works after 1759. It is probable that creamware was amongst the first of Wedgwood's productions as an independent manufacturer. The success of his early work enabled him to move to larger premises, the Brick House or 'Bell' Works, which were rented from William Adams. The exact date of the agreement is unrecorded, but it would appear to date from Christmas 1763 or New Year Tide 1764. Initially, in 1758 Josiah had entered into an agreement with his cousin Thomas Wedgwood to be his journeyman and on 11 November 1765 entered into a partnership with him for the manufacture of 'Useful Wares'.

B13 Tray of cream-coloured earthenware trials

Creamware pieces mounted in a wooden tray
Unmarked
About 1760
38.2 × 30 cm

Wedgwood's improved cream-coloured earthenware was the result of years of study and experimentation. The majority of his trials were completed by 1763, but individual experiments continued to be made until the 1770s. The trials are each marked with an experiment number – those on this tray running from 59 to 77 – which corresponds to entries in Josiah Wedgwood's 'Experiment Book' (Cat. B14). Trial no. 68, while not providing Wedgwood with the colourless glaze he desired, did result in a glaze which Josiah noted was less yellow than his creamware glaze. The ingredients of this particular trial

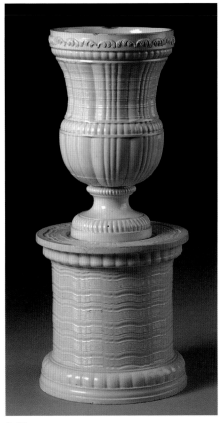

B 15

and the proportions were: 'India porcelain 5$\frac{1}{2}$/8, London crown glass 7/7, Flint glass 16/6, White enamel 4/67 and White lead 32 1/8/3'. It was not until trial number 411 that Wedgwood was able to write 'A Good Wt. Glaze!'

Trustees of the Wedgwood Museum, Barlaston, Staffordshire (No.4251F)
Lit: Science Museum 1978 Cat. 96

B14 'Experiment Book I' (also known as 'Josiah Wedgwood Memoranda 1772–74')

Manuscript volume
Begun 1759
32 × 22.5 cm (closed)

Although the first page is inscribed 'Feb 13-1759, at Fenton', the volume appears to have been used for recording a wide variety of experiments, covering numbers 1 to 837,

together with other contemporary jottings. See Cat. B13.

Trustees of the Wedgwood Museum, Barlaston, Staffordshire (MSS 26-19115)

B15 Vase and pedestal

Deep cream-coloured earthenware (Queen's Ware), with engine-turned decoration
Unmarked
About 1765
Overall height: 39 cm; height of pedestal: 15 cm

Josiah Wedgwood wrote to John, his brother and London agent, on 6 July 1765 referring to similar vases which were to be shown to Queen Charlotte: 'I shall be very proud of the honour of sending a box of patterns to the Queen, amongst which I intend sending two setts of vases, Creamcolour engine turn'd, & printed, ... I can adapt the Vases so that the designs & they will appear to be made for each other, & intended for Royalty, nor must you hint to the contrary'. Wedgwood introduced an eccentric or rose engine turning-lathe into his works in 1763. The eccentric motion allows a variety of repetitive patterns to be cut into the clay. He had originally seen the lathe, designed by James Taylor, in the workshops of Matthew Boulton in Birmingham. A garniture of similar vases is in the Saltram House Collection, National Trust.

Trustees of the Wedgwood Museum, Barlaston, Staffordshire (Vase: No.5384; pedestal: No.66)
Lit and refs: Wedgwood MS E25-18080; Reilly 1989 I pl. 40

B16 Vase and cover

Deep cream-coloured earthenware (Queen's Ware), of tall baluster form on a turned foot and with conical cover; applied ornament of floral swags suspended from lions' heads on the body, and acanthus leaves near the foot
Unmarked
About 1767
Height: 47.7 cm

Undecorated Queen's Ware vases were superseded at the end of the 1760s by those manufactured in emulation of agate, porphyry and other similarly veined and patterned stones (see Section E). Many of the Queen's Ware vases retain traces of gilding.

Trustees of the Wedgwood Museum, Barlaston, Staffordshire (No.70)

B17 Vase and cover

Cream-coloured earthenware (Queen's Ware), with turned band to the centre of the body; applied leaves to the base of the body, the band decorated with curtain swags supported by bows; conical lid
Unmarked
About 1765
Height: 25.4 cm

Josiah Wedgwood wrote to his friend Thomas Bentley of Liverpool, probably in November 1766, 'Vases with high crown'd hats! – Have you ever thought seriously, as you ought to do on that subject'.

Trustees of the Wedgwood Museum, Barlaston, Staffordshire (Vase: No.71; cover: No.72)

B18 Part of a coffee service

Printed in Liverpool by Guy Green (d. 1799)
Queen's Ware, with shell-pattern mouldings, transfer-printed in purple with exotic birds, and with traces of gilding
Marks: 'WEDGWOOD' and 'Wedgwood' impressed, the coffee pot also impressed 'L'
About 1775
Height of coffee-pot: 24.4 cm

The combination of the lighter-toned Queen's Ware body (which Wedgwood developed towards the end of the 1760s) and transfer-printed decoration enabled his creamware to provide serious competition with products of the English porcelain factories. Exotic birds such as these were a common subject on English transfer-printed porcelain.

Victoria & Albert Museum. Given by Lady

Charlotte Schreiber (Schr.II.406-409)
Lit: Honey 1948 pl. 24; Reilly 1989 I pl. 273

B19 Plate

Printed in Liverpool by Guy Green (d. 1799)
Queen's Ware, moulded feather edge with pierced border, painted with flowers in purple enamel; the centre transfer-printed in purple with *Corinthian Ruins*
Mark: 'Wedgwood' impressed
About 1770–75
Diameter: 23 cm

The *Corinthian Ruins* design shows the Temple of Pola in Istria.

Trustees of the Wedgwood Museum, Barlaston, Staffordshire (No.5793)
Lit: Reilly 1989 I pl. C26

B20 Plate

Printed in Liverpool by Guy Green (d. 1799)
Queen's Ware, transfer-printed in red, and enamelled in green, grey, purple and yellow
Mark: 'Wedgwood' impressed
About 1771–5
Diameter: 24.6 cm

One from a set of plates printed with illustrations adapted from Samuel Croxall's *Fables of Aesop and Others*, first published in 1722, the illustration here being of 'The Tiger and the Fox'. Several of these designs are also found on tin-glaze tiles (for which the prints were clearly originally intended) printed by Sadler & Green.

Victoria & Albert Museum. Given by Lady Charlotte Schreiber (Schr.II.401D)
Lit: Stretton 1994 pp. 205–09; Dawson 1984 pp. 20–21; Reilly 1989 I pls C59 and 367

B21 Jug

Printed in Liverpool by Guy Green (d. 1799)
Queen's Ware, transfer-printed in black
Marks: 'WEDGWOOD' and a trianglular workman's mark impressed

Inscribed below the lip: 'ELIZABETH LOWTHER' in black enamel
About 1770
Height: 19.4 cm

One side is decorated with the *Pretty Mantua Maker*, taken from an engraving by Charles Grignion (1721–1810) after Michel Vincent Brandoin (1733–1807). The other side bears *An Opera Girl of Paris in the character of Flora*, from an engraving by Grignion after Brandoin published by Robert Sayer in 1771.

Trustees of the Wedgwood Museum, Barlaston, Staffordshire (No.1041)
Lit: Wedgwood 1984 Cat. K2; Reilly 1989 I pl. 278; Drakard 1992 p. 93

B22 Teapot and cover

Queen's Ware, enamelled in red and black
Unmarked
About 1770
Height: 13.1 cm

The enamelling is in a style associated with David Rhodes, a partner in the Leeds firm of china dealers and decorators Robinson & Rhodes (later D. Rhodes & Co.), who bought Wedgwood creamwares for enamelling and resale during the 1760s. From 1768 until his death in 1777 David Rhodes supervised the day-to-day running of Wedgwood's London enamelling workshops, becoming in due course one of his most trusted employees. The several types of enamelled decoration traditionally associated with his name were probably common to a number of creamware painters working in Leeds and London, and possibly elsewhere.

Victoria & Albert Museum. Given by Mr C. Reginald Grundy (C.1407-1924)
Lit: Honey 1948 pl. 16

B23 Tureen and cover

Queen's Ware, enamelled in blue, and gilt
Mark: 'Wedgwood' impressed
About 1790
Height: 16.6 cm

In the '1802 Drawing Book' this shape is identified as 'Soup Tureen number 13'. For the 'Running Honeysuckle' pattern, see Cat. B24.

Victoria & Albert Museum. Given by Mr Sydney Vacher (C.97&A-1929)

B24 Punch-bowl and stand *(Pl. 11)*

Queen's Ware, enamelled in red and black with 'Running Honeysuckle' pattern, no. 341
Marks: 'WEDGWOOD' impressed on both pieces; 'C' impressed on stand; 'V' or 'Λ' impressed on bowl
About 1790–95
Diameter: 20 cm

Decorated with pattern no. 341, described in the pattern book Cat. D18 as 'Running Honeysuckle, red, black tracing, fine lines and double edge'. In the Wedgwood pattern books there are a considerable number of variations on this design which were inspired by the palmette ornament found on Greek vases. In the '1802 Drawing Book' the base section of this bowl and stand is recorded as 'Shape 1300', 'Ring for a Dish to stand on'.

Victoria & Albert Museum (3229&A-1853)
Lit and refs: Wedgwood MS 61-30635; Honey 1948 pl. 40B; Arts Council 1972 Cat. 1866; Reilly 1989 I pl. 344

B25 Tureen and cover

Queen's Ware, painted in black and red enamel with 'Etruscan' border pattern (no. 34)
Marks: 'WEDGWOOD' and two workmen's marks (a triangle and a 'V') impressed
About 1785–90
Overall width: 22 cm; height: 12 cm

The form of this tureen has been attributed to John Flaxman junior (1755–1826), but without conclusive evidence, based on a bill covering work for the period 28 April–6 September 1782, which includes 'moulding a Turin'. It is possible that this was actually work done for Wedgwood by Flaxman

senior (1726–95; see Cat. E31), as two other items on the same bill are also for casting and moulding.

Trustees of the Wedgwood Museum, Barlaston, Staffordshire (No.5315)
Lit and refs: Wedgwood MS 2-1334, see Clifford 1992 p. 54; Bindman 1979 p. 62; Reilly 1989 I pl. 348

B26 Jug

Pearl Ware, painted in polychrome enamels, on one side with exotic birds and on the other with *'Deutsche Blumen'*; 'JM' in monogram inscribed under the lip
Marks: 'WEDGWOOD' and a crescent-shaped workman's mark impressed
About 1780
Height: 21.9 cm

Pearl Ware was a refinement of the Queen's Ware body, which was developed by Wedgwood during the 1770s in response to demand for a whiter-bodied material, and the first was marketed in 1779. Both the exotic birds in a landscape and the *'Deutsche Blumen'* here are unusual for Wedgwood. The jug was probably painted in Wedgwood's Decorating Studio in Cheyne Row, Chelsea, London. In December 1769 the painters employed by Wedgwood & Bentley in the capital moved to larger premises complete with a muffle kiln. From March 1770 the decorating workshop was managed by David Rhodes, who was fully employed by Wedgwood & Bentley rather than working on commission.

Trustees of the Wedgwood Museum, Barlaston, Staffordshire (No.9116)
Lit: Reilly 1989 I C67, pls 411 and 411A

BLACK BASALT

Basalt was described by Josiah Wedgwood as 'A fine black Porcelain, having nearly the same Properties as the Basaltes [ie. the mineral rock], resisting the Attacks of Acids; being a Touch-stone to Copper, Silver and Gold, and equal in Hardness to Agate or

Porphyry'. It was the result of his experiments to perfect a fine-grained stoneware suitable for the production of ornamental pieces, one that would complement the Neoclassical styles then coming into vogue. Black clay was derived from 'Carr', an oxide of iron suspended in the water which had flowed through coal seams and mines. This was drained and dried and then sold by the cartload to potters for use in the production of Basalt pottery. Wedgwood made no secret of his recipe for Basalt, which he recorded on page 236 of 'Common Place Book I' (Cat. B61). The entry is dated 1777, and reads:

Our Black Body.
80 of ball clay (Hydes) sifted
80 of Carr (ochre) calcined & ground
9 of manganese
The above is one Blending

A second slightly different recipe, dated July 1787, is also recorded on page 327 of the same manuscript. In this second entry the ingredients are listed as:

White clay sifted 110
Carr 100
Black Marle sifted 47 [marle was a term used for a natural clay containing a high percentage of iron oxide]
Manganese 12 pounds.

When these ingredients were fired together at a high temperature they vitrified into a fine-textured black body. The distinctive colour of Wedgwood's Basalt, which has a deep purplish-black hue, is due to the high proportion of manganese included in the formula. It is probable that Wedgwood was experimenting with a Basalt body by September 1767. He wrote to Bentley, 'I am still going on with my tryals, & want much to shew you some of them'. Certainly within 12 months Basalt was generally available. The body was named in an invoice of ware sent by William Cox (the company clerk in Great Newport Street, London), dated 30 August 1768, where the term 'Etruscan' is used, suggesting that Josiah believed that all the ancient pottery excavated in Italy had been manufactured by the Etruscans.

The surface of 18th-century Black Basalt has a natural lustrous sheen, which Wedgwood explained in a letter to William Cox

B 18

B 26

B 20

B 23

B 25

dated 31 August 1769: 'NB, the polish is natural to the composition & is given in burning, they are never oil'd &c'. By the summer of 1770 leather was being used further to polish Basalt vases while they were in the 'cheese hard' state before firing. They were also being turned in a new and different way. Wedgwood explained the new procedure to Bentley: 'I am trying another method to render the surface smoother in general when no accidents happen in the fireing which is to burnish them when they are pretty hard, with steel burnishers, 'till they have the polish of a Mirror; but as this is done by hand, it is very tedious work but they take an admirable polish if the fire does not destroy it.' From 1773 Wedgwood's plain black body became universally known as Basaltes. Both ornamental and useful wares were produced in this versatile body and it was used to make virtually anything the public required. Wedgwood placed great confidence in his new material, predicting that 'Black is Sterling and will last for ever'.

Refs: Wedgwood MSS 50-32412, 39-28408 pp. 236 and 327, E25-18167, 46-17667, E25-18316

B27 Teapot

Black Basalt, with engine-turned base section to pot and relief decoration of *Bacchanalian Boys*; lion finial to lid, and over handle to the teapot
Mark: 'Wedgwood & Bentley' impressed
About 1776
Height: 15.25 cm

The subject of *Bacchanalian Boys* was among the designs supplied to Wedgwood by Lady Diana Beauclerk (1734–1808). Other similar figures are attributed to François Duquesnoy (1594–1643), known as 'Il Fiammingo', the Flemish sculptor.

Trustees of the Wedgwood Museum, Barlaston, Staffordshire (No.5647)

B28 Mug

Black Basalt, the body engine-turned and decorated with a relief of *Bringing Home the Game*; with silver rim
Marks: 'Wedgwood', '5' and 'G' impressed
About 1769
Height: 9.5 cm; diameter: 7.5 cm

For the relief decoration see Cat. B42.

Trustees of the Wedgwood Museum, Barlaston, Staffordshire (No.5084)

B29 Inkstand with inkwell and covered sander, the central handles formed round a vase for a 'wett sponge'

Black Basalt, with encaustic decoration of white and orange flowers and foliate scrolls
Marks: 'Wedgwood & Bentley' impressed on the base of each piece and '33' impressed on the stand
About 1778
Length: 16.8 cm

An early mention of inkstands occurs in a letter from Wedgwood to Bentley, dated 29 July 1772, in which he writes 'I am contriving some Inkstands in black'. An unnumbered drawing of this form occurs in a factory costings book which is dated 1776. In the 'Oven Books' (the firing records of the Etruria factory), inkstands of this form occur in the entries for 25 November–2 December 1780 when '5 dozen and 8 were fired of which 5 dozen and 6 were successful'. The small vase in the centre of the stand is referred to in a letter dated 10 April 1776 from the London manager, William Cox, to Thomas Bentley indicating that it was for 'a wett spunge' to be used 'to moisten the pens'.

Trustees of the Wedgwood Museum, Barlaston, Staffordshire (No.84)
Lit and refs: Wedgwood MSS E25-18383, 54-30023, LHP MS 14; Reilly 1989 I pl. 712; Ars Ceramica 1994 p. 26

B30 'Bulbous-root pot'

Black Basalt, with moulded relief of cupids, and painted with encaustic colours

Marks: 'WEDGWOOD' and 'K' impressed
About 1790
Height: 13.4 cm

These rectangular bulb pots are generally referred to as 'bulbous root pots', the collared cups being for hyacinths. On 19 November 1767 Wedgwood sent to Bentley for sale 'Root Flower Pots of various sorts, ornamented & plain'. Bentley was uncertain about their use, causing Wedgwood to write on 31 December: 'Your <u>Punch bowl</u> is a <u>Winter Flowerpot</u>, not to be fill'd with <u>water</u> & <u>branches of</u> flowers, but with <u>sand</u>, & bulbous roots & is to those baubles made in Glass for growing one bulbous root, what a <u>Garden</u> is to a <u>Flowerpot</u>.' The relief of cupids carrying a garland is adapted from a Classical Roman motif, one that was revived during the Renaissance: a version appears on the tomb of the Ilaria del Carretto by the early 15th-century Siennese sculptor Jacopo della Quercia.

Victoria & Albert Museum (1487-1855)
Ref: Wedgwood MS E25-18182

B31 Teapot (the spout broken and ground down) and cover

Black Basalt, with encaustic decoration in blue and white
Mark: 'Wedgwood & Bentley' impressed
1769–80
Height: 14.7 cm

The 'encaustic' decoration on Wedgwood's Basalt wares was painted in a mixture of enamel and kaolin clay slip (that is a suspension of clay in water). As Wedgwood acknowledged, the technique bore no relation to true encaustic painting, in which stained and heated waxes are worked on to a porous ground. Wedgwood's stated in the introduction to Class XIX of the 1777 Catalogue that his pigments were invented 'not only … to imitate the Paintings upon Etruscan Vases, but to <u>do much more</u>; to give to the Beauty of Design, the Advantages of Light and Shade in various Colours; and to render Paintings durable without the Defect of a varnished or glassy Surface'. The technique was patented in

November 1769, this being one of only two patents Josiah Wedgwood ever took out.

Victoria & Albert Museum (310&A-1867)
Lit: Honey 1948 pl. 53A

B32(A) Tray

Black Basalt, with encaustic decoration of anthemion ornament in orange-brown and white
Marks: 'Wedgwood' and 'K' impressed
About 1783
37 × 29 cm

Wedgwood and Bentley encountered difficulties with the manufacture of large Basalt trays, which tended to warp and crack in the firing. The trays were also heavy, which created additional problems, causing Josiah to write on 19 September 1772: 'We cannot make Canister tops <u>air tight</u> with the Canisters, nor <u>light, black</u> Dejuniers. <u>Black</u> ware will be heavy'. Four years later, in January 1776, Wedgwood reported the successful production of 'larger Tea Treas .... & furniture suitable'. See also Cat. B31.

Trustees of the Wedgwood Museum, Barlaston, Staffordshire (No.NY 4974)
Lit and refs: Wedgwood MSS E25-18407, E25-18643; see Reilly 1989 I p. 429

B32(B) Chocolate jug or coffee ewer

Black Basalt, with encaustic decoration of anthemion ornament in orange-brown and white
Marks: 'WEDGWOOD', '5' and a workman's mark impressed
About 1783
Height: 25 cm

This form is identified as a 'chocolate jug' in the 'Oven Books' (the factory firing records).

Trustees of the Wedgwood Museum, Barlaston, Staffordshire (No.1144)
Lit: Reilly 1989 I pl. 613

B32(C) Milk or cream jug, from a cabaret or tea-set

Black Basalt, with encaustic decoration of anthemion ornament in orange-brown and white
Mark: 'Wedgwood & Bentley' impressed
About 1778
Height: 8.9 cm

Although there was a considerable number of Black Basalt teawares listed in the catalogue of the Christie & Ansell sale of 1781 (which took place following the death of Thomas Bentley), very few lots of encaustic decorated teawares were included. Black teaware found great favour with aristocratic ladies, so much so that by the end of 1772 Wedgwood was enthusiastically writing to Thomas Bentley, 'I hope white hands will continue in fashion & then we may continue to make black Teapots'.

Trustees of the Wedgwood Museum, Barlaston, Staffordshire (No.89)
Lit and refs: Wedgwood MS E25-18430; Reilly 1989 I pl. 612

B32(D) Teapot

Black Basalt, with encaustic decoration of anthemion ornament in orange-brown and white
Marks: 'Wedgwood' and '2' impressed
About 1783
Height: 10.2 cm; overall length: 17.7 cm

Trustees of the Wedgwood Museum, Barlaston, Staffordshire (No.245)

B32(E) Cup and saucer

Black Basalt, with encaustic decoration of anthemion ornament in orange-brown and white
Mark: 'Wedgwood' impressed on both
About 1783
Diameter of saucer: 13 cm

Trustees of the Wedgwood Museum, Barlaston, Staffordshire (No.1088)

B32(F) Teacup and saucer

Black basalt, with encaustic decoration of anthemion ornament in orange-brown and white
Marks: 'Wedgwood', 'I' and '4' impressed
About 1783
Diameter of saucer: 12.9 cm

Victoria & Albert Museum. Jermyn Street Collection (2047&A-1901)

B33 Bust of Homer

Black Basalt
Marks: 'Wedgwood & Bentley' impressed and 'HOMER' impressed on bust; 'WEDGWOOD & BENTLEY' impressed on the socle
About 1779
Height: 34.4 cm

Library busts, which had earlier been made in plaster and other materials, were not made in pottery until Wedgwood began manufacturing them in Black Basalt in the early 1770s, the earliest reference to their production occurring in a letter dated 16 February 1771. Wedgwood obtained a cast of the bust of Homer from the plaster shop of Hoskins & Grant in 1774, and this was adapted by William Hackwood (about 1757–1839) before being produced in Black Basalt. Busts of Homer were listed in the 1779 *Catalogue of Ornamental Ware*, two sizes, 15 inches and 4½ inches being available.

Trustees of the Wedgwood Museum, Barlaston, Staffordshire (No.75)
Lit and refs: Wedgwood MS LHP 16th February 1771; Science Museum 1978 Cat. 137

B34 Bust of Marcus Aurelius (AD 120–180)

Black Basalt
Marks: 'WEDGWOOD & BENTLEY' impressed in two places and 'MARCUS AURELIUS' impressed in the back
1774–80
Height: 38.2 cm

The Roman Emperor Marcus Aurelius is

best remembered for his devotion to the Stoic Philosophy. Wedgwood produced two busts of him: this youthful version generally referred to as 'The Young Marcus Aurelius', and a larger figure 25 inches in height. Plaster models of both were supplied by Hoskins & Grant in 1774. The bust is listed under 'BUSTS' in Class XII, Section I of the 1779 Catalogue.

Trustees of the Wedgwood Museum, Barlaston, Staffordshire (No.1162)
Lit: Wedgwood 1984 Cat. H52

B35 Figure of Voltaire (François Marie Arouet; 1694–1778)

Black Basalt
Unmarked
In production by 1778; this example possibly later
Height: 29.4 cm

The model for a figure of Voltaire is mentioned by Wedgwood in a letter to Bentley dated 10 July 1777: 'The box by the Coach is arrived with the contˢ., and I shall be very glad to see the Statue of Voltaire, and we will endeavor to make you some copies of it ...'. The figure was possibly

modelled by William Keeling (active 1763–90), working from a drawing provided by Thomas Bentley of the marble sculpture of 1773 by Jean-Claude Rosset, called du Pont (1703/6–86). A companion figure of Jean-Jacques Rousseau (1712–78) was in production by October 1779. Wedgwood wrote on 16 of October of that year, 'We send you two small statues of Voltaire and Rousseau made of cane color clay'.

Victoria & Albert Museum (C.58-1915)
Lit and refs: Wedgwood MSS E25-18770 and E26-18931; Honey 1948 pl. 35; Dawson 1984 p. 86; Bindman 1989 p. 84

B 30

B 31

WHITE TERRACOTTA STONEWARE

One of the first references to the white terracotta stoneware body appears on 13 June 1770, when Wedgwood stated: 'I shall go about the white bisket immediately'. It is variously described in his *Catalogues of Ornamental Wares* as 'fine white terra-cotta' (1774), 'White waxen Biscuit Ware, or Terra Cotta' (1779), and 'White porcelain biscuit with a smooth wax-like surface' (1787). Although the different descriptions indicate developments with the same material, they have formerly been thought to refer to early forms of Jasper and Pearl Ware, the two other white bodies that Wedgwood was developing during the 1770s. The body itself is dense and hard, being similar in appearance to biscuit creamware, but fired at a higher temperature. It could take enamel colours and gilding as well as a clear glaze.

Terracotta was described by Wedgwood in the 1779 Catalogue as being 'of great beauty and delicacy, proper for cameos, portraits and bas-reliefs'. Initially it was used primarily for architectural plaques, cameos and medallions, but by the Christie & Ansell sale of Wedgwood & Bentley stock in 1781, the year after Bentley died, quantities of flower pots, vases, paint-boxes and other ornamental items were being manufactured in the terracotta body. It now seems probable that the large oval ceramic plaques made by Wedgwood for George Stubbs (1724–1806) to decorate were composed of the terracotta body.

B36 Paint box, with a tray containing a palette and 12 small pots for colours

White terracotta biscuit, decorated with a matt black slip; interior glazed; the lid decorated with a dolphin finial; the body engine-turned to reveal the white body underneath
Marks: 'WEDGWOOD' and 'S' impressed
About 1780
Length: 15.9 cm; height: 10.2 cm

Wedgwood made 'colour cups' for James 'Athenian' Stuart (1713–88) in January 1771. He was also prepared to make a considerable number of paint boxes for ladies' amusement. In the Christie & Ansell sale of the stock of Wedgwood & Bentley's partnership, which commenced 3 December 1781, Day 1 lot 7 reads: 'One

B 39

Box with an Apparatus for painting. The paint boxes contain in a very small compass, a neat apparatus for a Lady's painting or for the use of young people learning to draw and colour prints'. A further reference to these paint boxes occurs on 22 January 1779, when Thomas Byerley wrote to Peter Swift: 'The paint cups should be glazed within & on the edge for they say that the least roughness will injure a Camel's Hair pencil'.

Trustees of the Wedgwood Museum, Barlaston, Staffordshire (No.1360)
Lit and refs: Wedgwood MSS E25-18337 and 13-12428; Wedgwood 1984 Cat. H24; Reilly 1989 I pl. 497

B37 Vase

White terracotta stoneware, with applied and engine-turned decoration, dark brown slip and blue porphyry glazes; ornaments picked out in gold
Marks: 'WEDGWOOD' impressed, and 'K' incised
About 1785–90
Height: 16 cm

The shape is listed as no. 346 in the 'Shape Number One Book', where it is given in four sizes – large, 2nd, 3rd and 4th – under the column 'Pebble, gilt and black'. In the 'Shape Book' of 1790 the same shape is given again in four sizes: large, less, less, least; it is also described as 'diped & flu [fluted]'.

Victoria & Albert Museum (3528-1853)

B38 Plaque: *Silenus and Boys*

White terracotta stoneware, with oil-gilding
Mark: 'WEDGWOOD & BENTLEY' impressed
About 1774
12.2 × 16.2 cm

The subject of the relief seems to date from 1773, when Wedgwood obtained models of 'Silenus and Boys' from Mrs Landré (active 1768–74), a London mould-maker to whom he paid five shillings for each. In a letter to Bentley, postmarked 29 May 1776, Wedgwood makes reference to the plaque:

'The Tablet of Silenus, if it had been whole, would have been worth 4 or 5 Guineas. Nothing so fine can be had for five times the money, if at all, & these things can be had only from us, nor shall we have any competitors in haste'. The subject is listed as Class II, number 14, in the *Catalogue of Ornamental Wares*.

Holburne Museum and Crafts Centre, Bath
Lit and refs: Wedgwood MS E25-18671; Reilly 1989 I pl. 491

CANE WARE

Cane Ware is a dry-bodied stoneware, perfected from local North Staffordshire clays. Wedgwood commenced work on this body in the early 1770s, and on 9 September 1771 he was able to write to Thomas Bentley: '& am very happy to know the Fawn colour'd articles are agreeable to your wishes, – I believe they will sell, for all who have seen them here, have fall'n in love with them'. Cane Ware was used for both Ornamental and Useful pieces, many of which were decorated in imitation of bamboo. Major pieces do not seem to have been produced until 1779, and it was not until the summer of 1786 that the new body was totally established. It first appears in the 1787 edition of the *Catalogue of Ornamental Wares*, when it was the fifth in Wedgwood's list of ceramic bodies.

B39 Teapot and cover

Cane Ware, the lower part of the body, handle and lid moulded to resemble bamboo, the body with relief of *Bacchanalian Boys*, and with details picked out in blue
Marks: 'WEDGWOOD' and '2' impressed
About 1790
Height: 9.2 cm

The subject of *Bacchanalian Boys* had been taken from a mould supplied by Mrs Mary Landré (active 1768–74) after a design by François Duquesnoy (1594–1643), known as 'Il Fiammingo', a Flemish sculptor and

modeller who was one of the assistants to Bernini.

Victoria & Albert Museum (1505&A-1855)
Lit: Honey 1948 pl. 62

B40 Butter tub and cover

Cane Ware, the cover with recumbent cow knop, with enamelled decoration in blue and white
Marks: 'WEDGWOOD' and 'K' impressed and three dots painted in blue enamel
About 1785–90
Height: 10.2 cm; length: 15.3 cm

Butter tubs of this form are featured in the 'Shape Number One Book'.

On loan to the Wedgwood Museum, Barlaston, Staffordshire. From the Collection of Mr R. M. Stevenson

B41 Bowl

Cane Ware, enamelled in blue and white
Marks: 'WEDGWOOD' and '2' impressed
About 1785–90
Height: 9.3 cm; diameter: 19 cm

Victoria & Albert Museum. Jermyn Street Collection. Formerly in the Enoch Wood Collection (2385-1901)

B42 Mug

Cane Ware, with Sheffield plate mount, the body ornamented with a relief of *Bringing Home the Game* and with moulded 'bamboo' foot and handle. The canted rim and the interior are covered with an opaque white glaze; enamel decoration in blue comprising a variant of the 'egg and tongue' pattern around the rim; blue lines emphasize the bamboo moulding
Mark: 'WEDGWOOD' impressed
About 1786
Height: 25.4 cm

The relief subject, *Bringing Home the Game*, is the pair to *Hunting*. The first reference to these subjects occurs in a letter from Wedgwood to Bentley dated 13 March

1774: 'We have 4 Bass reliefs of Boys about 12 inches by 8 representing, War – Hunting – & the Arts & Sciences – Music. Out of these I propose making 4 or 6 Medallions ..... They will be in pairs & represent, Hunting in two Medall., Music & the Arts in two more & War – if you please to have so horrid a subject represented by innocent Babes, in two more.'

Trustees of the Wedgwood Museum, Barlaston, Staffordshire (No.1365)
Lit and refs: Wedgwood MS E25-18523; Reilly 1989 I pl. C117

ROSSO ANTICO

Wedgwood's *Rosso Antico* ('Old Red') body is a stoneware with similar properties to Black Basalt and Cane Ware. On 23 June 1770 Wedgwood informed Bentley that he had 'got a substance for lightening red Vases', adding 'The red Vases sho[d]. be an exact copy of the Etruscans'. Wedgwood was initially reluctant to manufacture *Rosso Antico* and even in March 1776 he wrote: 'I will try and imitate the Antico Rosso from your description. But when I have done my best, I am afraid where one spectator thinks of Antico Rosso an hundred will be put in mind of a Red Teapot.' Despite his lack of enthusiasm for the material he produced a wide range of objects in this body.

B43 Pot-pourri vase, with candle-holder lid

Rosso Antico, with a matt black surface dip, engine-turned with straight flutes to reveal the red body beneath; glazed interior
Unmarked
About 1780–85
Height: 21.2 cm

This form is listed in a factory 'Shape Book' as no. 144: 'Fluted shoulder from Plaister Vase'. Wedgwood observed to Bentley on 25 July 1772, 'you mention black & red fluted upon the English lathe in the Etruscan stile. I suppose you mean black and red upon the same piece in flutes so

//// but that is extremely difficult.'

Trustees of the Wedgwood Museum, Barlaston, Staffordshire (No.1332)
Refs: Wedgwood MSS 54-30019 and E25-18382

B44 Pot-pourri vase (without cover)

Rosso Antico, with a matt black surface dip, engine-turned with spiral flutes to reveal the red body beneath; glazed interior
Unmarked
About 1780–85
Height: 17.2 cm

See Cat. B43.

Trustees of the Wedgwood Museum, Barlaston, Staffordshire (No.1333)

B45 Bulb pot

Rosso Antico, dipped in black slip, and engine-turned
Mark: 'Wedgwood & Bentley' impressed
About 1775
Height: 12.1 cm

The bulb pot has a loose top with three cups for bulbs. The interior is glazed to make it impervious to water. The form is illustrated at the back of the 'Shape Number One Book' in a group of watercolour drawings illustrating the various bulb pot forms available during the 18th century.

Victoria & Albert Museum. Seawell Bequest (C.776&A-1917)

JASPER

With changes in architectural styles and the rise in popularity of Neo-classical styles of interior decoration, Josiah Wedgwood began a series of experiments to create a new ceramic material that would complement the new fashions. Thousands of meticulously recorded experiments were carried out to make a stoneware body that was capable of taking a mineral oxide stain throughout. The search for the Jasper body absorbed much of Wedgwood's energy and time, the result being his most important contribution to ceramic history.

The first reference to Jasper is generally assumed to be that written by Josiah on 13 January 1771, when he expressed his intention: 'To make a white body, succeptible of being colour'd & which will polish itself in burning bisket', although it is possible that this may relate to the terracotta stoneware he was working on simultaneously. Much of his experimental work was carried out in response to Bentley's request made late in 1772 for 'a finer body for Gems'. As late as December 1772 he had not made much progress in perfecting the material, but by the summer of the following year he had isolated, though not totally understood, the ingredients required. The majority of the actual trials were carried out between December 1772 and December 1774, Josiah writing on the 17 March of the latter year: 'I have for some time past been reviewing my experiments, & I find such Roots, such Seeds as would open & branch out wonderfully if I could nail myself down to the cultivation of them for a year or two'. Even in June 1776 he was commenting, almost in frustration, 'This Jasper is certainly the most delicately whimsical of any substance I ever engag'd with'.

By January 1775 he was 'absolute' in the production of Jasper with coloured grounds. He was also in a position to advertise that he could manufacture bas-reliefs, ranging from large plaques to small cameos for mounting as jewellery. The range of colours steadily increased, and by March 1776 Josiah was sending his first specimens of yellow to London. By September experiments were in hand for black Jasper, Wedgwood commenting that 'Black blue grounds are what I have been attempting a long time'. Certainly by the spring of 1777 he was carrying out further experiments to perfect a surface 'dip' to provide deeper coloured grounds for his cameos; and by the middle of December 1777, he was able to offer Bentley a choice of 'green – yellow – lalock [lilac] etc. to the colour of the rooms', referring to the tones favoured by their mutual acquaintance the architect Robert Adam (1728–92).

The introduction of American clay into the

Jasper composition was something Josiah felt worthy of advertising. He wrote, on 15 December 1777, 'I have often thought of mentioning to you that it may not be a bad idea to give out, that our small Jaspers are made of the Cherokee clay which I sent an agent into that country on purpose to procure for me, ... A portion of Cherokee clay is really used in all the small Jaspers so make what use you please of the fact.'

The number of plaques and tablets available rapidly increased, the number of models listed in the first Catalogue of 1773 and being more than doubled once Jasper was in production, 275 'Bas-relief Medallions Tablets etc.' being listed under Class II of the Catalogue of 1787. The tablets were important to Josiah, causing him to comment in August 1775: 'I am going upon a large scale with our Models etc. which is one reason why you have so few new things just now, but I hope to bring the whole in compass for your next Winter's Shew and ASTONISH THE WORLD ALL AT ONCE for I hate piddleing you know'.

Refs: Wedgwood MSS LHP 13 January 1771; E25-18521; E25-18673; E25-18701; E25-18803; E25-18802; E25-18614

B46 Tray of Jasper trials

79 Jasper pieces, mounted in a wooden tray
Unmarked
About 1773–6
39 × 30 cm

Each trial piece is marked with a number that corresponds to an entry in Wedgwood's 'Experiment Book'. Many pieces are also impressed with the firing instructions, for example 'TTBO' for tip-top of biscuit oven, the hottest part of the bottle oven. In nearly all of the sequence of trials to perfect a coloured Jasper body Wedgwood used between 120 and 200 parts of the white Jasper mixed together with one part of cobalt or zaffre, and usually 18 parts of coleothar.

Trustees of the Wedgwood Museum, Barlaston, Staffordshire (No.4228)
Lit and refs: Wedgwood MS LHP 13th January 1771; Science Museum 1978 pp. 56–7

B47 Two trial Jasper medallions: *Orestes at Delphi* **and** *Hercules and the Nemean Lion*

Pale blue Jasper with white reliefs
Unmarked
About 1775
11.4 × 8.9 cm

The blistering illustrates clearly the problems encountered by Wedgwood in producing his new Jasper body.

Trustees of the Wedgwood Museum, Barlaston, Staffordshire (No.5063 & A)
Refs: Wedgwood MSS E25-18443, E25-18521, E25-18578

B48 Demonstration plaque: *Cupid in his car drawn by lions*

Made by Bert Bentley
Jasper
Marks: 'WEDGWOOD' and 'O' impressed
1922
14 × 21 cm

The plaque shows the four stages of making a tri-colour Jasper dip cameo. This method of making cameos has remained unchanged for more than 200 years.

Trustees of the Wedgwood Museum, Barlaston, Staffordshire (No.5290)
Lit: Reilly 1989 I pl. C137

B49 Portrait medallion of John Flaxman junior (1755–1826) *(Pl. 4)*

After a model by John Flaxman junior
White Jasper with green dip and white relief
Mark: 'WEDGWOOD' impressed
About 1790–5
Diameter: 15.2 cm

John Flaxman junior's name first appears in the Wedgwood and Bentley correspondence in September 1771, when Josiah reported the visit of Mr Freeman of Schute Lodge to Etruria: 'He is a great admirer of young Flaxman & has advis'd his Father to send him to Rome, which he has promis'd to do. Mr Freeman says he knows young Flaxman is a Coxcomb, but does not think him a bit

the worse for it, <u>or the less likely to be a great Artist</u>'. Plasters of this portrait, and its pair of Mrs Anne Flaxman (née Denman), are in the Sir John Soane Museum, London. Both versions appear to have been taken from waxes executed during Flaxman's stay in Rome, 1787–94.

Trustees of the Wedgwood Museum, Barlaston, Staffordshire (No.W1/22)
Lit and refs: Wedgwood MS LHP 7 Sept 1771; Reilly and Savage 1973 p. 138; Bindman 1979 Cat. 53

B50 Chess figures from a set

Designed and modelled by John Flaxman junior (1755–1826)
White Jasper, with blue-dipped or lilac stands
Mark: 'WEDGWOOD' impressed
About 1785
Height of King: 9.5 cm; height of Queen: 9.5 cm

Josiah Wedgwood was obviously pleased with the set of chess figures, as a letter from John Flaxman dated 5 February 1784 indicates: 'I return you many thanks, for the liberal praise you bestow on my chess figures'. By 20 February, progress in the production was reported to the artist: 'We are getting forward with the Chessmen, & hope soon to send a complete set to Greek Street'. Pieces are mentioned in the 'Oven Books', the firing records, from December 1783. The designs for the figures came from a variety of sources including the Parthenon Frieze (the Knight), and the façade of Wells Cathedral. Flaxman was to exhibit a considerable knowledge of Gothic architecture in his lectures to the Royal Academy. The figures of the kings and queens are thought to represent John Philip Kemble and his sister Sarah Siddons, the celebrated 18th-century actor and actress. For Flaxman's presentation drawing of the set see Cat. D55.

Trustees of the Wedgwood Museum, Barlaston, Staffordshire (No.3943)
Lit and refs: Wedgwood MSS 2-30183 and 2-30189; Science Museum 1978 Cat. 212; Bindman

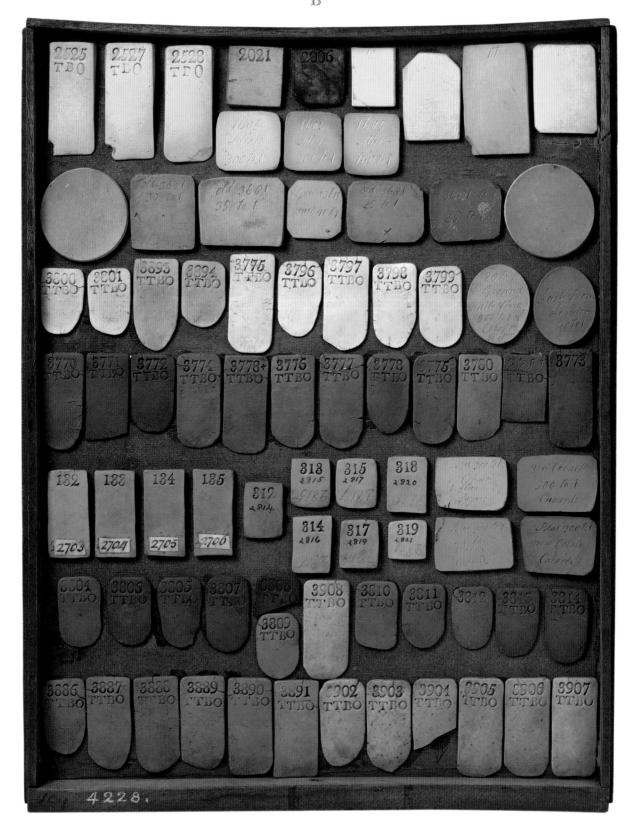

4228.

1979 Cat. 45; Reilly 1989 I pp. 636–7

B51 Vase

The reliefs after models by John Flaxman
junior (1755–1826)
Lilac Jasper, with white reliefs
Marks: 'WEDGWOOD' impressed twice
About 1790
Height: 28.5 cm

Josiah Wedgwood acquired a set of the
Muse figures by Edme Bouchardon
(1698–1770) by 1770, but he did not use
them until several years later. As Wedgwood
commented to Bentley at this time: 'I have
some objections to Bouchardons Muses
upon a more attentive inspection of them
which would prevent my giving them to
model. – They are not sufficiently finish'd
for an <u>unlearned</u> modeller to copy. Some of
them are essentially bad in other respects,
& from their being <u>left handed</u> I suppose
they are poor copies from Bouchardons
originals.' The letter continues: 'You may

permit Mr. Flaxman to proceed with the
Muses of the size he had begun, they will be
very useful to us & I would give half the
price of modelling extra to be in possession
of them now, so be so good to expedite him
all you can. We have Apollo, Melpomena,
Thalia & Terpshichore, so that we only
want 6 more to complete our suite.'

It is likely that the figures of the part set
were those Wedgwood had aquired from
Flaxman senior in March 1775, for which
he paid a half a guinea each. On 29 October
1777 Wedgwood commented to Bentley
that: 'Having laid all our bass-relief
Goddesses & ladies upon their backs on a
board before me in order to contemplate
their beauties, & to increase their numbers,
I instantly perceiv'd that the six Muses we
want might be produc'd from this lovely
group at half the trouble and expense they
will be procured from Flaxman, & much
better figures. For little more than 5/- each
we can complete them very well'. The
attribution of the modellers for the Muses is
complicated by another invoice headed

'Account of Letters from and to Mr. Angelo
Dalzamazzoni at Rome 1788–1790', in
which a payment to Guiseppe Angelini
(1742–1811) for a set of the Muses is
recorded in 1789. This second set was
probably copied from the Sarcophagus of
the Muses, then in the Capitoline Museum,
Rome.

*Trustees of the National Museums and Galleries
on Merseyside (Lady Lever Art Gallery)
Accession no.: LL1177
Refs: Wedgwood MSS E25-18788, 1-204, E25-
18789, W/M 1526*

B52 Plaque: *The Triumph of Bacchus*

Modelled by William Hackwood (about
1757–1839)
White Jasper with a blue surface dip; white
relief of Bacchus in his car accompanied by
Silenus and two single bacchanalian figures
Mark: 'WEDGWOOD & BENTLEY' impressed
About 1778
16.2 × 31 cm

B 52

The first mention of this subject occurs in a letter dated 6 January 1776: 'Hackwood has nearly finish'd the two Tablets of the birth & Triumph of Bacchus, but I am afraid we shall not be able to make either of them in one continued Tablet ... We could make them to fill a Frise very cleverly in seperate pieces'. For the *Birth of Bacchus* see also Cat. D56.

Trustees of the Wedgwood Museum, Barlaston, Staffordshire (No.WM 35)
Ref: Wedgwood MS E25-18641

B53 Teapot and cover

White Jasper with lilac dip and engine-turned decoration
Marks: 'WEDGWOOD', '8' and 'O' impressed
About 1785–90
Height: 15.9 cm

The subject of the decoration is *Domestic Employment*, two versions of which are listed in Wedgwood's 1787 Catalogue. One of these is stated to be 'from a design of Miss Crewe's', and the second 'from Lady Templeton'. Apart from these titles, nothing is known of Emma Crewe's work, and this design is generally attributed to Lady Templetown. Lady Templetown (1747–1823), an amateur artist, was the source of 14 sentimental, morally didactic and uplifting subjects, most or all of which were modelled by William Hackwood. In June 1783 Wedgwood wrote in self-abasing terms requesting more designs:

> Mr W presents his most respectfull comp to Lady Templeton & is very happy to learn ... that his attempt to copy in bas relief the charming groups of little figures her ladyship was so obliging as to lend him has met with the approbation which he durst not flatter himself with, & is sensible he owes much to Lady Templetons politeness on this occasion. Mr Wedgwood is afraid to trespass farther upon the goodness he has already experien'd & is sensible that nothing but experience could justify his expressing a wish to be indulged in copying a few more groups ...

Victoria & Albert Museum. Given by Lady Charlotte Schreiber (Schr.II.548)
Lit and refs: Wedgwood MS E.26-18958, see Reilly 1989 I p. 604

B54 Cup, cover cup, cover and stand

White Jasper with blue dip, engine-turned decoration and applied reliefs in white
Marks: 'WEDGWOOD' and 'H' impressed
About 1785
Height: 14.2 cm

A chocolate cup, lid and stand of this form is drawn in the 'London Pattern Book, 1787' (Cat. D19), where it is numbered as 329.

Victoria & Albert Museum. J. A. Tulk Bequest (Circ.744 to B-1965)

B55 'Ruined column' vase

White Jasper, the panels with blue wash
Marks: 'WEDGWOOD' and two lozenges impressed
About 1786–95
Height: 19.7 cm

There is little documentary evidence to assist in the dating of the introduction of ruined column vases. The problem is further compounded by the numerous different styles of ruined vases and ruined columns made by Wedgwood. The 'Oven Books', the 18th-century firing records, contain thumbnail sketches of this type of vase, which are described as 'Rute' or 'Flowerpots'. Between 10 and 17 December 1785 and 18 and 25 March 1786 three firings included ruined column cases, all of which are listed as blue and white, a total of 14 single, 6 double and 6 triple columns being successfully produced. The shape is recorded as no.1566 in the first 'Ornamental Ware Shape Book'. The contemporary cost of these types of vases is recorded by Thomas Byerley: 'prices recd. from Etrua. 29th June 1786, Ruin'd Vase 15/- Single Column 31/- – Double Columns – 42/-, Triple – 63/-'.

Victoria & Albert Museum (1519-1855)
Ref: Wedgwood MS No.45-29110

B56 'Ruined vase'

White Jasper, the panels painted with blue wash
Mark: 'WEDGWOOD' impressed
About 1786–95
Height: 16.5 cm

See Cat. B55.

Victoria & Albert Museum. Given by Mr J. H. Fitzhenry (131-1906)
Lit: Reilly 1989 I pl. 1005

B57 Water ewer ('Sacred to Neptune')

Blue Jasper, with white reliefs
Mark: 'WEDGWOOD' impressed
About 1790
Height: 38 cm

See Cat. E32 for a version in Black Basalt, and Cat. E31 for the derivation of the design.

Trustees of the National Museums and Galleries on Merseyside (Lady Lever Art Gallery)
Accession no.: LL1029

B58 Vase

Blue Jasper, with white Jasper handles and reliefs in white
Mark: 'WEDGWOOD' impressed
About 1790
Height: 35.8 cm

The relief of *Venus in her Chariot drawn by Swans* is after designs by Charles Le Brun (1629–90). The vase shape appears in both the 'London Pattern Book' (Cat. D19), and the 'Shape Number One Book', where it is no. 266. A Jasper vase of this design, and with the same relief, was illustrated in the 1787 English Catalogue, and in the French edition of the following year. This illustration was possibly after drawings by Henry Webber (1754–1826), a modeller who began work for Wedgwood early in 1782, as is recorded in an 'Extract of Memorandums by Mr. Webber to be presented to Mr Wedgwood ...'. This document contains a detailed description of the contents of Webber's sketchbook, for

B 55
B 56

which he was paid £16 9s 0d. A list of loose sketches at the bottom of the page covering the years 1782–4 includes 'A Sketch of a vase to Marine Venus'.

B59 Fan

The sticks and guards of ivory mounted with blue Jasper panels and medallions with white reliefs; the paper leaf painted with floral sprays in body colour
No visible marks
About 1790
Length of guards: 28.5 cm

The trapezoid shape of the Jasper mounts to the guards suggests that they were specially made for this purpose. No mention of fan mounts has been traced in the Wedgwood manuscripts, and no other fan with similar mounts is known. The reliefs include Aesculapius Flowers, Cupid and Psyche and Hercules and the Nemean Lion.

B 53

THE PYROMETER

Wedgwood's pyrometer was an instrument that used the degree of shrinkage of clay during firing as a means of determining kiln temperatures. It consisted of a gauge with a tapering slot which was used in conjunction with clay cylinders of a standard size. The cylinders were placed in the kiln and then removed one by one in succession. Once these had cooled they were placed in the pyrometer's slot, and the temperature was gauged from how far they would fit down the pyrometer's tapering slot, their shrinkage being proportional to the kiln's temperature. Prior to Wedgwood's invention of the pyrometer in 1782 the only means of assessing the temperature during firing was by observation of the colour of the fire.

B60 Pyrometer

Stoneware
Unmarked
About 1786
Length: 19 cm; width: 3.9 cm

From 1786 Wedgwood made stoneware pyrometer sets for sale and as gifts for his friends. In each boxed set two gauges, covering the range 0 to 120 and 120 to 240, were provided together with a supply of pyrometric clay cylinders. In July 1786 a set was presented to George III for the collection of scientific instruments under his patronage at the Observatory, Richmond, Surrey. Wedgwood's 'Common Place Book' includes the following note:

My Thermometer, prices, Settled May 1, 1788	
The gage	2 : 2 : 0
The pieces, 1½d each – 126 in a box	15 : 9
The cases, 2d each – 6 in a box	1 : 0
The box	1 : 3
	-----------
	3 : 3 : 0
	[sic]

Trustees of the Wedgwood Museum, Barlaston, Staffordshire (No.4805)
Lit and refs: Wedgwood MS 39-28408; Science Museum 1978 Cat. 48

B 60 / B 62

B61 Manuscript volume

Inscribed on the spine 'J.W Common Place Book I'
Begun about 1768
33.1 × 22 cm (closed)

The book contains jottings and observations on a wide range of topics, ranging from Wedgwood's draft papers on 'constructing a Thermometer upon a new principle for measuring high degrees of heat', to ceramic bodies and their composition, family and medical matters, details relating to the pottery works and a description of his 'Journey into Cornwall' undertaken in 1775. The book is written in Josiah's own hand, that of his wife, Sarah, and of his secretary, Alexander Chisholm.

Trustees of the Wedgwood Museum, Barlaston, Staffordshire (MS 39-28408)

B62 *Description and use of a thermometer for measuring the higher degrees of heat, from a red up to the strongest heat that vessels made of clay can support. By Josiah Wedgwood F.R.S and Potter to her Majesty. M.D.C.C.LXXXIV.*

1784
16.5 × 10.2 cm

About 650 of these pamphlets were printed in London by Joseph Cooper, the wording being largely taken from the paper read by Josiah to the Royal Society on 9 May 1782. Foreign language editions of the pamphlet were also produced, including 1,000 copies in French, translated in 1785, and 500 copies translated into German in 1786.

Trustees of the Wedgwood Museum, Barlaston, Staffordshire (No.29989/2-50)
Lit: Science Museum 1978 Cat. 54 and 55

B63 Medallion

White Jasper, inlaid with blue Jasper
Unmarked
1784
5.1 × 3.6 cm

The medallion bears the inlaid inscription 'BY J. WEDGWOOD F.R.S.' on the front and 'No 110' on the reverse. Production of these medallions is mentioned in the 'Oven Book' for 5 and 12 June 1784: '2dz & 3dz blue & white lybols Jos. Wedgwood F.R.S.'. Their exact purpose is not known, but they were probably designed to be inset into the top of boxes made to contain pyrometer sets.

Trustees of the Wedgwood Museum, Barlaston, Staffordshire (No.1233)
Lit and refs: Wedgwood MS 53-30015; Wedgwood 1984 Cat. F4

Josiah Wedgwood, A Lifetime of Achievement

The making of a master-potter

In October 1862, some 67 years after the death of Britain's greatest manufacturing potter, Godfrey Wedgwood responded to a request for information: 'I am fully satisfied that there are not materials for a really satisfactory life of my great-grandfather. I am sorry that such a man should have left so little to chronicle behind him'.[1] He was apparently unaware of the startling discovery, by Joseph Mayer of Liverpool in 1848, of many thousands of Wedgwood manuscripts that were being sold by a Birmingham scrap merchant to local grocers as wrapping paper. This extraordinary hoard, which includes most of Josiah Wedgwood's letters to his partner, Thomas Bentley, is now preserved at Keele University and forms the heart of one of the most important archives of the Industrial Revolution.

These archives yield an exceptionally full record of the Wedgwood factory at Etruria and an intimate portrait of Josiah Wedgwood, his way of life, his personal relationships, experiments and business methods; but they contain almost nothing of his early days. It is remarkable that even his sons do not seem to have known the date of his birth.[2] The parish register of St John's Church, Burslem, records the baptism of Josiah, son of Thomas and Mary Wedgwood of the Churchyard Pottery, on 12 July 1730.[3]

The youngest of 13 children[4] in a Staffordshire family whose ancestry has been traced back to the 14th century, Josiah was the great-great-grandson of Gilbert Wedgwood, who worked a small pottery in Burslem towards the end of the 17th century. Four successive generations of Wedgwoods worked the Churchyard Pottery, where Josiah was born, and, when his father died in 1739, Josiah's eldest brother, Thomas, inherited the family business. The Churchyard Wedgwoods were not as prosperous as some of their local kinsmen, but the purchase by Josiah's father of a family pew in the parish church for the substantial sum of £7 suggests that neither were they oppressively poor.[5]

Although no contemporary records of his education have survived, it is probable that the young Josiah walked the seven-mile round journey to and from a small school kept by one John or Thomas Blunt in Newcastle-under-Lyme.[6] There is no evidence that Josiah finished his schooling before the age of 14, when he was apprenticed to his brother, Thomas, in November 1744 to learn 'the Art of Throwing and Handleing' – the special skills of those expected to become master-potters. During this period, Josiah suffered a severe attack of smallpox,[7] which left his right knee so weakened that he was unable to use the 'kick-wheel', the mechanism that provided the motive power to the thrower's wheel. After the end of his apprenticeship, Josiah remained at the Churchyard Pottery for a further three years before entering into partnership with John Harrison and Thomas Allders. In 1754 he became the partner of Thomas Whieldon, one of the most creative and respected potters in Britain. The partnership lasted for five years and it was during his time at Whieldon's Fenton Vivian pottery that Wedgwood began his experiments, as he wrote in his 'Experiment Book': 'to try for some more solid improvement, as well in the <u>Body</u>, as the <u>Glazes</u>, the <u>Colours</u>, and the <u>Form</u> of the articles of our manufacture'.[8]

English pottery before 1760 has too often been dismissed as a peasant craft, but the tin-glazed or salt-glazed earthenwares and the work of John Dwight and the Elers brothers was certainly not lacking in invention, craftsmanship or a sense of design. There was, nevertheless, a great gulf in quality between any pottery made in Europe and the imported porcelains of China.

The search for the secret of 'white gold' (as 'true' or 'hard-paste' porcelain in imitation of the Chinese was known) helped to occupy the minds and empty the coffers of European kings and princes, and its discovery in 1708 by Johann Friedrich Böttger (1682–1719), while in the service of Augustus the Strong, Elector of Saxony, only increased the desire of almost every European ruler to finance his own factory. The composition was soon known to factories in Germany and the Palatinate, but the secret did not reach Sèvres, where the finest 'artificial' or 'soft-paste' porcelain was manufactured, until 1761. The Royal Saxon Porcelain factory at Meissen, founded in 1710, maintained its lead in the manufacture of porcelain in Europe until the beginning of the Seven Years' War. Supremacy then passed to the factory at Vincennes (moved to Sèvres in 1756), which likewise enjoyed court patronage, having been subsidized by Louis XV, who owned it from 1759.

All the major Continental porcelain factories were financed or owned by rich and aristocratic patrons, but no such patronage existed for the porcelain factories in England.[9] Pottery was not considered worthy of a nobleman's attention.

FIRST FACTORIES

When Wedgwood left Whieldon to set up on his own in May 1759, he had already embarked on a series of experiments which had led to the development of a fine transparent green glaze and improvements in the production of 'variegated' wares in imitation of natural stones, notably agate, but the principal object of his attention was the refinement of the lead-glazed creamcolour or creamware body that was beginning to compete with more traditional tin-glazed and salt-glazed wares. Josiah wrote later in the introduction to his 'Experiment Book': 'I saw the field was spacious, and the soil so good, as to promise an ample recompense to any one who should labour diligently in its cultivation'.[10] He entered that field by renting a small pottery, the Ivy House Works, for £15 a year and employing his cousin, another Thomas Wedgwood, as a journeyman at an annual salary of £22.[11]

'USEFUL AND ORNAMENTAL' PARTNERS

For the next ten years, at the Ivy House and from 1762[12] at the larger Brick House or 'Bell' Works (so named from Wedgwood's habit of summoning his workers by bell instead of the customary horn), Wedgwood laboured to perfect his creamware, improving the body, colour and glaze and introducing well-modelled tableware shapes, generally adapted from English and French porcelain, with polychrome enamelled or monochrome transfer-printed decoration. In 1765 he supplied Queen Charlotte with a 'complete sett of tea things'[13] in his refined creamware, and next year, after the official anouncement of his appointment as Potter to the Queen, he renamed it Queen's Ware. Cousin Thomas, who had become Josiah's principal assistant as well as a trusted friend, was promoted to partner in the manufacture of 'Useful Wares', later to be defined as 'such vessels as are made use of at meals'.[14] In 1767 Wedgwood wrote: 'The demand for this <u>Creamcolour</u>, Alias <u>Queen's Ware</u> ... still increases. It is really amazing how rapidly the use of it has spread allmost over the whole Globe, & how universally it is liked.'[15]

Pl. 12 (Cat. C2) Portrait of Thomas Bentley by or after John Francis Rigaud, undated.

In the spring of 1762, while visiting Liverpool, Josiah damaged his vulnerable right knee. Dr Matthew Turner, who attended him, introduced him to Thomas Bentley. Bentley was educated, cultured and sociable, a man of lively intellect, liberal views and considerable personal charm, who had travelled in Europe and spoke both French and German. His business experience included seven years indentured to a merchant in Manchester, where he had been trained in accountancy, and eight years in charge of his own business as a general merchant in Liverpool. This chance meeting was the start of the most intimate friendship of Wedgwood's life, and it initiated a business partnership and correspondence unique in importance in the history of British industry.

The Wedgwood & Bentley partnership was formed specifically for the production and marketing of 'Vases, Figures, Flowerpots' and other ornamental pieces.[16] Josiah had begun negotiations in July 1766 to buy the Ridgehouse Estate, a property of about 350 acres near Burslem, where he proposed to build a new factory – a 'Vase work' – especially for the new partnership. The site was well chosen. Conscious of the pressing need for better communications with London and the port of Liverpool, Josiah had taken a leading part in the promotion of turnpike roads and canals. The Trent & Mersey Canal, begun in 1766, was to link the Potteries with both Liverpool on the west coast and Hull on the east, as well as providing access, at greatly reduced cost, to clay and stone from the West Country. The Ridgehouse Estate lay directly in its path.

The cost of the land and the proposed buildings was to be more than £12,000 and it is clear that Wedgwood's accumulated profits from Queen's Ware could not have paid for it, especially since he was also to lend Bentley his share of the partnership capital. This problem was resolved by Josiah's marriage to his kinswoman, Sarah, the daughter (and, in due course, the sole heir) of a wealthy cheese merchant, Richard Wedgwood of Spen Green. The courtship was long and strongly opposed by Richard, who evidently viewed his young kinsman with suspicion, but he finally yielded and the couple were married on 25 January 1764.

There is strong circumstantial evidence that Sarah's fortune, settled at her marriage and inherited after her father's death, played a crucial part in the financing of Josiah's business; and Richard, who came to like and admire his son-in-law and occasionally to take an active part in the enterprise, may have made a direct investment in it.[17]

Sarah Wedgwood, just two years younger than Josiah, and handsome rather than beautiful, was intelligent, well-educated and strong-willed, but unspoilt by her comfortable family circumstances. She quickly learnt the

Pl. 13 (Cat. C1) Portrait of Josiah Wedgwood by Sir Joshua Reynolds, 1782.

Pl. 14 (Cat. D7) Portrait of Sarah Wedgwood, Josiah Wedgwood's wife, by Sir Joshua Reynolds, 1782.

Pl. 15 (Cat. D6) Portrait of Richard Wedgwood, Josiah Wedgwood's father-in-law, by George Stubbs, 1780.

code in which Josiah kept records of his experiments, so that she could help with their transcription, and was as ready with an opinion on property values as she was with suggestions for the shapes of teapots or the decoration of vases. She bore seven children who survived infancy, the eldest of whom, Susannah, born in January 1765, was to become the mother of Charles Darwin.

A NEW ETRURIA

The purchase of the Ridgehouse Estate, renamed Etruria, was completed in December 1767. It was no longer to be merely a 'Vase work' but a complete set of workshops for wares designated as 'Useful' or 'Ornamental', housed in three blocks, linked by walled yards, the whole stretch-ing about 150 yards along the intended course of the canal. Each workshop was designed as a distinct unit, arranged in sequence with others to provide a flowing line of production and to avoid inessential movement of workers or goods. Plans were made also for the building of Etruria Hall for Josiah's growing family, a house for Bentley (which he never occupied) and, in due course, a whole village of houses for workmen. When it was com-pleted in 1769, the factory was second to none in Europe (see Cat. D5). An industrial spy, visiting the factory in 1786, described it as 'an enormous building, practically a small town ... a marvel of organisation'.[18]

The building of Etruria and the establishment of the Wedgwood & Bentley partnership were both threatened in April 1768 when Josiah 'over walk'd & over work'd' his troublesome right knee.[19] His leg was amputated four weeks later, without anaesthetic, in his own house by a local surgeon. Six weeks later Josiah was dressing the wound himself and visiting his factories in a chaise. Shortly afterwards he was fitted with the first of the wooden legs which he wore for the rest of his life.

AN INTRODUCTION TO VASES

The particular inclusion of vases in the Wedgwood & Bentley partnership is significant for it signalled a departure from previous earthenware manufacture in Britain. The vase as an ornament was largely the invention of the 18th century. Ornamental vases were made at

Meissen during the first quarter of the century and the fashion spread through the European porcelain factories to Sèvres, where superb Rococo vases were produced. Some ornamental vases were made in earthenware by European potteries between 1730 and 1750, but there is no record of any pottery vases that could accurately be described as ornamental manufactured in England before 1765, when Wedgwood sent examples of his vases, 'Creamcolour engine turn'd, & printed', to Queen Charlotte for her approval.[20]

By the time the partnership books were opened in November 1768, Wedgwood already had three different types of vases in production: creamware (in declining quantities); variegated, of increasingly sophisticated

Pl. 16 (Cat. G289) Oval dish from the Frog Service decorated with a view of Etruria Hall.

Left: Pl. 17 (Cat. E2) Queen's Ware Vase 1769-80.

Below: Pl. 18 (Cat. C11) Canopic vase. Black Basalt, with encaustic decoration, about 1790.

colouring and quality, decorated in imitation of natural stones; and Black Basalt, a dense stoneware body resembling bronze in appearance, which Wedgwood had developed and refined from the earlier Staffordshire 'Egyptian black'.

Within 12 months he had added a new decorative technique – 'encaustic' painting in imitation of antique red-figure vase painting – which was applied to Black Basalt vases, tablets for chimneypieces and some tablewares. The formal inauguration of the Etruria factory on 13 June 1769 was marked by the production of six First Day's Vases (Cat. D2–3), thrown by Wedgwood with the help of Bentley, who turned the wheel, and decorated by the new encaustic process which was patented five months later.

WEDGWOOD IN LONDON

From the autumn of 1766 until Bentley's arrival in London in August 1769, Wedgwood's business in London was conducted from two rooms in Charles Street (now Carlos Place) off Grosvenor Square. In August 1768 a warehouse and spacious showrooms were opened at the corner of Great Newport Street and St Martin's Lane. Soon after Bentley's arrival to manage the London business, premises were acquired in Cheyne Row, Chelsea, where painters were employed to decorate encaustic Black Basalt vases and Queen's Ware tablewares; and it was at this Chelsea Decorating Studio that, in the following year, the first order from the Empress Catherine of Russia – for a dinner and dessert service of the Husk pattern (see Cat. D59) – was painted.

DISTINGUISHING MARKS

By 1772 virtually all ware for the partnerships with both Cousin Thomas and Bentley was marked with the name 'Wedgwood' or 'Wedgwood & Bentley'. Wedgwood was the first earthenware potter consistently to mark his wares, and the use of his own name impressed in the clay set him apart from English and Continental porcelain manufacturers, who used a painted device such as the anchor of Chelsea or the crossed swords of Meissen.

HUSKS AND FROGS

It was through the good offices of Lord Cathcart, Ambassador to the Court of St Petersburg (Cat. C19), and perhaps more particularly of his wife, Jane, that Wedgwood obtained his first order, for the Husk Service, from Catherine the Great of Russia in 1770, and their early efforts to promote his wares were no doubt largely responsible for the commission, received three years later, to produce the great Frog Service of nearly 1,000 pieces for the Empress (see Chapters 5 and 6), a Service still recognized as the most prestigious ever manufactured in earthenware.

'VASE MAKER GENERAL TO THE UNIVERSE'

By this time the Wedgwood & Bentley name had become as famous for the manufacture of ornamental wares as was that of Wedgwood for Queen's Ware. By August 1772 he could boast of 'upwards of 100 Good Forms of Vases'[21] for which he had handles and applied ornaments, many of which were interchangeable to provide even greater variety. Few of the shapes were original, being drawn principally from engravings, such as those illustrating the work of the Comte de Caylus and the collection of Sir William Hamilton,[22] or from examples of Sèvres porcelain. These were freely adapted, their sources disguised by altered handles and the use of applied swags, festoons and cameos. As early as May 1769 Wedgwood had noted the great gathering of coaches to his London showrooms to see his latest vases, and he announced to Bentley his intention to become 'Vase Maker General to the Universe'. 'We must,' he told his partner, 'endeavour to gratify this universal passion.'[23]

It was not, however, only for vases that Wedgwood & Bentley were becoming renowned throughout Europe. Library busts (Cat. B34), figures (some as large as 24 inches in height), tablets to be set in chimneypieces, decorative candlesticks, portrait medallions (Cat. C31), cameos and intaglio seals poured from the Etruria factory into the houses of the rich and fashionable, and of those who imitated them. Under Bentley's guidance and the influence of such knowledgeable patrons as Sir William Hamilton (1730–1803), Wedgwood had been converted to Neo-classicism. Wedgwood & Bentley became the high priests of the 'true style' in pottery, while many English and Continental porcelain manufacturers remained trapped in the mannerisms of Rococo. As manufacturers of ornamental wares, Wedgwood & Bentley had, by 1775, no serious rival in the pottery industry in Europe.

The refined Neo-classical styles, however, lacked sufficient colour greatly to appeal to female taste, and neither Wedgwood nor Bentley was likely to forget that, next to the King, their most important patrons were Queen Charlotte and the Empress Catherine of Russia. In December 1772 Bentley asked Wedgwood for a 'finer body for Gems' (cameos and intaglios).[24]

THE GREAT INVENTION

Josiah had already made some 'very promising experiments ... upon fine bodies for Gems and other things'[25] but production of the Frog Service and the establishment of the Greek Street showrooms in Portland House had obliged him to neglect his experimental work. In March 1774 he wrote: 'I have for some time past been reviewing my experiments, & find such Roots, such Seeds as would open & branch out wonderfully if I could nail myself down to the cultivation of them for a year or two'.[26] Some of these 'roots' had been 'selected & put into cultivation' but the science of chemical analysis was in its infancy and experimental work was both laborious and uncertain in its results. The identification and refining of materials and the lack of any method of measuring accurately the heat of the kiln during firing were among the most intractable of the problems involved in the creation of ceramic bodies, and Josiah was well aware of the financial disasters that had overtaken many of the porcelain factories. 'I cannot,' he wrote in frustration, 'work miracles in altering the properties of these subtle & complicated (though native) materials.' He added, in exasperation: 'If I had more time, & more heads I could do something – but as it is I must be content to do as well as I can. A Man who is in the midst of a course of experiments should not be at home to anything or anybody else but that cannot be my case ... I am allmost crazy'.[27]

By November 1774 his goal was plain. He was aiming for the appearance of a cameo, white bas-relief ornament on a coloured ground, in the style of the blue-and-white portrait medallions produced by the Doccia factory in the 1750s, examples of which he may have seen in the collections of patrons who had returned from the Grand Tour.[28]

Wedgwood's experiments and frustrations continued until 14 January 1776, when he wrote in triumph: 'I believe I can now assure you of a conquest & a very important one to us. No less than the firing of our fine Jasper ... with as much certainty as our Basaltes.'[29] He continued, however, to experience difficulties with firing, blistering, crazing, cracking and variations in texture and colour, complaining to Bentley: 'This Jasper is certainly the most delicately whimsical of any substance I ever engag'd with'.[30] The losses in production were frightening (75 percent of tablets for chimneypieces), and the high price of cobalt, the essential colouring of his blue Jasper, made it doubtful that Jasper could ever be made commercially credible.

Josiah's response to these problems was characteristically resolute and practical: further experiments would overcome the technical difficulties and, meanwhile, prices must be high 'to make the living pay for the dead'. This was possible while the secret of Jasper was safeguarded from rivals and its quality was 'fine enough to ask any price for'.[31] His introduction of a method of 'dipping' white Jasper in liquid dark blue clay ('slip') to give it a thin coating of colour lightened the costs of cobalt; the use of well-matured clay prevented cracking; the more careful regulation of firing, in a kiln built exclusively for Jasper, helped to improve colour and texture. With the number of his recorded experiments approaching 5,000, Josiah was at last able to tell Bentley on 3 November 1777: 'Sell what quantity you please. I would as readily engage to furnish you with this as any pottery I make'.[32]

During the last three years of the Wedgwood & Bentley partnership, Jasper was made in a wide variety of colours – three shades of blue, green, lilac, grey, yellow and chocolate-brown, the last three almost exclusively for portrait medallions, cameos and seals – chosen by Josiah 'to the colour of the rooms', a reference to the interiors designed by Robert Adam.[33] The techniques of applying ornament and engine-turning perfected for Basalt were adapted to Jasper and the range of articles produced was increased to embrace an extraordinary variety of decorative objects, further enlarged by the use of gold, silver, ormolu, cut-steel and pinchbeck mounts, often provided by Matthew Boulton's Birmingham factory.

In 1773 Wedgwood & Bentley had issued a *Catalogue of Ornamental Wares*, and this was followed in 1774 by Wedgwood's illustrated catalogue of Queen's Ware tablewares. The first catalogue to include Jasper was published in 1779. Private commissions were accepted for portrait cameos and medallions but the majority were of historical subjects or, as in the case of the 'Heads of Illustrious Moderns from Chaucer to the Present Time',

public figures – royalty, statesmen, poets, military heroes, physicians, philosophers, painters and architects – generally modelled from engravings or medals, or from relief portraits in wax or ivory. Wedgwood employed portrait modellers, notably William Hackwood (about 1757–1839), at Etruria and either bought or commissioned models from sculptors and modellers, of whom the most celebrated was John Flaxman junior (1755–1826). Both Hackwood and Flaxman also modelled Classical subjects for tablets and other ornamental pieces (Cat. B33).

The summit of Wedgwood's ambition for Jasper was the production of ornamental vases, but it was not until November 1777 that he discovered the use of a coarse body, which gave the vase sufficient strength to hold its shape under high temperatures, disguised by a thin 'dip' of a fine body.[34] Several years of trials were required before this technique could be satisfactorily applied to vases, and it was not yet perfected when Bentley died suddenly in November 1780.

Bentley's death robbed Josiah simultaneously of his dearest friend, his most candid critic and an incomparable business partner. Josiah had written to him almost every day of their partnership and Bentley's replies (now sadly lost) were probably not much less frequent. Wedgwood described them as 'my Magazines, Reviews, Chronicles, & I had allmost said my Bible.'[35] Their opinions diverged so seldom, and each was so ready to accept the advice of the other, that they seemed almost to be two halves of the same man. In the early days of their partnership Josiah wrote to him: 'I feel but like half of my self when we are separated'.[36] Bentley's abilities had been complementary to Wedgwood's: his commercial experience and entrepreneurial skills with Josiah's inventive genius and technical expertise; his education, taste and restraining good sense with Josiah's driving energy and urgent ambition; his perceptiveness with

Josiah's vision. Both as a partner and a friend Bentley was irreplaceable.

THE PORTLAND VASE

The Wedgwood & Bentley partnership stocks were sold by auction at Christie & Ansell in December 1781, and the first of Wedgwood's Jasper vases were shown when the Greek Street showrooms reopened shortly afterwards. During the following ten years Josiah continued to add shapes and to experiment with colours, ornament and the decorative effects obtainable by ingenious use of the engine-turning lathe. Between 1786 and 1790 much of his time was occupied by experiments and trials dedicated to the reproduction, in Jasper, of the Portland Vase. Whatever their artistic limitations, Wedgwood's first copies are ranked among the greatest technical achievements of the potter's craft (Cat. E33–39).[37]

Wedgwood's production of Jasper in general, and of his copies of the Portland Vase in particular, was greatly aided by his invention of a thermometer, or 'pyrometer' (Cat. B60), which employed the recorded shrinkage of clay cylinders during firing to measure temperature in pottery kilns. A paper describing this invention was read to the Royal Society on 9 May 1782, and in the following January Josiah was elected Fellow of the Society.

ARTISTS AND INDUSTRY

During the last 20 years of his life Wedgwood gave much of his time to the employment and patronage of artists. Flaxman was commissioned to model bas-reliefs for tablets and vases, including the exceptionally fine *Apotheosis of Homer* (Cat. C8) and *Hercules in the Garden of the Hesperides*;[38] Henry Webber (1754–1826), a sculptor and modeller recommended by Sir Joshua Reynolds, was employed at Etruria and became head of the ornamental department; and a series of costly experiments was undertaken to produce large white plaques for George Stubbs (1724–1806) to use as supports or 'canvases'. While he was at Etruria in 1780, Stubbs modelled two fine bas-reliefs, *The Fall of Phaeton*, (Cat. C22) and *The Lion and the Horse*, and painted portraits of Josiah and Sarah Wedgwood in ceramic colours on oval Wedgwood plaques. He also completed a more conventional portrait in oils of Richard Wedgwood (Cat. D6) and a large paint-

Pl. 19 (Cat. C8) Jasper tablet: 'The Apotheosis of Homer'. After a model by John Flaxman junior, about 1778.

Pl. 20 The Wedgwood Family in the grounds of Etruria Hall, by George Stubbs, 1780.

ing on panel of Josiah and Sarah with their seven children in the park at Etruria (Pl. 20). In 1782 Josiah and Sarah sat for their portraits to Sir Joshua Reynolds (Cat. C1 and D7). Three years later, Josiah bought four paintings by Joseph Wright of Derby, and the artist presented him with a fifth.[39]

In 1788 Wedgwood set up a modelling studio in Rome to supply him with casts and copies or adaptations of antique bas-reliefs. The studio was established by Webber, and Flaxman, who was also to be in Rome, promised to spare Wedgwood as much time as he could afford and to supervise the work of John de Vaere, a modeller hired to work full-time at the studio. Italian modellers, notably Camillo Pacetti, were also employed there, and the models they sent from Rome are among the most important to appear on Wedgwood Jasper tablets. Other new sources of bas-relief ornament were the designs in the fashionable Romantic style, obtained from three talented amateur artists: Lady Diana Beauclerk, Elizabeth, Lady Templetown, and Emma Crewe (see Cat. B27 and B53).

VENTURES IN POLITICS

In his early days as a manufacturer Wedgwood had enlisted the help of local magnates, chiefly Lord Gower, in his struggles to improve communications by road and canal to the Potteries, and he had reproduced portraits of leading political figures on Queen's Ware jugs or Jasper medallions; but, while Bentley lived, he was content to confine his part in the nation's politics to discreet discussion in their letters. He was an enthusiastic advocate of American Independence and, until 1792, a strong supporter of the Revolution in France. In some of his opinions he was years in advance of many of his contemporaries, favouring universal suffrage and annual parliaments.

Wedgwood lent practical support to the Society for the Abolition of the Slave Trade, of which he became a committee member, producing, in 1787, quantities of black-and-white Jasper cameos depicting a kneeling slave in chains. These were distributed free to those closely concerned with the cause and became fashionable mounted in rings, bracelets, hair-pins and the lids of snuff boxes. 'Thus,' as Thomas Clarkson commented drily, 'a fashion ... was seen for once in the honorable office of promoting the cause of justice, humanity and freedom.'[40]

Some of Wedgwood's ventures among the politicians were less judicious. In 1785 he had taken the chair at the first executive committee meeting of the General Chamber of the Manufacturers of Great Britain, formed at his suggestion. His use of this body to make public his passionate opposition to Pitt's worthy attempt to negotiate a liberal trade treaty with Ireland was widely seen as both ill-informed and basely motivated, and an abdication of his free trade principles. The assistance he gave to William Eden (later Lord Auckland) during the successful negotiation of the French Commercial Treaty of 1786 was more securely founded but exposed him to charges of treachery from a significant minority of the Chamber of Manufacturers who were violently opposed to it. Caught between the parochial interests of the manufacturers and the political lobbying of the professionals, Wedgwood was, as he told Matthew Boulton, 'buffeted & teased beyond human patience'.[41]

WEDGWOOD'S CIRCLE

Throughout his life Wedgwood made friends easily with men whose inquiring minds and innovative abilities matched his own. Second only to Bentley, his closest friend was Erasmus Darwin, Sarah's 'favourite Aesculapius', whose advice was sought whenever serious illness threatened any member of the family. He was an early advocate of inoculation, and it was probably on his advice that Josiah had his two eldest children inoculated against smallpox in 1767. Josiah consulted him on every subject from canals to education, and presented him with the first perfect copy of the Portland Vase in 1789. Their families were united when Darwin's son, Robert, married Josiah's favourite daughter, Susannah.

With Boulton, Darwin had been responsible for founding the Lunar Society, an informal gathering in Birmingham of some of the most inventive men of the period. Membership of the Society, which never exceeded 14 in its 25 years of existence, included Joseph Priestley, James Watt and Richard Lovell Edgeworth. Among visitors to their meetings were Benjamin Franklin, the astronomer Sir William Herschel, Sir Joseph Banks, President of the Royal Society, and Dr Daniel Solander, the Swedish botanist. Wedgwood's dictum, 'Everything gives way to experiment' might as suitably have been the motto of the 'Lunatics', as it was a guiding principle of the Enlightenment. His participation in their meetings, however, was probably occasional and as a visitor rather than as a member.[42] He was the only potter to have access to such a wealth of scholarship, wisdom and advice and the only one with both the ability and the determination to make full use of them.

FAMILY AFFAIRS

In the early days of Etruria, the upbringing of the Wedgwood children was primarily the work of Sarah. Josiah nevertheless took a part in their education, which he discussed with both Bentley and Darwin, and personally drew up the timetable for the 'Etruscan School' which he installed at home for the instruction of Susannah, her three brothers, John, Jos and Tom, and her younger sister, Kitty. The two elder boys were subsequently sent to boarding schools and to Edinburgh University, where they were followed by their youngest brother. All three spent time in the production departments of the factory and received a thorough grounding in the techniques and management of the business, but none showed any enthusiasm for life in the Potteries. Although all were intelligent, and Tom showed signs of exceptional ability, they were by nature indolent, and by far the most reliable members of the family were 'Useful' Cousin Thomas, who for more than 20 years directed the production of Queen's Ware, and Josiah's nephew, Tom Byerley, who had taken over the management of the London business after Bentley's death.

In 1788 Thomas Wedgwood died, leaving Josiah, for the first time in 22 years, in sole control of his business. Two years later he took his three sons and Byerley into partnership, but both John and Tom resigned three years later, and it was to Jos (Josiah II) that the firm was finally entrusted. Josiah Wedgwood died of cancer of the jaw on 3 January 1795.[43]

THE LEGACY

In 1863 William Ewart Gladstone described Josiah Wedgwood as 'the greatest man who ever, in any age or country, applied himself to the important work of uniting art with industry'.[44] The tribute has been considered extravagant but, despite the best efforts of revisionist historians, no credible rival has been found. There is no doubt that Wedgwood was far ahead of most of his contemporaries in factory organization, production management, cost accounting, marketing, public relations, industrial design and the training and care of his workforce, for whom he provided both housing and an early form of health insurance.

Surprisingly little of Wedgwood's work was truly original. He was, above all, a manufacturing innovator, a man who recognized opportunity and made it his own. Jasper was his single ceramic invention, but it was the most significant since the Chinese discovery of porcelain some 900 years earlier. Although he claimed the invention of Black Basalt, it was, like his Queen's Ware, white terracotta, *Rosso Antico* and Cane Ware bodies, a refined and sophisticated development of a ceramic body already in existence. Wedgwood alone understood the potential of these bodies and transformed them, through laborious experiments and trials, into wares that commanded an international market. Most of Wedgwood's designs for tablewares and ornamental pieces were adapted from engravings or examples of French or English porcelain, or remodelled from casts of antique models. It was their application and Josiah's insistence on the highest quality of materials, design and production that was new in pottery manufacture. Wedgwood's supremacy in the third quarter of the 18th century, in succession to Meissen and Sèvres, was founded on Josiah's personal ability to create, adapt and refine wares for the ascendant fashion.

In 1769, in the early days of their partnership, Wedgwood had suggested to Bentley that their days should be spent in the pursuit of 'Fortune, Fame & the Public Good'.[45]

He made a great fortune; he achieved abiding fame; and, by marrying art to industry and beauty to utility, he made a lasting contribution to public good. Gladstone's encomium needs, after all, no apologist.

Robin Reilly

CATALOGUE

C

Artistic Connections

The years of Wedgwood's work with Bentley saw new styles – founded on Classical art and fuelled by archaeological discoveries – introduced into British architecture and design. Wedgwood and Bentley were swift to sense the potential of this fashion, not only adopting and promoting the styles but developing a range of materials and products in order to satisfy this new and exacting market for pottery. In doing so they were aided by a tightly knit group of collectors, antiquaries and architects, men who played a key role in promoting the fashion, and gave them privileged access to prints, gems and vases to copy.

C1 Portrait of Josiah Wedgwood (1730–95)
(Pl. 13)

Sir Joshua Reynolds, PRA (1723–92)
Oil on canvas
1782
73 × 65 cm

It is not known how or when Reynolds and Wedgwood first met, but it has been suggested that they could have been introduced by Sir Watkin Williams Wynn (a patron and supporter of both potter and painter) or possibly by Sir William Hamilton, Sir William Chambers or John Flaxman. Reynolds's contributions to Wedgwood's work were small but significant. It is said to have been on the recommendation of Reynolds and Sir William Chambers that Wedgwood first employed Henry Webber (1754–1826) as modeller; and in June 1790, two weeks after Wedgwood had showed his first perfect copy of the Portland Vase to a select gathering of connoisseurs, Reynolds signed a

certificate declaring it to be 'a correct and faithful imitation, both in regard to the general effect, and in the most minute detail of the parts'. For the companion portrait of Sarah Wedgwood, Josiah's wife, see Cat. D7.

Trustees of the Wedgwood Museum, Barlaston, Staffordshire (No.5610)
Lit: Reilly 1992 pp. 309–10

C2 Portrait of Thomas Bentley (1730–80)
(Pl. 12)

By or after John Francis Rigaud
(1742–1810)
Oil on canvas
Unsigned
Undated
105.6 × 85 cm

This portrait of Bentley, Wedgwood's intimate friend from 1762, and partner from 1768, presents him as a scholar and connoisseur. The various books and works of art trace his philosophic and artistic inheritance through the writings of Shaftsbury and John Gilbert Cooper to its foundation in Socrates. He reads from Book I of Cooper's *Life of Socrates*, pointing to the phrases 'his celebrated Graces .../... were his Performances.' This rests on a volume of Shaftsbury's *Characteristics ...*, and medallions of the *Three Graces* and a portrait of Socrates rest against a further pile of books. Possibly the picture was not painted from life, but made after his death as a memorial and tribute. Bentley's cultivation, taste, contacts and diplomacy were of vital importance for the partnership's success, Wedgwood's adoption of Classical forms and prototypes during the 1760s and 1770s probably being

to a large extent due to his influence. Two versions of the painting exist, the other being at the Wedgwood Museum, Barlaston. Both have in the past been attributed to Joseph Wright of Derby. The present attribution of the portrait rests on its mention in the *Memoir of John Francis Rigaud* written by his son, Stephen Rigaud.

Trustees of the National Museums and Galleries on Merseyside (Lady Lever Art Gallery)
Accession no.: WAG 2548
Lit: Bennett 1978 pp. 51–3; Pressly 1984 pp. 53–4

C3 Portrait of Sir William Hamilton (1730–1803), Ambassador to the Court of Naples

William Hopkins Craft (1735–1811)
Painted enamels on copper
Inscribed: 'The R.ᵗ Hon:ᵇˡᵉ S.ʳ W:ᵐ Hamilton. W:H:Craft. fec:ʳ 1802'
Dated 1802
Height: 16.8 cm

Between 1764 and 1800 Hamilton was Ambassador to the Court of Naples, where he took a close interest in the archaeological excavations at Herculaneum and Pompeii and formed a vast collection of Greek and Roman vases. The collection was published in four volumes, the first of which appeared in 1766 (Cat. C5), and it was bought by the British Museum in 1772. Hamilton is today chiefly remembered today as the cuckolded husband of Nelson's Emma.

William Hopkins Craft (who painted this portrait), worked in Wedgwood's Chelsea Decorating Studio between 1769 and 1771, when his artistic airs and temperament provoked Wedgwood to express to Bentley his anger and disgust.

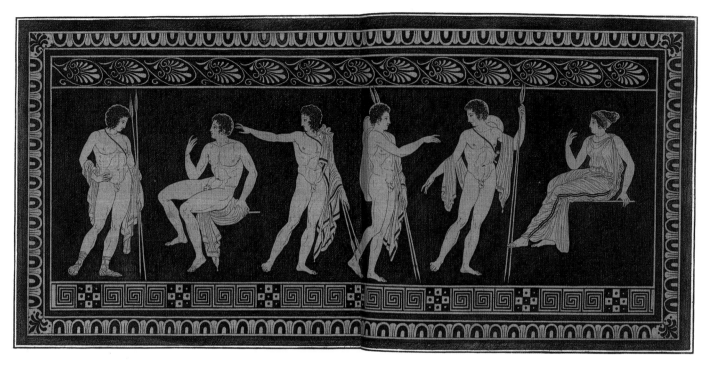

The Trustees of the British Museum. Presented by A. W. Franks (1890-8-10-21)
Lit and refs: Toppin 1959 pls 13–14; Wedgwood MS E25-18279, see Reilly 1989 I pl. 55

C4 Portrait medallion of Sir William Hamilton (1730–1803), Ambassador to the Court of Naples *(Pl. 5)*

Modelled by Joachim Smith (active 1758–1803)
White biscuit stoneware
About 1772
Height: 16.5 cm

A version of this portrait in Black Basalt with an encaustic-painted ground was presented to Sir William Hamilton in 1772. This bears the following dedication by Bentley:

> Wedgwood & Bentley beg Sir Wm. Hamilton will do them the honor to accept of an Etruscan Bas-relief Portrait of himself, as a small testimony of Respect and gratitude to a Gentleman who has conferred obligations upon this <u>Kingdom in general</u> and upon <u>themselves in particular</u> which may be the means, not only of <u>improving</u> and <u>refining</u> the <u>Public Taste</u> but of <u>keeping alive</u> that Sacred Fire, which his Collection of unestimable models <u>has</u>

<u>happily kindled</u> in Great Britain, so long as <u>burnt Earth</u> and <u>Etruscan Painting</u> shall endure. Great Newport Street, April 30, 1772.

Victoria & Albert Museum (275-1866)
Lit and refs: for the encaustic-painted example see Reilly and Savage 1973 p. 182 and Adams 1992 p. 76; compare also Reilly 1989 I fig. 485

C5 *Collection of Etruscan, Greek and Roman Antiquities from the Cabinet of the Honble William Hamilton ...*

Sir William Hamilton (1730–1803) and P. H. d'Hancarville (P. F. Hugues, 1719–1805), etchings by Guiseppe Brachi
First published 1766; this edition 1801
48.3 × 28.8 cm (closed)

The first part of the four-volume catalogue to Hamilton's collection of Greek and Italian vases was published by Hamilton and the self-styled Baron d'Hancarville between 1766 and 1776. A copy of the first volume was presented to Wedgwood by his patron Sir Watkin Williams Wynn in 1769, early proofs of illustrations having previously been lent to Wedgwood by Lord Cathcart, brother-in-law of Hamilton and

Ambassador to St Petersburg (Cat. C19). Hamilton's collection was the most important source of designs for Wedgwood's encaustic vases. He sent Wedgwood drawings and models during the 1770s, and in 1786 he wrote to him:

> It is with infinite satisfaction that I reflect on having been in some measure instrumental in introducing a purer taste of forms & Ornaments by having placed my Collection of Antiquities in the British Museum, but a Wedgewood and a Bentley were necessary to diffuse that taste so universally, and it is to their liberal way of thinking & ... acting that so good a taste prevails at present in Great Britain.

National Art Library, Victoria & Albert Museum
Lit and refs: Ramage 1990 p. 76, quoting Wedgwood MS E30-22495, and passim

C6 Vase (Volute Krater)

Black Basalt, with encaustic decoration in red, white and blue
Marks: 'WEDGWOOD' and 'Z' impressed
About 1785
Height: 87.4 cm

This Krater, the largest of the encaustic-painted vases made at Etruria, is a copy of a

C 6

4th-century BC Apulian (south Italian) vase from the collection of Sir William Hamilton. That Wedgwood copied the decoration from Hamilton's *Antiquities*, and not from the vase in the British Museum, is proven by his repetition of the engraver's mistake in running the Vitruvian wave pattern under the rim from left to right (Cat. C5). According to Hamilton's biographer in the *Dictionary of National Biography*, Wedgwood stated that in two years he had himself brought into England, by sale of imitations of the Hamilton vases, three times as much as the £84,000 paid for the antiquities by Parliament. The vase was formerly in the collection of the glassmaker Apsley Pellatt.

Victoria & Albert Museum. Jermyn Street Collection (2419-1901)
Lit: Zeitlin 1968 pp. 147–51; Science Museum 1978 Cat. 132; compare Reilly 1989 I pls C101–2

C7 'The Pegasus Vase'

Solid pale blue and white Jasper, with white reliefs
Marks: 'WEDGWOOD' and two workmen's marks impressed
1786
Height: 46.4 cm

Joisah Wedgwood regarded this vase sufficiently highly to offer it in 1786 to the British Museum, who accepted it despite their general policy then of not accepting objects of contemporary manufacture. The relief on the front is an adaptation of *The Apotheosis of Homer* (Cat. C8), which had been modelled by John Flaxman in 1778 after the decoration of a vase from Sir William Hamilton's collection. In 1779 Wedgwood presented a tablet with this subject to Hamilton, an idea first broached in a letter to Bentley of October 1778: 'Suppose we were to make Sʳ. Wᵐ. Hamilton a present of an Etruscan tablet, Homer &c. The expence to us would be trifling in comparison to the value of the present, & the compliment paid to him, which he well deserves at our hands, & it would be the best introduction they could have in the country where he resides.'

C8 Tablet: *The Apotheosis of Homer (Pl. 19)*

After a model by John Flaxman junior
(1755–1826)
Solid blue Jasper, with white reliefs
Mark: 'Wedgwood & Bentley' impressed
About 1778
19.5 × 36.6 cm

The composition was copied from a calyx
crater described and illustrated in
d'Hancarville and Hamilton's *Antiquities*.
From a letter written by Thomas Bentley to
Sir William Hamilton and dated 26
February 1779 it is evident that the subject
had been known to the partners for some
time and that they were acquainted with
d'Hancarville himself:

> Having modelled a large Tablet from one of the
> unpublished Designs in your excellency's collection
> at the British Museum, which we copied from a
> drawing lent by Mr D'Hankerville, and which we
> consider as one of the most perfect specimens of the
> present state of our Ornamental Manufactory ....
> We understand the subject to be some honour paid
> to the Genius of Homer, but perhaps your
> Excellency will have the goodness to inform us
> more exactly what this fine composition represents.

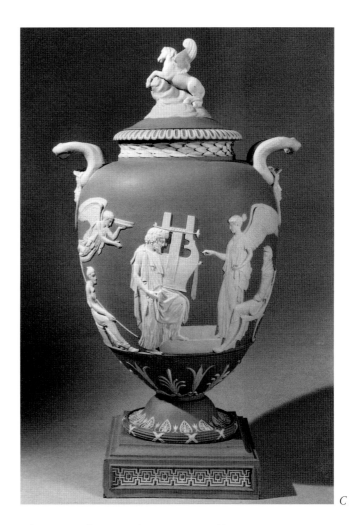

C 7

A later letter from Sir William Hamilton
to Josiah Wedgwood confirms Flaxman as
the modeller. Written on 24 July 1786, this
states: 'I should have thought that my
Friend Flaxman would have been of use to
you in your present undertaking, for I must
do him the justice to say that I never saw a
bas-relief executed in the simple antique
style half so well as that he did of the
Apotheosis of Homer from one of my
vases'.

C9 Self-portrait

John Flaxman junior (1755–1826)
Terracotta
Signed and dated in Latin
1778
Diameter: 18.7 cm

John Flaxman junior, the most gifted British
sculptor of his generation, supplied models
for portrait medallions and figure subjects
to Wedgwood from 1775, an early
ambitious commission being *The Apotheosis
of Homer* (Cat. C8). This precocious self-
portrait roundel was formerly in the
collection of Sir William Hamilton, an early
supporter and admirer of the artist.
Wedgwood's successful exploitation of the

C 9

'true' or 'antique' taste in his Jasper reliefs was made possible by his access to a pool of extremely talented modellers, their task being to rework Classical themes for modern manufacture and render modern subjects in a Classical style. Flaxman is the best known of them, but other notable talents included Joachim Smith (Cat. C4), John Bacon, John Charles Lochée and Henry Webber (1754–1826).

Victoria & Albert Museum (294-1864)
Lit: Deutsch 1943 p. 38; Bindman 1979 Cat. 4A

C10 The members of The Society of Dilettanti

William Say (1768–1834) after Sir Joshua Reynolds, PRA (1723–92)
Mezzotint (proof impression on india paper)
Lettered: 'Sir Joshua Reynolds pinx^t. Say sculp.' and with the names of the sitters
Undated
Cut to 57.4 × 41 cm

The Society of Dilettanti was founded in 1732 as a dining club for gentlemen who had travelled to Italy on the Grand Tour. From 1751 the architects and antiquaries James Stuart and Nicholas Revett were members, and the Society sponsored their expedition to Greece and the subsequent publication of their *Antiquities of Athens* (1762–1816). Reynolds was elected a member in 1766, and between 1777 and 1779 he painted two portrait groups of the society, of which this print reproduces one. At the centre of the composition is Sir William Hamilton, seated before a volume of his *Antiquities* and a Greek vase. The figure on the far left is Sir Watkin Williams Wynn, who presented Wedgwood with a copy of Hamilton's *Antiquities*, lent him 245 cameos and intaglio gems to copy and had the architect Robert Adam include an encaustic-decorated Basalt tablet in a fireplace that he designed for Williams Wynn's London house in 1772. Wedgwood and Bentley's deft courtship of the praise and support of such 'legislators of taste' as Williams Wynn and Hamilton was of

C 10

fundamental importance for the aesthetic and fashionable success of their ornamental wares.

Victoria & Albert Museum (24256.1)
Lit: Penny 1986 Cat. 109–10

C11 Canopic vase *(Pl. 18)*

Black Basalt, with encaustic decoration

Unmarked
About 1790
Height: 34 cm

In addition to Hamilton's *Antiquities*, Wedgwood drew on a number of archaeological publications for the design and decoration of his Black Basalt wares. A list headed 'Books belonging to W&B the 10th August 1770' includes an impressive number of works on Classical architecture, gems and antiquities alongside Jacques Stella's *Livre de Vases* (Cat. E9) and the *British and Irish Peerage*. Heading the list are the 15 volumes of Bernard de Montfaucon's *L'Antiquité Expliquée* (1719–24), Volume II of which illustrates an Egyptian canopic jar (made for storing viscera removed in the process of mummification), on which both the design and decoration of this piece were based. The vase formerly belonged to Wedgwood's friend the physician and poet Erasmus Darwin.

Trustees of the Wedgwood Museum, Barlaston, Staffordshire (No.1944)
Lit and refs: Wedgwood MS 55-31201 repr. in Chellis 1962; compare Allen 1962 p. 69; Connor 1983 Cat. 27; repr. Reilly 1989 I pl. 581

C12 Medallion: *Ganymede and the Eagle*

White Jasper, with blue-grey dip and white reliefs
Mark: 'WEDGWOOD & BENTLEY' impressed
About 1778
Height: 17.7 cm

Wedgwood was careful always to reciprocate when aided by connoisseurs and leaders of fashion. In April 1778 he presented a medallion of this subject to his patron Sir Roger Newdigate (1719–1806), who two years earlier had invited him to take casts from his collection of antique sculpture at Arbury Hall. Wedgwood wrote to Bentley: 'We shall send you three pieces of Jasper to day from Sʳ Roger Newdigates models, which with the Eagle & Ganimede should be sent with our compliments to that good gentleman.' The design is ultimately derived either from a Roman sardonyx in the Duke of Marlborough's collection, or from an engraving by Bellori and Bartoli, but Wedgwood probably took his model from a glass paste medallion by James Tassie (for Tassie, see Cat. D44–46).

Nottingham City Museums. Felix Joseph Bequest (NCM 1892.329)
Lit and refs: Reilly 1972 pl. 4; Wedgwood MSS E25-18790, E25-18822, see Reilly 1989 I pl. C154

C 12

C13 Vase: plate 29 from *Vasi, candelabri, cippi ...*

Giovanni Battista Piranesi (1720–78)
Etching
Lettered with dedication to Sir Watkin Williams Wynn (1748–89)
Published 1778
Cut to 41.2 × 30.5 cm

Piranesi's *Vasi* was a highly influential compendium of vases, candelabra, sarcophagi and other objects. Some of these were genuine Roman antiquities, but many were objects assembled by Piranesi from surviving Roman fragments and sold to collectors and antiquarians living in Rome or taking the Grand Tour. Among the latter category were the massive candelabra sold in 1775 to Wedgwood's patron Sir Roger Newdigate (1718–1806). Many plates in the book bear dedications to English *milordi* including several from Wedgwood's circle: this print is dedicated to Sir Watkin Williams Wynn, a patron and mentor of Wedgwood's; and another bears a tribute to Sir William Hamilton, who had earlier praised Piranesi's *Diverse Maniere* for its usefulness to English designers. Piranesi exercised a vital influence on early Neo-classical architects, notably Sir William Chambers (1723–96) and his great rival Robert Adam (1728–92). Piranesi and Adam were on close terms, and the artist dedicated his *Campo Marzio* of 1762 to Adam, who returned the compliment by using trophies designed by Piranesi for the ante-room at Syon.

Victoria & Albert Museum (E.1527 A 250-1885)

C 16

C14 Vase *(Pl. 9)*

Solid agate ware, with Queen's Ware
handles formed as crouching panthers
Unmarked
Probably 1770s
Height: 19 cm

Vases of this design were illustrated by
Piranesi in his *Vasi, candelabri, cippi* of 1778
(Pl. 8) and in an etching of 1763 by Jean
Claude Richard de Saint Non (1729–91).
Either could have been the source, although
in view of the fact that Wedgwood
mentioned 'two lamps from St Non' being
modelled in November 1774 – which
indicates that he had access to prints by
Saint Non – the latter is perhaps more
likely. A pair of Wedgwood & Bentley vases
of the same design in the British Museum
have their original covers, which are
surmounted finials in the form of a bird
feeding its chicks, as in the Piranesi and
Saint Non prints. The panther handles are
completely out of character for a Roman
marble vase, which is what Piranesi's print
purports to show. The same vase later
appears in drawings made at Rome in 1795
by the architect C. H. Tatham.

*City of Stoke-on-Trent Museum and Art Gallery
(No.2994)*
*Lit and refs: Reilly 1989 I pl. 446; compare
Dawson 1984 fig. 15; Wedgwood MS W/M 1449,
see Wedgwood 1984 Cat. E23*

**C15 Double portrait of Thomas Hollis,
FRS, FSA (1720–74)**

After Giovanni Battista Cipriani, RA
(1727–85)
Engraving
'Lettered: 'I. B. CIPRIANI' and with Latin
dedication
Dated 1767
Size of platemark: 27.6 × 22.8 cm

In April 1770 Wedgwood and Bentley
called on Thomas Hollis – the Milton
scholar, promoter of republican literature
and antiquary – to view the 'Etruscan' vases
in his miniature museum, Hollis having
earlier visited their showrooms and found

the newly introduced Etruscan ware a 'very
imperfect imitation'. Hollis records that
Wedgwood and Bentley followed his
suggestion of engaging G. B. Cipriani to
draw designs for them according to antique
models. Whether they actually did so is not
recorded. At least one piece by Wedgwood
can be linked to a design by him, but this
could well have been taken from an
engraving (Cat. C16–17). There are several
references to a 'Mr. Hollis' in Wedgwood's
letters to Bentley. The earliest of these dates
from June 1769, but there is also a
reference to a 'Mr. Hollis' in October 1780,
six years after Thomas Hollis died. Hollis is
also known to have collaborated with the
architect James 'Athenian' Stuart (1713–88)
on the design of medals and similar work.
Cipriani, an Italian-born designer and
history painter, came to England in 1755 in
the company of the sculptor Joseph Wilton
and Sir William Chambers. He is best
known for his designs engraved by
Francesco Bartolozzi, but he also painted
allegorical works for houses designed by
Chambers and Adam. His strange
emblematic portrait of Hollis includes
devices he designed for use in the latter's
bookbindings.

Victoria & Albert Museum (29718.11)
*Lit and refs: Bond 1990 p. 107 and fig. 4;
Wedgwood MSS E17-15865, E25-18296, E25-
18484, LHP MS 5 Oct 1780*

C 18

**C16 Tablet: a winged figure garlanding a
male term**

After a design by Giovanni Battista
Cipriani, RA (1727–85)
Black Basalt, painted in encaustic colours;
in a gilt-metal frame
Unmarked
About 1775
Length: 34.8 cm (unframed)

The subject of the composition has not
been identified. The design matches that in
Cipriani's print Cat. C17. The blue ground
is highly unusual.

*Trustees of the British Museum (English Pottery
Cat. I 571)*
*Lit: Dawson 1984 pl. 6a and p. 94; Reilly 1989 I
pl. 577*

**C17 A winged figure garlanding a male
term**

Engraving and etching
Francesco Bartolozzi (1725–1815) after
Giovanni Battista Cipriani, RA (1727–85)
Lettered: 'G. B. Cipriani inv. F. Bartolozzi
sculp.'
About 1770–75
Image size: 12.2 × 15.2 cm

See Cat. C16.

Victoria & Albert Museum (21029.17)

**C18 Plaque: a female centaur and
bacchante**

White terracotta stoneware
Unmarked
About 1772
Diameter: 40.5 cm

From a series of 14 medallions based on
wall paintings excavated at Herculaneum.
These were illustrated by Thomas Martyn
and John Lettice in *The Antiquities of
Herculaneum*, to which Josiah Wedgwood
subscribed in 1773. By that date
Wedgwood's 'Herculaneum Bass-reliefs'
were already in production, the source for
the models being a set of plaster reliefs
owned by Lord Lansdowne, whose help in

this respect was gratefully acknowledged by Wedgwood in the 1787 *Catalogue of Ornamental Wares*. In September 1771 Wedgwood wrote to Bentley suggesting that he show examples of the reliefs to the architect Robert Adam (1728–92) in the hope of provoking 'some new idea of disposing of them'.

Victoria & Albert Museum (279-1866)
Lit and refs: Hawes 1965 passim; Reilly 1989 I pl. 487 and pp. 369–70 and 484

C19 Portrait of Charles, 9th Baron Cathcart, British Ambassador at St Petersburg (1721–76) *(Pl. 40)*

Sir Joshua Reynolds, PRA (1723–92)
Oil on canvas
Unsigned
1753–5
124 × 99 cm

Lord Cathcart married Jane Hamilton, William Hamilton's sister, in 1753. He and Wedgwood first met in March 1768, the latter remarking to Bentley that 'we are to do great things for each other'. Lord Cathcart provided Wedgwood with proof illustrations of Hamilton's *Antiquities*, and both he and his wife did much to promote Wedgwood's wares in Russia, where he was Ambassador to St Petersburg from 1768 until 1771. It was through their influence that Wedgwood obtained the commission of the Husk Service, made for Catherine the Great in 1770 (Cat. D59–60).

Manchester City Art Galleries (1981.36)
Purchased with the aid of a government grant and the National Heritage Memorial Fund
Lit and refs: Wedgwood MS E25-18196; Manchester 1983 Cat. 65

C20 Soup tureen with cover and stand

Queen's Ware
Marks: on the stand 'WEDGWOOD' impressed; on the tureen '88' incised; on the cover '41' incised
About 1770–71
Height of tureen: 16 cm; length of stand: 36.2 cm

C 20

The design is based on a Sèvres porcelain tureen given by Louis XV to the Duchess of Bedford, wife of the British Ambassador, after the negotiation of the Treaty of Paris in 1763. In 1765 Wedgwood wrote to Bentley: 'I have been three Days hard & close at work takeing patt^ns, from a set of French China at the Duke of Bedford's, worth at least £1500, the most elegant things I ever saw, & am this evening to wait & be waited upon by designers, modellers &c.'

Victoria & Albert Museum. Jermyn Street Collection (2335 to B-1901)
Lit and refs: Wedgwood MS E25-18093, see Mallet 1975 pp. 46–8 and fig. 8

C21 Tablet: *Bacchanalian Boys*

After designs by Lady Diana Beauclerk (1734–1808)
Blue-grey Jasper, the upper face with pale-blue Jasper wash; white reliefs
Mark: 'WEDGWOOD' impressed
About 1787–90
15.2 × 57 cm

During the 1780s Wedgwood introduced a number of new subjects after designs by amateur artists, all of them women from the upper levels of society. Lady Diana Beauclerk – who supplied him with designs of bacchanalian boys at play – was the daughter of the second duke of Marlborough. Miss Emma Crewe – about whose work for Wedgwood little is known – was the daughter of one of the most celebrated beauties of her time, the Whig hostess Frances Anne Crewe. For Lady Templetown, the final member of this trio, see Cat. B53.

Nottingham City Museums. Given by Mrs Lucy West in memory of Mr William Lees (NCM 1949-149)
Lit: Reilly 1989 I pl. C158

C22 Tablet: *The Fall of Phaeton*

Designed and modelled by George Stubbs (1724–1806)
Solid blue Jasper with white reliefs
Marks: 'WEDGWOOD' impressed twice
About 1785
26 × 48.3 cm

Stubbs visited Etruria in July 1780 and stayed

C 22

for several months. During this time he painted a large portrait of Wedgwood and his family (Pl. 20) and modelled two tablets, of which this is one. Wedgwood informed Bentley in October 1780 that Stubbs 'wishes to employ some of his evenings in modeling a companion to his frighten'd horse, & has fixed upon one of his Phaetons for that purpose, but cannot proceed until he has the print of this subject'. In November 1780 he told Bentley that the 'model of Phaeton is in some forwardness – He works hard at it every night almost 'till bedtime.' The composition of the print was in turn based on Stubbs's painting in enamel on copper of the same subject.

Trustees of the National Museums and Galleries on Merseyside (Lady Lever Art Gallery)
Accession no.: LL1508
Lit: Tate Gallery 1974 Cat. 18; Wedgwood 1984 Cat. L15; Reilly 1989 I pl. 860

C23 Griffin candlestick *(Pl. 42)*

Modelled by William Hackwood (about 1757–1839) after a design by Sir William Chambers (1723–96)
Black Basalt
Mark: 'WEDGWOOD' impressed
First produced 1771; this example possibly 19th century
Height: 34 cm

A design for an almost identical candlestick was illustrated in the third edition of Sir William Chambers' *A Treatise on Civil Architecture* (1791; Cat. C24). The attribution of the design to Chambers is further supported by a letter to Bentley of November 1771 in which Wedgwood wrote: 'The Griffin Candlestick is alter'd sure enough, for Hackwood was oblig'd to new model it. I hope all the world will not have Mr Chambers's Eyes.' A letter of 9 July 1771 records the problems Wedgwood had in firing the candlestick: 'The tips of the Griffins wings will not stick to the top of the head in our metal as they are in the Lead or Wood pattern, they all fly off. I do not know what may be done respecting the ornament on its breast & shoulders but will try.' The pearwood model from which Hackwood worked (attributed to John Coward) is in the Wedgwood Archives. Similar griffins also occur in Matthew Boulton's ormolu.

Sir William Chambers, the King's architect, was an important influence on the design of Wedgwood's Ornamental Wares; not only did he lend Wedgwood models to copy, but he also played a significant role as a mentor and critic. The views of the gardens and his buildings at Kew, published in 1763, were much used on the decoration of Frog Service (see Cat. G42–57).

Victoria & Albert Museum. Jermyn Street Collection (4789-1901)
Lit and refs: Wedgwood MSS LHP (30 or 31 Nov 1771, 9 July 1771), see Reilly 1989 I pl. 680; Hayden 1909 p. 8 fig. 30, shows the pearwood model before it suffered extensive damage

C24 *Various Ornamental Utensils,* supplementary plate II from *A Treatise on Civil Architecture* (third edition; 1791)

P. Bigby after Sir William Chambers (1723–96)
Engraving and etching
Published 1791
Cut to 39.8 × 27.6 cm

See Cat. C23.

Victoria & Albert Museum (29365.7)
Lit: Harris 1970 p. 67 and pl. 67

C25 Presentation drawing of a griffin candlestick *(Pl. 6)*

John Yenn (1750–1821) after Sir William Chambers (1723–96)

C 24

C 26

C 27

Pen and ink and watercolour
Undated
41.2 × 28.2 cm

See Cat. C23.

Victoria & Albert Museum (E.5029-1910)
Lit: Clifford 1974 pl. 69 and p. 765

C26 Three-part model for a soup tureen

Attributed to John Coward, after a design
by Sir William Chambers (1723–96)
Carved pearwood
About 1770
Height: 17 cm; length: 29.6 cm

The model – one from a small group
preserved in the Wedgwood Archives –
follows Chambers' design of about 1768–9
for a silver tureen (Cat. C27). Echoes of the
design are found in some Wedgwood
creamwares, but it does not seem to have
been put into production. These pearwood
models have been attributed to John
Coward, a carver who is said to have
worked also for Robert and James Adam.
He is first mentioned in the Wedgwood
letters in 1765, and by 1770 Wedgwood was
expressing dissatisfaction with his work:
'models in wood are of very little service to
us, or none at all farther than patterns to
look at for in most cases it is less trouble to
make new models than to repair the presses

out of moulds taken from Wood models'.
He was later employed to repair Basalt
vases that had been damaged in the firing,
and his name occurs in connection with the
Catherine or Frog Service, for which he is
believed to have carved models for shell-
edged compotiers.

Trustees of the Wedgwood Museum, Barlaston,
Staffordshire (No.3123)
Lit and refs: for Coward see Reilly 1989 I pp. 195
and 269, where Wedgwood MS E25-18318 is
quoted

C27 Design for a soup tureen

John Yenn (1750–1821) after Sir William
Chambers (1723–96)
Pen and ink and watercolour
About 1768–9
27.2 × 38 cm

A pair of silver tureens was made to this
design for Chambers' and Wedgwood's
patron the Duke of Marlborough in 1769.
These differ from the tureen in the drawing
principally in having a Vitruvian scroll in
place of the awkward key fret indicated
here by John Yenn, Chambers' draughtsman and assistant. The combination of
naturalistic and heavy geometric Classical
ornament is characteristic of Chambers'
designs for silver, as is also the gadrooning

on the cover. This last feature finds echoes
on Wedgwood Queen's Ware tureens of
about 1790, in a number of the patterns
illustrated in the '1802 Shape Book', and on
the cream bowls of the Frog Service (Cat.
G207–10 and G329).

Victoria & Albert Museum (E.4992-1910)
Lit: Young 1987 pp. 396–400, figs 1 & 2

C28 Tureen and cover

Printed in Liverpool by Guy Green
(d. 1799)
Queen's Ware, transfer-printed in black
Marks: 'WEDGWOOD' impressed and '487'
painted in black enamel
About 1791
Diameter: 35.6 cm; height: 28 cm

The cover echoes Chambers' design for a
tureen, Cat. C27, drawn over 20 years
earlier. The transfer-printed pattern has
been identified as the 'Landscape with oak
borders' that appears in an invoice for work
done by Guy Green in May–October 1791.

Trustees of the Wedgwood Museum, Barlaston,
Staffordshire (No.5539)
Lit: Reilly 1989 I pl. 257

C 28

C29 'Michelangelo' lamp

Black Basalt
Mark: 'WEDGWOOD' impressed
In production from about 1772; this
example possibly 19th century
Height: 35.5 cm

The caryatid figures are copied from the
base of a silver-gilt crucifix made by the
16th-century Italian goldsmith Antonio
Gentile, but which was believed in
Wedgwood's time to have been made by
Michelangelo. Similar caryatids occur in
Matthew Boulton's ormolu (Cat. D32).
The models for the smaller versions of these
were supplied by John Flaxman senior
(1726–95), who was probably also the
source for those used by Wedgwood. Three
of Gentile's figures are illustrated in Sir
William Chambers' *A Treatise of Civil
Architecture* (1759), where they are stated to
have been 'cast from models of Michael
Angelo Buonarroti, and repaired either by
himself, or under his direction'.

A similar grouping of the figures also
occurs in a highly problematic drawing, the
back of which is inscribed 'Stuarts Sale
1788'. The Stuart referred to is presumably
the architect James 'Athenian' Stuart, who
died in that year, and who lent models to
Wedgwood, who mentions this in a letter of
June 1770. The lamp is no. 180 in the
factory 'Shape Book'.

*Victoria & Albert Museum. Jermyn Street
Collection (4790&A-1901)*
*Lit: Montagu 1954 p. 380; Goodison 1974 pp.
108–12; Clifford 1974 p. 764; compare Reilly 1989
I pl. 678*

C30 Plaque: *Bacchus and Panther* (also known as *Dionysus and Panther*)

Black Basalt, with integral gilt frame
Unmarked
About 1772–80
Width: 36.2 cm

The design is adapted from a sculpture on
the frieze of the 4th-century BC Monument
of Lysicrates in Athens, detailed engravings
of which were included in the first volume
of James Stuart and Nicholas Revett's
Antiquities of Athens, published in 1762.
Stuart built a replica of this monument in
the grounds of Shugborough for Thomas
Anson, and in 1771 Wedgwood supplied a
Basalt bowl for the tripod that was made to
surmount its roof. Wedgwood was on good
terms with both Stuart and his patron
Thomas Anson, visiting him regularly at
Shugborough, and enrolling him as a
promoter of the Trent & Mersey Canal.

C 29

C 30

Several views of Stuart's monuments and
Anson's grounds are among those painted
on the Frog Service (Cat. G208, G261 and
G276). The first medallion of this subject
was said to have been made in November
1772 for Sir Watkin Williams Wynn.

Victoria & Albert Museum (4-1884)
*Lit: Hawes and Schneidemantel 1969 pp. 29–34;
Wedgwood 1984 Cat. H29; compare Reilly 1989 I
fig. 484; Edwards 1994 fig. 64*

C31 Portrait medallion of James 'Athenian' Stuart (1713–88) *(Pl. 10)*

White Jasper with green dip and white
relief
Marks: 'WEDGWOOD' impressed and '7-9'
incised
About 1785
Height: 10.5 cm

Stuart was one of the first architects to
revive Classical Greek detailing in his
buildings. Although he built little he was
influential through his publications. He was
a friend, advisor and supporter of
Wedgwood's, his name heading the list of
those who proposed Wedgwood's election
as a Fellow to the Royal Society. He
incorporated Jasper tablets in his work at
Montagu House – one of his rare
commissions – and he was sufficiently close
to Bentley to compose an epitaph for the
latter's memorial tablet at Chiswick Church,
which he may also have designed.
Wedgwood issued two portrait medallions
of Stuart, one being listed in the first
Catalogue of 1773.

C32 Portrait medallion of Robert Adam (1728–92)

James Tassie (1735–99)
Moulded opaque white glass paste mounted on glass backed with paper
Marks: the truncation impressed 'ROBERT ADAM ARCHITECT.DIED 3 MARCH 1792 IN HIS 64 YEAR' and 'Tassie F[ecit]'
About 1792
Height: 10.2 cm

In 1771 Wedgwood described Robert Adam as 'a Man of Genius & Invention & an excellent Architect'. In the following year he supplied terracotta stoneware and encaustic Basalt tablets for chimneys designed by Adam, writing at that time: 'I suppose it is very much in Mr Adams's power to introduce our things into use & am glad to find he seems so well dispos'd to do it ...'. His Jasper medallions and tablets found obvious echoes in the painted medallions of the interiors designed by such fashionable architects as Robert Adam and James Wyatt (1746–1813), the colours of these being chosen 'to the colours of the rooms'. Wedgwood had high hopes that his Jasper tablets would be taken up by leading architects. However, he failed to 'prevail upon the architects to be godfathers to our child ...'. Previously, in 1770, Wedgwood and Bentley had considered taking premises in the Adelphi, James and Robert Adam's development of a site between the Strand and the River Thames, a plan that came to nothing.

Victoria & Albert Museum. Given by Lady Charlotte Schreiber (Schr. II 605)
Lit and refs: Wedgwood MS W/M 1441, see Edwards 1994 p. 39; Wedgwood MS E25-18394 and E26-18898, see Reilly 1989 I pp. 578–9

C33 *Design of a Ceiling for the Drawing Room at Mamhead in Devonshire*

Robert Adam (1728–92)
Pen and ink with water- and body colour
Inscribed with title
About 1768–77
46.3 × 60.4 cm

The influence of such fashionable architects as Robert Adam and James Wyatt on the design and vocabulary of ornament of Wedgwood's Jasper was enormous. It was perhaps this that the engraver, publisher and self-styled 'Professor of Ornament' Matthias Darley was referring to when he commented in the dedication to his *Book of Architecture* of 1773 that: 'Some of the present Architects of this Nation by their Introducing the Ornaments made Use of by the Ancients, have done more good than all the other polite Artists put together ... Witness the Pottery of this Kingdom, there is now performances in Clay which would make the heavy handed Silversmith blush ...'.

Victoria & Albert Museum (D.2171-1896)
Lit and refs: Darley is quoted in Clifford 1978 p. 162; Rowan 1988 Cat. 132

C34 Grecian sphinx

Black Basalt
Unmarked
In production by 1773
Length: 31.2 cm

Pairs of Grecian sphinxes are listed in Wedgwood & Bentley's first Catalogue of 1773. Their design is related to four lead sphinxes designed by Robert Adam for Osterley Park House, and to others designed by Adam for Syon House, but eventually added to the bridge at Compton Verney, Warwickshire, in 1760–65. Very similar sphinxes were also made in Bristol hard-paste porcelain in 1768–70, the models for these probably being bought for the Bristol factory from David Crashley's plaster shop in Long Acre in 1768. Since Crashley's shop was very close to Wedgwood's showrooms in Great Newport Street it has been suggested that the model for Wedgwood's Grecian sphinxes may have come from Crashley. The London plaster shops of John Flaxman senior, Hoskins & Grant and John Cheere were an important source of models for Wedgwood's Basalt figures and library busts; and his productions were frequently made in direct competition with theirs.

Victoria & Albert Museum. Jermyn Street Collection (2389-1901)
Lit: Wills 1982; Poole 1986 Cat. C14; Reilly 1989 I p. 464

C 34

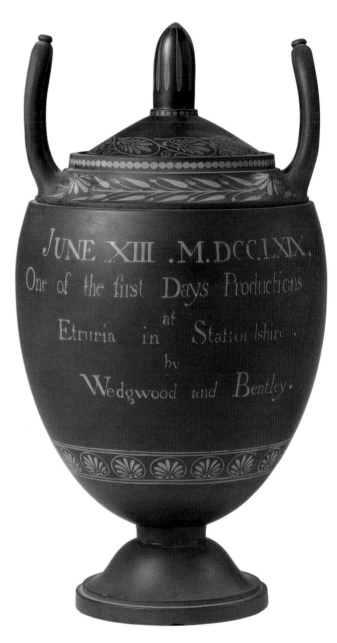

D 2

D 4

Wedgwood's great reputation as a entrepreneur is founded on his rational planning of his manufactory at Etruria, his involvement in the transport improvements that opened up the Potteries to the rest of the world, his establishment of a massive export empire, and his skill as a marketeer. During the years of his partnership with Bentley his production was divided between the 'Useful' works – run in partnership with his cousin Thomas in the manufacture of Queen's Ware tablewares – and the 'Ornamental' partnership run in partnership with Bentley, who also managed the London Decorating Studio. The products of the partnership for ornamental wares are closely related to those of competitors with Wedgwood in the market for luxury goods, notably Matthew Boulton and William Duesbury, who on occasions made use of the same designs, patterns and modellers as Wedgwood.

THE FOUNDING OF ETRURIA

D1 Manuscript letter

Dated 31st December 1767
34 × 21 cm

The letter from Josiah Wedgwood is addressed to Thomas Bentley, 'Merch. in Liverpool'. It covers various topics of common interest to the two men and discusses in some detail the proposed 'Elevation of our Works' for the newly designed Etruria Manufactory, as well as the advantages, plans and location of the canal which was to pass through the Ridgehouse Estate, Burslem, on which the manufactory was to be built.

From its inception, progress was slow on Wedgwood's plan to expand his manufacturing activities by constructing a new works outside the main pottery conurbation. He had considerable difficulties to overcome in respect of the area of land he had chosen and contracted to purchase by Michaelmas 1766. Eventually the matter was settled, and the Ridgehouse Estate of about 350 acres was formally purchased by Josiah Wedgwood in December 1767 for the sum of £3,000. One of the advantages of this site was that the planned Trent & Mersey Canal was to pass through the property. Wedgwood kept an extremely tight control of the plans and proposed designs for his Etruria Works. Ideas, sketches and details passed regularly between himself, Thomas Bentley and the architect, Joseph Pickford. During the planning of the new factory, Bentley's opinion was sought on all matters of taste, even down to the shape of the hovels for the kilns, and whether or not they should be decorative as well as functional. After many letters and alterations Wedgwood was able to write on 23 January 1768: 'We have now settled my plans for the house & works, & Mr. P[ickford].: takes them with him to make the Estimates'. Bad weather throughout the summer of 1768 plagued the building programme, and it was not until November that the works were roofed. By January 1769 significant progress had been made, causing Josiah to comment: 'We are making saggars at Etruria, building the steps, glazing the windows and getting forward as fast as possible'. The new works were officially opened on 13 June 1769.

Trustees of the Wedgwood Museum, Barlaston, Staffordshire (MS E25-18182)

D2 'First Day's Vase'

Black Basalt, with encaustic decoration
Unmarked. Inscription as given below
Dated June 1769
Height: 25.4 cm

The vase is one of six thrown by Josiah Wedgwood himself to mark the opening of the Etruria manufactory on 13 June 1769. It is inscribed on one side in encaustic enamel:

JUNE XIII .M.DCC.LXIX
one of the first Days Productions
at
Etruria in Staffordshire,
by
Wedgwood and Bentley.

and with 'Artes Etruriae renascuntur' (The Arts of Etruria revived), on the other. Wedgwood refers to the vases in a letter to Bentley dated 19 November 1769: 'The six Etruscan vases ... three handled sent to you a fortnight since were those we threw & turn'd the first at Etruria & sho^d. be finished as high as you please, but not sold, they being <u>first fruits</u> of Etruria.' The form is based on a Greek *Lebes gamikos*, and is listed as 'Shape Number 49' in the 'Shape Number One Book'. The vases were painted in the London Decorating Studio, the figure subject – of Hippothion, Antiochus and Clumenos – being taken from Hamilton's *Antiquities* (Vol. I, left-hand half of pl. 29; see Cat. C5).

Trustees of the Wedgwood Museum, Barlaston, Staffordshire (No.73)
Ref: Wedgwood MS E25-18269

D3 'First Day's Vase'

Black Basalt, with encaustic decoration
Unmarked. Painted with inscription
identical to that on Cat. D2.
Dated 1769
Height: 25.5 cm

The figures are taken from the right-hand
half of the plate from Hamilton's
Antiquities used for Cat. D2. Another 'First
Day's Vase' painted with the same group of
figures is on loan to the City Museum and
Art Gallery, Stoke-on-Trent.

Private collection

D4 Plaque with a view of Etruria Hall

Attributed to James Bakewell (active
1750–75)
Enamel on biscuit earthenware
Unmarked
About 1773
19 × 36.9 cm

The plaque shows Josiah Wedgwood's own
home, designed by Joseph Pickford of
Derby and completed in 1769, together
with the Trent & Mersey Canal in the
foreground. It clearly shows the proximity
of the Etruria site to the canal that
Wedgwood played such a key role in
promoting.

   The painting of this plaque has previously
been attributed to Edward Stringer (see
Chapter 5, note 11), but without any
documentary proof. On stylistic grounds it
does not appear to be by his hand, and it is
possible that it is by James Bakewell. Partial
confirmation of this is in a letter from
Benjamin Mather at the Chelsea Decorating
Studio to Josiah Wedgwood and dated 5
November 1774:

> We have but very little work to employ our hands
> upon and they must I am afraid stand still some
> time if no Orders should not come in for Enamel
> Ware. – Jas. Bakewell would be glad to do
> Landscape ware; if you think proper to imploy him
> at that Work – he has just finished a Tablet painted
> with a Landscape in Colours; which suceeded very
> well in the Colour, & in Workmanship the best that
> has been done yet; I have asked him what he
> thought he could finished plates for a Piece in
> Colours and he thought the lowest would be 3s/6d a

Piece, including the Landscape the inside Border
the same pattern as the Russian Dessert Service wth
... Ivy Border in Colour & Edging. I should be glad
if you will let us do Dessert Service with Landscapes
in Colours, I am allmost certain it will be done to
please if not to what you would wish it; you will
never be able to fix a Price upon it; by the Service
that J. Simcock is upon for I see no probability of
the plates laying in less than upwards of a Guinea p.
Piece for the Workmanship –.

The plaque is recorded as having been
found in the works of Etruria in 1905.
Another polychrome enamelled landscape
panel was formerly in the collection of
Frank Hurlbutt: this was painted with a
view of Fingal's Cave, and was inscribed on
the reverse, apparently by Thomas Pennant,
'The gift of Mr. Wedgewood in return for
some small service I had done him'. For
Pennant and Fingal's Cave see Cat. G237;
for polychrome pieces painted in the style
of the Frog Service see Cat. G320–30.

*Trustees of the Wedgwood Museum, Barlaston,
Staffordshire (No.4110)*
*Lit and refs: Wedgwood MS 6-42333; Tate Gallery
1974 Cat. 13; Science Museum 1978 Cat. 241;
Reilly 1989 I pl. 65; Hurlbutt (n.d.) p. 3*

D5 View of Etruria

Anonymous
Watercolour
Late 18th century or early 19th
43 × 60.7 cm

The painting clearly shows Etruria Hall and
Bank House (the home built for Thomas
Bentley in Staffordshire), as well as the
Etruria Manufactory, as viewed from across
the Trent Valley.

*Trustees of the Wedgwood Museum, Barlaston,
Staffordshire (No.5389A)*

D6 Portrait of Richard Wedgwood
(1701–82) *(Pl. 15)*

George Stubbs, RA (1724–1806)
Oil on panel
Signed 'Geo Stubbs pinx 1780'
Dated 1780
71.2 × 58.5 cm

Richard Wedgwood was a merchant and
cheese factor from Spen Green. He was the
eldest brother of Thomas and John
Wedgwood of the Big House at Burslem,
notable manufacturers of salt-glazed
pottery, and father of Sarah Wedgwood.
The details of his settlement on his
daughter are not known, but she was
heiress to a considerable fortune, and this
played a crucial part in the financing of
Josiah Wedgwood's business. Richard's
account shows that he had a turnover of
between £1,200 and £1,800 a month. Josiah
wrote to Thomas Bentley on 9 January 1764
about the negotiations to marry Sarah: 'If
you know my temper, & sentiments on
these affairs, you will be sensible how I am
mortify'd when I tell you I have gone
through a long series of bargain makeing –
of settlem[ts]. Revisions – Provisions &c: &c:
Gone through it did I say! wo[d]. to Hymen I
had, No I am still in the Attorneys hands,
from which I hope it is no harm to pray
"good Ld. deliver me".' Two weeks later
Wedgwood reported: 'All matters being
amicably settled betwixt my Pappa (Elect)
& my self.'

*Provenance: Painted for Josiah Wedgwood; by
descent to Dr Ralph Vaughan-Williams, who
bequeathed it to the Wedgwood Museum in 1944*

*Trustees of the Wedgwood Museum, Barlaston,
Staffordshire (No.5612)*
*Lit and refs: Wedgwood MSS E25-18055 and E25-
180560; Tate Gallery 1974 Cat. 13; Reilly 1989 I
pl. 38*

D7 Portrait of Sarah Wedgwood
(1734–1815) *(Pl. 14)*

Sir Joshua Reynolds, PRA (1723–92)
Oil on canvas
1782
75 × 63 cm

Sarah Wedgwood was the wife and cousin
of Josiah. They were married on 25 January
1764 at Astbury Church, Cheshire. After
their marriage Sarah became involved in the
ceramic business, causing Wedgwood to
comment in March of the following year
that: 'Sally's my chief mate in this as well as

other things, & that she may not be hurried by haveing to many <u>Irons in the fire</u> as the phrase is. I have ord^d. the spinning wheel into the lumber room.' Three years later, in January 1768, he added: 'I speak from experience in Female taste without which I should have made but a poor figure amongst my Potts, not one of which of any consequence, is finished without the Approbation of my Sally.' She was a devoted wife, and a shrewd lady. She bore eight children, only one of whom died in infancy. For the companion portrait of Josiah see Cat. C1.

Trustees of the Wedgwood Museum, Barlaston, Staffordshire (No.5609)
Lit and refs: Wedgwood MSS E25-18070 and E25-18183; Reilly 1989 I pl. C5

TRANSPORT AND COMMUNICATIONS

D8 View of the Potteries, from Etruria South, Newcastle Road

Etching and engraving, hand-coloured
F. Wrighton after Frederick Calvert (active 1827–d. about 1845)
Lettered: 'F. Calvert del. F. Wrighton Sc.'
About 1830–45
13.5 × 18.5 cm

Josiah Wedgwood was an active supporter and promoter of turnpike roads, particularly those that connected the Potteries with the ports, including Liverpool and Chester, through which clay from Cornwall was imported and his finished products were exported. Josiah addressed the local North Staffordshire inhabitants at the Town Hall of Newcastle-under-Lyme in 1763, and his forceful speech outlining the advantages of such a road system for tradesmen and manufacturers is recorded in full in his 'Common Place Book'. Wedgwood went on to enlist the help of Lord Gower in seeing the new turnpike bill through Parliament. He became one of the leaders, amongst potters, in the various campaigns to improve the road system. Nine turnpike

acts were passed by Parliament in 1766. Later acts of 1777 and 1783 were specifically aimed at linking the local road system to the main London route. It is interesting to note that amongst the 130 Trustees named in the 1791 Turnpike Act were Josiah Wedgwood I and his three sons. This 19th-century print shows the type of conditions that pack horses laden with pottery and raw materials had to cope with.

Private collection

D9 *A SHORT VIEW of the general advantages of inland navigations; with a Plan of a NAVIGABLE CANAL intended for a communication between the ports of LIVERPOOL & HULL*

Written by Thomas Bentley, with corrections by Dr Erasmus Darwin
Manuscript
Undated
33.1 × 19.1 cm

The Trent & Mersey Canal connected the land-locked Potteries with the ports of Liverpool on the west coast and Hull on the east coast. The first full meeting of those men interested and involved with the development of 'the Navigation from the Trent to the Mersey' was called for 10 June 1766 at The Crown, a coaching inn in Stone, Staffordshire. At the inaugural meeting, the committee which was appointed included many eminent men of the district. Officers were also nominated, amongst them James Brindley as surveyor general and his brother-in-law, Hugh Henshall, as clerk to the works. Wedgwood was elected as treasurer, as he comments 'at £000 p.ann. out of which he bears his own Expences'. He wrote to his brother, John, on 3 April 1765: 'This scheme of a Navigation is undoubtedly the best thing that could possibly be plann'd for this country & I hope there is a great degree of probability of its being carried into execution'.

The Bill for the Trent & Mersey Canal was presented to Parliament on 18 February 1766 and was authorized on 14

May. On 26 July 1766 Wedgwood cut the first sod of earth to commence the canal construction. Rival schemes and opposition to the proposed canal led Josiah to call in the assistance of Thomas Bentley to prepare a pamphlet to help popularize the proposal. The draft was sent to Erasmus Darwin for his comments, and the surviving manuscript exhibits both authors' hands. Darwin's comments provoked a quarrel between the two men, causing Josiah to comment to Bentley on 15 October 1765: 'I am my good friend very sorry that this Pamphlet turns out so troublesome an affair to you whom I am sure have full employm^t. for every moment of your time'. He continues, 'Away with such hyper criticisms, and let the press go on, A Pamphlet we must have, or our Design will be defeated.'

It took 11 years to complete the canal, which involved the construction of one of the engineering feats of the 18th century, Harecastle Tunnel, completed by 1775. The opening of a navigable waterway reduced dramatically the cost of carrying heavy materials such as clay and finished ceramics.

Trustees of the Wedgwood Museum, Barlaston, Staffordshire (MS 24151)
Refs: Wedgwood MSS E25-18072 and E25-18117

D10 Map: *A Plan of the GRAND CANAL from the Trent to the Mersey*

Engraving
1771
20 × 39 cm

Taken from *The Gentleman's Magazine* for July 1771. See Cat. D9.

Private Collection. On loan to the Wedgwood Museum

D11 Portrait of Francis Egerton, 3rd Duke of Bridgewater, promoter of the Bridgewater and Trent & Mersey Canals (1736–1803)

Anonymous
Engraving and etching
Lettered in English and Latin with

identification of the sitter
1766
Cut to 23.9 × 12.7 cm

See Cat. D9. Cut from R. Whitworth's *The Advantages of Inland Navigation ... to shew that an Inland Navigation may easily be effected between the three great Ports of Bristol, Liverpool, and Hull ... (1766).*

Trustees of the British Museum (1869-10-9-22)

D12 Portrait of James Brindley (1716–72)

John Taylor Wedgwood after a painting by Francis Parsons, FSA (active 1763–d.1804)
Engraving
Lettered: 'Engraved by J. T. Wedgwood. From a Print by R. Dunbarton 1773, after a Picture by F. Parsons', and with sitter's name and publication line
19th century
Sheet size: 27.6 × 19.2 cm

A portrait of the engineer of the Trent & Mersey Canal engraved by J. T. Wedgwood, the son of Josiah Wedgwood's partner, 'Useful' Thomas. The original painting was exhibited at the Society of Artists in 1771. The vase is after a print by the 16th-century artist Polidoro da Caravaggio.

Trustees of the British Museum (1920-12-11-278)

PRODUCTION

D13 'JW's Experiments, Potters' Instructions Etc 1780'

Manuscript volume
Dated 1780
29 × 24 cm (closed)

Wedgwood's manufactory at Etruria was an exemplary piece of modern planning. Separate workroom spaces were allocated to separate processes, these being laid out in a logical order that echoed that of the manufacturing processes – beginning with preparation of materials and ending with finishing and packing. Such a system presupposed a high degree of specialization and division of labour. In order to ensure the smooth running of the factory Wedgwood drew up a set of rules governing the conduct of his employees at Etruria, copies of which are included in this volume. Covering every aspect of the workforce's activities, these were intended to eliminate waste, irregular working practices and fraud and to ensure that cleanliness, punctuality and sobriety prevailed. The date given on the spine of the manuscript is significant,

1780 being the year in which Bentley died.

Trustees of the Wedgwood Museum, Barlaston, Staffordshire (E26-19114)
Lit: McKendrick 1963 pp. 12–13

D14 View of Etruria factory

The Rev. Stebbing Shaw (1762–1802)
Watercolour
1794
20.3 × 33 cm

The use of a windmill for grinding materials at Etruria is recorded in 1773. It was superseded during the course of the next two decades as steam power was introduced, the first steam engine – made by Boulton & Watt – being installed in 1784. By 1793 steam power was being used to grind the flints used in the Queen's Ware body, and to grind enamel colours, pound broken kiln saggars (cases of baked fire-proof clay, enclosing pottery while it is baked) and temper clay; it is not known to have been used at Etruria in the manufacture of pottery – as opposed to preparation of materials – until the early 19th century. Shaw's view was probably prepared for inclusion in the unpublished second part of volume 2 of his *History and*

D 18

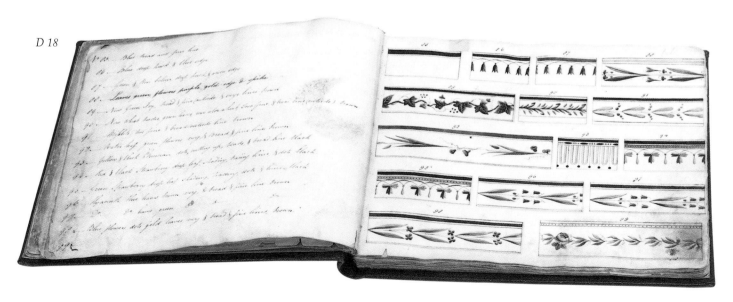

Antiquities of Staffordshire. It is the only record of the windmill's appearance.

Trustees of the William Salt Library (Staffs. View, Vol. 4, p. 184)
Lit: Science Museum 1978 Cat. 188; Thomas 1971 pp. 46–8

D15 Plate

Queen's Ware, moulded with bead edge
Marks: 'WEDGWOOD', '3' and 'C' impressed
About 1765
Diameter: 23.5 cm

The production of 'Useful Wares' – defined as 'such vessels as are to be made use of at meals' – was excluded from Wedgwood's partnership with Bentley by the terms of their agreement (although some teawares were made by the Wedgwood & Bentley partnership in apparent contravention of this). Between 1766 and 1788 Wedgwood's 'Useful Wares' in Queen's Ware were made in partnership with his cousin Thomas. In addition to the range of tablewares decorated with border patterns, a vast amount of undecorated Queen's Ware was made by this partnership, some of it being plain and aimed at a relatively unprosperous market.

Trustees of the Wedgwood Museum, Barlaston, Staffordshire (No.1601)

D16 Cup and saucer

Queen's Ware, moulded with shell edge
Marks: 'Wedgwood' and a workman's mark impressed on both
About 1765
Diameter of saucer: 12.2 cm; height of cup: 6 cm

See Cat. D15.

Trustees of the Wedgwood Museum, Barlaston, Staffordshire (No.5433)
Lit: Wedgwood 1984 Cat. C3

D17 Plate

Queen's Ware, moulded with 'New Feather' edge
Marks: 'WEDGWOOD' and '9' and 'K' impressed
About 1765
Diameter: 15 cm

See Cat. D15.

Trustees of the Wedgwood Museum, Barlaston, Staffordshire (No.3441)

D18 'First Pattern Book'

Pen and ink and watercolour
Compiled between 1810 (date of watermark on one page) and 1814
30 × 24 cm (closed)

The book was made as a factory record of creamware border patterns and their reference numbers. It would have been used to ensure standardization of the patterns painted in the decorating studio at Etruria and of the numbers used in ordering and stock control; and it was possibly also shown to prospective clients visiting the factory. Although the volume was compiled early in the 19th century, it must duplicate the contents of an earlier pattern book or books, which would have been replaced when they became worn or damaged through normal factory use. The numbering here runs from 1 to 663. The number of patterns that had been developed by this date is in fact larger than this, as certain of the those known to have been introduced before the 1773 move to Etruria of the 'Useful Works' do not appear in the book.

Wedgwood was one of the first manufacturers to use simple repeating patterns of plant or Classical architectural ornament as border decoration on wares that were otherwise left plain. This form of decoration is still with us today.

Trustees of the Wedgwood Museum, Barlaston, Staffordshire (MS 13-12085)
Lit: Reilly 1989 I pls 338 and C54

D19 'London Pattern Book, 1787'

Manuscript volume
About 1787
41 × 17 cm (closed)

The 'London Pattern Book, 1787' contains numbered outline drawings of ornamental wares. It was probably made to standardize the shape reference numbers used in the showrooms. The numbers and shapes tally with those in the 'Shape Number One Book', which was kept at Etruria.

Trustees of the Wedgwood Museum, Barlaston, Staffordshire (MS 61-30635)

D 21

D 22

D20 Vase and cover

Black Basalt, with encaustic decoration
Mark: 'WEDGWOOD' impressed
About 1780–90
Height: 31.1 cm

The figure group here is taken from
Hamilton's *Antiquities* (Cat. C5; Vol. I pl.
109). The same scene occurs on the
following two exhibits, and also on one side
of Cat. D29, each of these four vases being
of a different shape. The handles here are
repeated from another earlier vase, the
design of which is loosely based on a print
by the 17th-century artist Jacques Stella
(Cat. E9). Few of Wedgwood's vases were
archaeologically exact reproductions;
rather, the stock of models for cast and
moulded parts and reliefs, and the patterns
for painted decoration, were used in a
variety of combinations on the factory's
range of thrown, cast and moulded forms.

*Nottingham City Museums. Felix Joseph Bequest
(NCM 1892-198)*
Lit: Nottingham 1975 Cat. 457

D21 Amphora

Black Basalt, with encaustic decoration
Mark: 'WEDGWOOD' impressed
About 1785
Height: 30.8 cm

Victoria & Albert Museum (1506-1855)

D22 Vase (Volute Krater), one from a pair

Black Basalt, with encaustic decoration
Marks: 'WEDGWOOD' and 'A' impressed
About 1795
Height: 32.5 cm

*Trustees of the National Museums and Galleries
on Merseyside (Lady Lever Art Gallery)*
Accession no.: LL1151
*Lit: Victoria & Albert Museum 1959 Cat. 33;
Reilly 1992 p. 207*

THE LONDON DECORATING STUDIO

D23 Plate

Queen's Ware, with a moulded rose motif in
the centre and feather edge; painted in
yellow and black enamels
Mark: a cross within a diamond impressed
About 1770
Diameter: 22 cm

The enamelled decoration was probably by
James Bakewell (active 1750–75). This
painter was initially employed in the
summer of 1768 to decorate Etruscan vases,
but on 23 May 1770 Wedgwood wrote that:
'Bakewell has set his mind much upon
being a good enamel Painter and really
improves very much both in flowers & in
Coppying figures'.

*Trustees of the Wedgwood Museum, Barlaston,
Staffordshire (No.9009) (Formerly in the
D. Towner Collection No.351)*
*Lit and refs: Wedgwood MS E25-18302; Towner
1978 pl. 13B*

D24 Shell dish *(Pl. 21)*

Queen's Ware, enamelled in purple with
sprays of flowers
Marks: 'WEDGWOOD' impressed and 'g'
painted in purple
About 1770
Length: 19.9 cm

The dish is identical to those in the Husk
Service ordered in 1770 by Catherine the
Great, part of which survives at the Palace
of Petrodvorets (Peterhof), St Petersburg.
See Cat. D59.

*Victoria & Albert Museum. Gift of Miss Lily
Antrobus (C.70-1914)*
*Lit: Towner 1978 pl. 13A and pp. 58 and 223;
Reilly 1989 I pp. 268–9*

D25 Dish

Queen's Ware, enamelled in purple with
sprays of flowers
Marks: 'WEDGWOOD' impressed and 'B'
painted in purple
About 1770
Length: 32.5 cm

Decorated en suite with Cat. D24

*Victoria & Albert Museum. Jermyn Street
Collection (2322-1901)*

D26 Oval dish or stand

Queen's Ware, with pierced border
moulded to resemble basket weave; painted
with floral sprays in monochrome pink;
alternate sections of the border picked out
in pink enamel
Marks: 'WEDGWOOD', and '4' impressed
and 'N' painted in pink enamel
About 1772
22.9 × 25.4 cm

Decorated in the London Decorating
Studio, Little Cheyne Row, Chelsea. In
May 1770 Wedgwood commented to
Bentley: 'You observe very justly that few
hands can be got to paint flowers in the
style we want them.' Flowers of this type
were painted by numerous hands, including
Joseph Cooper, who was described as a

'good flower painter', and Ralph Unwin (active 1770–1812), who 'will do flowers, under a Master very prettily'.

Property of Mr Robin Reilly on loan to the Wedgwood Museum, Barlaston, Staffordshire
Lit and refs: Wedgwood MS E25-18301; Reilly 1989 I C51

D27 Pair of knife rests

Queen's Ware, painted with a broad and fine brown line and an armorial crest
Mark: 'WEDGWOOD' impressed
About 1780–85
3.5 × 6.5 cm

The crest, which was commissioned by the Reverend M. Duglass, is recorded in the 'Crest Book Index'. Initially Wedgwood would not undertake armorial decoration, writing on 25 September 1766:

> Crests are very bad things for us [potters] to meddle with & I never take any orders for services so ornamented – Plain Ware if it sho^d. not happen to be firsts, you will take off my hands as seconds, which if Crested wo^d. be as useless as most other Crests, and Crest wearers are, for this & other reasons the additional expence is more than the buyer can be perswaded to believe it ought to be.

Ten years later, on 12 September 1776, Wedgwood wrote that: 'painting of Arms is now become a serious business, & I must either lose or gain a great deal of business by it – However, I must, at all events, come into it.'

Trustees of the Wedgwood Museum, Barlaston, Staffordshire (No.6634c)
Refs: Wedgwood MSS 45-29101, E25-18129, E25-18692

D28 Tureen with cover and fixed stand

Queen's Ware, decorated in brown with the 'Bedford Grape' pattern and the crest of Lord William Russell
Marks: 'WEDGWOOD' and 'F' impressed
1789–90
Height: 12 cm; overall length: 19.3 cm

The association between the Dukes of Bedford and Wedgwood can be traced as far back as 1765, when Josiah was

D 28

permitted to take patterns from one of their 'French China' services (Cat. C20). A series of invoices and receipts for wares supplied to the Dukes of Bedford survives, the earliest being dated 1786. These include orders for Basalt and Jasper, but the largest single order was that placed in 1789 for a Queen's Ware armorial service painted with a border pattern which has subsequently been called 'Bedford Grape'. The order involved the painting of 1,334 crests and coronets at a cost of £55 13s 0d plus £1 13s 6d delivery charge.

Trustees of the Wedgwood Museum, Barlaston, Staffordshire (No.5419)
Lit: Wedgwood 1973 Cat. A10

D29 Vase

Black Basalt, with encaustic decoration
Mark: 'WEDGWOOD' impressed
About 1785
Height: 34.6 cm

Despite the importance of the decoration in London of Queen's Ware, it was the development of the Black Basalt body for ornamental wares that gave the Cheyne Row Decorating Studios a new challenge. Within a month of sending the first good Black Basalt vases to Bentley, which he had done in August 1768, Josiah was admonishing William Cox, the company clerk, not to forget to call them 'Etruscans'.

Wedgwood patented two methods of decoration in 1769 for his newly refined ornamental body, the best known of which was his encaustic enamelling. This was made in emulation of Greek red-figure pottery, which was then the subject of renewed interest as a result of archaeological discoveries and the publication of works such as Hamilton's *Antiquities*. In the introductory remarks to the 1777 Catalogue, Wedgwood stated that the method had been developed 'completely to imitate the Painting upon Etruscan Vases, but to do much more; to give to the Beauty of Design, the Advantages of Light and Shade in various Colours; and to render Paintings durable without the Defect of a varnished or glassy Surface'. This was, he observed, 'an object earnestly desired by persons of critical taste in all ages'. The pigment used by Josiah to achieve the desired effect was, according to the surviving specifications, made of part-enamel and part slip, and it also contained a small portion of the Cherokee clay brought to Staffordshire from North Carolina by Thomas Griffiths.

D 29

Initially, the decoration of these vases was a time-consuming and expensive process. Bentley suggested that they should be less sophisticated and thus less expensive and easier to produce. Wedgwood readily agreed, indicating that the bulk of the vases could be painted in 'Simpler style or we shall never have very many done'. To assist in the decoration, William Hopkins Craft (see Cat. C3) suggested that the outlines of the figures could be transfer-printed or drawn in chalk and then filled in and shaded by less skilled hands. For the next two years various methods of easing the task were tried, and in September 1772 Josiah commented that he had obtained 'Punches to cut Etruscan shapes & borders in paper'. He told Bentley that 'by means of some of these punches & some other contrivances we have here made very decent Etruscan Vases at a guinea & half a sett of five'. Further ideas were pursued, including the proposal that some of the simpler Etruscan vases could be decorated at Etruria, whilst 'you might do the fine & expensive ones, & such subjects as may be particularly admir^d. at Chelsea'. The scene of a warrior and woman here is taken from Hamilton's *Antiquities* (Cat. C5, Vol. II, pl. 61). The figure scene on the reverse of the vase is same that on Cat. D20–22.

Victoria & Albert Museum (1408-1855)

PEER COMPETITORS AND ALLIED MANUFACTURERS

D30 Portrait of Matthew Boulton (1728–1809)

Peter Rouw the younger (1770–1852)
Modelled in pink wax
Inscribed on the truncation 'P. Rouw sculptor London 1814'
Dated 1814
Diameter: 37 cm

A posthumous portrait of the Birmingham industrialist, who was both Wedgwood's

D 3

friend and keen rival in the market for luxury ornaments. Wedgwood and Matthew Boulton collaborated on certain schemes, notably the production of Jasper and cut-steel jewellery and dress ornaments. When Boulton planned to make black vases Wedgwood wrote: 'It doubles my courage to have the first Manufacturer in England to encounter with – The match likes me well – I like the Man, I like his spirit. – He will not be a mere sniveling copyist like the antagonists I have hitherto had.' Several of Boulton's productions in ormolu have elements in common with Wedgwood's, among them the 'Michelangelo' caryatids, and the griffin and tritons (Cat. C29, C23, D39). Much of his metalwork was sold abroad, especially in Russia, where Lord Cathcart was a useful ally. In financial terms his ormolu business was a failure, but the contacts he made laid some of the foundations for his later success in other spheres.

Victoria & Albert Museum. Given by Mr Charles Vine (1058-1871)
Lit and refs: Pollard 1970 p. 317, n. 1; Wedgwood MS E25-18261, see Reilly 1989 I p. 445; Goodison 1974 passim

D 32

D31 Candlestick

Made at Matthew Boulton & John
Fothergill's Soho Works, Birmingham,
probably after a design by James Wyatt
(1746–1813)
Fused plate ('Sheffield plate')
Unmarked
About 1780
Height 32.2 cm

Sheffield plate is a substitute for solid silver
made from copper that has been faced with
silver, rolled into sheet form and shaped in
dies or moulds. Matthew Boulton was the
foremost manufacturer of this material from
the 1760s onwards, this work being directly
analogous to Wedgwood's more lavish
Queen's Ware productions – both in terms
of price and market, and in design and
finish. Like Wedgwood, Boulton's business
empire embraced the manufacture of luxury
goods aimed at the highest levels of society,
and well-designed and considerably cheaper
goods that were produced in bulk and sold
to a much wider market. And again like
Wedgwood, Boulton enlisted the support of
the taste-makers of the day, including the
architects Sir William Chambers (1723–96)
and James Wyatt. The design of this
candlestick, which appears as no. 973693 in
the Boulton & Fothergill catalogue of 1779,
is attributed to the latter.

Victoria & Albert Museum (M.287-1976)
Lit: Snodin 1987 p. 26 fig. 4

D32 'Persian' candle vase

Made at Matthew Boulton & John
Fothergill's Soho Works, Birmingham
Blue-john (Derbyshire fluorspar) and
marble, mounted in ormolu
Unmarked
1772
Height: 81 cm

In 1770, when both Matthew Boulton and
Josiah Wedgwood were considering taking
showrooms in the Adelphi, Robert and
James Adam's development near Charing
Cross, Wedgwood was clearly worried by
the possibility of losing sales to Boulton. He

consulted the architect James 'Athenian'
Stuart on the subject, and they concluded
that 'those customers who were more fond
of shew & glitter, than fine forms, & the
appearance of antiquity wo[d]. buy Soho
Vases, And that all who could feel the
effects of a fine outline & had any
veneration for Antiquity wo[d]. be with us. –
But these we were afraid wo[d]. be a
minority.'

Reduced versions of the 'Persian' figure
occur on Boulton's 'Geographical' clock of
1770–72, which he was at one time
considering sending to Catherine the Great.
The models for these were supplied by John
Flaxman senior in December 1770, and they
occur again on Wedgwood's 'Michelangelo'
lamps (Cat. C29). This vase is one of a pair
supplied to Sir Lawrence Dundas in 1772
for his Arlington Street house (remodelled
by Robert Adam 1763–6); for Moor Park,
his country seat, see Cat. G323.

Victoria & Albert Museum (W.23-1934)
*Lit and refs: Goodison 1974 pp. 161–3 and pl. 84;
Wedgwood MS E25-18335, see Clifford 1978
p. 161 and McKendrick 1982 p. 115*

D33 Jewellery

Probably mounted at Matthew Boulton &
John Fothergill's Soho Works, Birmingham
Blue Jasper with white reliefs, mounted in
cut steel
No visible marks
About 1785–95

A   Buckle, with central medallion of opal
    glass back-painted in *grisaille*

    Width: 11.3 cm

B   Buckle
    Height: 6.8 cm

C   Six buttons
    Diameter: 2.1 cm

Boulton & Fothergill were important
customers of the Wedgwood factory, buying
cameos for mounting in metal from 1772.

*Victoria & Albert Museum. D57A given by Lady
Charlotte Schreiber (Schr.II.504; 5818-1853; 277-
1866)*

D34 Court sword and scabbard

Cut steel hilt mounted with blue Jasper
cameos and beads, steel blade, and vellum
scabbard
No visible marks
About 1790
Full length: 97.8 cm

The case for the hilt bears a trade label for
'I. DAWSON, small steel worker, Goldsmith
and Jeweller, 21, Hyde Street, Bloomsbury,
London'.

*Nottingham City Museum. Gift of Felix Joseph
(NCM 1879-168)*
*Lit: Nottingham 1975 Cat. 445; Reilly 1989 I
pl. C139*

D35 Clock pendulum

Blue Jasper medallion with white reliefs,
mounted in cut steel
No visible marks
About 1790
Overall length: 17 cm

The cameo is ornamented with Signs of the
Zodiac, a model of which was supplied to
Wedgwood by Mrs Landré (active 1768–74)
in 1774. The beaded cut steel mount is
attributed to Matthew Boulton.

*Trustees of the Wedgwood Museum, Barlaston,
Staffordshire (No.5393)*
Lit: Reilly 1972 pl. 41

D36 Pot-pourri vase and cover

Chelsea or Chelsea-Derby
Soft-paste porcelain, enamelled and gilt
Unmarked
About 1765–75
Height: 27.9 cm

Tripod-vases similar to this one were made
in Basalt by Wedgwood & Bentley (Cat.
D37). Possibly one factory copied the other,
but more probably they arrived at the
design independently, taking it from an
etching by Vien (Cat. D38). This vase was
probably made during the Chelsea-Derby
period of production (which followed the
sale of the Chelsea factory to Derby in

D 34

1770). Such vases are also known to have been made at Chelsea: they are recorded in Nicholas Sprimont's sale of stock in 1770, where they are described as 'small antique urns upon pedestal, crimson and gold, decorated with women's heads and flowers'. In a letter of April 1772 Wedgwood expressed concern about being eclipsed by 'the Glare of the Derby & other China shews', adding 'What heads, or Eyes could stand all this dazzleing profusion of riches and ornament if something was not provided for their relief, to give them at proper intervals a little relaxation, & repose. Under this humble idea then, I have some hopes for our black, Etruscan, & Grecian Vases still ...'

Victoria & Albert Museum. Given by Lady Charlotte Schreiber (Schr.I.372)
Lit and refs: Mallet 1975 pp. 54–5; Wedgwood MS E25-18365, see Clifford 1978 p. 161; ibid p. 171 and pl. 83A & C

D37 Tripod incense burner

Black Basalt, with engine-turned decoration
Mark: 'WEDGWOOD & BENTLEY: ETRURIA' in an applied circular seal
1770s
Height: 21 cm

See Cat. D36.

Nottingham City Museums. Normand Collection (NCM 1896-19)
Lit: Nottingham 1975 Cat. 40

D38 Design for a vase: plate 12 from *Suite de Vases Composée dans le Goût de L'Antique*

Marie Therèse Reboul Vien (1729–1805)
after Joseph Marie Vien (1716–1809)
Etching
Lettered: 'Vien in. R. Vien. S.'
1760
Size of platemark: 18.6 × 13.3 cm

The design was used by Wedgwood and the Chelsea-Derby factories (Cat. D36–37; see also Cat. E19).

Victoria & Albert Museum (25378.3)
Lit: Clifford 1978 p. 171 and pl. 83A & C

D 37

D39 Triton candlestick

Solid blue and white Jasper
Mark: 'WEDGWOOD' impressed
About 1790
Height: 28.6 cm

Wedgwood refers to this pattern in a letter of November 1769: 'Mr Chambers lent me the model of the Triton Candlestick, & was to have the first pair as a present, pray make my comp[ts]. with them'. These were presumably made in Basalt, and versions in Jasper were in production by 1787. Triton candlesticks are listed in the 1773 Catalogue, where they are said to be 'from Michael Angelo'. The pair to the triton supplied by Chambers to Wedgwood was probably modelled by John Bacon, a sculptor who also worked for Duesbury's Derby factory, where the design was produced in porcelain (Cat. D40). Similar tritons also appear in the pattern books of Boulton & Fothergill, who in 1771 sold a 'tryton in dark bronz'; the model for this was probably obtained from either Wedgwood or Chambers.

Nottingham City Museums. Felix Joseph Bequest (NCM 1892-330)
Lit and refs: Goodison 1974 p. 102; Clifford 1974

D 38

p. 764; Nottingham 1975 Cat. 472; Wedgwood MS E25-18269, see Wedgwood 1984 Cat. H55; Clifford 1985 pp. 292 and 294; Reilly 1989 I p. 463

D40 Triton candlestick

William Duesbury's Derby Porcelain factory
Soft-paste porcelain, enamelled
Mark: 'G' incised
About 1775–85
Height: 22.3 cm

See Cat. D39.

Victoria & Albert Museum. Given by Lady Charlotte Schreiber (Schr.I.347)

D41 Ewer

Queen's Ware, with porphyry glaze, and applied decoration picked out with gilding, on Black Basalt plinth
Mark: 'WEDGWOOD & BENTLEY, ETRURIA' impressed
About 1775
Height: 38.8 cm

The shape, with its ovoid body, high loop handle and flared mouth, is listed as no. 60 in the factory 'Shape Book'. It was also made in Basalt by Wedgwood & Bentley, by their competitors Palmer & Neale, and is found in Derby porcelain (Cat. D42) and Boulton's ormolu.

Trustees of the National Museums and Galleries on Merseyside (Lady Lever Art Gallery)
Accession no.: LL1016

D42 Ewer

William Duesbury's Derby porcelain factory
Soft-paste porcelain, painted in blue and grey enamels, and gilt
Marks: 'D' under a crown painted in gold, 'No 92 [?]' incised
About 1780
Height: 27.2 cm

The shape parallels that of Wedgwood & Bentley's agate ewer Cat. D41, and this in turn is echoed in the design of ewers made by Boulton in ormolu-mounted blue-john. The *grisaille* landscape and figure painting have traditionally been attributed to Zachariah Boreman and Richard Askew respectively.

Victoria & Albert Museum. Herbert Allen Collection (C.264-1935)

D 41

D 43

D43 Barometer

Made and probably designed by Benjamin Vulliamy (1747–1811)
Marble and ormolu, with Derby biscuit porcelain figures, and Wedgwood Jasper medallions with black dip, white reliefs and lapidary polished edges (the original painted and inlaid satinwood plinth not exhibited)
Inscribed: 'VULLIAMY LONDON'
The companion clock to this is dated 1787
Height (excluding plinth): 41 cm

Benjamin Vulliamy, clockmaker to George III, coordinated all aspects of design and production of his clocks and barometers, drawing on the services of a remarkable pool of designers and modellers, including the architect Robert Adam, the sculptors Deare, Bacon, Peart and Rossi and the services of William Duesbury at the Derby factory and of Josiah Wedgwood at Etruria. The Derby biscuit porcelain figures here were modelled by John Deare after a design by John Bacon, who also supplied models to Duesbury's great rivals Josiah Wedgwood and Matthew Boulton. The Wedgwood Jasper medallions are of *Aurora* and *Bellerophon watering Pegasus*.

Victoria & Albert Museum (W.16-1958)
Lit: Reilly 1989 I pl. 770; Clifford 1990 pp. 230–31 and passim

D44 Portrait medallion of James Tassie (1735–99)

William Tassie (1777–1860)
Moulded opaque white glass paste mounted on glass, backed with paper and in a turned wood frame
Mark: the truncation impressed 'JAMES TASSIE DIED 1 JUNE 1799 IN HIS 64 YEAR and W. Tassie F[ecit] 1799'
Dated 1799
Height: 15.2 cm

James Tassie, a manufacturer of glass paste cameos and intaglios, and John Voyez, a modeller and manufacturer of Basalt seals, who had at one point worked for Wedgwood, were the only serious rivals of Wedgwood in the production of portrait medallions and seals. In 1776 Wedgwood wrote to Bentley that 'Mr. Tassie & Voyez, between them, have made terrible depredations upon our Seal trade'. In the 1779 Catalogue he stated that the figures in his own cameos were 'much sharper than those that are made of Glass', clearly a reference to Tassie's work. However, in spite of their rivalry, the two men were friends, and they exchanged models for reproduction. Relations with Voyez, on the other hand, were strained almost to the point of litigation, when he was found to be forging Wedgwood & Bentley's mark in 1776. Tassie's business was carried on after his death by his nephew William.

Victoria & Albert Museum. Given by Lady Charlotte Schreiber (Schr.II.620)
Lit and refs: Wedgwood MS E25-18657, see Reilly 1989 I p. 477 and Edwards 1994 p. 82

D45 Trade card of James Tassie (1735–99)

Edward Malpas (active 1773–88)
Engraving
Lettered: 'Malpas Sc' and 'JAˢ. TASSIE Nᵒ. 20 The East side of LEICESTER FIELDS'
Probably 1788
10.2 × 15.6 cm

Tassie developed his glass paste formula in Dublin in 1763. He moved to London in 1766 and took rooms in Great Newport

D 46

Street, Soho, where Wedgwood also had showrooms between 1768 and 1774. Tassie moved to 20 Leicester Square, the address on this card, in 1788. His greatest commission came in 1781, when Catherine the Great ordered 12,000 gems and intaglios. According to Tassie the cabinet made to contain them was to have been fitted with nearly '100 heads and figures ... purchased from Mr Wedgwoods for the purpose'.

Victoria & Albert Museum (1601-1892)
Lit: Holloway 1986 passim and p. 13

D46 Vase

Coconut, mounted in silver-gilt, and set with pale blue Jasper medallions, with white reliefs of the *Three Graces* and *Omphale, Queen of Lydia*
Unmarked
About 1785
Height: 19.7 cm

The medallion of the *Three Graces* is copied

from an impression of the gem by James Tassie, this being signed 'Pichler' in Greek, probably for Giovanni Pichler (see Cat. E35). The work of this engraver was known to Wedgwood, who wrote to Bentley in July 1771 about a gem from the Albani Collection which had been 'patched by Old Pickler'. According to Raspe's *Descriptive Catalogue*, the source for Tassie's impression was a gem in the collection of Prince Stanislas Poniatowski, the nephew of Stanislas Augustus Poniatowski whose interest in English landscape gardening possibly influenced Catherine the Great's commission of the Frog Service (see p. 139). Mounted coconut cups are well known in 17th-century English silver, but 18th-century examples are virtually unknown. The maker of this exceptional piece has not been identified.

Victoria & Albert Museum (815-1891)
Lit and refs: Wedgwood MS E25-18481; Raspe 1791 no. 6443

MARKETING

D47 Portrait medallion of Queen Charlotte (1744–1818)

After a model by William Hackwood (about 1757–1839)
White Jasper with blue dip and white reliefs, in gilt-metal mount
Marks: 'WEDGWOOD' and 'Q. CHARLOTTE' impressed
After a model of about 1776
Height: 10 cm including mount

Wedgwood's first royal order came in the summer of 1765, when he made a 'complete sett of tea things with a gold ground & raised flowers upon it in green' for Queen Charlotte. This commission did much to ensure the fashionable status of Wedgwood's creamware, and he capitalized on its value in the marketing of his wares (Cat. D48). In June 1766 he was officially made Potter to the Queen, and he renamed his creamware 'Queen's Ware' in her honour. The name was taken up as a general

term for creamware, and it appears as such on the trade cards of a number of Wedgwood's competitors. Queen Charlotte was an occasional visitor to the Wedgwood showrooms, attending the exhibition of the Frog Service in July 1774. This medallion, the third in a series of seven portraits of Charlotte issued by Wedgwood, is mentioned in a letter to Bentley in June 1776. Despite all his efforts to the contrary, the appointment of Potter to the King eluded Wedgwood throughout his career.

Victoria & Albert Museum. Given by Lady Charlotte Schreiber (Schr.II.517)
Lit: Reilly and Savage 1973 p. 96 and fig. c; Reilly 1992 pp. 41–2

D48 Two bills for wares 'Bought of Josiah Wedgwood, Potter to her Majesty'

Engraved bill heads with manuscript additions
Dated 1787 and 1789
21 × 17 cm; 21 × 33 cm

The bills are for wares bought by the Duke of Bedford (see Cat. D28).

Trustees of the Wedgwood Museum, Barlaston, Staffordshire

D 47

D49 Trade card of Augustus Cove

Anonymous
Engraving
Late 18th century
6.3 × 9.3 cm

The card of Augustus Cove, 'late E. Smith & Cº., 62 Grace-church Street' advertises the sale of 'Wedgwood (or Queens) ware of all kinds', in addition to foreign and English china, red and brown stoneware and cut glass. Wedgwood sold his pottery from Etruria, his London showrooms, and also, at times, through Mr Neuenberg or Nuenberg at No 75 Cornhill and (as his bill heads state) 'at no other place in town'. Cove was therefore probably using 'Wedgwood' and Queen's Ware as generic terms for Staffordshire wares made by Wedgwood's imitators. In September 1769 Wedgwood proposed to Bentley the use of a business card of this type, but no example is known: 'A card will be very necessary – "Vases, Urns, & other Ornaments after the Etruscan, Greek, & Roman models" I like the best – it shoᵈ. be in French certainly as well as English'.

Trustees of the British Museum. Heal Collection (Heal 98.1)
Ref: Wedgwood MS E25-18257

D50 Cream bowl, lid and stand

Queen's Ware, 'Royal' shape, painted in pink enamel with the 'Antique' border pattern
Marks: 'WEDGWOOD' impressed on both and a crescent incised on stand
1773
Height: 15.3 cm; diameter: 19.7 cm

Wedgwood named three of his patterns in honour of his royal commissions. The 'Royal' pattern is said to have been specially made for George III in 1770, the plates of this being a variant on the 'Queen's Pattern' plates. The 'Queen's Pattern' plates are similarly said to have been specially made for Queen Charlotte, although they were possibly in production from 1765. A further variant was the 'Catherine' shape, made for

the Frog Service in 1773. All the plate forms in turn derive from earlier patterns known in Staffordshire salt-glaze, silver and pewter. Large quantities of 'Royal' pattern domestic ware were sent worldwide. 'Invoices of Queen's ware sent to Mr. Thoˢ. Byerley' refer to '43 Doz. Royal Pattern Flat Plates' being sent to London on 17 May 1790.

Trustees of the Wedgwood Museum, Barlaston, Staffordshire (No.1532)
Lit: Wedgwood 1984 Cat. C13

D51 'Devonshire' garden pot

Pearl Ware, decorated to resemble a barrel, covered in brown slip, the bands in green
Mark: 'WEDGWOOD' impressed
About 1780–85
Height: 24.2 cm

One of the marketing strategies adopted by Wedgwood was to increase the social status of his pottery by naming particular lines after leading members of high society, as with the Devonshire flower pots and vases named after Georgina, Duchess of Devonshire. On 4 February 1778 he wrote to Bentley: 'The articles I should propose are a few sets of Vases ... – New flowerpots, brown with green hoops & 2 or 3 bulbous root pots when we have them right!' Five days later he wrote again: 'I do not know what to advise concerning the price of the green hooped flower pots ... they want a name – A name has a wonderfull effect I assure you – Suppose you present the Dˢ of Devonshire with a set & beg leave to call them Devonshire flowerpots. You smile – Well call them Mecklenberg – or what you please so you will but let them have a name. As the ground is the Devone brown you may without leave call them by that name.' Wedgwood confidently wrote on 17 February 1778: 'I have the greatest expectations from the Devonshire flowerpots, & shall make some large Bouquet & cheap window flowerpots in the same stile.'

Trustees of the Wedgwood Museum, Barlaston,

Staffordshire (No.3306)
Lit and refs: Wedgwood MS E25-18809 and E25-18811, see McKendrick 1982 p. 112; Wedgwood 1984 Cat. H1, and Reilly 1989 I pp. 379 and 433

D52 'Devonshire' vase

Pearl Ware, covered with brown slip, the bands in green
Marks: 'WEDGWOOD' impressed and with incised workman's mark
About 1780–85
Height: 18.4 cm

See Cat. D51.

Trustees of the Wedgwood Museum, Barlaston, Staffordshire (No.1429)
Lit: Wedgwood 1984 Cat. H2

D53 *A Catalogue of Cameos, Intaglios, Medals, Bas-reliefs ... After the Antique, made by Wedgwood & Bentley ...*

1773
17 × 10.5 cm (closed)

Wedgwood proposed to Bentley in 1772 that they should have a printed catalogue of cameos and medallions, and the first edition, which was the earliest catalogue to be issued by an English ceramic manufacturer, was published in the following year. The copy exhibited here has an advertisement for the 'Second Edition with Additions', cut from a contemporary newspaper, pasted in adjacent to the first page. The Catalogue ran to six editions between 1773 and 1779, some of these appearing also in French, German or Dutch translations. The 1788 French translation contained a supplement on the Portland Vase, which appeared as an appendix in subsequent English editions.

Provenance: Formerly in the library of Gilbert R. Redgrave; presented to the Etruria Museum by Sir R. L. Wedgwood 27 June 1932

Trustees of the Wedgwood Museum, Barlaston, Staffordshire (MSS 50-32412)

D54 Six plates from *A Catalogue of different Articles of Queen's Ware manufactured by Josiah Wedgwood, Potter to her Majesty*

Etched by John Pye (1745–after 1775)
Etching and engraving
1774
Sheet size: 24.3 × 19.9 cm

The 1774 *Catalogue of Queen's Ware* contained 10 plates illustrating 35 shapes, a small percentage of the range then available. These were bound separately from the text, which was published in both English and French. A new edition was prepared for the partnership of Wedgwood, Sons & Byerley sometime after 1790, but no complete copies of this are known.

The 1774 Catalogue was one of the first of its kind. The earliest illustrated manufacturers' catalogues proper date from the mid-1760s, those by Chippendale and similar designers and craftsmen being at least in part intended as pattern books of designs. In 1767 Wedgwood informed Matthew Boulton that he had sent engraved prints abroad to advertise his wares, but nothing more is known of this remarkably early scheme. John Pye, who etched the plates of the 1774 Catalogue, is recorded as working for the Liverpool transfer-printers Sadler & Green, and he supplied Wedgwood with prints and 'sundry drawings' for use on the Frog Service.

Trustees of the Wedgwood Museum, Barlaston, Staffordshire
Lit and refs: Reilly 1989 I pp. 274, 329–33; Reilly 1992 p. 214; Snodin 1987, passim and p. 32 n. 4

D55 Presentation drawing of a set of chessmen

John Flaxman junior (1755–1826)
Pen and wash
Signed 'Flaxman Invt et Delint'
1783–5
Sheet size: 17 × 52 cm

It is probable that this highly finished drawing was executed after the production of the first Jasper chess figures, possibly as

D 55

D 56

a record of the figures themselves or to show to prospective customers in the London showrooms. The first evidence for a chess set occurs in a manuscript dated 30 October 1783: 'A figure of a Fool for chess, £1: 5: 0', implying that the subject had been modelled in wax. On the same bill, but dated 1 December 1784, Flaxman charged for 'Three days imployed in drawing bas relief vases, chessmen, etc. £3: 3: 0.' Flaxman charged Wedgwood for another drawing in an invoice dated 8 March 1785 – 'Drawing for Chessmen £6: 6: 0' – possibly after Josiah decided to retain the sketch in *trompe l'oeil* style. See also Cat. B50.

Trustees of the Wedgwood Museum, Barlaston, Staffordshire (No.4316)
Lit and refs: Wedgwood MSS E25-1339 and 2-1339; Constable 1927 pp. 21–2; Bindman 1979 Cat. 45d; Science Museum 1978 Cat. 211; Irwin 1979 p. 27; Reilly 1989 I pl. 962 and p. 637

D56 Tablet: *The Birth of Bacchus*

Modelled by William Hackwood (about 1757–1839)
White Jasper with green dip and white reliefs
Unmarked
About 1776
12.8 × 27 cm

The pricing of this panel was discussed by Wedgwood and Bentley in 1776. On 21 February of that year Wedgwood wrote: 'The Birth of Bacchus, & 6 figures in his Suite will at once shew you the state of Hackwoods Modelling. And the largest piece of Jasper we have yet made.' On the same date, in a letter sent on the afternoon coach, he added: 'You will judge better than I can what the Tablet Birth of Bacchus ought to be charged, by comparing it with other things'. On 10 March he returned to the subject, stating that: 'The Birth of Bacchus will be quite cheap of 36 [shillings]. The modelling of these things, so highly finish'd as ours are, is very expensive, beside all the risques in these delicate articles'. By 3 November of the following year the technical problems seem to have been overcome. Wedgwood wrote to Bentley: 'We put into a box a Birth of Bacchus, 14 in. by 5 3/4 & have a Triumph of the same dimensions, both straight, & perfect, without a single crack or flaw!'

The composition is ultimately derived from the frieze of a Hellenistic marble vase signed by the Athenian sculptor Salpion. But it is closer still to the frieze on Matthew Boulton's 'Bacchanalian Vase', which in turn is probably copied from or shares the same design source as a vase made by Giacomo or Giovanni Zoffoli, Italian bronze-founders, whose workshop specialized in pieces for the tourist market in Rome.

Trustees of the Wedgwood Museum, Barlaston, Staffordshire (No.32)
Lit and refs: Wedgwood MSS E25-18655, E25-18656, E25-18660, E25-18790; see Wedgwood 1984 Cat. H75; Macht 1957 pp. 45–6; compare Goodison 1977 pls 3–6; Reilly 1989 I pp. 593–5 and pl. C156

EXPORTS

D57 Punch bowl

Printed in Liverpool by Guy Green (d. 1799)
Queen's Ware, transfer-printed in black with *The Sailor's Farewell*, *The Pipe and Punch Party*, *The Triumph of Amphitrite* and *Neptune in his Car*, and with enamelled inscription: 'JURRY PARKER EN ELISABETH PARKER EGTE LUYDEN BINNEN DE STAD ROTTERDAM 1779'
Mark: 'WEDGWOOD' impressed
About 1779
Diameter: 26.7 cm

The bowl was transfer-printed in England and exported to Holland, where the inscription celebrating a marriage was added.

Samuel Taber, an English merchant of Rotterdam, was one of Wedgwood's earliest overseas agents. The first surviving letter was written on 22 April 1763: 'Having heard the Character of your house a very good one, I take the liberty of writing to you on the articles of your manufactory. I do considerably in this Branch & have a mind to make tryall of your goods. if the price & terms suit me.' The long and successful business association provides a good insight into the wares being sent. These included large quantities of cauliflower and pineapple moulded teaware and subsequently nearly every form and shape of the creamwares produced.

In 1769 John du Burk became Wedgwood's agent in Amsterdam, an association that lasted from 1769 to 1777. Du Burk's name appears in the *Amsterdamsche Courant* in 1770, where he advertised an assortment of wares exclusive to 'Mr. Wedgwood, Burslem'. The association was not a particularly satisfactory one, and by August 1770, after only 16 months of trading, Josiah was expressing concern at shipping large quantities of ware without payment, asking Bentley: 'Do you think we are quite safe in entrusting so many thousands to du Burk?' Two years later, possibly to protect their investment, Wedgwood and Bentley found

D 57

a partner for du Burk in Joseph Cooper, a printer of Drury Lane. Cooper was later responsible for printing in 1773 and 1774 respectively the *Catalogue of Ornamental Wares* and the Catalogue that accompanied the Frog Service. By 1776 Josiah had sufficient evidence to condemn du Burk as 'a bad man, as well as a fool', and he was ultimately sent to prison for embezzlement.

It is evident from the manuscripts that, apart from large quantities of 'Useful Ware', ornamental vases and flower containers were particularly popular, 'Devonshire' garden pots among them (see Cat. D51). In September 1777 Cooper wrote: 'pack for us green hooped flowerpots of the Barrel pattern ... We thought ourselves tolerably stocked with them, but we have a demand for them lately, which had quite reduced us'.

In 1777, Wedgwood decided to make Lambertus van Veldhausen his sole agent, an arrangement that continued until 1820. A wide range of wares was retailed through the Dutch warehouses but most particularly large quantities of Queen's Ware and a range of 'Ornamental Wares', many of which had Dutch associations. These were portrait medallions of the Dutch royal family and other notables such as Cornelius and Maarten Tromp, Johan de Witt, Egbert Kartenaar and library busts of their famous admirals such as Johan van Oldenbarneveld. The Netherlands was to become one of the most reliable and enduring European markets for Wedgwood's wares.

Victoria & Albert Museum. Given by Mr Sidney Hand (C.391-1923)
Lit and refs: Wedgwood MSS 7-30343 and 93-17182B; Reilly 1989 I pl. 222

D58 Mug

Printed in Liverpool by Sadler & Green
Deep cream-coloured earthenware (Queen's Ware), transfer-printed in black with a portrait of William Pitt, afterwards first Earl of Chatham (1708–78), within an elaborate cartouche of scrollwork and trophies; the rim outlined in red

Unmarked; the print lettered: 'THE RIGHT HON. WILL^M. PITT ESQ.'
About 1765
Height: 12.7 cm

Lord Chatham was one of George III's principal secretaries of state and a privy seal. He emerged from retirement to defend the American colonists, making his celebrated speech in the House of Lords on 20 January 1775, in which he said 'To impose servitude to establish despotism over such a mighty continental nation must be in vain, must be fatal. We shall be forced ultimately to retreat, let us retreat while we can, not when we must'. Pitt was a particularly popular subject with American customers. Josiah commented on this phenomenon on 18 July 1766, writing to Bentley:

> What do you think of sending Mr. Pitt on Crockery ware to America; a quantity might certainly be sold there now, and some advantage made of the American prejudice in favour of that great man. Lord Gower brought his family to see my works the other day and asked me if I had not sent Mr. Pitt over in shoals to America. If you happen to do anything in that way, we can divide a tolerable profit and sell at the same price with Sadler.

While the Americans had portraits of Pitt on their creamware, the English preferred the motto 'Let us spit on Mr. Pitt'.

The surviving manuscripts provide some indication as to the wares being exported to America in the 18th century. A letter from Bentley and Boardman, merchants in Liverpool, which is dated 25 September 1764, seems to be the earliest surviving order specifically for Boston. The order specifies all sorts of 'Useful' wares, especially cauliflower and pineapple from moulded sets as well as cream-coloured earthenware to the value of £27.

By 1766, after the development of the improved creamware body, it is evident from the letters that Wedgwood was intent on exporting those pieces which were no longer popular or finding a ready market at home, writing to Bentley in Liverpool on 18 July: 'I am quite clear in my warehouse of coloured ware, am heartily sick of the commodity (Tortoishell, agate, green glaze)

and have been so long but durst not venture to quit 'till I had something better in hand, which thanks to my fair customer I now have and intend to make the most of it'. The green glaze ware was rapidly despatched, much to the joy of Wedgwood, who wrote to Bentley: 'I am rejoiced to know you have shipped off the Green & Gold – May the winds and sea be propitious & the invaluable cargo be wafted in safety to their destin'd markets, for the emolument of our American Bretheren & friends & as this treasure will no longer be locked up, or lost to the rest of the world I shall be perfectly easy about the returns, be they much, little or nothing at all'.

News of Wedgwood's Queen's Ware had reached New York by the autumn of 1769, as indicated by a letter from James Rivington, 'Bookseller in New York, North America', dated 9 September 1769: 'Sir, Upon receive of this letter I desire you to send me a list of all the articles which you make and sell under the denomination of the Queen's Ware. You have lately furnished my good friend Mr. Mortimer the paymaster general of the forces in this country, with a perfect & beautiful sett of all articles which has occasioned a demand for them in our city'.

Bentley and Boardman continued to act as agents forwarding new orders from American clients, including a large consignment of 25 crates of cream-coloured earthenware for Philadelphia. A letter from Boardman, which is dated 2 September 1771, reads: 'The annexed order is for a Gentleman at Philadelphia, who was in Staffordshire last Summer amongst the manufacturers – therefore is well conversant with the prices & quality which we desire may be of the best thirds and charged as low as possible'. The order was for large quantities of Queen's Ware plain and transfer-printed ware in black. There is a gap in the surviving accounts as the next specific order for America occurs in a letter from Samuel Boardman to Wedgwood, dated 2 April 1780, in which he wrote from Liverpool asking for Jasper portrait medallions:

A friend to American Liberty and I believe I may add to the liberty of every Country asked me this day if I had got Doctor Franklin, – G. Washington, Lawrence, or any of the exposuer of that cause – He would like to have them properly ranged in his parlour; so that his friends might not be at a loss to know his sentiments when they pay him a visit. ... the first of the above Heroes I have out, it is blue ground, charged 10/6. – I should like to know if you have any more of the same stamp & the price, for I think my friend, Tho' warm in the cause will not lay out his money extravagantly on the occasion.

Jasper proved very popular in North America and the manuscript of 'Sales 1792–1794' provides some indication of the quantities and range of items being ordered by John Bringhurst of Philadelphia alone, from small cameos and intaglios to figures and ornamental items.

Victoria & Albert Museum. Given by Lady Charlotte Schreiber (Schr.II.366)
Refs: Wedgwood MSS 632-1E, E25-18124, E25-18167, 74-12736, 7087-9

D59 Pair of plates

Queen's Ware, painted in rose-purple enamel with floral sprays and a husk swag border
Marks: 'WEDGWOOD' and '3' impressed and on the other 'WEDGWOOD' impressed
About 1770
Diameter: 24.7 cm

From the Husk Service, a dinner and dessert service made for Catherine the Great in 1770, part of which is today preserved at the Palace of Petrodvorets (Peterhof), St Petersburg. The service was of 'Queen's Pattern', each piece being painted with rose-purple floral sprays.

Wedgwood owed the order to the promotion of his wares and the advocacy of Lord and Lady Cathcart (Cat. C19). His letters between April and mid-June provide ample evidence that the service for Russia was to be decorated with husks. On 4 May he offered to send more painters to London: 'Mr Rhodes has hands who can do husks, which is the pattn of the Table service, & I think I shall not wait yr reply to send you two or three for flowers.'

Mrs A. Solanko, the wife of the

Counsellor to the Legation of Finland, bought part of the Husk Service from the Soviet government's Antique Store in Moscow in 1931. These pieces represented an excess not needed for display. Mrs Solanko took the objects back to Finland with her, where they were in storage when the country was invaded by the Soviet Union in 1938. By 1955 she was able to get some of her possessions to the United States of America, including the pieces from the Husk Service. The Wedgwood Company purchased her entire collection in 1956.

Trustees of the Wedgwood Museum, Barlaston, Staffordshire (No.1737 & A)
Lit and refs: Wedgwood MS E25-18298; Wedgwood 1984 Cat. G1; Reilly 1989 I p. 266

D60 Cream bowl, lid and pierced stand

Queen's Ware, painted in rose-purple with botanical sprays
Marks: 'WEDGWOOD' impressed and monogram 'M' painted in rose-purple enamel on the stand
About 1770
Length of stand: 26 cm; height of tureen: 15 cm

The bowl matches those from the Husk Service at the Palace of Petrodvorets (Peterhof), St Petersburg (see Cat. D59).

Trustees of the Wedgwood Museum, Barlaston, Staffordshire (No.9117)
Lit: Reilly 1989 I pl. 325

D61 Epergne, stand, covered cups and baskets

Queen's Ware, the reeded borders picked out with enamelling in blue and green
Mark: 'WEDGWOOD' impressed
About 1790
Height: 60.3 cm

A table centrepiece to contain sweetmeats, jellies and delicacies. The form is 'Shape No 52' in the 1790 *Catalogue of Useful Wares*, and it is also illustrated in the '1802 Shape Drawing Book', where it is shape no. 371: 'Pineapple Epergne'. From the evidence of

surviving orders for the Russian market, pineapple epergnes appear to have been popular. For example two were ordered on 3 July 1784, another being requested on 6 August 1770: 'A high Pickle frame or Apurne with Baskett at the top'.

Epergne and stand: Victoria & Albert Museum. Jermyn Street Collection (2336-1901); covered cups and baskets: Trustees of the Wedgwood Museum, Barlaston, Staffordshire (No.1472, 1473, 1475, 1477, 1487 & A)
Refs: Wedgwood MSS 61-30635, 12-10221, 5-3762

D62 Portrait plaque of Peter the Great (1672–1725), Tsar of Russia

Black Basalt
Mark: 'WEDGWOOD & BENTLEY' impressed
About 1779–80
38 × 30.5 cm

This is probably the largest portrait medallion ever made by Josiah Wedgwood. Peter the Great visited England in 1689 and made strenuous efforts to diffuse Western culture through Russia. He founded a new Russian capital at St Petersburg in 1703.

Trustees of the Wedgwood Museum, Barlaston, Staffordshire (No.182)
Lit: Reilly and Savage 1973 p. 273; Science Museum 1978 Cat. 136; Reilly 1989 I pl. 691

D63 *Catalogue des Came'es, Intaglio, Medailles, Bustes, Petit Statues, et Bas-reliefs; ... Vases, et Autres Ornemens d'apres les Antiques, Fabrique's par Wedgwood et Bentley ... 1779*

1779
21.5 × 14 cm (closed)

The Catalogue is a French translation of the 6th edition of Wedgwood & Bentley's *Catalogue of Ornamental Wares*. Wedgwood had earlier issued a French edition of the 1774 Catalogue; and the Queen's Ware catalogues of 1774 and 1790 were prepared with texts in both English and French. Wedgwood first made reference to trade with France in a letter to Bentley of 16 March 1768, where he stated: 'I have been

honour'd with a pretty long audience with the President of the Council, he will take care of the grants in a certain quarter, & has ord'd. a large service of Q-S ware to go as a present to Paris'. A letter written on 7 April 1769 to Bentley suggests that Wedgwood had some of his wares on show in the French capital, the slightly obscure reference reading:

> As Mrs. B. has liberty to send but one parcl. or package carre free she shod undoubtedly make it as large as possible to go safe, & the higher pris'd the goods, the better for her, if she can send them, but that must be left to her choice, the articles I wod recommend to her are Vases, for at present there is only one shop in Paris that has them, & I wish to put them in more.

Wedgwood was keenly interested in entering the French market. In a letter of 13 September 1769, he wrote to Bentley:

> And do you really think that we may make a complete conquest of France? – Conquer France in Burslem? – My blood moves quicker, I feel my strength increase for the contest – Assist me my friend, & the victorie is our own. We will make them (now I must say Potts, & how vulgar it sounds) I won't though, I say we will fashn our Porcelain after their own hearts & captivate them with Elegance & Simplicity off the Ancients. But do they love simplicity ? – Are you certain the French nation will be pleased with simplicity in their Vessells ? Either I have been greatly deciev'd or a wonderfull reformation has taken place amongst them – French & Frippery have jingled together so long in my idea I scarcely know how to separate them, & much of their work which I have seen cover'd over with ornament, has confirmed me in the opinion.

From the mid-1770s Josiah Wedgwood was exporting wares to a number of French cities, receiving his first orders from Paris by 1774, Dunkirk in 1775, Marseilles in 1775 and Boulogne in 1789. In 1776 Thomas Bentley made a trip to Paris, staying at the Hotel de Modina, Rue Jacob, from where he kept an informative diary. The main purpose of this visit was reconnaissance – to see what was being produced in France and to purchase samples to bring back to England. Certain French subjects Wedgwood introduced were particularly popular exports to France, and in a letter to Bentley of 8 May 1779 Josiah commented: 'Add several heads to our list ... such as Voltaire to match Rausseau'. Later he produced statues of the same subjects (see Cat. B35), writing on the 23 August 1779: 'We have nearly finish'd the Herboriseur [i.e Rousseau] it will be an excellent companion for Voltaire'.

Less well known is Josiah Wedgwood's relatively large trade in 'Useful' wares, especially Queen's Ware. A notable commission was the order placed by Sykes and Maynard, merchants in Paris, for dairy ware for the Duke of Orleans's new building at Raincy, which was ready by January 1789. Wedgwood also supplied a considerable number of Jasper buttons for the French court: in a private ledger of 1786 there is a reference to Monsieur Darnaudery, 'Button makers to the King at Paris'.

Apart from Wedgwood's natural interest in French commerce he followed closely the political events that culminated in the Revolution (see Cat. D67–68). After the storming of the Bastille he wrote to Erasmus Darwin: 'I know you will rejoice with me in the glorious revolution which has taken place in France'. Two different Jasper medallions depicting the fall of the Bastille were issued, both of which had French inscriptions indicating that they were aimed at the French market.

Trustees of the Wedgwood Museum, Barlaston, Staffordshire (MSS 50-29997)
Ref: Wedgwood MS E.25-19252

D64 Plaque: *Mercury Uniting the Hands of Britain and France*

Designed and modelled by John Flaxman junior (1755–1826)
Solid blue Jasper with white reliefs
Marks: 'WEDGWOOD' impressed twice
1787
25 × 25 cm

The design was commissioned by Wedgwood from John Flaxman to celebrate the Anglo-French Commercial Trade Treaty of 1786, which had been strongly advocated by Wedgwood, and which relaxed restrictions governing the importation of English ceramics by France. Flaxman

initially sent a sketch that showed not only the three figures used in the final plaque but also the personification of Peace and the burning of the implements of war. Josiah suggested that the two aspects would be better as separate groups and that some alterations should be made to the other figures. He wrote on 2 November 1786:

> We must take care not to shew that these representations were invented by an Englishman; as they are meant to be conciliatory, they should be scrupulously impartial. The figures for instance which represent the two nations sh[d]. be equally magnificent and important in their dress, attitude, character & attributes; and Mercury should not seem more inclined to one than the other, but shew a full front face between them, and if you think there is non impropriety in it, I should wish France to have her helmet and shield as well as Britannia, & the Fleur de lis upon the latter.

Wedgwood was charged 13 guineas for the model. The finished article was included in the 1788 French version of the Catalogue (Class II, no. 256 or 257).

Nottingham City Museums. Felix Joseph Bequest (NCM 1892-404)
Lit and refs: Wedgwood MS L2-30193, see Bindman 1979 Cat. 52; Bindman 1989 p. 85

D65 Dress buckle

White Jasper medallion, with pale blue dip and white relief of *Poor Maria*; mounted in cut steel with beads of steel, crystal and Jasper
Mark: 'WEDGWOOD' impressed
About 1785
Height: 8.9 cm

The design by Lady Templetown (1747–

1823) of *Poor Maria* is based on Joseph Wright's painting of 1777, *Maria and her dog, Sylvio*, which depicts the central character from Lawrence Sterne's *Sentimental Journey* (published 1768). A very similar buckle is depicted on a *Portrait of a Lady* by Marie Louise Elizabeth Le Brun (née Vigée; 1755–1842), painted in 1789, now part of the Samuel H. Kress Collection, National Gallery of Art, Washington DC.

Trustees of the Wedgwood Museum, Barlaston, Staffordshire (No.5185)
Lit: Reilly 1989 I pl. C133

D66 Snuff box

Ivory, mounted in gold, and inlaid with Jasper medallion with blue dip and white reliefs
No visible marks
About 1789
Diameter: 7.2 cm; height: 2.5 cm

The medallion of France and Liberty holding hands before an altar was produced to celebrate the French Revolution. The design follows a suggestion made by Josiah II on 28 July 1789. It was probably modelled by Henry Webber (1754–1826), as Josiah II wrote:

> Do you choose to have anything modelled ... which should relate to the late revolution in France & to the support given to public credit by the national assembly? What do you think of Public faith on an alter & France embracing liberty in the front? Mr. Byerley says we ought to do something & that quickly. I will get Mr. Webber to make a sketch & send it to you tomorrow.

In a letter written on the following day he described the subject: 'The figure on the alter with the Caduceus in one hand & the Cornucopia in the other is Public Credit or Faith & instead of the caduceus on the Altar there ought, I think to be the words Fid.Pub. for dies publica, the goddess of liberty with the cap of liberty of her left hand takes hold of France in her right ... The story appears to me to be well told and to make good composition.'

Trustees of the Wedgwood Museum, Barlaston, Staffordshire (No. 5208)
Lit and refs: Wedgwood MSS LHP and W/M1460; Reilly 1989 I pl. 904

D67 Portrait medallion of Louis-Phillipe-Joseph, Duc d'Orléans (1747–93)

White Jasper with blue dip and white reliefs; lapidary polished edge
Marks: 'WEDGWOOD' and 'H' impressed
About 1790
Diameter: 5.5 cm

Louis-Phillipe-Joseph succeeded to the title of Duc d'Orléans in 1785. His reputation for debauchery made him unpopular at the court of Louis XVI, and it seems that he took advantage of the weakness of the French King and the unpopularity of Marie Antoinette to aspire to the crown. With the onset of the French Revolution he gave it his active support, and in 1792 when hereditary titles were removed he adopted the title of Phillipe Egalité. He was arrested and guillotined in 1793. He was responsible for introducing many English fashions and promoting English taste in France. The medallion is one of a group of portraits of key figures in the French Revolution, which Wedgwood issued in 1789–90. See also Cat. D66.

Trustees of the Wedgwood Museum, Barlaston, Staffordshire (No. 3297A)
Lit: Reilly and Savage 1973 p. 266; Bindman 1989 p.98

D68 (A–C) Three medallions: portrait of Leopold II (1747–92), Holy Roman Emperor; *The Coronation of Leopold II*; and *Leopold the Lawgiver supported by Wisdom and Benevolence*

White Jasper with blue dip and lapidary polished edge
Marks: A and B with 'WEDGWOOD' impressed; C also impressed with '1'
About 1790
A: 4.3 × 3.3 cm; B: 7 × 3.8 cm; C: 4.7 × 4 cm

In the absence of ambassadorial channels that could be used to promote his goods, Wedgwood adopted a different approach to promoting his wares in the German states. In 1771 a plan was conceived of sending a thousand parcels, each containing £20 worth of earthenware, to Germany. Wedgwood wrote:

> The object is very great indeed, & my general idea upon it is to close heartily with it to the utmost verge of prudence, or rather beyond – The rest you will be so good to manage as circumstances occur – But I think we shd not sell all to Italy & neglect the other Princes in Germany & elsewhere who are waiting with so much impatience for their turns to be served with our fine things ...

The idea of flooding the market was again put into effect in 1790, when a group of commemorative medallions was made to mark the coronation of Leopold II as Holy Roman Emperor. Wedgwood hoped that those attending the ceremonies would take the medallions away with them to the various parts of the empire, and that 'the rememberence of our fine things will be implanted with sufficient force upon their minds'. A complete list of the medallions, dated 11 September 1790, has survived.

Trustees of the Wedgwood Museum, Barlaston, Staffordshire (Nos. L11, 919, L13)
Lit and refs: Wedgwood MS LHP; Mosely Collection MS (Josiah Wedgwood to his son Josiah II, dated 11 Sept 1790) and Wedgwood MS E26-19010; Reilly 1989 I pls 908 and 910

D69 Portrait medallion of Maria I, Queen of Portugal (1734–1816)

After a model by John Flaxman junior (1755–1826)
White Jasper with black dip and relief in white
Mark: 'WEDGWOOD' impressed
About 1787
10 × 7.8 cm

Maria Francisca was the eldest daughter of Joseph Emmanuel. She married her uncle, Pedro, in 1760 and they were crowned as joint sovereigns in 1777. She was considered weak-minded, and power was seized by her mother, Marianne Victoria.

Her portrait was modelled by John Flaxman junior in 1787. The wax arrived at the Etruria manufactory during the first half of 1787 (an invoice dated 1 June reads 'A Model of the Queen of Portugal £3:3'), and the finished medallions were available for sale before the end of the year. Wedgwood was well aware that portrait medallions would always sell well in the countries of origin of the sitters. Writing on 2 July 1776 he commented: 'We can make other Kings & Queens, & eminent Heads for other Countries, & such subjects will be the most likely to go in quantities, for People will give more for their own heads, or the Heads in fashion, than for any other subjects, & buy abundantly more of them'.

A fascinating insight into Wedgwood's methods of promoting his wares, and his means of access to the Portuguese market, is found in a letter to Bentley dated 9 September 1771. This reads:

> I must first ask you whilst it is in my head, whether you have done anything to⁰ˢ. makeing the most of our exellent letter from Portugal? – what would I do with it – Why I wo⁰. take it in one hand, & Kents Directory in the other & shew it to every Portuguese Merch⁰. in London, & tell them that we were introduceing a new manufacture at every Court in Europe, & When we have done this, they wod. be wanting to themselves, & to the interests of their Country if they did not do the rest.

Trustees of the Wedgwood Museum, Barlaston, Staffordshire (No.4083)
Lit and refs: Wedgwood MS E25-1339; Reilly and Savage 1973 p. 228; Bindman 1979 Cat. 49

D 69

THE LONDON
DECORATING STUDIO

edgwood's expansion to the Etruria manufactory, which opened on 13 June 1769, was intended to meet the increased demand for his wares. As sales in London grew during the 1760s and 1770s he leased a succession of showrooms in increasingly large and more suitably located premises. With the demand for specially created armorial services it became important for the firm to have a method of adding decoration to pieces once they had been transported to London. The first small decorating studio was established behind the company showroom at no. 1 Great Newport Street, where a special muffle kiln had been built for the firing of enamelled ware. By this date, attaching decorating departments to the London warehouses of major manufacturers of ceramics was well-established practice. This was certainly the case with the porcelain producers and the more prestigious earthenware manufacturers, as well as some of the retailers.

The development of muffle kilns made it possible to add enamelled decoration after the objects had left the factories. A 'muffle' refers simply to the refractory, often a fire-clay box similar in principle to a saggar but built as a permanent part of the kiln, which was to protect ware from direct contact with the flames. The outer part of the muffle kiln was generally constructed of iron. In Wedgwood's time these were small portable kilns which were fed with either billetwood or charcoal. They fired at relatively low temperatures and were used exclusively for the firing of delicate enamel colours and sometimes gold. Locating these small kilns within the retailing

establishment enabled the personalizing of services to be carried out with reasonable speed and efficiency.

The enthusiastic correspondence of 1768 about Great Newport Street and the securing of a 40-year tenancy for 100 guineas details how the wares were to be presented and the great advantages of being close to a fashionable part of the city. Wedgwood wrote jubilantly to Bentley from Charles Street, London, in March 1768: 'we shall not want so many <u>long Rooms</u> I think of making habitations for a Colony of Artists, – Modelers Carvers &c. I have already agreed with one very usefull Tennant, A Master Enameler, & China piecer, – He joins old valuable pieces of China, not with Rivits, but a white glass, & burns them till the glass vitrifys, & they are as sound as ever they were'.[1] The new tenant was David Rhodes, formerly of Robinson & Rhodes, 'Chinamen' or decorators in Leeds. Tantalizingly, only fleeting references are made to the decoration of creamware on the premises and the exact location of the muffle kiln. It is unclear whether this was placed in the cellar or, as is more probable given the risk of fire, in the yard to the rear of the premises. The only surviving Sun Assurance Company insurance policy for these premises issued on 30 October 1771 makes no specific reference to the kiln. It reads: 'Item 304306. Josiah Wedgwood and Thomas Bentley of Great Newport Street, manufacturers of Earthen ware (utensils and stock in their Brick warehouse on the corner of Little St Martins Lane in Newport Street) £3,000.' Perhaps slightly stronger evidence of there being a kiln on site occurs in the advertisement for Queen's Ware which states that 'Orders are executed on the shortest notice'.[2]

Some years later, in 1776, Wedgwood wrote to Bentley confirming that armorial wares had by then been decorated in London for some considerable time. He wrote:

The painting of Arms is now become a serious business …. The question now with me, is, whether they should be done in London, or Liverpool. I should prefer the former on many accounts, but the enormous difference in the prices, not less than 6 to 1, put it out of my power, unless a method can be hit upon of coming something near the Liverpool prices. Mr. Green Prints, & then colors the Arms, & we must do the same in London, or transfer near half our business from thence to Liverpool.[3]

From the surviving 'Crest Book Index' it is obvious that Green's methods were also employed in London. This is confirmed by Josiah's own comment, 'I have not his name at hand he that paints & prints the out lines in the little Chamber'.[4] He was referring to the work of David Rhodes and his assistant, of whom he enthused: 'The having of such a man as this under the same roof with the warehouse, to do Crests or any other patterns by order – to take sketches etc – is the most convenient thing imaginable'.

In Wedgwood's 'Common Place Book I' there is a list of 'Workman's Prices of Enamelling different kinds of ware in London', which is dated August 1784, the entry carrying the note 'and which have continued the same for five years past'. Under the heading 'For painting Crests, Cyphers &c.' the following is given: 'Single letter – ½d, 3 & 4 letters – 1d; Simple crest on wreath – 1½d; Palm branch or Ring – ½d',[5] the list continuing with every conceivable variation of crests, monograms and embellishments.

The alliance and partnership from 1769 between Josiah Wedgwood and Thomas Bentley was to bring a new importance to the London Decorating Studios, and Bentley's influence was immediately apparent. Within a month of arriving at Great Newport Street in August 1769 he was actively scouring London for new premises for the decorating studios. An undated letter, though from the context almost certainly written in 1769, and addressed to Samuel Cox at Southampton Buildings, Chancery Lane, gives a full description of a possible site, for which negotiations were obviously fairly near completion: 'Mr. Bentley presents his compliments to Mr. Cox, & if it would be convenient will wait upon him to meet Mr. Green at Mr. Cox's house tomorrow at 4 o'clock to treat about the House at Chelsea'.[6] The letter continues with a list of essential repairs and alterations to make the premises tenable. Wedgwood & Bentley would take a lease for seven, fourteen or twenty-one years, with the provision to quit at the end of any of the above periods.

The property under consideration was no. 2, Little Cheyne Row, Chelsea (now renumbered as no. 26, Upper Cheyne Row), or 'Little China Row' as Wedgwood preferred to call it. The choice of location may have been influenced in part by the closure of Nicholas Sprimont's Chelsea porcelain manufactory earlier in the year, to which Wedgwood had drawn Bentley's attention in April: 'The Chelsea Moulds, Models &c &c are to be sold, but I'll enclose you the advertisement, there's an immense fund of fine things'.[7] It is evident from the manuscript that Wedgwood was assuming the area would have a trained workforce, especially of painters, who would be available for new employment.

The stringent list of requirements and alterations was obviously completed and the tenancy resolved, as a surviving receipt indicates: 'Received of Josiah Wedgwood Esq. this 6th December 1770 the sum of Ten Pounds for ½ a years rent for the House in Little Cheney Row due to me at Michaelmas day last past'.[8] A similar sum was paid by Wedgwood on 20 April 1771. A later draft advertisement to re-let the premises, probably written about 1776, gives a good indication of the extent and nature of the property. It reads:

To be Let or Sold

Pleasantly situated, in a refined part of Chelsea, a good house, with Stable, Coach House and other Buildings convenient for the Workshops &C – with two large Gardens. Enquire of Mr. David Rhodes in Little Cheyne Row Chelsea.

By December 1769 the workrooms and a muffle kiln, which had been bought at Lambeth, were ready at Chelsea, and from this date enamellers and craftsmen were transferred from Etruria and Great Newport Street. The principal painters were David Rhodes and his partner, William Hopkins Craft (1735–1811). Craft is described as a man 'who has Enamel[d] at Paris &c and does it with great Elegance &c, & wants to begin upon some small plates immediately which you'l please to furnish them with'.[9] Wedgwood constantly refers to the partner as 'Mr. Croft' or 'Crofts', but to judge from three receipted invoices from Rhodes to Wedgwood, dated 18 January to 17 April 1769, January 1770 and March 1770, he was almost certainly William Hopkins Craft. Wedgwood considered that the salary of £200 per annum paid to Craft was 'too extravagant to be lasting'.[10] It seems likely that he was the best painter in the Chelsea Studios and was responsible for some innovations in the decoration of Black Basalt encaustic vases, causing Wedgwood to admit grudgingly that: 'If that coxcomb Crofts would be made anyway bearable I apprehend we could find him constant employment'.[11] The hope was not to be fulfilled, as Craft left in the late spring (probably late April or early May) 1771 to become an independent decorator; but by then the Chelsea Studio had taken on sufficiently talented painters for it to continue successfully without him.

Rhodes remained in the employment of Wedgwood and Bentley for over ten years, and was appointed manager of the Cheyne Row Studio with responsibility for the day-to-day running of the business, but he was directly answerable to and worked under the direction of Thomas Bentley. He became one of Wedgwood's most trusted employees, and he was expected to deal with confidential matters, including negotiations and purchases. He was also entrusted with closely guarded secrets, as is clear from a memorandum to Bentley, dated 22 January 1770, which reads: 'I must beg the favour to have Mr Rhodes to prepare me some colours for the sake of privacy chiefly'.[12]

From the surviving manuscripts it would appear that the Chelsea enterprise was proving to be a successful venture for the partners, and it soon became necessary to transfer painters to London from the Brick House Works, Staffordshire, in order to cope with the ever-increasing volume of work. When recruiting painters Josiah was conscious that he demanded a higher quality of work than many of the other manufacturers. He told Bentley in May 1770: 'You observe very justly that few hands can be got to paint flowers in the style we want them. I may add, nor any other work we do – We must make them. There is no other way. We have stepped forw[d] beyond the other manufacturers & we must be content to train up hands to suit our purpose.'[13] This became increasingly evident as the quality of Queen's Ware was recognized and widely appreciated, and orders for special services such as the Husk Service were commissioned.

Two Liverpool painters were engaged at 45 shillings and 27 shillings a week respectively – Joseph Cooper, who was initially described as a 'good flower painter', and Ralph Unwin. They were sent to London in May 1770 as 'outside passengers'[14] on the stage coach. Ralph

Pl. 21 (Cat. D24) Queen's Ware dish with enamelled decoration, about 1770. The dish is identical to those in the Husk Service ordered in 1770 by Catherine the Great.

Unwin (active 1770–1812) was a miniaturist and enameller who was known also to paint landscapes. He was described in 1770 as someone 'who will do flowers, under a Master very prettily'.[15] Two more painters, Joseph Barret and Thomas Glover, walked to London from Burslem, a distance of about 150 miles, to augment the artists already employed there. Again in May, Josiah commented: 'I intend likewise to send you Ja^s Bakewell for six weeks or 2 months'.[16] At the end of 1769 James Bakewell had completed the decoration of a dessert service in yellow and black enamel, which did not satisfy Josiah. But less than six months later he was reporting to Bentley: 'Bakewell has set his mind on being a good enamel Painter and really improves very much both in flowers & in coppying figures. I have not taken him from his painting of some time past he has set his heart so much upon it, & makes so quick a progress both in improvement, & in a dispatchfull method.'[17]

In order to increase the staff at the Chelsea Studio Rhodes was instructed to advertise and 'mention that any hands who have been employ'd in painting figures, or flowers upon Coaches, Fans, Waiters [papier-mâché trays] might have constant employment by applying to him in Little China Row, Chelsea'.[18] Initially all the people employed at the Great Newport Street Decorating Studio were men; however, this changed when Sarah and Ralph Wilcox arrived from the Worcester Porcelain factory via Etruria on 24 June 1769. Ralph had made a good impression on Josiah, who commented: 'I like his appearance much, he seems a sober solid man, & has nothing flighty or Coxcomical in his dress, or behaviour of which most of this Class are apt to contract a small tinture'.[19] Sarah was the daughter of Thomas Frye, the mezzotint engraver and founder of the New Canton porcelain factory at Bow. Her husband readily admitted that Sarah was by far the better and more skilful painter, and that she was 'an excellent coppyer of figures & other subjects, & a much better hand than himself'.[20]

Three months later, in September, Wedgwood realized that her talents could be put to better use in London. Writing to Bentley he stated: 'Mrs. Willcox is loosing time here as she might as well paint figures upon Vases as upon paper as I am perswaded you will be convinc'd from the drawings I sent you. If she does such things of

Pl. 22 (Cat. G30) Triangular dish from the Frog Service, decorated with a view of Dolwyddelan Castle, Gwynedd.

her self, what may not be expected from her under the tuition of a Bentley & a Crofts – Pray let me know when I shall send her & her Goodman.'[21]

On receipt of the first major commission from Catherine the Great of Russia in 1770 – the creamware Husk Service (Cat. D24 and 60) – the pieces were all manufactured in Burslem by 'Useful' Thomas before being sent to London to be painted in monochrome pink enamel with botanical sprays. The first surviving reference to the Husk Service in the Wedgwood and Bentley correspondence occurs in a letter to Bentley dated 28 April 1770, where the employment of newly engaged artists to work on the service is discussed: 'I dare not trust to a <u>new man</u> & a <u>new manufacture</u> as enameling must be with him for the Russian service, & therefore the separation you mention, however desirable, & practicable it may be, <u>in due time</u>, cannot I think take place <u>at present</u>, nor all at once, 'till we know more of Mr. Shaw, & his abilities.'[22] A day later, Wedgwood wrote again, obviously anxious that the service for Catherine should be completed on time: 'I

tremble as well as you for the Russian service, & wo[d]. rather Mr. Rhodes set up two or three Iron Kilns than it sho[d]. not be done in time. I think hands may be got to do it, if you are short I could send you three from hence who can paint flowers very well from good patterns, & might assist in this service, all I can say further is that you shall not want the <u>plain ware</u>.'[23] Further reference is made to the creamware production in a letter to Bentley postmarked 23 April 1770: 'We shall send you the Russian Table & desert service faster than you will get it enamel'd. I think I can promise with certainty that no part of it shall wait of us, if you'l be so good to push Mr. Coward on with his carving,'[24] the Mr Coward referred to being John Coward, a woodcarver, of London.

Orders for additional individual pieces were being forwarded from London by Peter Swift, Wedgwood's 'Cashier, Paymaster General and Accountant General', notably on 9 June 1770: 'Wanted for the Empress of Russia's service for Enam[l]. 12 cushions [small oval tureens] with covers betwixt the 1/- & 2/- size, 4 largest sauce

Bowls &c at 3/- quite plain Edge, some more Plain Double salts and Ladles, 16 Round 11 inch Dishes.' Within ten days Wedgwood refers to the actual manufacture of the pieces: 'We are making the cushions (cover'd) & the few other things for the Russion service you ord[d] with a shell cream & sugar bowl & some of the new fruit baskets, or bowles, pray let us know in time if anything else is wanted to complete this service.'[25]

Also in June 1770 Josiah was planning 'to treat myself with a sort of pleasure journey to London to have a peep at the Russian Service, & your enamel works at Chelsea'.[26] Wedgwood had also proposed that the Husk Service should be displayed in their London showrooms: 'The idea of our shewing & making the most of this service at home as well as abroad appears to me of more consequence every time I think of it. I have therefore set it

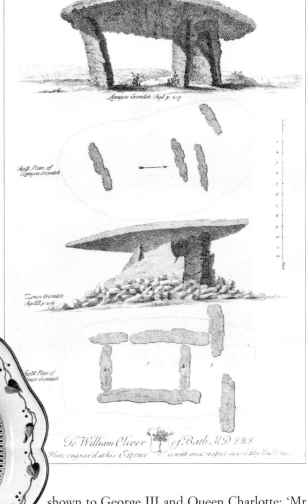

Pl. 23 (Cat. G231) Dessert plate from the Frog Service decorated with a view of Lanyon Quoit, Cornwall.

Far right: Pl. 24 (Cat. G228) Lanyon and Zennor Quoit, from William Borlase's 'Observations...'

down as sterling which I do by most things that will bear that test.'[27] Sadly there is no record of whether the service was ever displayed in London, although according to a letter dated 24 July 1770 and written by Ben(jamin) Mather, head clerk in the showroom, the service was shown to George III and Queen Charlotte: 'Mr Wedgwood & Mr Bentley have this day waited on their Majesty at Richmond with some Patterns of ye Enam[d]. service for the Empress, & they are much pleased with it & have Order a Large Table & Desert of the same'.[28]

The complexities of the manufacture and painting of the Frog Service, the second service for Catherine the Great of Russia, between 1773 and its despatch in October 1774 are now well documented. The result was an undisputed triumph, despite Wedgwood's initial misgivings about the

Pl. 25 (Cat. G287) Glacier from the Frog Service decorated with a view of Harewood House, N. Yorks.

ability of the London decorators to achieve the topographical views. He wrote on 9 April 1773:

> Dare you undertake to paint the most embellished views, the most beautifull Landskips, with Gothique Ruins, Grecian Temples, & the most Elegant Buildings with hands who never attempted anything beyond Huts & Windmills, upon Dutch Tile at three halfpence a doz! – And this too for the first Empress in the World? – Well if you dare attempt & can succeed in this, tell me no more of your Alexanders, no nor of your Prometheus's neither for surely it is more to make <u>Artists</u> than mere <u>men</u>.[29]

As early as 23 March 1773 Wedgwood was consulting Bentley about the shape and decoration: 'I suppose it must be painted upon the Royal pattern & that there must be a border upon the rims of the dishes & plates of some kind, & the buildings &c in the middle only. The Child & Frog, if they are to be all in the same attitudes, may perhaps be printed.'[30] Discussions ensued on the best method of obtaining views to copy for the centres: 'Do you think the subjects must all be from <u>real views, & real buildings</u>, & that it is expected from us to send draftsmen all over the Kingdom to take these views – if so, what time, or what money? wo[d]. be sufficient to perform the one, or pay for the other.'[31] The actual gathering of the views was a relatively expensive process. Various accounts have survived including 'Sundary Accounts paid for the Russia Service to which Mr. Wedgwood stock is debited', which refers to: 'Original Drawings, Copying pictures & Drawings & Books on Natural History & Prints suppose half the Expence – £100',[32] and

Pl. 26 (Cat. G147) Dish from the Frog Service, decorated with a view of Studley Royal, N. Yorks.

'For prints purchased in London an additional £63-5-8d'.[33] A memorandum of London costs from 1771 to 1774 taken by Ben Mather includes 'Mr Wedgwoods Expenses to Noblemen & Gentlemans House to take Views &c for Russian Service £85-1-0'.[34]

Whilst the source material was being gathered, the pieces for the Service were being manufactured in the 'Royal' shape at Etruria. On his return from a visit to London, Josiah commenced the organization of the more elaborate items for the Service, including new forms of compotiers, tureens, fruit dishes for the dessert service, and glaciers with a finial comprising three seated female figures. By 8 March 1774 orders from London specified: 'Wanted for the Russian Service; 4 Royal Pattern Ice pails – 4/-; 8 Cream & Sugar Bowls (of a new pattern); 12 Oblong cover'd dishes 3/-'.[35] Other references include:

'All things wanted for the Russia Service Except Jugs, Turines, Sauce Boats & Bowls & Table Plates'.[36] With the volume of objects being transported to London, Josiah suggested that it would be advantageous for him to have a list of the Service, with the quantity of each item completed, and with its landscape marked in the margin .

It seems probable that as many as 33 artists were employed at the Chelsea Decorating Studio to complete the entire Service. Some specialized in borders, including the frog crests in green enamel. Among them were Nathaniel Cooper, who received '½ pence to 3 pence per border', presumably according to the size and complexity, and Samuel Armstrong, who appears to have added the enamel line outlining the shape of each plate. The central landscapes were painted in monochrome sepia by several artists, including some of the women employed at Chelsea: Miss Glisson was paid 12 shillings a week, and Miss Pars received slightly less at 10 shillings and 6 pence per week for painting ruins. Ralph and Catherine Wilcox, who were paid some of the highest wages at 18 shillings per week, tackled both the borders and the landscape centres. The painters' wages on the Service alone came to considerably more than the cost of manufacturing the plain Queen's Ware, which for the table service amounted to £36 6s 0d, and for the dessert service £15 2s 4d, making a total of £51 8s 4d for the manufacture of the 952 pieces comprising the service.[37]

An undated manuscript provides a complete breakdown of the number of painted scenes on each shape of Queen's Ware, confirming that 952 pieces were decorated with '1,244 enamel views & Paintings at 5/3d, 10/6d, 21/-, 31/6d & 42/-', giving a total of £1,306 4s 0d, with the additional note: 'say at 21/- upon an average'. The painting of the frog crests and the border was equally expensive: '1244 Green Frogs in and compartments at 1/-, 5/-, 10/-, 15/-, 20-, 25/-', in all £933 0s 0d, which worked out, according to their accounting, at '15/- each upon an average'. The amount for the painting alone for the service was £2,239 4s 0d.[38]

The total amount eventually paid by Catherine the Great is not recorded, although the company did receive payment in full on 8 October 1774. The account submitted was for £2,290 12s 4d.[39] This included a number of interesting details, such as a discount to Mr Alexander Baxter for organizing the order of the Service, £2 18s 6d for insurance on the items whilst in the London Decorating Studios, and £7 5s 7d for the cost of the packing crates.[40] A bill also details the cost 'for printing and translating as £9 14s 0d',[41] this being for the catalogue – prepared by Thomas Bentley and translated into French for the Empress – which identified the view and gave the reference number painted in brown enamel on the reverse of each piece.

On successful completion, the dinner and dessert Service was placed on display at the new showrooms in Portland House, Greek Street, London, marking its opening in June 1774. Josiah visited London for the event, commenting on 31 May to his father-in-law, Richard Wedgwood: 'At last we have fitted up our new Rooms at Greek Street so far as to be able to set out the Russian service with some vases &c, to be seen there, and tomorrow we advertise and open them for that purpose'.[42] The set created immediate interest amongst the aristocracy. Wedgwood wrote to Bentley: 'I am very much oblig'd to you for the particular account you have been so obliging to give me of this visit, & the disposition of the Rooms, which I am sure must have a charming effect & do not therefore so much wonder at Her Majesty, & the Prince her Bror. expressing their approbation in pretty strong terms.'[43] After its display the Service seems to have been despatched in the early autumn of 1774 in 22 crates.

It is likely that once the Service had left London some attempts were made to ensure that something similar was retained in the Portland House showroom. In a detailed 'Inventory of Goods on hand at Chelsea, taken 26th October 1774 an acc^t of the Wedgwood, by Benj Mather' the following reference occurs: '4 doz & 3 Flat plates R.P ['Royal' pattern] with small Landscapes in the Middle, done at the first begining of the Russian service'.[44] They were reckoned at 4 shillings the dozen. Apart from the duplicate pieces and plates of unsatisfactory quality, as described by Wedgwood – 'They will not be worth shewing – I think the <u>fine-painted</u> pieces condemn'd to be set aside, whether it be on account of their being blister'd, or duplicates or any other fault'[45] – a small number of plates decorated in a similar manner, but with polychrome topographical scenes, have survived. From extant documentary evidence it seems that these pieces were manufactured in the second half of 1774 specifically for public display in the London showrooms in order to illustrate the abilities of the decorators employed. Josiah wrote to Bentley in June 1774 about the Russian Service, adding: 'we may paint more, without the Frog to be shewn in Greek Street'.[46]

The successful completion of the Russian Service undoubtedly brought Wedgwood & Bentley considerable additional prestige and publicity. The use of their Queen's Ware body as a canvas for topographical painting was an undertaking that arguably only Wedgwood was capable of achieving during the 1770s, with the extensive resources and the remarkable skills of the craftsmen employed at his establishments.

Although the Chelsea Decorating Studios were officially closed and the painters moved to the Greek Street premises in 1774, it is obvious that the company had difficulties in sub-letting, or assigning the lease for the remaining two years and disposing of Cheyne Row. A detailed list of expenditure on London properties indicates that by 1776 the rent had decreased to £49 19s per annum, excluding the water rate and the window tax. There is also a rather terse but interesting letter concerning the poor state of repair of the premises. Perhaps the condition of the house can be attributed in part to the fact that Wedgwood & Bentley had used it almost in the capacity of a small factory and had constructed kilns and several workrooms there.

The situation was possibly further complicated by an explosion that wrecked the muffle oven at the Chelsea Decorating Studio and probably led to considerable disruption, causing Bentley to complain irritably: 'We are always too much in a hurry to do anything right – Things done in a hurry are never well done'. 'Who says so?' Josiah rejoined. 'Never? First thoughts are often best & many things must be done now or never, – Take time by the forelock or he will slip through your fingers – But I have not time for any more old proverbs or I would string you a necklace of them ...'. For good measure he added: 'It was not precipitation in making but in firing the kiln at Chelsea which blew it up'.[47]

No conclusive evidence seems to survive as to exactly why the Chelsea Decorating Studios were closed long before the expiration of the lease, although several speculative suggestions can be put forward. It can be argued that the pollution had increased. 'Foul air', to quote contemporary sources, was proving problematical, with the increase of diverse industries such as brewing and tanning along the edge of the Thames. After all, Josiah Wedgwood did consider London to be a 'Dismal, smoky place'. It is far more probable that the partners were spreading themselves too thinly in view of the periodic cash-flow crises, and that it was felt better to consolidate their activities in the capital into one location, Portland House, in Greek Street, rather than pay rent and rates on two separate buildings. It is also conceivable that Josiah Wedgwood's business sense led him to conclude that however successful Thomas Bentley was at overseeing and managing both establishments, it was difficult for him to supervise two premises located in different parts of London simultaneously and effectively.

The closure of the Chelsea workshop did not mean the cessation of decorating special pieces within the London showrooms, but the output was severely curtailed. Certainly there is evidence in a plan of the Greek Street premises of 1792–3 which shows two circular buildings in the yard which would, most probably, have been enamel-firing kilns.[48]

After 1774 the majority of the pieces manufactured were subsequently decorated in Staffordshire and only sold in London. Never again was such a large presence of decorators to be gathered by Wedgwood in London.

Gaye Blake Roberts FMA, FRSA

Wedgwood's variegated and Black Basalt vases of the late 1760s and 1770s were the first pottery vases made in England. His move into vase production coincided with the fashionable world taking up the vase as a symbol or leitmotif of the new and fashionable 'antique' style. So great was this demand for antique vases that, in addition to copying surviving Classical antiquities, Wedgwood, like other manufacturers, took designs from printed designs of the 17th-18th centuries, some which were highly fanciful inventions that were perhaps not seriously intended for production. Wedgwood announced his intention of becoming 'Vase Maker General to the Universe' in a letter to Bentley in May 1769, and his vases met with enormous success when they were first shown in his London showrooms. It was reported in May 1769 that 'there was no getting to the door for Coaches, nor into the rooms for Ladies and Gent^n & ... Vases was all the cry'. Wedgwood's most celebrated vase was his reproduction of the Portland Vase, perfected in 1790, one of the final achievements of his career.

'VASE MADNESS'

E1 Vase and cover

White terracotta stoneware, with applied reliefs and porphyry glaze, on a Black Basalt plinth
Mark: 'WEDGWOOD & BENTLEY: ETRURIA' in applied circular seal
About 1773–5
Height: 31.7 cm

E 1

For Wedgwood, the vase form itself bore elevated and refined connotations. Referring in 1771 to the agate and marbled teawares, a popular product in mid-18th century Staffordshire, and his own vases with similar finishes and patterns, Wedgwood wrote to Bentley that: 'it is the <u>forms</u> more than the <u>colours</u> of many of the Vases which has raised, & unvulgariz'd them – Make exactly the same pebbles [pottery with mottled glazes] into Tea ware & they are let down to the class of common Pott ware again, many degrees below <u>Queens Ware</u>'.

Victoria & Albert Museum. Jermyn Street Collection (2386&A-1901)
Lit: Wedgwood MS LHP (2 Nov 1771), see Reilly 1989 I p. 344

E2 Vase *(Pl. 17)*

Queen's Ware, with porphyry glaze, on a Black Basalt plinth, the applied ornament with traces of original gilding
Mark: 'WEDGWOOD & BENTLEY: ETRURIA' in applied circular seal
1769–80
Height: 37 cm

The gilding on Wedgwood & Bentley's early marbled and 'pebbled' vases attracted criticism from such connoisseurs as Sir William Hamilton. Wedgwood wrote to Bentley in April 1772: 'I hope we shall be able to make a good use of his hints respecting the Pebble Vases, by greatly reduceing, if not totally banishing this <u>offensive Gilding</u>.' He added: 'I do not find it an easy matter to make a Vase with the colouring so natural, vairied, pleasing & <u>un-</u>

pot-like & the shape so delicate, as to make it seem worth a great deal of money, without the additional trappings of handles, ornaments, & Gilding.' For use in their London showrooms Wedgwood proposed 'a Curtain ... which you may open or shut, inlarge or diminish the shew of gilding as you find your customers affected.'

Victoria & Albert Museum. Given by Lady Charlotte Schreiber (Schr. II 454)
Lit and refs: Wedgwood MS E25-18365, see McKendrick 1982 p. 119 and Reilly 1989 I p. 347

E3 Josiah Wedgwood's 'Price Book of Workmanship'

Manuscript
August 1772
34 × 45 cm

The overwhelming success of Wedgwood's vases in the period 1769–72 led to over-expansion of vase production and created cash-flow problems, with much of the partnership's capital resources being tied up in materials and overheads. Wedgwood responded to this crisis by drawing up a 'Price Book of Workmanship' in which the costs incurred in manufacturing and selling his wares are itemized. This is one of the earliest cost accounting documents to survive from any British manufacturer.

Trustees of the Wedgwood Museum, Barlaston, Staffordshire (W/M 1780)
Lit: Reilly 1989 I pp. 350–62 and pp. 694–5

E4 Vase

Queen's Ware, with applied ornament and porphyry, on a Black Basalt plinth; with traces of original gilding
No visible marks
About 1775–85
Height: 28.4 cm

Victoria & Albert Museum (1102-1855)

E5 Vase and cover

Solid agate ware, with gilded putto finial
Mark: 'WEDGWOOD & BENTLEY' impressed
About 1774
Height: 21 cm

Trustees of the Wedgwood Museum, Barlaston, Staffordshire (No.160)
Lit: Reilly 1989 I pl. 457

E 8

E 5

E6 Urn

White terracotta stoneware, with blue-grey porphyry glaze; the winged-figure handles, torch finial and applied ornament picked out in contemporary gilding
Mark: 'WEDGWOOD' impressed
About 1785
Height: 50.8 cm

Trustees of the Wedgwood Museum, Barlaston, Staffordshire (No.1619)
Lit: Reilly 1989 I pl. C86

E7 Vase

White terracotta stoneware, with surface agate decoration in brown, cream and black slips; the cream-coloured handles with entwined snakes picked out in gold; the applied ornament and rouletted decoration to the body neck and foot also picked out in gold
Mark: 'WEDGWOOD' impressed
About 1780
Height: 36.6 cm

The vase is shape no. 266 in the 'Shape Number One Book'. The vase is probably earlier than the white terracotta base to which it is bolted.

Trustees of the Wedgwood Museum, Barlaston, Staffordshire (No.5158)
Lit: Reilly 1989 I pl. 453

E8 Ewer ('Stella's ewer')

Black Basalt
Mark: 'WEDGWOOD & BENTLEY: ETRURIA' in applied circular seal
About 1775–80
Height: 32.7 cm

The design is based on a vase on the title-page to Stella's *Livre de Vases* (Cat. E9). Wedgwood further dramatised Stella's design by adding scales to the fish tail and increasing the height of the plinth. It is paradoxical that the extraordinary concoctions in Stella's book – which owe

E 6

E 7

much more to the fantastic Mannerist inventions of the 16th-century artist Giulio Romano than they do to Classical antiquity – should have found favour with a man often perceived as being solely dedicated to the revival of Classical design. In fact Wedgwood used a wide range of sources for his vases, and was by no means solely committed to the 'antique style'. Such was the mania or 'madness' for vases in the years around 1770 that virtually any vase design had some marketing potential, and many much earlier designs were seized upon by printsellers and manufacturers alike. 'Stella's ewers' are referred to as being made in September 1770.

Victoria & Albert Museum. Jermyn Street Collection (2398-1901)
Lit: Clifford 1978 p. 164 and passim

E9 *Livre de Vases ...*, open at titlepage

Françoise Bouzonnet Stella after Jacques Stella (1596–1657)
Etching and engraving
Lettered: 'Inventé par Mr. STELLA Chevalier et peintre du Roy A Paris ... francoise bouzounet, sculp ...'
Dated (in manuscript) 1667
Platemark: 28.1 × 20.7 cm

Wedgwood owned a copy of Stella's Book of Vases: on 22 August 1770 he wrote to Bentley: 'I am glad you have met with such a Treasure in Stella, & shall be glad to have it here for our edification – Cannot Mr Coward [Cat. C26] offtrace the heads and handles & so we may have the book allmost immediately, for I long to see it'. Seven days later, on receiving the volume, he described it as 'an admirable one indeed', adding 'many good things may be made out of [it]'. At least four of Wedgwood's vase shapes were taken from Stella's designs, including Cat. E8, E11, and E12.

Victoria & Albert Museum (26597)
Lit and refs: Wedgwood MSS E25-18319, E25-18322, see Clifford 1978 p. 164; ibid. pp. 164–6 and pls 71A

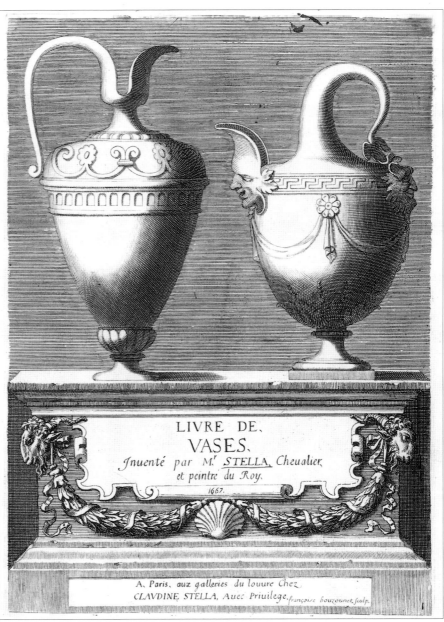

E 9

E10 Ewer ('Stella's ewer')

Queen's Ware, with applied ornament, sprinkled 'Lapis Lazuli' underglaze decoration, and traces of gilding, on a Black Basalt plinth
Unmarked
About 1770–75
Height: 29 cm

In 1770 Wedgwood attempted to define the various glazes made in emulation of natural stones: 'Pebble Vases – Suppose we call those barely sprinkled with blue and ornam.ts Gilt – Granite – when Vein'd with black, Vein'd Granite – with Gold Lapis Lazuli – With colours & Vein'd – Variegated pebble – those with colours & Vein'd without any blue sprinkleing,

E 11

E 14

In Bronzo

background device in Sir Joshua Reynolds's 1764–5 portrait of Lady Diana Beauclerk (1734–1808) – an amateur artist whose designs of bacchanalian boys were reproduced in Jasper by Wedgwood (Cat. C21) – in order to signify her modernity and commitment to the 'antique'.

Private collection
Lit: Clifford 1978 p. 165

E13 Design for stucco panelling for the hall at Syon House, from *The Works in Architecture* by Robert and James Adam (Vol. I, Pl. VII)

Engraved by A. Finnie
Etching and engraving
Published 1778
Cut to 26.6 × 17.3 cm

Wedgwood was far from alone in plundering prints by Mannerist artists of the 16th and 17th centuries for his vase designs. Robert Adam's vase here was adapted from an etching in Stella's *Livre de Vases*, one that was also copied by

Egyptian Pebble.' The design of the vase here is taken from Stella's print, Cat. E9.

Trustees of the National Museums and Galleries on Merseyside (Liverpool Museum)
Accession no.: M2940
Lit and refs: Reilly 1989 I pl. C74; Wedgwood MS E25-18289, see Reilly 1989 I p. 345

E11 Vase

Black Basalt, the body engine-turned, and with lion-headed handles terminating in bacchanalian masks
Mark: 'WEDGWOOD & BENTLEY: ETRURIA' in applied circular seal
About 1770
Height: 42.5 cm

The design appears to be loosely based on one published in Jacques Stella's *Livre de Vases* (Cat. E9). Variations of this shape are found in Black Basalt made by Wedgwood's

rival and imitator Humphrey Palmer, and probably also by Neale & Co.

Trustees of the Wedgwood Museum, Barlaston, Staffordshire (No.77)
Lit: Clifford 1978 p. 165; Wedgwood 1984 Cat. E13; Reilly 1989 I pl. 530

E12 Ewer

White terracotta stoneware, with blue porphyry glaze, and with traces of gilding, on a Black Basalt plinth
Mark: 'WEDGWOOD & BENTLEY: ETRURIA' in applied seal around bolt
Probably around 1775
Height: 30.5 cm

This ewer, versions of which were also manufactured in Black Basalt, is based on the design published as no. 10 in Stella's *Livre de Vases* (Cat. E9). A gigantic version of Stella's design was included as a

E 17

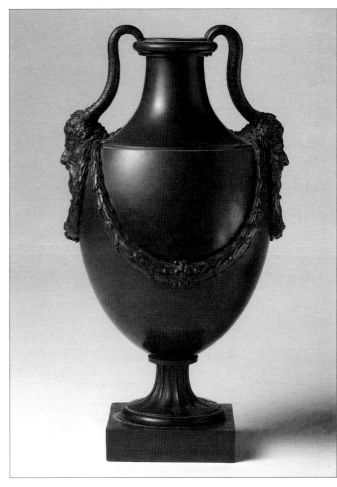

E 19

E 20

Wedgwood (Cat. E11); and Adam, like Wedgwood, also borrowed from etchings by Stefano della Bella. The body of the vase was later repeated in Adam's two designs for the Richmond Race cup for 1770, one of which features extraordinary panther handles copied directly from an engraving by the 16th-century Italian artist Enea Vico.

Victoria & Albert Museum (28263.161)
Lit: Clifford 1978 p. 165 and pl. 72C

E14 Set of six prints of vases

Anonymous
Etching and engraving
Early 19th century
Platemark of tallest print: 16.2 × 6.6 cm

Although some of the vases are shown as being weathered with age, and the prints are variously inscribed *'del Museo Grimani'* and *'In Bronzo'*, each print in fact shows a vase shape well-known in Wedgwood's Black Basalt or 'pebbled' wares. One of the vases depicted has engine-turned decoration (which is most unlikely to be found in bronze), and another shows Wedgwood's lion-handled vase, made after a design by Stella (Cat. E11). It is interesting to note that by the beginning of the 19th century Wedgwood's productions could be confused with, or passed off as, Classical antiquities.

Victoria & Albert Museum (E.1527 A 184-189-1885)

E15 Sheet of designs for vases: plate 6 from *Raccolta di Vasi diversi* ...Stefano della Bella (1610–64)

Etching
Lettered: '[Stef.] de la Bella invent fecit'
First published about 1646
Cut to 8.5 × 20.2 cm

This tiny etching was a rich source of designs for Wedgwood. Both the vase with goats' heads and festoons, and that with the high loop handles, were produced at Etruria (Cat. E16–18); and the seated figures on the cover of the vase are frequently found on Wedgwood's Basalt wares, appearing also on the glaciers of the Frog Service (Cat. G286–88).

Victoria & Albert Museum (E.1527 A 18-1885)
Lit: Clifford 1978 pp. 166–7 and pl. 76

E16 Vase ('Goats head vase')

White terracotta stoneware, with applied
ornament, and sponged blue and black
underglaze decoration; with later gilding
Mark: 'WEDGWOOD & BENTLEY: ETRURIA'
in applied circular seal
About 1775
Height: 39 cm

The design, no. 14 in Wedgwood's 'Shape
Number One Book', is taken from the print
by Stefano della Bella, Cat. E15. 'Goats
head vases' with variegated glazes are
priced at £3 3s 0d in a list of wares fired on
4 December 1769.

Trustees of the National Museums and Galleries
on Merseyside (Lady Lever Art Gallery)
Accession no. LL1056
Lit: Reilly 1989 I pl. 471 and p. 347

E17 Vase ('Goats head vase')

Queen's Ware, with applied swags and
goats' head handles (damaged), and with
purple and red sponged; on a white marble
base
Unmarked
About 1770
Height: 42 cm

The colour and finish of the glaze is in
imitation of porphyry. In an undated letter
to Bentley (probably October 1769),
Wedgwood wrote: 'Porphiry Vases will be
very Clever; but we must proceed with
some method'. On 29 August of the
following year he wrote again of his
intention to imitate porphyry, asking
Bentley: 'Have you visited L^d. Bassborough
[Bessborough] yet, when you do pray
borrow the Porphiry (late Lady Germains)
Vase & send it down to mould off. I will be
answerable for its safety.' Lord Bessborough
visited Wedgwood's London showrooms on
6 February 1769, Wedgwood writing to
Bentley: 'My last, & best chap was L^d.
Bessborough, a fine old Gentleman ...
admires our vases & manufacture
prodigiously. Says, he sees we shall exceed
the Antients, that friezes & many other
things be made, that I am a very ingenious

man ... & that he will do me every service.'
The design here is taken from Stefano della
Bella's print, Cat. E15.

Trustees of the Wedgwood Museum, Barlaston,
Staffordshire (No.1205)
Lit and refs: Wedgwood MSS E25-18252, E25-
18318, E25-18227, see Wedgwood 1984 Cat. E11
and H42; Reilly 1989 I pl. 443

E18 Two vases

Queen's Ware in imitation of agate with the
addition of green copper oxide staining;
applied Queen's Ware handles and swags;
Black Basalt plinths
Marks: 'Wedgwood & Bentley' impressed;
and 'WEDGWOOD & BENTLEY: ETRURIA'
impressed in applied circular seal
About 1775
Height: 26 cm and 28.3 cm

Wedgwood commented on this type of
body in a letter dated 3 January 1769:
'There is much sin to be commited in the
Marble way, as you will guess by the
patterns L. have merecy on our Old Stock
say I'. The popularity of marbled vases is
apparent from a letter Wedgwood sent to
Bentley in Liverpool describing how he has
just received 'a piteous letter last night from
Mr Cox – not a Vase scarcely of any sort to
sell, Blue Pebble, & Marbled all gone'. The
design of these vases was adapted from one
in Stefano della Bella's print, Cat. E15. The
same design was also taken up by English
silversmiths' work from about 1770–71; a
set of three such silver vases, now in
Nottingham City Museums, was presented
to John Flaxman junior by Wedgwood in
1776.

Trustees of the Wedgwood Museum, Barlaston,
Staffordshire (No.176, 5086)
Lit and refs: Wedgwood MSS E25-18222 and E25-
18237; Clifford 1978, compare pls 76 b-c;
Nottingham 1975 Cat. 475.

E19 Design for a vase: plate 13 from *Suite de Vases Composée dans le Goût de L'Antique*

Marie Thérèse Reboul Vien (1729–1805)
after Joseph Marie Vien (1716–1809)
Etching and engraving
Lettered: 'Vien in. R. Vien. S.'
1760
Size of platemark: 18.9 × 13.4 cm

Vien's satyr-handled vase was copied by
Wedgwood & Bentley as their 'No. 1'
shape, in production from 1769 (Cat.
E20–21).

Victoria & Albert Museum (25378.1)
Lit: Clifford 1978 p. 171 and pl. 82A

E20 Vase ('No. 1' shape)

Black Basalt, with satyr's head handles, the
body with applied swags of husks; engine-
turned foot
Mark: 'WEDGWOOD & BENTLEY: ETRURIA'
in applied circular seal
About 1769
Height: 32.5 cm

The vase is no. 1 in the Etruria factory
'Shape Number One Book'. It was evidently
much liked by Wedgwood, as he had
George Stubbs include it in his portrait of
the Wedgwood family, painted in 1780 (Pl.
20). It was produced in eight sizes from 6½
inches to 16½ inches in height, and in four
bodies – 'Pebble and Gilt', 'Black', 'Jasper'
and 'plain Bisque'. The design is taken from
the print by Vien, Cat. E19.

Trustees of the Wedgwood Museum, Barlaston,
Staffordshire (No.5173)
Lit: Clifford 1978 p. 171; Reilly 1989 I pl. 529

E21 Vase and cover ('No. 1' shape)

White terracotta stoneware, the body
covered with a porphyry glaze; applied
ornament and satyr's head handles, with
traces of gilding, on a Black Basalt plinth
Mark: 'WEDGWOOD & BENTLEY: ETRURIA'
in applied circular seal
About 1770–5
Height: 40.6 cm

E 22

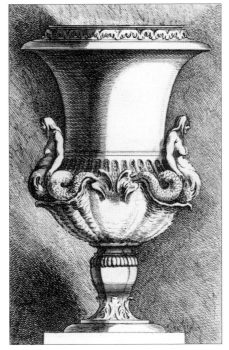

E 23

After the same source as Cat. E20. 'Satyrs head Vases Variegated N°. 1' are referred to in a letter to Bentley of December 1769.

Trustees of the Wedgwood Museum, Barlaston, Staffordshire (No.178)
Lit and refs: Wedgwood MS E25-18273, see Wedgwood 1984 Cat. E2

E22 Vase

Black Basalt, the body engine-turned, with applied handles formed as mermen with double entwined tails
Unmarked
Probably about 1775–80
Height: 24 cm

The design is based on the print by Bouchardon, Cat. E23, but with the substitution of male figures in place of the mermaids designed by Bouchardon. At least one vase made to this design is fitted with a disc pierced to take flowers, indicating that some were originally intended as bough

pots. The vase is no. 11 in the Wedgwood 'Shape Number One Book'.

Trustees of the Wedgwood Museum, Barlaston, Staffordshire (No.1114)
Lit: Clifford 1978 pl. 78A

E23 Design for a vase: plate 11 from *Second Livre de Vases*

Gabriel Huquier (1695–1772) after Edme Bouchardon (1698–1762)
Engraving and etching
Lettered: 'Bouchardon.in. avec Privilege du Roy. Huquier Sculp'
Before 1737
Cut to 19.3 × 12.5 cm

Wedgwood may have known Bouchardon's vases through pirated copies issued in about 1771 by the London printseller and publisher François Vivares. Bouchardon, a sculptor working at the Court of Louis XV, was the subject of a biography by the Comte de Caylus, whose *Receuil*

d'Antiquités (1752–67) was used by Wedgwood as a source of designs.

Victoria & Albert Museum (14466.11)
Lit: Clifford 1978 pp. 167–8 and pl. 78A

E24 Design for a vase: plate 8 from *Second Livre de Vases*

Gabriel Huquier (1695–1772) after Edme Bouchardon (1698–1762)
Engraving and etching
Lettered: 'Ed. Bouchardon.in. avec Privilege du Roy. Huqier sculp. et ex'
Before 1737
Cut to 19.3 × 12.5 cm

The design was used as the source for Cat. E25. Bouchardon's vase designs combine antique and Baroque elements in a highly individual way. They were probably influential on the better-known vase designs of Jacques Saly, whose designs were realized in Derby porcelain during the period of 'Vase madness', about 1770. Vase designs by both Bouchardon and Saly were in the Matthew Boulton and family collection.

Victoria & Albert Museum (14466.8)
Lit: Clifford 1978 pp. 167–8 and pl. 78C; Jordan 1985 passim; Christie's 1986

E25 Vase

White Jasper with green dip, the wrythen 'tendrils' in white Jasper
Mark: 'WEDGWOOD' impressed
About 1790
Height: 16.5 cm

Although Jasper was in production from 1776, Wedgwood did not attempt to make vases in this material until about 1781. The first Jasper vases were put on display in the London showrooms in 1782, having probably been held back from sale in order not to compromise the success of the auction of the Wedgwood & Bentley partnership's stock – which took place in December 1781 – and so as to demonstrate to his public that Wedgwood's partner's death had not affected the firm's ability to initiate fresh fashions. Wedgwood's Jasper

E 26

vases post-date the period when 'Vase madness' was at its height, and, compared with those in Basalt and the variegated wares, far fewer are based on printed designs. In being based on a print – Bouchardon's design Cat. E24 – this vase is exceptional. The biscuit model for the shape is preserved in the Wedgwood Archives.

Trustees of the National Museums and Galleries on Merseyside (Liverpool Museum)
Accession no.: M2824
Lit: Reilly 1989 I pl. 987, and pp. 642–3

E26 Vase and cover

Solid agate ware, with Queen's Ware satyrs' heads, and traces of gilding; on a marble plinth
No visible marks
Probably about 1770–75
Height: 27.2 cm

The design here is taken from an etching by Friedrich Kirschner, Cat. E27. The vase was formerly in the collection of the politician and statesman W. E. Gladstone (1809–98).

Victoria & Albert Museum (Circ.1&A-1923)
Lit: Clifford 1978 p. 172; Reilly 1989 I pl. 462A

E 27

E27 Design for a vase

Friedrich Kirschner (1748–89)
Etching
Lettered: 'F. Kirschner'
Undated
Cut to 16.1 × 11.4 cm

Friedrich Kirschner's design was adapted by Wedgwood & Bentley for production in engine-turned Black Basalt and agate ware (Cat. E28 and E26). Basalt watch stands that copy the design more faithfully were also made. Variants on this design were made by Wedgwood's competitor Humphrey Palmer of Hanley.

Victoria & Albert Museum (24880.9)
Lit: Clifford 1978 p. 172 and pl. 85A

E28 Vase and cover

Black Basalt, engine-turned and with applied reliefs; satyr's head handles and acorn finial
Mark: 'WEDGWOOD & BENTLEY' impressed
About 1770
Height: 19 cm

Wedgwood & Bentley's engine-turned adaptation of Kirschner's design for a vase (Cat. E27) was also closely copied in silver-gilt by an unidentified London silversmith in 1772–3, an indication of the degree to which Wedgwood was leading developments in design, and the prestige accorded to his products. English silver and ceramic designs are often closely related, but until Wedgwood's wares came on the market it was much more frequently the silversmith that led the way. The vase is no. 26 in the factory 'Shape Number One Book'.

Trustees of the Wedgwood Museum, Barlaston, Staffordshire (No.90)
Lit: Clifford 1978 p. 172 and pls 85–6; Reilly 1989 I pl. 553

E 30

E29 Design for two vases: Plate 3 from Part 5 of *Entwerff einer Historischen Architektur*

After Johann Bernhard Fischer von Erlach (1656–1723)
Engraving and etching
Lettered: 'J: B: F: vᵒ: E. del.' and 'C.P.S. C.M.' and inscribed with title
Published 1721
Size of platemark: 28.5 × 41.5 cm

Fischer's *Entwerff einer Historischen Architektur*, an ambitious comparative history of architecture, was translated into English in 1730. Although the two vases here are stated to be from the collection of the Marquis de Carpio, Viceroy of Naples, and made of Egyptian porphyry, four palms in height, they are in fact fantastic creations of the artist's own invention. The vase on the right, identified as 'L'Immortalité de l'Ame', was the design source for Wedgwood's vase Cat. E30.

Victoria & Albert Museum (17197)
Lit: Connor 1983 Cat. 24

E30 Vase and cover

Rosso Antico with Black Basalt relief decoration
Mark: 'WEDGWOOD' impressed
About 1785
Height: 32 cm

The vase is based on the print Cat. E29, but although the basic shape of Fischer von Erlach's bogus Egyptian design has been closely followed, it has been further embellished with a wealth of Egyptian detailing, some of which was taken from Bernard de Montfaucon's *L'Antiquité Expliquée* (1719–24). The use of Egyptian motifs is particularly associated with the early years of the 19th century, following Napoleon's expedition of 1798 and the subsequent publication of Baron Dominique Vivant Denon's *Voyage dans la basse et la Haute Egypte* (1802), but they have appeared sporadically in Western European art since the Renaissance.

Russell-Cotes Art Gallery and Museum, Bournemouth (BORGM 8186)
Lit: Allen 1962 pp. 75–7; Humbert 1994 Cat. 93

E 29

E31 Presentation drawing of a ewer

Attributed to John Flaxman senior (1726–95)
Pen and ink
Unsigned
About 1775
39.5 × 22 cm

The drawing shows the model for a water ewer ('Sacred to Neptune', Cat. B57). The models for this together with that for the companion wine ewer were supplied to Wedgwood by John Flaxman senior. On the invoice they were described as 'A pair of Vases, one with a satyr & the other with a Triton Handle £3.3', this being countersigned by John Flaxman junior on behalf of his father and dated 3 January 1775. Flaxman senior's models were in turn copied or cast from bronzes, the original models for which were probably those shown by Sigisbert Michel (1728–1811), the nephew of Claude Michel (called Clodion), in the Salon de l'Académie de Saint-Luc in Paris in 1774. Flaxman's plasters are in the Wedgwood Archives.

Trustees of the Wedgwood Museum, Barlaston, Staffordshire (No.4548)

Lit and refs: Wedgwood MS Invoice L1-204, see Reilly 1989 I p. 408 and Clifford 1992 pp. 53–4; Poulet and Scherf 1992 p. 182

E32 Pair of wine and water ewers ('Sacred to Bacchus' and 'Sacred to Neptune')

Black Basalt; the water ewer with a triton clasping the neck, the body with swags of aquatic leaves, and with an applied mask of a marine monster below the lip; the wine ewer with a satyr at the neck, the body with swags of fruiting vine, and with an applied goat's head below the lip
Mark: 'WEDGWOOD & BENTLEY' impressed
About 1778
Height: 40.5 cm

Wine and water ewers were made in Black Basalt from the 1770s until well into the 20th century. Examples in Jasper were sold at 105s (5 guineas) each, and in Black Basalt at 42s (2 guineas) each. They are no. 236 in the 'Shape Number One Book'. For the derivation of the model see Cat. E31; for an example in Jasper see Cat. B57.

Trustees of the Wedgwood Museum, Barlaston, Staffordshire (No.5161 and 5762)
Lit: Reilly 1989 I pl. 556

E 32

E 31

E 39

THE PORTLAND VASE

E33 Frontispiece to the catalogue to the sale of the Duchess of Portland's collection

Charles Grignion (1721–1810) after
Edward Francis Burney (1760–1848)
Etching and engraving
Lettered: 'Burney del^t. Grignion Sculp^t.'
and with publication line
Dated April 8th 1786
Image size: 18.8 × 13.5 cm

The Portland Vase, a Roman cameo cut-glass vase of about 30–20 BC, is probably the most celebrated artefact to have survived from ancient Rome. It is shown here as the star exhibit of the heterogeneous collections of the Duchess of Portland, who had bought it from Sir William Hamilton in 1784 (the latter having owned it only briefly). The Duchess died in July of the following year and the vase was bought by her son, the third Duke of Portland, at the sale of her collection; the vase was Lot 4155, which was offered on 7 June 1786. By 10 June it had been lent to Wedgwood, who had possibly conceived the idea of reproducing the vase in Jasper as early as February 1784, when John Flaxman had drawn his attention to it. On the 5th of that month Flaxman wrote to Wedgwood: 'I wish you may soon come to town to see W^m. Hamilton's Vase, it is the finest production of Art that has been brought to England and seems to be the very apex of perfection to which you are endeavouring to bring to your bisque & jasper; it is the kind called "Murrina" by Pliny, made of dark blue glass with white enamel figures. The vase is ... engraved in the same manner as a Cameo & the grandest & most perfect Greek Sculpture.'

Victoria & Albert Museum (E.273-1886)
Lit and refs: Dawson 1984 pl. 87; Reilly 1989 I pl. 1029; Wedgwood MS E2-30188; Painter and Whitehouse 1990 I, II passim

E 33

E34 The Portland Vase

Francesco Bartolozzi (1725–1815) after
G. B. Cipriani, RA (1727–88); published
by John Boydell
Engraving and etching
Lettered: 'G. B. Cipriani delin. Bartolozzi
Sculp.' and with publication line
Dated April 20th 1786
Cut to 31.1 × 22.8 cm

From a set of prints commissioned by Sir
William Hamilton and published
immediately before the sale of the Duchess
of Portland's collection, which commenced
on 24 April 1786. At least four different sets
or single-sheet prints of the Portland Vase
were issued in the 1780s, an indication of
the level of public interest in the object.

Victoria & Albert Museum (E.260-1886)
*Lit: Painter and Whitehouse 1990 I pp. 42 and
44–5*

E35 Cast of the Portland Vase

James Tassie (1735–99), from a cast taken
by Giovanni (or Johannes) Pichler
(1734–91)
Plaster
About 1782
Height: 24.8 cm

The gem engraver Giovanni Pichler was
commissioned to make a mould of the
Portland Vase by the antiquary and art
dealer James Byres. It was from the latter
that Hamilton acquired the vase in 1783,
Byres having bought it three years earlier
from the Barberini family, in whose
possession it had been since 1627. Byres
commissioned an edition of 60 copies from
Tassie, and these were sold at 10 guineas
each. Tassie's reproductions have the mould
seams clearly visible and do remarkably
little justice to the subtlety of the original.
This cast was Tassie's own.

Trustees of the British Museum (OA.10, 755)
*Lit: Reilly 1989 I pl. 1028; Holloway 1986 p. 11;
Painter and Whitehouse 1990 I pp. 38–9*

E36 Three medallions with trial reliefs for the Portland Vase:

A: dark blue Jasper, with relief in white of
the Phrygian cap; B: blue Jasper with black
'dip', front and reverse, and relief in white
of a satyr's mask; C: blue Jasper, with black
'dip' on upper surface only, and relief in
white of a male figure's legs
Marks: A: incised 'No 6'; B: incised 'old'
and in ink three 'A's; C: no visible marks
Dimensions: A: 11 cm high; B: 6 × 4.5 cm;
C: 6.5 × 6 cm

*Trustees of the Wedgwood Museum, Barlaston,
Staffordshire (Nos 1650, 1366&A)*

E37 Trial of the Portland Vase

Black Jasper dip, with white reliefs (no
base)
Unmarked
About 1787
Height: 26 cm

Although he had borrowed the Portland
Vase as early as June 1786, it was not until
October 1789 that Wedgwood and his
artists succeeded in making the first good
copies. Difficulties with the Jasper body
ranged from cracking to blistering (clearly
visible here) and 'lifting' of the reliefs
during firing.

*Trustees of the Wedgwood Museum, Barlaston,
Staffordshire (No.4949)*
Lit: Reilly 1989 I pl. 1031

E38 Copy of the Portland Vase

Blue-black Jasper dip, with white reliefs
Unmarked
About 1790
Height: 26 cm

An unnumbered copy of the Portland Vase,
apparently from the 'first edition' of those
potted during Josiah I's lifetime. In 1786
Wedgwood had expressed his fears that
Jasper bas-reliefs could never be applied
sufficiently thinly to match the subtlety and
delicacy of the original. On the 'first
edition' vases this effect was achieved by a
combination of undercutting and shading
the reliefs with a grey slip. Wedgwood's
Portland Vases are generally held to be
among the greatest of his achievements;
they were also among his last. For
Wedgwood's exhibition of the vase see Cat.
F17–19.

*Victoria & Albert Museum. Jones Collection (854-
1882)*
Lit: Eatwell 1983

E39 Copy of the Portland Vase

Blue-black Jasper dip with white reliefs
Unmarked
About 1790
Height: 25.4 cm

A 'first edition' vase said to have come from
the collection of the naturalist Charles
Darwin, whose father, Dr Robert Waring
Darwin, bought it from Wedgwood in 1793.

*Victoria & Albert Museum. Jermyn Street
Collection (2418-1901)*
Lit: Eatwell 1983

A RAGE FOR EXHIBITIONS
The Display and Viewing of Wedgwood's Frog Service

The display of Wedgwood's Frog Service in 1774 in the newly opened showrooms in Portland House, Greek Street, was not an isolated phenomenon. Some impression of the exhibition's context in the late-18th century is provided by a characteristically vivid passage in one of Horace Walpole's letters.[1] Writing on 6 May 1770 to his friend Horace Mann, Walpole commented on the similarity of contemporary English 'luxury and extravagance' with that of the ancient Romans and then proceeded to list a range of currently fashionable goods, activities and diversions. He first mentioned that there had 'lately been an auction of stuffed birds, and as natural history is in fashion, there are physicians and others who paid 40 or 50 guineas for a single Chinese pheasant'. After adding that you 'may buy a live one for five,' he continued: 'After this it is not extraordinary that pictures should be so dear. We have at present three exhibitions ... The rage to see these exhibitions is so great, that sometimes one cannot pass through the streets where they are.' The relationship between these exhibitions and that mounted by Wedgwood four years later was already anticipated here by the reference a few lines later to the 'Etruscan vases, made of earthen ware in Staffordshire, [available] from two to five guineas; or <u>or moulu</u>, [presumably Matthew Boulton's] never made here before, which succeeds so well'. Walpole's remarks not only registered the enthusiasm for such exhibitions among a rapidly growing public of viewers and consumers in 18th-century London. They also indicate, through the juxtaposition of stuffed birds and the ambitious narrative paintings of Benjamin West ('who paints history in the taste of Poussin') the diversity of such events.

The 'shows' that attracted these audiences represented one aspect of the 'public sphere', a concept that has been employed in many recent discussions of 18th-century culture.[2] In the first half of the century the notion of the 'public sphere' had involved ostensibly shared assumptions about public virtue and its representations in public culture, albeit assumptions that legitimized the interests of a landed élite. But by about 1750 this apparent consensus was being challenged and disrupted, especially in urban centres, by the commercialization of 'polite culture' and its greater accessibility to those 'of the middling sort'. While the notion of the 'public', as opposed to the 'private', could be invoked in discussions of moral and political issues, it could also be expressed in terms of urban life through the establishment of spaces such as Vauxhall Gardens, Covent Garden or the nave of Westminster Abbey. During the second half of the century such spaces were being frequented by an increasingly wide range of people, and discussion about them frequently centred around who should be admitted and who excluded, just as Wedgwood was concerned about the relation between exclusivity and wide appeal in his plans for the exhibiting of the Frog Service.

The 'shows' available in London around 1770 in their remarkable variety were intended to attract different ranges of visitor, and viewing in these public spaces sometimes involved spectators from very different social

Pl. 27 (Cat. F1) Sir Ashton Lever's Museum, engraving by William Skelton, 1789. The opening of the Museum in London was enthusiastically noted by Wedgwood in a letter of 1774.

groups.[3] In Westminster Abbey, for example, a recently erected monument might be inspected by a 'gentleman' for the beauty of its inscription, while the wax effigies of various monarchs be gawped at by a group of astonished artisans, as they are shown in a caricature of the 1780s. Situated between these two classes of fictional viewer were perhaps those who bought the guide book to the monuments in the Abbey, which was published in no less than five editions between 1754 and 1784. Many shows, however, were evidently aimed at relatively specific audiences. The display in 1790 of a painting 'on a large scale by Mr Dodd' of a procession to St Paul's, accompanied by 'real Portraits and Dresses, as worn on that memorable Day' was evidently intended for a popular market.[4]

So too was the 'mechanical tarantula' shown by Weeks's Museum (Cat. F3), judging from the language employed in the advertisement for it. Even in the case of exhibitions that included a uniform type of material, a range of different audiences may have been envisaged and choices made about advertising or admission arrangements so as to control this. During the 1760s such differentiation between different levels of audience is apparent in the published accounts of the exhibitions of painting at the Society of Artists from 1760 and those mounted by the Royal Academy following its foundation in 1768.[5] While the Society of Artists exhibited a variety of subjects, including genre scenes or 'conversations', with a wide appeal, the Royal Academy from the start set out to show history paintings, works representing grand themes in an elevated style. As David Solkin has remarked, this combination not only 'conferred nobility on the painter ... [but] was also meant to define his chosen viewers as individuals who were morally, socially and intellectually superior to that part of mankind attached to more vulgar, material concerns'.[6] The distinction between the exclusive audience sought by the Academy and that which viewed the exhibitions of the Society of Artists and others is suggested by Reynolds when he commented that 'Exhibitions, while they produce such admirable effects by nourishing emulation and calling out genius, have also a mischievous tendency, by seducing the Painter to an ambition of pleasing indiscriminately the mixed multitude of people who resort to them'.

By exhibiting the Frog Service before it went to Russia, Wedgwood was taking advantage of the enthusiasm for the various types of exhibition that were so numerous in late 18th-century London. Which type of exhibition did he wish to be associated with and which was the right level at which to pitch his exhibition? Through their familiarity with the range of exhibitions outlined above, viewing publics in the 1770s would have been finely attuned to subtle differences between the places in which works were displayed, the manner in which they were shown, the ways in which they were publicized and the arrangements made for admission. Just as Wedgwood had to decide the extent to which he followed the marketing practices of his rival potters, so he had to chose between different modes of exhibiting. While he evidently wished to avoid the popular audience attracted by the St Paul's procession show, he also had to take account of the different publics that visited the Society of Artists and Royal Academy exhibitions. If the culture reflected in Wedgwood's display strategy was one in which consumption and commerce were changing, it was also a culture in which both aesthetic categories and practices of viewing were being newly formulated.

A sensitivity to these issues underlies the anxieties expressed by Wedgwood in his letters to Bentley, particu-

Pl. 28 Invitation card for an exhibition of shellwork by Mrs. Dard, 1779.

120

The Public Advertiser.

Numb. 13038

WEDNESDAY, June 1, 1774. Price Two-pence Halfpenny.

KING's THEATRE.

AT the King's Theatre in the Haymarket, on Friday next will be performed a new Serious Opera called

L'OLIMPIADE

The Music by the most celebrated Composers, Under the Direction of Signor GIORDANI.
The principal Characters by
Signor Millico, Signor Schiroli, Signora Galli, Signor Michelli, Signora Marchetti, and Signora Cecilia Davies, detta Inglesina.
With new Dances by Monf. PITROT.
End of Act I. A Grand Serious Ballet called L'Embarras du Choix, in which Monf. Fierville and Mademoiselle Nina Favier will dance the principal Entree.
End of Act II. A new Field Dance, by Signor Mariottini and Signora Mazzoni.
End of Act III. A new grand Serious Ballet, by Monf. Fierville and Mademoiselle Nina Favier.
With magnificent new Scenes, Decorations and Dresses, both for the Opera and Dances.
Pit and Boxes to be put together; and no Person to be admitted without Tickets, which will be delivered at the Office at Half a Guinea each.
First Gallery 5s. Second Gallery 3s.
By Their MAJESTIES Command,
No Person whatsoever to be admitted behind the Scenes, or into the Orchestra.

DRURY-LANE.

The last Time of the Company's performing this Season.
BY PARTICULAR DESIRE.
NOT ACTED THESE TWO YEARS.
For the Benefit of Mr. BANNISTER.

AT the Theatre Royal in Drury Lane, To-morrow will be presented

LOVE in a VILLAGE.

Hawthorn, Mr. BANNISTER;
Justice Woodcock, Mr. WESTON;
Sir W. Meadows, Mr. J. AICKIN;
(Being his 1st Appearance in that Character)
Young Meadows, Mr. DU-BELLAMY;
Eustace, Mr. OWENSON;
Hedge, Mr. KING;
Margery, Miss POPE; Deb. Woodcock, Mrs. LOVE;
Lucinda, Mrs. SCOTT;
Rosetta, Mrs. SMITH;
(Being her 1st Appearance in that Character.)
In Act I. a Dance incidental to the Opera.
End of the Opera, Imitations, Vocal and Rhetorical By Mr. Bannister.
To which will be added,

The REGISTER OFFICE.

Capt. Le Brush, Mr. KING;
The Irishman, Mr. MOODY,
(In which he will introduce the Description of a Man of War.)
Gulwell, Mr. Fearon; Scotchman, Mr. Moody;
Frankly, Mr. Courtney;
Frenchman, Mr. BURTON,
(Being his 1st Appearance in that Character)
Margery Moorpout, Mrs. LOVE.
Mrs. Doggerel by Miss POPE.
The Doors will be opened at Half after Five. To begin exactly at Half an Hour after Six o'Clock.
Tickets and Places for the Boxes to be had of Mr. Johnston, at the Theatre.

HAY-MARKET.

AT the Theatre Royal in the Hay-market, This Day will be presented

The BANKRUPT.

The principal Characters by
Mr. FOOTE,
Mr. KENNEDY,
Mr. AICKIN, Mr. JOHNSON,
Mr. FEARON, Mr. COURTNEY,
Mr. DAVIS, Mr. EVERARD,
Mr. WESTON,
Mr. JACOBS, Mrs. WILLIAMS,
Mr. BANNISTER, Miss AMBROSE,
Mr. LLOYD, Miss PLATT,
Mr. JONES,
And Mrs. JEWELL.
PROLOGUE to be spoken by Mr. FOOTE
End of the Play, a modern, operatical, sentimental, crying Comedy, of one Act, called
PIETY in PATTENS.
Butler, Mr. Weston: The 'Squire, Mr. Fearon: Mrs. Gandy, Mrs. Palmer: Polly Pattens, Mrs. Jewell.
After the Interlude, a Dance by Sig. Giorgi's Scholars.
To which will be added

The LYING VALET.

Gayless, Mr. DAVIS:
Justice Guttle, Mr. Lloyd: Cook, Mr. Jacobs: Beau Trippit, Mr. Everard: Melissa, Miss Ambrose: Mrs. Trippit, Mrs Weston: Mrs. Gadabout, Mrs. Palmer: Kitty, Mrs. GARDNER.
Places to be taken of Mr. Jewell, at the Theatre.
Boxes 5s. Pit 3s. Gall. 2s. Upper Gall. 1s.
No Admittance behind the Scenes, nor any Money to be returned after the Curtain is drawn up.
The Doors to be open at Six. To begin at Seven.
Servants to keep Places to be at the House at Five.
Vivant Rex & Regina.

SADLER's WELLS.

THE DIVERSIONS of this Place will be continued This and every Evening: Consisting of
Ladder Dancing by Monsieur Richer.
Singing by Mr. Lowe, Mr. Kear, Mrs. Burnett, and Miss Dowson.
Dancing by Mr. Atkins, Mr. Lepeltier, Mr. Delegal, Mrs. Stephens (late Miss Capon) Mrs. Huntley, Miss Collett, Miss Valois and others.
Tumbling by Mr Rayner, Mr. Risher, Mr. Oliver, and Mr Garman.
Several surprising and pleasing Performances by Messrs. Siegls, lately arrived from Paris
And Rope Dancing by Mr. Ferzi, and others.
With an Entertainment of Music and Dancing, call'd

The Cave of Enchantment.

The Music by Mr. DIBDIN,
And the Decorations entirely new.
The Doors to be opened at Five.
To begin precisely at Six.
Places for the Boxes to be taken at the Wells.

Exhibitions in the Cities of London and Westminster.
By Desire of several Persons of Distinction,

BRESLAW and his ITALIANS new great Performances, and the celebrated Miss Rose's Infant Imitations will be performed (for a few Nights only) in the Great Ball Room at the King's Arms Tavern, opposite the Royal Exchange, Mondays, Wednesdays and Fridays in the Evenings.— Likewise Breslaw and his Italians will continue their Performances as usual at his Exhibition Room, Cockspur-street, in the Hay-market, Tuesdays, Thursdays and Saturdays, in the Evenings. At each Place the Doors will be opened at Six o'Clock, and begin precisely at Seven. The Rooms will be illuminated with Wax. Admittance Half a Crown each Person. Tickets to be had at both Places of Performance.

SPRING-GARDENS, VAUXHALL.

THE EVENING ENTERTAINMENTS of this Place will be continued every Day, (Sundays excepted.)
Each Person to pay One Shilling Admittance.
The Doors will be opened immediately after Five.

THE Society of ARTISTS, associated for the Relief of their distressed Brethren, their Widows and Children, give Notice, that their annual Exhibition (being the 15th) is now open at Mr. Christie's Great Room (next Cumberland House) in Pall-mall, and will continue every Day (Sundays excepted) from Seven in the Morning till Eight in the Evening until further Notice.
Admittance 1s. Catalogue gratis.
By Order of the Society,
J. FURMAN, Sec.
☞ Plans of the Institution may be had of the Secretary, in the Inner Temple.

INCORPORATED SOCIETY of ARTISTS of GREAT BRITAIN.

THE President and Directors give Notice, That their annual Exhibition (being the 15th) is now open at their Room near Exeter Exchange, Strand, and will be continued every Day (Sundays excepted) from Eight in the Morning till Seven in the Evening.
W. THOMSON, F. S. A. Assistant Sec.
Admittance 1s. Catalogues gratis.

DARLY's COMIC EXHIBITION. No. 39, Strand, near York Buildings,

IS opened this Day at One Shilling each Person, with a Catalogue gratis, which entitles the Bearer to any Print not exceeding One Shilling Value. This droll and amusing Collection is the Production of several Ladies and Gentlemen, Artists, &c &c. and consists of several laughable Subjects, droll Figures, and sundry Characters, Caracatures, &c. taken at Bath, and other watering Places, and at the public Places of Resort in Great-Britain.
N. B. By the kind Assistance of Ladies, &c there are near 200 new Subjects added to the Collection this Year.

THE Gentlemen who served with the late Admiral BOSCAWEN are desired to dine on Saturday next at the St. Alban's Tavern, St. Alban's-street.
It is requested they leave their Names at the Bar of the said Tavern on or before Friday, that it may be better known for what Number to provide Dinner.

MONEY.

THE Nobility, Gentry, Officers of Rank in the Army, Clergymen, and all Persons entitled to any certain Income for Life, may be immediately supplied with Sums of Money to any Amount, upon the strictest Honour, and with the greatest Secrecy, by applying in Person or by Letter to Mr. FREEMAN, No. 1, Crown and Scepter Court, St. James's Street.
Wanted to purchase immediately, for the Seller's Lives, one Annuity of 500l. one ditto of 300l. and five ditto of 10 l. each.

TO be SOLD, a House in GROSVENOR PLACE. It is almost in the Centre of that delightful Row. The Premises cannot be viewed except between the Hours of Eleven and One on Mondays, Wednesdays, and Fridays.
Ask at the Sun in Chapel-street, near the Lock Hospital for Mr. Grews, Joiner.

A Medal of her Royal Highness the Duchess of Cumberland.
This Day is published, Price 6d.
(In which is given a fine Medal of her Royal Highness the Duchess of Cumberland, finely executed by Mr. Kirk. Also, an elegant Copper-plate, entitled Summer, designed by a capital Master, and engraved by Collier.)
Numb. XVI. (To be continued Monthly) of

THE SENTIMENTAL MAGAZINE, or General Assemblage of Science, Taste, and Entertainment, for May, 1774.
Containing, among Variety of other Articles, A Dialogue between Zeno and Epicurus in the Regions of the Dead. The mysterious Delay, &c. &c.
Printed for the Authors, and sold by G. Kearsly, No. 46, in Fleet-street; and by all other Booksellers in Great Britain and Ireland.

This Day is publish'd, Price 1s.
Containing Eighty Pages of Letter-Press, printed on an elegant Type.
Number VI. (To be continued the First of every Month) of

THE MEDICAL MAGAZINE, or General Repository of Practical Physic and Surgery. Calculated for the Aid and Assistance of the Physician, the Surgeon, the Apothecary, the Chemist, the private Gentleman; Medical Students, and Hospital Pupils.
By a SOCIETY of GENTLEMEN of the different Branches of the Profession.
London, printed for the Authors, and sold by G. Kearsly, No. 46, Fleet-street; and by all other Booksellers in Great Britain and Ireland.
☞ Among other Articles, this Work will contain the modern Practice of Physic, on a new Plan; a complete System of Surgery, &c. &c.

This Day is publish'd, Price 6d.
(To be continued Monthly.)
Embellished with the following elegant Engravings: 1. An elegant new Pattern for an Apron 2. A beautiful Historical Print, entitled, The Unwary Sleeper. And, 3. A new Song, set to Music by Mr. Hudson.
Number XLIX. For May, 1774, of

THE LADY's MAGAZINE; or, Entertaining Companion for the Fair Sex, appropriated solely to their Use and Amusement.
Containing the usual Variety of useful and entertaining Articles.
Printed for G. Robinson, No. 25, Paternoster Row: By whom Favours from Correspondents will be received.

This Day is published, Price 6d.
No. LXXI. (To be continued Monthly) of

THE TOWN and COUNTRY MAGAZINE, or Universal Repository of Knowledge, Instruction, and Entertainment. For May, 1774.
Illustrated and embellished with the following beautiful Engravings: 1. A striking Profile of the Martial Orator. 2. An elegant Portrait of Miss G——. And, 3. A beautiful Historical Picture, entitled, The Intercepted Letter, founded on Fact.
Containing, amongst a great Variety of original and interesting Articles, History of the Tête à Tête, or Memoirs of the Martial Orator and Miss G——. Letters from an American Gentleman to his Friend in London, Letter IV. History of Dick Wildfire. The Observer, No. 11. A Letter from Peter Ploughshare, &c. &c.
Printed for A. Hamilton, jun. near St. John's Gate; and sold by G. Robinson, No. 25, Paternoster-Row.

RANELAGH HOUSE.

THIS DAY, the 1st of June, will be performed a Concert of
Vocal and Instrumental MUSIC.
Admittance 2s. 6d. each Person,
Coffee and Tea included.
To be continued on Mondays, Wednesdays and Fridays.
The Doors to be opened at Half past Six.
The Music to begin at Seven.
A Horse Patrol to guard the Roads.
☞ Ladies and Gentlemen may walk in the Rotunda, Gardens, &c. every Day (Sundays excepted) at 1s. each.

MUSEUM LOTTERY

By the Authority of Parliament, consists of

			£
2	Prizes of the Value of	5000	10,000
2	Ditto	3000	6000
12	Ditto	1500	18,000
18	Ditto	750	13,500
52	Ditto	450	23,400
100	Ditto	300	30,000
212	Ditto	150	31,800
2	Ditto	50	100
2	Ditto, first drawn	100	200
2	Ditto, last drawn	750	1500
120,000	Tickets of Admission to the Museum, at 10s. 6d.		63,000
120,404	Amounting in all to		197,500
60,000	Tickets A } 120,000 at 1l. 1s.		126,000
60,000	Ditto B }		
	Balance in favour of the Public		71,500
			197,500

Lottery Tickets are now selling at the Museum, Spring Gardens, and at the Lottery-office, Shoe-lane, Fleet-street; and by most of the principal Jewellers, Goldsmith, and other Shop-keepers in Town and Country.
With every Lottery Ticket will be delivered a descriptive Inventory of the great and valuable Prizes in the Museum Lottery; also a Copper-plate Print of the Perpetual Motion, with an Account of that astonishing Piece of Art, together with a Model of the fine Pair of Brilliant Ear-rings, for which Mr. Cox allows Five Thousands, if they are relinquished to him, and the Public are requested to observe, that there are only two Prizes of 50l. two of 100l. and 212 of 150l. each, the rest being all high Prizes, from Three Hundred to Five Thousand Pounds; and whoever is in Possession of the duplicate Numbers, both A and B, that is, two Tickets of the same Number, one of which being entitled to Five Thousand Pounds, the two will be entitled to Ten Thousand Pounds for their two Guineas, to be paid in Cash, without any Deduction, at the Bank of England, within three Months after the Drawing of the Lottery.
If the Twenty and Fifty Pound Prizes in the State Lottery are excluded the Prizes in the Museum Lottery will amount to more than those of the State Lottery, though the Price of Tickets is so trifling in one to what it is in the other; besides, that each Ticket of one Guinea and a Half admits two Ladies or Gentlemen, and one young Person, and the duplicate Ticket admit six Persons; thus the younger Branches of Families at an easy Expence, may be put in Fortune's Way, and gratified with a Sight that at the same Time that it recreates the senses, and improves the Understanding of Youth, heightens the Pleasure of the Parent, in observing the Looks of Rapture exchanged by his astonishing Offspring when that Scene of Wonder is unfolded.
N. B. Persons occasionally accommodated with Lottery Tickets, with Admission, or with Tickets of Admittance only, and those Persons who after seeing the Museum think proper to pay the Difference, may have the Lottery Tickets delivered to them. Quarto Inventories adorned with Copper-plates, are given with every duplicate Ticket. Lists of the Prizes with every Particular relative to the Lottery, are delivered to the Public gratis at the above Offices. Light Gold taken at 3l. 18s. per Ounce, and Tickets registered.
☞ The Museum will continue to be seen by Candle-light till Saturday the 11th of June next, and the Exhibition at Eleven in the Morning, and Two in the Afternoon, be continued to that Day.

Cavendish-square, or Holles-street.

WANTED to purchase, the Freehold, or the Remainder of a Lease in Possession of a small House, with the Appurtenances, in either of the above Situations.
Particulars to be sent to Mr. Barnard, at the Golden Cup in Air-street, Golden-square.

THE Letter signed "A Neighbour and Well-wisher," directed to a Gentleman in Berners-street, has been received. The Person to whom it was addressed desires the Writer of it to accept his most hearty Thanks, and intreats the Favour of an Interview with the Person who wrote it, not only to testify his Gratitude in Person but, as the Writer must be sensible such Outrage deserves legal Punishment, he wishes much for an Opportunity to carry his just Resentment into Execution. If Secrecy is required it may most assuredly be relied on.
May 31, 1774.

Monday June 6, will be published, Price 1s.

A Copy-Book for Youth, by which they may learn to write without the Assistance of a Master, and properly adapted for Schools, as it will save the Teacher much Time and Labour.
By BENJAMIN WEBB, junior,
Master of an Academy in Bridgewater Gardens, Aldersgate-street.
Printed for T. Carnan and F. Newbery, junior, at No. 65, in St. Paul's Church-yard.
∴ This introductory Method for Teaching the Art of Writing, having been practised Thirty Years in Mr. Webb's Academy, with the utmost Success, is therefore now submitted to the Public.

This Day are published,

A VOYAGE to the HEBRIDES, in the Year 1772.
By THOMAS PENNANT, Esq;
In which is included an Account of STAFFA, communicated by JOSEPH BANKS, Esq;
Illustrated with Forty-five Copper Plates, engraved by the most eminent Artists, from original Drawing, and printed in Quarto, on a fine Writing Paper.
Also (the 3d Edition) A TOUR in SCOTLAND in 1769. By Thomas Pennant, Esq; Illustrated with 23 Copper Plates, being new Designs from original Drawings, and printed also in Quarto, on a fine Writing Paper.
Printed for B. White, at Horace's Head, in Fleet Street.

PANTHEON.

THE Building may be seen every Day (Sundays excepted) from Ten in the Morning 'till Four in the Afternoon, at 5s. each Person.
The Decorations used at the Masked Ball given by the Society at Boodle's, will remain for a short Time only.

PALL-MALL.

THE Resort of Company was so great, the latter End of last Week, to see that inimitable Piece of Art, the Microcosm, (before its Departure from this Kingdom) that many Parties were obliged (for want of Room) to return without seeing it, which has induced the Proprietor to exhibit that wonderful Piece of Mechanism till Saturday Night next, and positively no longer. Every Age, Rank, and Sex, behold it with Delight, and declare the Pleasure which its Performances afford to a rational Mind is inexpressible. It may be seen any Time of the Day, by four or more Persons, at 1s. each; and at the Hours of Twelve, One, Two, Three, and Seven o'Clock. It will be shewn to any Number of Persons, at the Proprietor's House, the third Door East of John-street, opposite the Golden-ball, Pall-Mall.

MR. JERVAIS's Exhibition of curious Stained Glass which every Admirer of the Polite Arts universally allows to exceed any Production of that Sort ever before exhibited, and which is now to be seen in Mr. Pinchbeck's Repository, Cockspur-street, from Ten in the Morning till Eight in the Evening, Admittance 1s. The major Part of the Pictures in this Exhibition, are done from original Drawings, designed for this Purpose, among which the following Effects are attempted, Sunshine, Moon-light, Fire-light, and Candle-light, after original Pictures of Teniers, Braklenkamp, Gerard-dow, Le Naine, Van Goen, &c. and a St Cecilia, after Dominichino, nearly as large as Life, calculated either for a Church or a Music-room. And, as many Persons have expressed it as their Opinion, that it is impossible to examine the Merits of the various Pieces at once seeing them, any Person who has paid, may come as often as they please gratis, bringing other Company with them that do pay.

WEDGWOOD and BENTLEY inform the Nobility and Gentry, that those who chuse to see a Table and Desert Service, now set out at their new Rooms, in Greek-street, may have free Tickets for that purpose, at the Ware-house, in Great Newport-street, and that none can be admitted without Tickets.

PHILOSOPHICAL TRANSACTIONS.

THE first Part Vol. LXIV. for the Year 1774, will be ready to deliver to the Members of the Royal Society, on Thursday next, the 2d of June, 1774. Copies to be had at their House, in Crane-court, Fleet-street.

This Day at Noon will be published,
Price Sixpence,

FREEDOM; a POEM. Inscribed to JOHN WILKES, Esq.
Printed for the Author; and sold by T. Evans, No. 54, Pater-noster-row; and J. Plummer, No. 100, Fenchurch-street.

This Day is published,
In Three Volumes Folio,
(Adorned with a Head in Profile, engraven by Mr. Baire, from a Model by Mr. Gosset, taken from the Life, 1756, when the Author was in his 8_th Year)

THE WORKS of BENJAMIN HOADLY, D. D. successively Bishop of Bangor, Hereford, Salisbury and Winchester. With an Index, and an Account of the Author and his Family prefixed.
Published by his Son, JOHN HOADLY, L. L. D.
Chancellor of the Diocese of Winchester.
Printed for W. Bowyer, and J. Nichols; and sold by R. Horsfield, No. 5, Stationers Court; also by J. Wilkie, No. 71, St. Paul's Church-yard
Where may be had, Bishop Hoadly's Sermons, three Vols, and some of his other Pieces in Octavo.

This Day is published, Price 6d.
(To be continued Monthly,) Number XVIII. of

THE WESTMINSTER MAGAZINE; or, the Pantheon of Taste. For May, 1774.
Embellished with, 1. A beautiful and striking Likeness of Lewis XVI. the present French Monarch. 2. The Friendly Rivals, an Historical Print.
Containing, a great Variety of original, interesting, and entertaining Articles, &c.
London, printed for W. Goldsmith, No. 24, Paternoster Row, and sold by Richardson and Urquhart, at the Royal-Exchange.

This Day is published, Price 1s.
Containing Eighty Pages of Letter-Press, which is almost double the Quantity, in Proportion to the Price that is usually given in Law Books.
Number XI. (To be continued the First of every Month) of

THE LAWYER's MAGAZINE, or General Repository of Practical Law. By a Society of Gentlemen of the Middle Temple.
Printed by Mess. Strahan and Woodfall, Law-Printers to the King's Most Excellent Majesty, for G. Kearsly, at No. 46, in Fleet-street.
☞ In this Work will be given, the Practice of the Courts of Law and Equity. A complete Body of Conveyancing. Also a new Law-Dictionary. The Rules and Orders of the different Courts. The present Practice of Distress and Replevin. Curious Precedents of original Writs, &c. &c.

To the Printer of the Public Advertiser.
SIR,

THE late Resolutions with respect to the Coin will probably, if carried into Execution, produce endless Trouble and Perplexity. But the greatest Evil attending them will be the Increase of our Paper Currency. This is a new Thing in the History of the World, and in some measure peculiar to this Kingdom. It is frightful to think how much we depend upon it, and to what Danger it exposes us.
"Bank Notes in particular (as Dr. Price "observes in the additional Preface just pub-"lished to his Pamphlet on the National "Debt) make a principal Part of our Cash, "and were they to lose their Credit, all the "Money in the Kingdom would not much "exceed the annual Amount of the Taxes, "and the Revenue would fall to nothing, and "general Devastation would take place.
"Paper-Money (as the same Writer goes "on) having only a local and imaginary Va-"lue, can bear no Shock. It shrinks at every "Approach of Danger; and the Condition of

Pl. 29 Page from the 'Public Advertiser' for 1 June 1774 carrying Wedgwood's advertisement for the exhibition of the Frog Service.

Pl. 30 (Cat. F9) 'Mr Cox's Perpetual Motion...', engraving by J. Lodge of a clock exhibited in James Cox's Museum in 1774.

larly in the year or so before the opening of the Frog Service exhibition, when he was writing about the size and nature of the showroom and the possible responses of the potential viewers to both the display and other visitors.

The cultural context in which the exhibition of the Frog Service took place is represented in a typographical form on the front page of the *Gazetteer and New Daily Advertiser* for Monday 6 June 1774 (Pl. 29).[7] Here the announcement of Wedgwood's exhibition is placed alongside advertisements for 'A new Musical Piece, call'd the Surprize' (to be performed at Sadler's Wells along with acts by 'Mr Ferzi on the tightrope'), James Mad-

dock's 'Grand Collection of Ranicula, now in Bloom' and the auction of the stock of a bankrupt linen draper. But in the same column are also several more closely comparable exhibitions. One was the annual exhibition of the Society of Artists already mentioned. The contents are not specified but from the published catalogue we know that in 1774 it included a 'Portrait of a horse' by Stubbs, 'Venus attired by the graces, in inlay' by the cabinet-maker Christopher Fuhrlogh, some models in wax by Diemer for chandeliers, Miss Davies's 'A head of Psyche, in human hair' and engravings by Mazell for some of the plates in Pennant's *Tour in Scotland* (Cat.

F20). More detail is given in the *Gazetteer* about 'Mr Jervais's exhibition of Stained Glass' (see also Cat. F13). Among the pieces shown here were copies after Teniers, Gerard Dou and Le Nain, 'a St Cecilia after Domenichino, nearly as large as life, calculated for either a church or music room', along with pictures in which the effects of sunshine, moonlight, firelight and candlelight were attempted. If the Royal Academy presented itself as consciously distinct from an exhibition such as Jervais's, there was far less difference between this and shows at the Society of Artists. Alongside the works already mentioned, these included several paintings exhibited there (rather than at the Royal Academy) by Joseph Wright of Derby that make use of the same effects as those described in the advertisement for Jervais's glass. Juxtaposed in this way, the announcements for these various exhibitions suggest a continuum of visual – and, more specifically, showing and viewing – culture in which Wedgwood's display of the Frog Service may be situated.

Distinctions may, however, be discerned in the language employed as well as the conditions of admission that are given, whether explicitly or not. The size of Wedgwood's advertisement is very modest; no mention is made of the fact that the Service had been commissioned by the Empress of Russia and, compared with the way in which other attractions are announced on the same page, there is a notable absence of hyperbole or even very elaborate description. The manner of the announcement is very much in accord with Wedgwood's careful attitude to advertising, acknowledging its usefulness but wary of forms such as handbills – 'a mode of advertisement I never approv'd of' – which were associated with 'common Shopkeepers'.[8]

Wedgwood's advertisement also differs from the others on the page in referring to the public for which it was intended. While Jervais's show was simply for 'the Curious' and the others, including the Society of Artists, for as wide a social range as possible, Wedgwood makes specific mention of 'the Nobility, and Gentry'. Similarly, it is the only one to state that admission tickets had to be obtained elsewhere. The exclusivity of admission was an important part of Wedgwood's strategy, and in this he and Bentley – particularly the latter – were perhaps aware of the more exclusive audience for the Royal Academy's exhibitions than that for either other exhibitions or the displays of works in the auction rooms. In a letter of 1767 Wedgwood agreed with Bentley that the

> reasons you have given against my fixing upon an Auction Room, or any other which has been a place of public resort, are solid ... and there is another nearly as strong as any of them. At present the Nobility, and Gentry recommend one another to my rooms, & they never meet with any other Company there, but every body wo[d]. be apt to stroll into an Auction room – one that they had ever free access into, & that wo[d]. be the most effectual method for keeping present sett of Customers out of it. For you know well they wil not mix with the rest of the World any farther than their amusements, or conveniences make it necessary to do so.[9]

One exhibition advertised on the same page as the Frog Service display engaged Wedgwood's close attention and offers an instructive case for comparison. This was the exhibition at Cox's Museum (see also Cat. F7). Although the announcement on 6 June states only that the Museum in Spring Gardens will continue to be open for viewing by candlelight until the end of the week, the exhibition of mechanical toys and automata would already have been well known to most readers/viewers through many other announcements and 'puffs' in the press, as well as through several editions of Cox's own catalogue. Originally apprenticed as a goldsmith, James

Cox began in the late 1760s to produce elaborate and richly mounted mechanical clocks (see Cat. F8), with the assistance of Merlin,[10] his 'first or principal mechanic'. Between 1772 and 1774 these formed the contents of his Museum (Cat. F8 and 9), admission to which cost the large sum of a half-guinea, although this was later reduced to a quarter-guinea.[11]

Cox evidently ran into financial difficulties, not least through his short ownership of the Chelsea porcelain factory, which he had purchased from Nicholas Sprimont in 1769 only to sell it to William Duesbury five months later. Despite these problems, Wedgwood was evidently impressed by both Cox's exhibition and the display mounted by Duesbury of Derby. On 11 April 1772 he commented in a letter to Bentley on the contrast between Matthew Boulton's success and that of 'Mr Cox [who] has so far outshone him', adding ironically:

I am not without pain for our Nobility & Gentry themselves, for what with the fine things in Gold, Silver & Steel from Soho, the almost miraculous magnificence of Mr. Coxes Exhibition, & all the Glare of the Derby & other China shews – What heads or Eyes could stand all this dazzleing profusion of riches & ornament if something was not provided for their relief, to give them at proper intervals a little relaxation, & repose.[12]

At this point Wedgwood was thinking of the less dazzling effect that 'our black, Etruscan, & Grecian vases' might have as a contrast to the 'golden surfeit' of Cox's display. But the opportunities for publicity offered by an exhibition were far from lost on him.

Two years earlier, Boulton too had been contemplating the possibility of mounting an exhibition in London, and the exchange of letters between him and James Adam, who was attempting to persuade him to set up a showroom in the new Adelphi development, articulates the arguments for and against such a plan.[13] These let-

ters also refer to the different ways of presenting objects and the extent to which different strategies of display attracted different publics. Adam argued that a 'show shop on the Strand' would serve as 'an useful appendix to the ware-house as it is certainly in the best part of town for chance custom'. In his view:

all the shopkeepers, especially those who deal in the silver and toy way, put great stress upon chance custom. In this way it might be useful for common things, and likewise for those of our own patterns that might be after a time become common, or perhaps at first exposing some few things in a new stile in the show shop, might serve as decoy to lead people to the warehouse.

Adam's remarks were made in response to a rather different assessment made by Boulton, who favoured 'a large elegant room, without any other window than a sky light. By this sort of concealment you excite curiosity.' Apart from having the advantage of safeguarding new designs from 'street walking pirates', such a showroom would be more attractive to the nobility who 'like that less publick repository'. Set apart in this way, the 'novelty would please more and last longer than the present mode of exhibition'. Arguing for a more exclusive mode of display, Boulton contrasts practices in London and Paris and apparently favours the Parisian model as that most appropriate for his ormolu and vases:

The great customers for plate are such as are not to be caught by shew as they walk along the street and you know that unprivate shops are only customary in London, for at Paris all their finest shops are upstairs.[14]

For these reasons he was more attracted by premises on two levels, in which the 'lower parts might be appropriated to the sale of grosser articles of our manufacture and for the reception of gentlemens servants. The upper handsome room for plate d'or moulu and such other fine toys as we make'. In the event Boulton did not proceed with this plan but chose instead to sell his 'gilt and chased vases and various other pieces of ornamental furniture' by auction at Christie & Ansell's saleroom, with viewing by ticket and the first two of three days reserved for the nobility.

The exchange between Boulton and Adam makes explicit a concern about the degree of openness offered by different types of shop; this concern underlies much of Wedgwood's thinking about the display of his work in London. Already by the 1740s, shop interiors were becoming increasingly elaborate, and visiting the shops of tradesmen such as mercers was becoming a steadily more familiar way of viewing and buying.[15] But while such shops may have been catering for the growing numbers of middle-class consumers of luxury goods, the nobility and gentry that Wedgwood and Boulton wished to attract were apparently far less enthusiastic. For Wedgwood the dilemma as to how to draw as many potential customers as possible, while maintaining a unambiguous exclusivity, was nowhere more acute than in decisions concerning the physical organization of the showroom and the extent to which this was accessible or visible from the street. Although the popularity of the Frog Service exhibition is well documented, the evidence about the way in which it was arranged in the showroom is neither detailed nor precise. The Service was shown on both the ground and first floors, but the size and regular arrangement of the windows along the Portland House façade meant that it would not have been seen from the street. Within the showroom the Service was laid out not on large formal dining tables, as it would have been when used, but rather on small tables so that the individual pieces, with their different scenes, could be viewed closely.[16]

By thus maintaining exclusivity and encouraging close examination of views, Wedgwood was not displaying wares for sale as in a shop but exhibiting the results of an exceptional technical and artistic undertaking to an informed and discerning public that was accustomed to viewing works of art in a gallery setting. The interest of the Service lay as much in the images with which it was decorated as in its qualities as a ceramic ensemble. Presented as representations, these scenes were literally framed by the two different types of border and metaphorically 'framed' within the setting of an exhibition space. While not denying the production of the Service as a highly impressive technical feat, Wedgwood was through its display making a claim for it as art. Here, then, we may detect Wedgwood negotiating a position within a commercial and industrial culture in which, as Ann Bermingham has suggested, 'the relationship between the fine arts and other forms of artistic practice' was ambiguous.[17]

By presenting his work as art rather than craft Wedgwood was invoking the power and associations of a newly emerging aesthetic. The institutional framework for this category of the aesthetic was provided by bodies such as the Free Society of Artists and the Royal Academy and their exhibitions. Wedgwood's exhibition might at first sight seem have had a closer affinity with the former, not least because it was there that the paintings of Joseph Wright of Derby, from whom Wedgwood commissioned the *Corinthian Maid*, were shown. But the range of publics encouraged by the Free Society was not what Wedgwood wanted. His far more exclusive audience had more in common with that which was admitted to the Royal Academy.[18]

What expectations and assumptions did Wedgwood's audience bring to the display and how were these grounded in other viewing experiences? One set of associations in the minds of viewers may have been the status of the Service as an imperial commission. Although this was not mentioned in the advertisement, Wedgwood may have relied on this being known and passed on by word of mouth. The imperial connections are unlikely to have been ignored by those who had visited, or even read the publicity for Cox's Museum (Cat. F7–9), in which the earrings made for the Empress of Russia were given particular prominence.[19]

Eighteenth-century publics would also have been familiar with the presentation in various forms of innovations in technology and materials. Alongside accounts of antiquities, poetry and digests of recently published books, 'polite' periodicals, such as the *Gentleman's Magazine*, carried descriptions about processes of manufacture and new inventions. During the 1760s, for example, the *Universal Magazine* included articles on the 'Arts and Sciences which may render it useful to Gentry, Merchants, Farmers and Tradesmen', and published a series of accounts of various trades and manufactures, each illustrated with an engraving of working processes. Attitudes towards new materials and innovations would also have been shaped by the activities of the Society of Arts and Manufactures, which offered 'premiums' for technological inventions as well as proficiency in design, a combination paralleled by Wedgwood's activities, and by the public lectures on 'natural philosophy' that were being advertised in the same newspapers as Wedgwood's exhibition.[20] Audiences familiar with technological innovation would therefore have been alert to the technical qualities of the wares that Wedgwood was so keen to stress.

But the individual pieces of the Service, each with its unique scene, were also topographical representations. Contemporary responses to the exhibition suggest that the images were considered as much a cause for wonder and comment as the plates, dishes and tureens themselves. Lady Grey's comment, for example, that the Service made the strongest impression when one looked at it from close quarters rather than from a distance,

implies that what was most important was the detail of the scenes.[21] Painted in a monotone on flat surfaces, surrounded by a frame, the scenes on the plates in particular must have appeared not too dissimilar from framed prints. The relationship between Wedgwood's display and exhibitions of other two-dimensional images served to enhance the status of the Service and Wedgwood's achievement. But there were also of course marked and striking differences. The Frog Service pieces were displayed in such a way as to allude to their function. A further difference emerges if the scenes on the Service are considered as a series, or at least a loose grouping, of topographical images. Topographical prints were certainly grouped together, either in portfolios or in a published form such as Pennant's *Tour in Scotland* (Cat. F20), which was advertised on the same page as Wedgwood's announcement in the *Public Advertiser* of 1 June 1774 of the Frog Service show. The viewing of these prints would, however, have been a private activity and the images looked at by an individual or small group, perhaps in a library. Seen as a series of topographical representations, the scenes on the Frog Service are remarkable in constituting not only an exceptionally large number of images but also in being publicly shown.[22]

Lady Grey's comment that 'The whole together does not make a Shew nor strike you at first with beauty, being only painted with Black Colour heightened with a Purplish Cast, but each Piece is separely extremely pretty & generally very well executed'[23] reinforces the impression that the imagery of the Service meant that the scenes themselves provided the focus of attention for many visitors. What connotations did these subjects have for different groups of viewer, and how might they have been read? As Wedgwood was very aware, many of the nobility and gentry that he was anxious to attract would have had a particular interest in the representations of their own properties or the landscape gardens of their neighbours. Even those gentry and viewers 'of the middling sort' who were not themselves landed owners would presumably have brought to the display a concern with, and certain assumptions about, the estates and topography of their own locality and a set of attitudes towards landscape that had been determined by other forms of representation and interpretation. As Peter de Bolla has suggested, the viewing of landscape gardens was not straightforward but mediated in a variety of ways. [24]

In writings about gardens, the link between the construct of the English landscape garden and notions of English and (sometimes) British national identity was already well-established by the 1770s. It was most explicitly stated in Horace Walpole's statement that the 'English Taste in Gardening is thus the growth of the English Constitution, & must perish with it'.[25] Presented in the form of images on a service destined for a foreign ruler, which were displayed in urban London, these representations of gardens that were in themselves highly artificial constructs of the natural and rural, must have carried a still heavier ideological weight of meaning.[26]

The viewers would also have been conditioned by other well-developed modes of presenting landscapes and country properties.[27] One such mode was the type of topographical print in volumes such as Pennant's (Cat. F20). Another consisted of the guide books issued for individual properties, which during the course of the 18th century were being visited by an increasingly wider public. A third type of presentation took the form of the county histories (Cat. F21), in which houses and parks were described and illustrated alongside accounts of antiquities and family lineages. The viewing of the scenes on the Frog Service was not directly, or simply, connected with the experience of viewing actual gardens but involved the familiarity of Wedgwood's audience with a range of other interpretations of landscape as well as certain expectations about exhibitions and other forms of display.

One advantage of displaying the Frog Service in this way was its association with legitimate classes of high art, which Wedgwood hoped would attract the nobility and gentry he mentioned so often. But there were further potential gains. While the Frog Service's scale, lavishness and inaccessibility (since it was not for sale) meant that it was hardly typical of domestic wares, it was intended to have an appeal for women consumers as a set of objects for use in the dining room. The assumed attraction of ceramics for women was indeed acknowledged by Wedgwood himself when he stated that the exhibition would please the ladies.[28] But, in addition, by decorating it with scenes of British landscapes that had much in common with prints, he was also able to draw in a élite male audience, by appealing to their concern with land and property, their identification with civic humanist values in the public sphere and their activities as collectors of prints and antiquities.

Guided by Bentley's sensitivity to the responses of London viewers, Wedgwood realized the possibilities and problems of exhibiting. While acknowledging that 'Every new show, Exhibition, or variety soon grows stale in London, & is no longer regarded after the first sight, unles utility, or some such variety... continue to recommend it to their notice', he nonetheless took advantage of the increasing enthusiasm for exhibitions and the opportunities they provided for exploiting changing ways of looking and a reformulation of notions of art and the aesthetic.[29] The exhibiting of the Frog Service in London in 1774 was not merely an astute and carefully planned act of marketing. It was also an event that was intricately connected with modes of exhibiting and viewing in the culture of late-18th century London.

Malcolm Baker

CATALOGUE
F
'Business & amusement hand in hand'

When Wedgwood was displaying the Frog Service and other wares in his showrooms during the 1770s and 1780s a wide range of exhibitions were being mounted to attract a rapidly growing public of consumers and viewers. The enthusiasm for such events among the viewing public was already evident in 1770, when Horace Walpole commented that the 'rage to see these exhibitions is so great, that sometimes one cannot pass through the streets where they are'. These exhibitions ranged from the most elevated 'history paintings' shown at the Royal Academy to displays of shellwork or mechanical toys. Although they differed in their nature and the audiences they sought to attract, they all took advantage of that growth in public viewing which was an important aspect of 'polite' culture in late 18th-century London.

F1 Sir Ashton Lever's Museum (Pl. 27)

William Skelton (1763–1849) after Charles Reuben Ryley (1752–98) and Miss Stone
Engraving
Lettered: 'Miss Stone & C. Ryley del' and 'W. Skelton sculp.'
Dated 1789 in manuscript
Platemark: 21.2 × 16 cm

Sir Ashton Lever's Museum, with its displays of stuffed birds and fossils, was characteristic of the more ambitious of late 18th-century displays. Opened in 1774 in Leicester House, it was moved in 1788 to the rotunda at Blackfriars and then dispersed by lottery in 1806. In August 1774 Wedgwood wrote to Bentley: 'Do you hear that Mr. Lever is coming to Town to add another museum to the many already

establish'd there. I had heard of it some days since, but did not believe it till now ... The shew in Town ... is to be at 10/6 per head ... and Mr. Lever expects to clear 6 or £8,000 per Ann^m. by it and to sell the whole when he thinks proper for £30 or £40,000'.

This print of the interior, based on a drawing by Miss Stone (probably an amateur artist) and executed by the same draughtsman and engraver responsible for the admission ticket (Cat. F2), was presumably issued as publicity. It represents the display in the interior of the building at Blackfriars as a place for the elegant and fashionably dressed, who formed the 'polite' audience the organizers were hoping to attract.

Trustees of the British Museum. Banks Collection (C2-645)
Ref: Wedgwood MS E25-18551

F2 Admission ticket to Sir Ashton Lever's Museum, Blackfriars

William Skelton (1763–1849) after Charles Reuben Ryley (1752–98)
Etching and engraving
Lettered with title and 'C. R. Ryley inv.' and 'W. Skelton sculp.'
The mount dated 1788 in manuscript
11.4 × 14 cm

This ticket was probably issued in 1788, since this was the date written alongside it by Sarah Banks, the sister of the naturalist Sir Joseph Banks. It seems, however, to repeat the design used on earlier admission tickets issued before the move from Leicester House.

Trustees of the British Museum. Banks Collection (C2-644)

F3 Broadsheet for an exhibition at Weeks's Museum

Letterpress
The reverse dated 1798 in manuscript
14.7 × 18.5 cm

This broadsheet or handbill advertises the display of a 'Curious and Surprising Mechanism ... . A Tarantula Spider, Made of Steel' at Weeks's Museum, described here as 'similar to that unrivalled and brilliant assemblage exhibited by Mr James Cox in Spring-Gardens 1773'. Wedgwood evidently intended the exhibition of the Frog Service to be regarded in a rather different way from displays of this type, writing to Bentley on 7 December 1772 that the use of handbills 'will sink us exceedingly ... it being a mode of advertisement I never approv'd of'. His promotion of the Frog Service and its display was allied to that of exhibitions of paintings.

Trustees of the British Museum. Banks Collection (C2-694)
Lit and ref: Wedgwood MS E25-18427, see McKendrick 1982 p.24

F4 A Representation of MR. LUNARDI'S BALLOON, as Exhibited in the PANTHEON, 1784

Etching and aquatint
Francis Jukes (1746–1812) and Valentine Green (1739–1813) after Frederick George Byron (1764–92)
Lettered with title, dedication and publication line dated 1785, and 'Drawn by F. G. Byron. The Acquatint by F. Jukes. Engraved by V Green ...'
1785
Cut to 42.7 × 55.3 cm

The exhibition of Lunardi's balloon – held in what Horace Walpole regarded as 'the most beautiful edifice in England'– was one of the most remarkable of such spectacles. Events at the Pantheon, including a display of the 'Decorations used at the Masked Ball at Boodle's', were advertised on the same page of the *Public Advertiser* for 1 June 1774 that carried the announcement of Wedgwood's exhibition of the Frog Service.

Guildhall Library, City of London
Lit: Altick 1978 p.84

F5 *An auction in Mr Christie's rooms*

Thomas Rowlandson (1757–1827)
Pen and ink and watercolour
Probably 1790s
20.5 × 29.1 cm

By the 1770s Christie's auctions were a well-established location for viewing works of art as well as a fashionable place for meeting, as Rowlandson's image makes clear. It was for this reason, as well as the cost of maintaining a London showroom, that Matthew Boulton chose in 1770 not to display his 'gilt and chased vases' in premises of his own – as did Wedgwood – but to exhibit them at Christie's for three days prior to their sale by auction.

Christie, Manson & Woods Ltd.

F6 *The Exhibition of the Royal Academy in the Year 1771*

Richard Earlom (1743–1822) after Michel Vincent (called Charles) Brandoin (1733–1807)
Mezzotint
Lettered with title, publication line dated 20 May 1772 and 'Charles Brandoin invt. ... Richd. Earlom fecit'
1772
46.9 × 55.7 cm

Earlom's print shows the Academy's third exhibition held in Lambe's auction room in Pall Mall, before the move to the newly completed Somerset House in 1780. The exhibition is represented here as full of

F 8

'polite' and fashionably dressed visitors, although some of the more gauche figures refer mockingly to those 'of the middling sort' who were increasingly visiting exhibitions. The display is dominated by the closely packed paintings. Sculptor's models in terracotta and plaster would also have been shown, but many other categories of work – such as models in coloured wax, which may have carried associations with popular exhibitions of waxworks – were excluded; so too were artificial flowers and needlework, partly because these were seen as feminine occupations.

Royal Academy of Arts
Lit: Whitley 1928 I pp. 283–4; Altick 1978 p.103; Penny 1986 pp. 365–6; Solkin 1993 pp. 274–6

F7 Admission ticket to James Cox's Museum

Francesco Bartolozzi (1727–1815) after Biaggio Rebecca (1735–1803)
Engraving
Lettered 'B Rebecca inv. F. Bartolozzi sculp.'
Dated 1772
9.1 × 13.4 cm

Originally a goldsmith, James Cox (active 1749–91/2) opened his Museum of automata,

clocks and 'Pieces of Mechanism and Jewellery' in February 1772 and, partly through his own effective self-advertisement, it became the subject of much comment. Its fame was certainly registered by Wedgwood, who commented to Bentley on 11 April 1772 about 'the almost miraculous magnificence of Mr. Coxes Exhibition'. In 1774 Cox obtained an Act of Parliament to sell the exhibits by lottery, and several catalogues were issued listing as many as 56 items, including the Silver Swan (now in the Bowes Museum) and the Perpetual Motion clock (Cat. F9). The lottery, which finally took place in 1775, was widely advertised in the newspapers, along with the Museum. These advertisements, announcing that the Museum 'will continue to be seen by Candlelight' in the evenings, appear alongside Wedgwood's for the Frog Service in June 1774.

Trustees of the British Museum (1977-U-1067)
Lit and refs: Wedgwood MS E25-18365, see Mallet 1975 p.55; Iveagh Bequest 1985 Cat. E3

F8 Design for a centrepiece with clock with automata

Attributed to the workshop of James Cox (active 1749–91/2)
Pencil and bodycolour
About 1770
44.5 × 28 cm

With its combination of mechanical devices, tiers of fantastic beasts and goldsmith's work, this design is characteristic of the more elaborate works shown in Cox's Museum (Cat. F7). The attribution of the drawing to Cox here is based on close similarities to the descriptions of the exhibits given in the several editions of the Museum's catalogue, and to the design of a number of mounted hardstone boxes supported by bulls, made in Cox's style, which were sold from the Strogonoff Collection in 1931.

Victoria & Albert Museum (E.3985-1906)
Ref: compare Grigorii Stroganoff Collection, Lepke's, Berlin, 12–13 May 1931

F 10

F10 Presentation design for the 'King's vases'

John Yenn (1750–1821) after Sir William Chambers, RA (1723–96)
Pen and ink and wash
About 1770
43.7 × 33 cm

This highly finished drawing by an assistant to Sir William Chambers shows one of the 'King's Vases', made for George III by Matthew Boulton in 1771 after designs by Chambers, and preserved today at Windsor Castle. Possibly the drawing was among the 'Various Vases, &c to be executed in ormolu, by Mr Bolton, for their Majesties' which were exhibited by Chambers at the Royal Academy in 1770. The Academy's annual exhibition consisted largely of painting and sculpture, the most prominent place being given to 'history paintings' such as Benjamin West's *Death of General Wolfe* (Cat. F11), these being considered the most important in the hierarchy of genres. On occasion, however, architects such as Chambers, one of the Academy's founding members, exhibited designs for decorative works.

In the same year that these vases were begun, Boulton was himself considering opening a showroom in James and Robert Adam's Adelphi development for the display of his ormolu and ornamental goods to the nobility. In the event, he chose instead to sell his ormolu and vases by auctions at Christie & Ansell's.

Victoria & Albert Museum. C. J. Richardson Collection (3436-408)
Lit: Clifford 1974 p. 765 and fig. 68; Goodison 1974 pp. 158–61

F9 *Mr Cox's Perpetual Motion ... (Pl. 30)*

J. Lodge, probably John Lodge (d. 1796)
Engraving, pasted into the 1772 edition of 'A Descriptive Catalogue of the Several Superb and Magnificent Pieces of Mechanism and Jewellery, Exhibited in the Museum at Spring-Gardens, Charing Cross'
Lettered with title and 'J. Lodge sculp.'
Dated (on the verso) 1774
Sheet size: 22 × 14.5 cm

This clock, now in the Victoria and Albert Museum's collection, was exhibited in James Cox's Museum in 1774. The print, which describes it as 'A Prize in the Museum Lottery', was probably published as part of Cox's advertising campaign.

Victoria & Albert Museum. National Art Library (208.H.7)

F11 *The Death of General Wolfe*

William Woollett (1735–85) after Benjamin West, PRA (1738–1820); published by Wollett, Boydell and Ryland
Engraving and etching
Lettered: 'Engraved by Wᵐ. Woollett.', 'Painted by B. West' and with title and publication line dated 1776
Cut to 47 × 61 cm

West's painting was exhibited at the Royal Academy in 1771, where it attracted huge attention and was perhaps the most viewed contemporary painting. Boydell took advantage of the sensation created by the exhibition by employing Woollett to engrave this print, which enjoyed great popularity, thereby earning the publisher £15,000. When Boydell launched a subscription for this print, and that by John Hall after West's painting of *William Penn's Treaty with the Indians*, he exhibited smaller versions of both paintings at his shop at 90, Cheapside.

Victoria & Albert Museum (27189)
Lit: Alexander and Godfrey 1980 pp. 33–4; Solkin 1993 pp. 209–12

F 12

F12 Shepherdess and country boy

Attributed to William Collins (1721–93)
Relief in white and coloured marbles
Probably about 1761
41 × 64 cm

This may be the relief 'for a chimney-piece; a clown and country girl' exhibited by Collins at the annual exhibition of the Society of Artists at Spring Gardens in 1761 (no. 144). Comparable works were shown in the Society's 1774 exhibition, which was advertised alongside Wedgwood's announcement of the display of the Frog Service in the *Gazetteer and New Daily Advertiser* (6 June 1774). Collins worked for Henry Cheere, whose workshop produced elaborate chimneypieces in different coloured marbles, each with a central tablet of this sort. According to J. T. Smith, Collins was 'the most famous modeller of his day', executing 'pastoral scenes which were understood by the most common observer'.

Although made to form part of the decorative ensemble of a chimneypiece, a relief such as this could also be shown separately within the context of an exhibition. As with Wedgwood's vases, this context allowed a new status to be given to works otherwise regarded as 'useful' and decorative. In introducing two-colour

Jasper tablets and plaques, which were intended to be used in fireplaces and interior decoration, Wedgwood was undoubtedly attempting to break into a market previously dominated by sculptors and masons, such as Cheere and Collins, who carved low reliefs like this one in white marble set against coloured grounds.

Victoria & Albert Museum (1152-1882)
Lit: Smith 1828 II p. 313; Victoria & Albert Museum 1984 Cat. S49.

F13 Rural scene

Probably by Thomas Jervais (active 1760–99) or James Pearson (active 1739/40–1837)
Stained and painted glass
About 1770–80
34.3 × 28.3 cm

Panels such as this would have been among the stained glass shown by Jervais in a series of exhibitions in the 1770s. An advertisement placed adjacent to Wedgwood's for the Frog Service exhibition in the *Gazetteer and New Daily Advertiser* for 6 June 1774 announced 'to the curious' that 'Mr. Jervais's Exhibition of Stained Glass (which is entirely new)' was open 'at Mr Pinchbeck's Repository in Cockspur Street'. In addition to copies after

Netherlandish paintings or prints (such as this), the 'pictures' shown included many 'done from original drawings, designed for this purpose' and imitating the effects of sunshine, moonlight, firelight and candlelight. Admission cost 1s (apparently without tickets) and also allowed visitors to see Pinchbeck's 'mechanical exhibition'.

Victoria & Albert Museum (C.108-1978)

F14 Vase of flowers

Mrs Beal Bonnell
Shellwork
1779–81; the glass dome added in 1841
Height: 70 cm

The use of natural materials to represent scenes, figure subjects or other natural forms was a common feature of late 18th-century exhibitions. Shellwork, representing different marine creatures 'from the Prawn to the Porpoise', was shown by Mrs Dard, and an admission ticket to her exhibition in the Sarah Banks Collection at the British Museum (Pl. 28). Such work was intended to intrigue and astonish the viewer through the virtuoso technique employed as well as the simulation of one material by another. According to the entry for 23 February 1781 in the Journal of Miss Harvey Bonnell,

F 15

this vase of shell flowers was made over two years by Mrs Beal Bonnell of Old Windsor and retained by her family; it closely resembles shellwork shown in contemporary exhibitions.

Victoria & Albert Museum. Gift of Mrs Mavis Hudson (W.70-1981)

F15 Trade card of Duesbury & Co.

Engraving, hand-coloured
About 1774
9.5 × 14 cm

As 'Manufacturers of Derby and Chelsea Porcelain', Duesbury & Co. continued the established practice of the porcelain factories in seeking their customers among the nobility and gentry. The company's trade card, decorated with examples of their wares – including a number of elaborate vases and tripods – announced their newly opened 'large & elegant suite of Rooms' at 8 Bedford Street, Covent Garden. Here they exhibited a 'great Variety of Capital as well as Useful and Ornamental Articles ... Biscuit Groups

[and] Derbyshire Fluors'. The issue of this trade card was accompanied in June 1774 by a series of advertisements for this 'commodious and new Warehouse' in the *Gazetteer and New Daily Advertiser* and the *Morning Post*. Wedgwood's new showroom in Portland House was in direct competition with that of Duesbury (see also Cat. D36–42).

Victoria & Albert Museum (E.1638-1907)

F16 The exterior of Portland House, Greek Street, in 1799

Charles Tomkins (b. about 1750)
Pen and ink and watercolour
Signed and dated 'C. Tomkins 1799', the reverse also inscribed 'Wedgwood's House Greek Street Soho' and erroneously dated 1797
1799
19.8 × 21.2 cm

Wedgwood signed the lease for Portland House, Greek Street, on 16 June 1774, two weeks after having first announced the exhibition of the Frog Service in these

rooms. According to Mrs Delany, the exhibition consisted of: 'three rooms below and two above filled with it, laid out on tables ...'. In accordance with his strategy of limiting admission to those with tickets, the pieces displayed would not have been visible from the street, Wedgwood no doubt agreeing with Boulton that there should not be 'a shew to the street for the nobility are more at their ease in a private shop'. From as early as 1770, Wedgwood was well aware of the value of exhibiting his most prestigious commissions; on 23 April of that year he wrote to Bentley about the Husk Service, also made for Catherine the Great, commenting that the 'idea of shewing, & making the most of this service at <u>home</u> as well as <u>abroad</u> appears to me of more consequence every time I think of it'. Nothing further is known of these plans.

William Drummond
Lit and refs: Mary Granville, Mrs Delany Autobiography and Correspondence, *see Reilly 1989 I p. 281; Boulton MSS see Goodison 1974 p. 93; Wedgwood MS E25-18295, see Reilly 1992 p. 104; Wedgwood 1984 p. ii*

F17 Copper plate for printing admission tickets for Wedgwood's exhibition of his copy of the Portland Vase

Engraving and aquatint
Lettered: 'Admission to see Mr Wedgwood's Copy of THE PORTLAND VASE, Greek Street, Soho, between 12 o'Clock and 5'; the reverse stamped: 'IONES PONTIFEX No4Y SHOE LANE LONDON'
1790
9 × 6.5 cm

Following the private views of the copy of the Portland Vase, Wedgwood showed it to a wider public in his showroom. Admission was still restricted, however, to those who had obtained tickets. A total of 1,900 admission tickets was printed.

Trustees of the Wedgwood Museum, Barlaston, Staffordshire (No.1354)

F 18

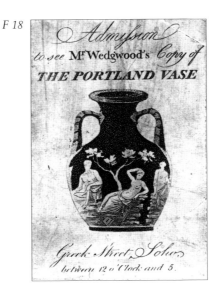

F 19

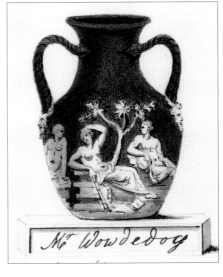

F18 *Catalogue of Cameos, Intaglios, Medals, Bas-reliefs ... By Josiah Wedgwood, F.R.S., and A.S.*

1787
21 × 13.3 cm

Bound into the catalogue is one of the original invitation tickets to see Wedgwood's Portland Vase.

Victoria & Albert Museum. National Art Library (96.M.23)

F19 Three imitation admission tickets with different views of the Portland Vase

Attributed to Sarah Banks (1744–1818)
Watercolour, bodycolour and pencil
About 1790
12.1 × 7.9; 12.3 × 7.9; 7.9 × 12 cm

Each of the cards is illustrated with a different view of the Portland Vase, consisting of the two sides and the disc with the head of Paris. Below each view is a name-plate inscribed with a different humorous anagram of Wedgwood's name. They are mounted in one of Sarah Banks's folders containing exhibition tickets and invitations, together with a copy of Wedgwood's pamphlet on the imagery of the vase. Evidently parodies of invitation cards or admission tickets, it is likely that they were produced around 1790, probably by Sarah Banks herself, when Wedgwood showed his first perfect copy of the Portland Vase to a 'numerous company' at Sir Joseph Banks's house in Soho Square.

Trustees of the British Museum. Banks Collection (C.688, 689, 690)

F20 *A Tour in Scotland, and Voyage to the Hebrides MDCCLXIX*

Thomas Pennant (1726–98)
1774 edition (first edition 1771)
23.3 × 37.5 (open)

The images on the Frog Service were viewed by a public familiar with them through both descriptions and illustrations in topographical works such as Pennant's

Tour or the county histories being produced at this date (Cat. F21). The way in which the scenes on the Service were viewed was conditioned not only by the experience of visiting exhibitions of various types, but also by the practice of looking at the representations in these publications. This edition of Pennant's *Tour* was advertised on the same page of the *Public Advertiser* for 1 June 1774 as the exhibition of the Frog Service and so was available to the same audience. It contains a number of views not included in the first edition; some of these also appear on the Frog Service, Pennant having instructed his printer to lend Thomas Bentley all the engravings not yet published (see Cat. G237 and D4).

Victoria & Albert Museum. National Art Library (264.B)

F21 *A New History of Gloucestershire, comprising the Topography, Antiquities, Curiosities, Produce, trade & Manufactures*

Samuel Rudder (d. 1801)
1779
43 × 60.5 cm (open)

Rudder's work is characteristic of a number of county histories published in the late 18th century, many of them with illustrations of country houses as well as antiquities. The engraving of Battesford Park displayed here is juxtaposed with a text that not only describes the house but

gives an account of the family's lineage. For at least some of the visitors to Wedgwood's showroom, the meanings of the scenes on the Frog Service would have been informed by a familiarity with such a set of connections and ideas.

Victoria & Albert Museum. National Art Library (51.D.17)

F22 *A New Description of the Pictures, Statues, Bustos, Basso-Relievos and other Curiosities at the Earl of Pembroke's House at Wilton*

James Kennedy
1758
19.2 × 25.4 cm (open)

During the second half of 18th century increasing numbers of houses could be viewed by members of a 'polite' public who were not known personally by the owner. Tickets were issued for such visitors and guide books such as this were produced for their use. Many of the visitors looking at the scenes on the Frog Service may have visited such properties in this way, and their viewing of these representations would have been informed by the experience of seeing actual houses under these conditions, with certain features brought to their attention through the language and arrangement of the guide book.

Victoria & Albert Museum. National Art Library (255.D)

THE FROG SERVICE
AND ITS SOURCES

In March 1773 Josiah Wedgwood and Thomas Bentley were approached by Alexander Baxter with a commission from Catherine the Great of Russia. Baxter was a member of the Russia Company and an accredited agent of the Russian government in Britain, who had officially been appointed consul on 19 January that year.[1] Wedgwood & Bentley had been trading with Russia since 1769, marketing vases through the British Embassy in St Petersburg (helped by Lady Cathcart, wife of the British Ambassador and sister of Sir William Hamilton), and they had supplied an enamelled service for 24 people to the Empress (the Husk Service, see Cat. D59–60) in 1770.[2] But this new commission was of a quite different order: they were asked to supply a dinner and dessert service for 50 people, all the pieces decorated with views of Britain. For Catherine, the Frog Service, as it has become known, offered an opportunity to advertise her enthusiasm and friendship towards a nation which, in its own view and that of many admirers abroad, had achieved a position of political, economic and industrial pre-eminence thanks to its enlightened constitution and to the natural vigour and industry of its inhabitants, uncorrupted by the indulgence of an all-powerful court and idle aristocracy. The very fact that an imperial service was to be made in pottery, rather than porcelain, decorated in virtual monochrome, with no gilding, itself suggested a deliberate antithesis to luxury. Furthermore, as will be demonstrated, the Gothic style carried connotations of uncorrupted strength and virtue, while the English landscape garden had become

Pl. 31 (Cat. G39, 40, 41, 38) Items from the Service decorated with views taken from Thomas Robins' engraving of King Alfred's Hall (Cat. G37).

a celebrated emblem of liberty. As an enlightened monarch, Catherine wanted to demonstrate her sympathy with these ideals.

Although they had considerable concerns about the commission, Wedgwood and Bentley decided to undertake it. There are no surviving documents to show just what instructions came from the Empress, but Wedgwood's first letters to Bentley indicate that the principal characteristics of the Service as executed were stipulated from the start. On 23 March 1773 he wrote:

> a few words ... about this s^d. service for my Great Patroness in the North, which the Consul has been so obliging to bring me. ...
>
> I suppose it must be painted upon the Royal pattern & that there must be a border upon the rims of the dishes & plates &c of some kind & the buildings &c in the middle only. The Child & Frog, if they are to be all in the same attitude, may perhaps be printed.
>
> I have no idea of this service being got up in less that two or three years if the Landskips & buildings are to be tolerably done, so as to do any credit to us, & to be copied from painters of real buildings & situations – nor of its being afforded for less than £1000, or £1500. – Why all the Gardens in England will scarcely furnish subjects sufficient for this sett, <u>every piece having a different subject</u>.[3]

A week later (29 March) he talked of a price of £1500 or £2000 and asked:

> Do you think the subjects must all be from <u>real views, & real Buildings</u>, & that it is expected from us to send draftsmen all over the Kingdom to take these views – if so, what time or what money? wo^d. be sufficient to perform the one, or pay for the other. –
>
> As to our being confin'd to Gothique Buildings only, why there are not enough I am perswaded in Great Britain to furnish subjects for this service.[4]

In his first letter he had suggested that his partner should discuss the price with Baxter, and it appears that from the very first this was Thomas Bentley's project. He ran the Decorating Studio in Chelsea with David Rhodes as his chief enameller, procured most of the pictures on which his artists based their decorations and handled negotiations with the Consul. He was surely well aware of the numerous views that were available on the London print market, and by the beginning of April he had already started his painters on trials.[5] It is clear from Wedgwood's letters that the principal subjects depicted on the Service were to be landscape gardens and Gothic (i.e. ancient) buildings, that they were to be painted on 'Queen's Ware' with decorative borders and that there was to be a device incorporating a frog (the accompanying child was left off) – this green frog was a reference to the palace for which the service was destined, located at Kekerekeksinen, a name meaning (in Finnish) the 'frog marsh'. He does not mention the colour for the main decoration, but a visitor who saw the Service displayed in Wedgwood's London showroom at Portland House before it was sent to Russia described it as 'Black ... heightend with a Purplish Cast'. She also reported what Wedgwood or Bentley had no doubt told her: 'The Empress's directions were all from herself. She chose the Colours, orderd the views to be confin'd to this Island, & to contain all that could be of Gothic Remains, of Natural Views, & of Improved Scenes and Ornaments in Parks & Gardens Which they say are what she wants to collect & Imitate.'[6]

If all of this was clear from the start, the cost still had to be estimated and a price agreed – and Alexander Baxter was not at first expecting the price to be more than £400–500.[7] Work stopped at the end of May, and not until the end of July did approval come through. On the 30th Wedgwood thanked Bentley for 'the good account from St. Petersburg. The Empress has again prov'd her self to be what we had before all the reason in the world to believe she was – A Woman of sense – fine taste, & spirit.' He continued:

> The Consul should not talk of <u>doing them as much lower as we can</u> – If his Mistress heard him she wo^d rap

his knuckles – we could do them as much lower as he pleases but to do them in the manner the Empress wishes to see them; & as we (I mean the Consul & all of us) may recieve due honor for the execution of the noblest plan ever yet laid down, or undertaken by any Manufactures in Great Britain – The price agreed upon is cheap beyond comparison with anything I know, & you will I make no doubt of it convince the Consul of it in due time.[8]

No delivery date is mentioned in the correspondence, but Josiah was understandably worried about the stability of Catherine's position and the possibility of undertaking the commission and not being paid. Whether the Empress or the partners set the delivery date, it is clear from the way work proceeded that they planned to finish it by the following summer. The first task was to find sufficient sources for the decorators to copy, and this was something they had already looked into quite carefully. One of Josiah's first suggestions had been that they should perhaps find some way of printing on the ware from existing plates: 'if you could get the old plates, or the use of them for an impression from each of Stow Gardens &c something clever might perhaps be done at a tolerable expence.'[9] He seems to have discussed this early in April with Guy Green in Liverpool, who did much of their transfer-printing and even suggested that if Baxter paid for new plates (which they would be able to re-use) they would not charge for the enamelling of the views,[10] but this proposal was patently impractical. Next he looked into the possibility of all the views being drawn from scratch. On his return from Liverpool he went to see an artist friend in Knutsford, Samuel Stringer (1750–84),[11] to discuss having the views (which he estimated to amount to 2,000) drawn specially for the Service. 'He said it was a very arduous undertaking, & must be a most expensive one if we did tolerable justice to the designs. – That there were very few Men in England clever at painting Buildings, & on asking his opinion about the expence of painting each View upon our Ware, he said it would be necessary to have each view sketched out from any that were now published, by some good draftsman in order to adapt it to the piece, to take and leave with skill & judgment &c. & that this wo^d. deserve half a Guinea for each design. The painting it upon the ware perhaps as much more … at a rough guess he supposed it could not be done for less than 3 or £4000 nor in less time than 3 or 4 years.'[12]

This was out of the question, but once final agreement from the Empress had been received, Wedgwood came back to Stringer. In his letter of 30 July he said he would go ahead and 'have some real views taken', and two weeks later he asked whether Stringer should be engaged for a few months 'to paint & instruct our hands in London. Upon this plan I would bring him up to London, – have a Camera Obscura with us, & take 100 views upon the road.'[13] Bentley rejected Josiah's suggestion, for with David Rhodes in charge at the Decorating Studio in Chelsea they had no need of Stringer's instruction. As for views, there was a wealth of material in printed sources for the decorators to start from: for 'antiquities', there were the collections of prints issued each year from 1726 to 1742, county by county, by Samuel and Nathaniel Buck; for 'improved landscapes', there were several collections of prints and individual engravings issued since the 1750s that depicted some of the most celebrated landscape gardens; while for 'natural landscapes', there were the views of the Peak District and Yorkshire by Thomas Smith of Derby.

Buck's Antiquities (Cat. G1), which contained views of over four hundred buildings, mostly castles and abbeys, was the source on which Bentley's painters made their start, and work began with a run of some 80 flat plates copied from these engravings. Samuel Buck had begun

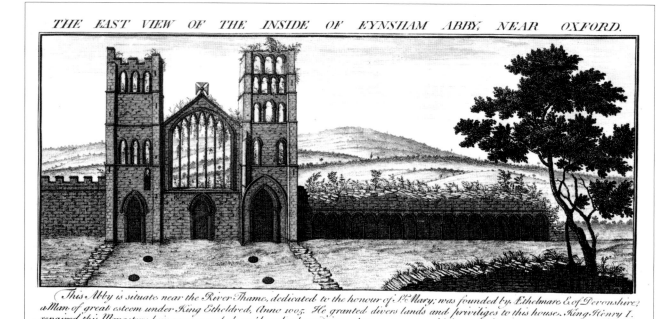

Pl. 32 (Cat. G1) 'The East View of...Eynsham Abby', from 'Buck's Antiquities', 1730.

the enterprise on his own, as draughtsman and engraver, and the first issue of 24 prints, published in 1726, was devoted to Yorkshire. Two years later Samuel was joined by his younger brother, Nathaniel, and they shared the work, each generally engraving the other's drawings.[14] The Bucks' views were a little old-fashioned in style, especially those done in the early years of the project, but they had moved on from the formalized convention that had been current in late 17th-century works such as *Britannia Illustrata* (by Johannes Kip and Leonard Knyff), where a bird's-eye view was generally chosen for the building that formed the principal subject, while a lower point of view was chosen for its surroundings. However, the Bucks usually emphasized the contrast between the main subject in the foreground and the distant landscape, with no intervening middle ground.

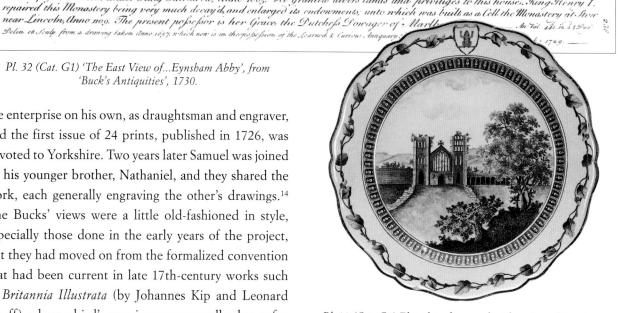

Pl. 33 (Cat. G2) Flat plate decorated with a view of Eynsham Abbey, Oxon.

No special policy seems to have governed Bentley's choice of the prints to be copied, although they are fairly evenly divided between the different issues,[15] and the Bucks' views continued to be used right up to the final

stages of the decoration of the Service. Even small details from the distant landscapes would be copied on
small items, such as the bowls of spoons, but the Bucks'
superb panoramas of towns, drawn on the same expedi-
tions as the *Antiquities* and issued year by year, were
never used, although they are crammed with suitable
details. Towns, like modern buildings, clearly did not fall
within the Empress's terms of reference.

Gardens, as can be seen from the first of Wedgwood's
letters already quoted, were Catherine the Great's
especial interest. The earliest first-hand reports she had
received of English landscape gardens were no doubt
from Stanislas Poniatowski, with whom she had a passionate love affair in 1755–8. The year before coming to
Russia, in the entourage of the new British ambassador,
Sir Charles Hanbury Williams, Stanislas had visited

England, and in the memoirs he composed much later
he recalled visiting Prior Park near Bath, Wilton, Oxford
and 'Stone-Hinge' as well as Lord Temple's estate at
Stowe, the most celebrated of all the English gardens. He
wrote that Stowe was 'regarded with veneration, since it
was the cradle of the new style, which had no use for
"jardins symétrisés".... This new style, which consists
mainly in producing artificial landscapes in the places
one wishes to embellish, had become a kind of new cult,
with almost all the concomitant fanaticism and intoler-
ant antipathy towards old beliefs.'[16]

More recently, in June 1772, Catherine had written to
Voltaire, telling him: 'I love English gardens to the point
of folly: serpentine lines, gentle slopes, marshes turned
into lakes, islands of dry ground, and I deeply despise
straight lines. I hate fountains which torture water to

Pl. 34 (Cat. G126) Oval dish decorated with a view of Stowe, Bucks.

make it take a course contrary to nature; in a word, my plantomania is dominated by anglomania.'[17] She had also taken some practical measures to introduce the English style of garden design in Russia. She had hired a number of English gardeners and was eager for reports of English gardens from Russian visitors to the country. In 1771 she sent Vasily Ivanovich Neelov, who had worked in the gardens at Tsarskoe Selo since 1744, on an expedition to look at English gardens with his son,[18] and on his return the following year he apparently brought back a number of prints, including views of Stowe, Kew, Studley Royal and Wilton.[19]

The first batch of prints of gardens that Bentley used included groups by William Woollett (1735–85) and Luke Sullivan (1705–71) done around 1760 that had been reprinted by Robert Sayer and other leading printsellers and sold as 'Fine prints in sets': 'Six *Delightful Views* of elegant *Gardens*, drawn from nature, and engraved by W. Woollett ...' etc.[20] The gardens depicted included Wilton, but were otherwise mainly close to London – among them West Wycombe and Cliveden in Buckinghamshire, Painshill, Esher Place and Woburn Farm in Surrey (Cat. G97–116), gardens that received many visitors who might be expected to buy the prints. Some views of Twickenham were also acquired as models for the decorators, and one curiosity, an engraving by Thomas Robins (1716–70) of the first sham Gothic ruin in England, 'King Alfred's Hall' in Cirencester Park (Cat. G37). They also worked from the set of prints of Windsor Park engraved after drawings by Thomas Sandby (1723–98; see Cat. G93–96), and from the book Sir William Chambers had published of the garden buildings in Classical, Chinese and Moorish styles that he had designed for the royal gardens at Kew (a copy of which the Empress had ordered through her ambassador in London;[21] see Cat. G42–57).

Before embarking on the celebrated gardens at Stowe,

Bentley inserted a whole group of views by Thomas Smith (d. 1767), a painter from Derby who undertook estate views, but who had also done some remarkable prints of wild picturesque landscapes, especially in the Derbyshire Peak. Many of his prints had first been issued in the 1740s, but the enterprising publisher John Boydell appears to have acquired his plates and reissued them; and they remained in his catalogue for another 30 years. It is not quite clear whether these landscapes really conformed to the Empress's instructions. Later on, when Wedgwood located a set of the six Welsh views by Richard Wilson that had as yet been published only on subscription, he questioned whether they could be included: 'most of them being <u>mere Landskips</u>, without any the least <u>Pleasure ground</u> I am afraid they are not proper for you.'[22] However, Bentley had no hesitation about Smith (nor, later, about Wilson), and some 65 views, including those on some of the most magnificent dishes in the whole Service, are based on just over 30 of Thomas Smith's engravings. It is quite possible these were prints that Bentley already owned, as he was, too, a native of Derbyshire, and the finest series of Thomas Smith's engravings was devoted to Dovedale, the district where Bentley had been born. In the catalogue he later prepared for the Service, Bentley's descriptions are usually brief and factual, but when it comes to the views of his home county they become quite lyrical: 'View of the upper part of Dove-Dale; This is one of the most charming and romantic of valleys, in the midst of which runs a fairly rapid river, which meanders for several miles, between the slopes which form this valley' (see Cat. G59–62).

Among Smith's prints were two devoted to Colebrookdale (see Cat. G82), and throughout the Frog Service there is a small but highly significant sub-category of landscape views devoted to industrial sites. These would certainly have had a special appeal to Wedgwood and

Bentley, but they were quite right in assuming they would also interest the Empress. One of Alexander Baxter's principal functions had been to try and recruit English technicians who were willing to go to Russia – falling foul of the British government, who thoroughly disapproved of such activities – and he was also responsible for the Empress's purchase in 1774 of Joseph Wright's painting of *An Iron Forge, Viewed from Without* for 150 guineas.

Now, having decorated around 180 plates and dishes, the painters turned to Stowe. More than one set of prints of the gardens had been published, but the most up-to-date was the collection of 16 engravings by George Bickham junior (d. about 1769) after drawings made by Jean-Baptiste Claude Chatelain (1710–71) in 1752 and published the following year by Bickham's father, George senior (Cat. G117). They show the gardens much as they would have looked when Stanislas Poniatowski visited them and tactlessly regretted the lack of any alignment in the canals or avenues. Every one of the Chatelain prints was copied for the Service, and details from many of them – especially the temples and other garden buildings – eventually appeared again and again on the sides of sauce tureens or on the ends of covers for tureens and dishes.[23]

But as yet the decorators confined their work to flat plates, soup plates and oval and round serving dishes, making use of the sources already described and a few others they were able to obtain through the print shops. One of the most interesting artists, although only a few views on the Service are actually based on his paintings, was George Lambert (1700–65), the chief scene-painter at Covent Garden. Working together with Samuel Scott (1710–72), he had done a series of views of the gardens at Mount Edgcumbe, overlooking the Plymouth dockyards (Cat. G135–7), which had been engraved in 1755, but his most interesting views are of three castles, Saltwood (Cat. G86) and Dover in Kent and Longford (Cat. G87) in Wiltshire (the last of which was only privately engraved). These are far more sophisticated than the Bucks' views, and the paintings themselves show a sense of composing the landscape similar to that of contemporary garden designers. It is no coincidence that many painters of 'real views', including of course Canaletto, were by training theatrical scene-painters – for the garden was in every sense a living theatre, creating an idealized illusion of the real world in order to simulate Arcadia and convey its moral message.

An outlay of some 20 guineas gave Bentley plenty of material to work from, but with so many views needing to be painted – well over one thousand – the decorators made the most of what was available. Frequently the left half of a print would be copied on one plate, the right half on another, while the whole view was used on an oval dish. Most of the figures in original prints were omitted, and trees and other incidental features (boats etc.) were often transferred or altered to balance the composition. The results were not always successful, and when the final selection of pieces for the Service was made, a few of these early plates were omitted. Other pieces were set aside when there were imperfections in the firing.[24]

Nevertheless, there were limitations to the material that was readily available: the Bucks' views were rather old-fashioned in style, while the choice of garden prints was limited to no more than 20 places. Furthermore, as was to be expected of a form of art which was so fashionable, styles in garden design were changing rapidly. The profusion of allegorical buildings that had characterized Stowe or Kew in the 1750s and early 1760s was giving way to a taste for more natural effects, whether on the intimate scale of the poet William Shenstone's garden at the Leasowes, near Birmingham, or in the grander plans of Lancelot Brown, who had been head gardener at Stowe throughout the 1740s and whose hand was by now evident in 40 or 50 other gardens where he had been called in as designer. There were virtually no prints of

Pl. 35 (Cat. G84) Flat plate decorated with a view of Colebrookdale, Salop.

these new gardens, although Sayer and Boydell thought it worthwhile reissuing the older views, and Wedgwood pursued the idea he had originally had of having drawings specially made. He even considered applying to Brown himself, who 'could pro'cure us a great number of designs, tell us who had had the views of their pleasure grounds taken, & might lend us a hand to take others, or perhaps do more, & we must pay him by inserting his name to the seats he has imbelish'd, in our index'.[25]

The most important thing, as far as Wedgwood was concerned, was to get views of the estates of his influential Staffordshire neighbours that could be used on the Service. Undertaking to produce and decorate the Service for the Empress was obviously quite a serious commercial risk: there was going to be very little margin of profit, and there was a real danger that they would never receive payment. It was therefore important to make the most of all the opportunities for using the Russian commission to strengthen contacts among people of influence at home.

Since his suggestion of sending Samuel Stringer to London had not been taken up, in August 1773 Wedgwood began making arrangements for Stringer to visit estates in the neighbourhood of Etruria, to make drawings that could be copied by Bentley's artists in London. He himself accompanied Stringer on some of his journeys, most of which were done in the autumn of that year. On 4 November he wrote to Bentley that 'for some time past young Stringer has taken up a good deal of my time' and that he expected to be with him for another ten days or a fortnight, 'it being abo[t]. two days work to fix upon a situation, take a rough sketch, & copy & finish another from that, which is the course he takes.'[26] Bentley was impatient for more material and ten days later Wedgwood wrote: 'You say in yours of the 8th. that you shall finish the Russ[n]. service with such things as you have if we do not send you some views immediately. I am afraid you are not in much danger of doing so …' He continued: 'We could not send you the views we have taken, for the Gent[n]. here will see, not only the views of their own seats, but their neighbours likewise, to compare them together, so that we must finish our Staffordshire views, at least those about us, before we can send you any of them. The Gent[n]. seem highly pleas'd with the compliments, as they are pleas'd to say I am paying them, & from what I percieve in the little we have done, I could make it worth my while to pursue the same plan all over the Kingdom, & I believe that of any Painters to accompany me.'[27] Wedgwood was disappointed that Stringer failed to capitalize on the opportunities the project offered him, 'but he is a sad, untutor'd raw young fellow'.[28]

One of the local magnates, Lord Stamford of Enville, suggested that, rather than have Stringer draw new views, Wedgwood should use the drawings that had already been done of his estates. These views of Enville and of Lord Stamford's old family estates at Bradgate in Leicestershire had been made, probably quite recently, by Anthony Devis (1729–1816), a younger half-brother of the portrait painter Arthur Devis. Although none of the original drawings used for the Service has come to light, another drawing of Enville (see Cat. G170) by Devis shows a delicacy and sensitivity that is of a completely different order to the rather clumsy drawings of Stringer's or to the much more sharply defined and stylized engravings of Woollett and Sullivan. The studio in Chelsea responded to these drawings in a remarkable way – the artist responsible was almost certainly James Bakewell – and Devis's qualities are reflected in the far more subtle handling of the enamels, with a range of tones and textures that are hardly ever seen in the views based on engravings or on less accomplished drawings. Lord Stamford suggested that Wedgwood might be able to borrow other drawings from Devis, but he appears not to have been able to do so.[29]

A decision had been made right at the start that the pieces should not bear a caption, but they were num-bered on the back, so that they could be identified in the catalogue that it was planned should accompany them. Rather than all the numbers being allocated in advance, the pieces were numbered as they were decorated, so that the numbers are a fairly accurate guide to the sequence in which individual pieces were done, although the situation is complicated by the fact that numbers were sometimes reallocated when pieces were set aside for technical reasons.[30] By matching references in letters and documents – even the publication dates of prints[31] – to the numbered sequence of pieces, it is possible to determine what progress had been made by particular dates. For example, the first item decorated from one of Devis's drawings is an 11-inch oval dish numbered 312, which comes at the start of a batch of dishes decorated from drawings by Devis and by Stringer – also the first use made of the work of Josiah's protégé. Wedgwood's letter to Bentley telling him about the Devis drawings is dated 22 November, so that work from the drawings

Pl. 36 (Cat. G154) Round cover decorated with a view of Tabley, Cheshire.

must have started around the beginning of December. This date would make sense for the first Stringer drawings too, which included drawings of Trentham and Keele in Staffordshire and some drawings of estates in his native Cheshire done a few years earlier – at Tabley, Booth Hall and Tatton Park.

Progress so far had been fairly slow: some 240 of the required 288 dinner plates had been decorated,[32] but apart from these, apparently, only about 20 soup plates and 30 serving dishes. While the work-rate in the Decorating Shop needed to be improved considerably if the Service was to be completed by mid-1774, Bentley also needed to find new sources of illustrations. On 19 January a batch of prints was bought – '8 Views of Lakes 2 of Chatsworth and London Hospital', all reissues of engravings first published in 1761 or earlier, and on 2 February there is a record of a payment to the publisher Samuel Hooper for the first 25 issues of a new series of prints of antiquities by Francis Grose.[33] Grose (1731–91) was a huge, genial character, the son of a jeweller from Bern, a captain in the militia and an indefatigable traveller. He not only compiled all the texts on the buildings included in his volumes, but he himself had made the vast majority of original drawings on which the prints of them were based, travelling through England and Wales for this purpose from the late 1750s. Furthermore, he made watercolour copies of all the original drawings to the size they were to be engraved.[34] The style is much more up-to-date than the Bucks' views, less schematic and more natural, owing much to the example of Paul Sandby (1731–1809), whom Grose knew well and who provided a number of drawings (chiefly in Yorkshire and Wales) for reproduction. Sandby, in a development that again mirrors trends in garden design, was one of a group of English draughtsmen who rendered scenes in a way that was far less deliberately composed – more 'natural'. Although many of the subjects that had been engraved

for *Buck's Antiquities* also appeared in Grose's work, there were many that did not, and these new prints meant that in this field at least there was no shortage of material. However, the choice of subjects to copy seems again to have been quite arbitrary: there are new views of some of the buildings that had already been copied from the Bucks as well as ones they had not included, and their prints continued to be used as a source alongside Grose's. As his work was still in progress during 1774, it is evident that Grose allowed Bentley to borrow some of the drawings he had made for the engravers (or possibly the original drawings) before the prints were made (see Cat. G188–9).

Another new source, details from which were well suited to the small spaces on the sides of sauce tureens, was the collection of engravings of villages around London by Chatelain (see Cat. G211–19) – one set, first published in 1745, of Hampstead and Highgate, another, published in 1750, of views on the Thames. However, for the most part, as the decorators began to work on the hollowware, they simply reused details from the prints they had already copied on to the plates and dishes. But when these were painted on the convex surfaces they were treated with greater freedom, and there were also several different hands at work, so that there is no sense of repetitiveness in the decoration.

From December to February, around 300 more pieces must have been decorated (with some 450 views), leaving 80–90 more pieces of the dinner service to be done. During February Bentley also engaged William Shuter (active 1771–9), an established painter who exhibited at the Society of Artists, probably to provide some examples for the other enamellers to follow, particularly in the handling of architectural views. He was paid three guineas on account on 5 February and appears to have done some individual dessert pieces as models. Later he undertook a series of round dishes (see Cat. G116), being paid four times as much as the other painters, and was also employed to copy paintings in a number of London houses.[35] Work started properly on the dessert service during March. The painters in Chelsea were now so well into the routine that the first dessert plate had to be rejected: they had forgotten that this service was to have different border patterns – an ivy-leaf outer border, rather than the oak-leaf motif of the dinner service, and a more simply geometric inner border (Cat. G204). Again, a start was made with the simpler items, and a run of 115 dessert plates was painted, after which some additions were made to the dinner service.

The smaller size and pronounced octagonal moulding of the dessert plates demanded a more delicate handling of the views, and while many of the old sources were still used, a further distinction was drawn as two important new collections of prints were now called into play. William Borlase (1695–1772) was a Cornish antiquary, who had published several books on Cornwall and the Scillies during the 1750s. His *Natural History of Cornwall* contained views of a number of Cornish country houses set in their gardens, while the *Observations on the Antiquities Historical and Monumental of the County of Cornwall* (Cat. G228) reproduced views of dolmens and natural phenomena that Borlase associated with the Druids, giving an entirely new dimension to the antiquities depicted on the Service. The other new source was a folio of prints (Cat. G259) put together by John Boydell (1719–1804) in 1770 and consisting largely of views he himself had made in the early 1750s. More than half were views on the Thames, both upstream and downstream from London, but there were also pictures of Oxford, Blenheim and Chelsea, some landscapes in the Peak District and Wales, and even a view of Jersey, which appears on one of the dessert plates. The prints in these books do not conform quite so closely with the instructions that Wedgwood and Bentley appear to have re-

ceived, but it was quite evident at this stage that new sources of material had to be found.

Little progress had been made in locating more original drawings from artists or patrons,[36] but Mr Anson of Shugborough (who, with Lords Gower and Stamford, was one of the promoters of the Grand Trunk Canal, for which Wedgwood acted as treasurer) had had views of his garden (see Cat. G276–82) made in 1768 by Nicholas Thomas Dall (d. 1777). Shugborough had been on Stringer's itinerary, but Wedgwood had written to Bentley in December 1773, 'I suppose the objects will be found much better done in Mr. Ansons views which was the reason I wrote to you not to paint them.'[37] Dall was a Scandinavian artist born in the first half of the century who had come to England around 1760. He painted scenery for Covent Garden (where he must have worked with George Lambert) and, like other scene painters, also made views of gentlemen's country estates (there are records of his travelling in Yorkshire in 1766, 1767 and 1773 and in the Midlands in 1768 and 1770). It appears that Bentley was able to make contact with him in London and that Dall made available not only the drawings of Shugborough but others too for the artists at Chelsea to copy.[38] Dall's work is typical of the estate painters of this period, considerably more accomplished than Samuel Stringer, but with none of the exquisite draughtsmanship of Anthony Devis. His helpfulness (and that of George Barret, see Cat. G.290) is acknowledged in Bentley's introduction to the catalogue of the Service he prepared for the Empress, in that they 'obligingly permitted us to copy a great Variety of original Drawings that had never been given to the Public'.

More generous help was forthcoming from Thomas Pennant (1726–98), a traveller and naturalist who in 1771 had published an account of a tour of Scotland he had made two years previously. Up to this point there had been no source available to Bentley for any views in

Scotland, and Pennant was able to make good this deficiency. He had made a second tour in 1772, on which he had been accompanied by his servant, Moses Griffiths (1747–1819), whom he had had trained as a draughtsman at the Artists' Society. A new edition of the first volume was published in 1774, together with a volume on the second tour, which also included some views in the Hebrides drawn by the artists on Sir Joseph Banks's 1772 expedition to Iceland. Bentley used the first edition of volume 1 (there are views based on eight of the prints which appear in it), but since the second volume and the new edition of the first were not published until 1 June,[39] Pennant arranged for the printer to make the engravings available to Bentley[40] (see Cat. G237). There is an acknowledgment to Pennant too in the catalogue: a view of his own house, Downing in Flintshire, appears on a dessert plate, and Bentley describes it as the 'country house of the celebrated naturalist, Mr. Pennant, who has contributed to the utmost of his power to the perfection of this work'.[41]

One other new publication, a two-volume history of Dorset by John Hutchins, vicar of Wareham, published early in 1774, was used for the decorations, probably in late April, but while it was now clear that there was enough material to complete the decoration of the Service, Wedgwood and Bentley began to think again about the patrons whose goodwill might be gained by reproducing their estates on prominent pieces on the Service. It is not always clear whether it was the owners or the artists themselves who made drawings available – probably the owners in most cases – but original drawings were provided of estates owned by, among others, the Duke of Northumberland, the Marquess of Rockingham, the Earl of Exeter, the Earl of Carlisle, Henry Hoare, Sir Lawrence Dundas, Sir William Mayne, Sir George Osborn and Peter Taylor, the MP for Portsmouth. However, when it came to the largest dishes of all, the estates that were given pride of place were Syon (Duke of Northumberland) and Trentham (Earl Gower) with two dishes each, and Butterton Hall (belonging to the local Staffordshire magnate Mr. Swinnerton).[42] The invidiousness of this choice had always bothered Wedgwood; on 1 December 1773 he had written to his partner:

> It is a Pity but we had more large Dishes in the service. As it is, it will seem, & be in reality, too great a partiality for a Country Esqr. though he does happen to be ones Neighbour, & a good man, to occupy so Capital a situation as a large Dish when there is but 2 or 4 in the Whole Service. If we can afford [it] one of them to L^d. Gower will be as much as the Bargain, for we have in my opinion been guilty of a Capital omission in not waiting upon his Majesty to acquaint him with the Comm^{ds}. we have rec^d. from the Empress & to know his Maj—s pleasure if he would permit us to take any views from the R—l Palaces or Gardens – but it is better later than never & I am firmly of the opinion it ought to be done, & beg leave to submit it to your consideration.[43]

This matter was evidently not pursued, for with the exception of the views of Kew, there are very few views of royal palaces and none that is given special prominence. There was a well-known series of engravings of Hampton Court by John Tinney after Anthony Highmore that might well have been copied, but Bentley decided for some reason not to use them.

When Wedgwood was visiting his neighbours with Samuel Stringer the previous autumn, several of them had said they would come to London to see the Service if it were put on display before being sent to Russia. Wedgwood, as usual, carefully weighed the pros and cons:

> On one side, it would bring an immence number of

People of Fashion to our Rooms – Wo[d]. fully complete our notoriety to the whole Island, & help us greatly, no doubt in the sale of our goods, both usefull & ornamental. ... We should shew that we have paid many comp[ts]. to our Freinds & Customers, & thereby rivet them more firmly to our interests, but then we must do this pretty universally, or you see the danger. For suppose a Gent[n]. thinks himself neglected, either by the omission of his seat, when his Neighbours is taken, or by puting it upon a small piece, or not flattering it sufficiently. He then becomes our enemy – Gains some of the Artists to his party, & Damns it with the R[n]. Ambass[r]. & with every one he is able. – This is a Rock, & a dangerous one too . . .[44]

In the event, an ingenious solution was found. When the Service was put on display during June 1774 it was not yet complete – there were as many as 150 views still to be painted. This allowed time for influential customers whose estates had not yet appeared on the Service to offer drawings to be copied. This was the case with Marchioness Grey, whose letter was quoted near the beginning of this essay. Her daughter, whose drawing-master was Alexander Cozens, had done views of their gardens at Wrest and Wimpole, and Lady Grey immediately asked her to send these to London, so that they could be used.[45] Other landowners whose estates were portrayed on some of these latest pieces included the Duke of Buccleuch, the Duke of Portland, the Duke of Atholl, the Earl of Leicester, the Earl of Radnor, the Earl of Cathcart (former ambassador to Russia), Viscount Bateman, Lord North, Sir William Codrington and Sir John Griffin. Work was finally completed on Friday 6 August, and the level of activity at Chelsea can be gauged from the fact that one of the firemen for the kilns had to work 98 hours that week.[46]

Throughout the colossal task of making and decorat-ing the Service, Wedgwood and Bentley had had to keep in mind the stipulations they had received from the Empress, and, as was indicated earlier, these were clearly quite specific. As a result, it is a remarkably consistent view of Britain that is presented by the Service as a whole, entirely suited to its destined home – a palace built in English Gothic style, which was later renamed to celebrate a Russian naval victory to which English seamen had made an important contribution.[47] The commission was not simply an indulgence of Catherine's taste for English style, her fashionable anglomania. Taste in the 18th century did not have the moral neutrality it has today, and imperial taste also had a political significance that was anxiously observed at court. In August 1772 the new British ambassador in St Petersburg, Robert Gunning, had noted in a coded message sent back to his minister: 'The service of Porcelaine lately presented by the King of Prussia to the Empress, has been exposed in the Palace for several days; where persons of every Rank have been admitted to see it.' And again four weeks later he reported: 'Her Imperial Majesty has ordered to be made in Porcelaine a Group consisting of herself and the King of Prussia accompanied with many symbols and emblems of Union with an inscription in the French language which is to eternize their friendship.'[48]

The Frog Service enshrines not only an English style but also the very idea of a nation, and this was an idea that existed at a general, popular level. The figure of the free-born Englishman had come into being through an accretion of disparate, often contradictory, characteristics elaborated and disseminated by philosophers, politicians, artists and writers, but also in popular literature, newspapers and prints. The constitution of 1688, which had effectively eliminated the dangers of both absolutism and republicanism, had indeed done much to create a far more balanced structure of society, at least for the upper and middle classes, who liked to see themselves as heirs to the ancient Romans in the heroic days of the Republic before the corruption of the Emperors. Their most prized virtue was public spirit, and the welfare of the 'common people' was a part of this – however ineffectively it may have been considered in practice. Furthermore, Britain's antagonism to France meant that the country had, to some extent at least, shaken off French cultural imperialism. Certainly, in the popular mind, British virtues were simply the antithesis of French vices – symbolized, at one level, in garden design. What made the myth far more potent outside Britain was that it had received much of its impetus from dissident French writers, particularly Voltaire's *Letters Concerning the English Nation* (1733) and Montesquieu's *The Spirit of Laws* (1748). It was through the dominance of French culture in Europe that the idea of British freedom was spread.

However, the Glorious Revolution had occurred almost within living memory, and a much fuller history needed to be uncovered, one that would demonstrate that freedom was an age-old inheritance of the inhabitants of these islands and would provide a link with the heroes of ancient Rome. The revival of antiquarianism from the 1720s, which the work of the Bucks did so much to promote, helped to create these roots, and 'Gothic' remains began to acquire their own symbolism. Medieval castles were a reminder of the struggles between kings and barons – Magna Carta had already assumed its mythical status – but also of the recent wars between King and Parliament, in the course of which so many of them had been slighted. Ancient abbeys recalled both primitive piety and the corruption which had necessitated their Dissolution in Tudor times – and how much more useful monastic estates were in the hands of English lords than in those of the Roman church. Thus, while classical temples in a gentleman's garden were a testimony to his taste, the Gothic remains were a reminder of his lineage and the virtues of the ancient Britons.

The importance of the medium of print in diffusing images which represented and reinforced this idea of Britain to a far broader public cannot be overemphasized. It is an idea implicit throughout James Thomson's *Seasons* (1726–30), said to have been the most popular book in the 18th century after the Bible and *Pilgrim's Progress*, while the contributions of the Welsh and Scots to the united heroic nation were celebrated most famously in Thomas Gray's ode 'The Bard' (1757) and in James McPherson's Ossian epics (1760s), whose authenticity was widely accepted. These same images appeared in pictorial form, and there was a large and expanding market for engravings. If a sizeable proportion of this was devoted to prints after Old Master paintings – another demonstration of English taste – the prints of English gardens, views and antiquities, with all the associations that they carried, reinforced the self-image that the British had created. It was also an image that was enormously powerful abroad, leading many other countries, particularly in northern Europe, to develop a new sense of their own national identity.

It goes without saying that the ideals of liberty, individuality, unprejudiced scientific thought, industriousness, public spirit and social consciousness were reflected only very dimly in the everyday politics and everyday life of 18th-century Britain. But the significance of the Green Frog Service, an amalgam of the artistic, cultural and commercial intentions of several hundred different individuals, potters and painters, draughtsmen and engravers, patrons and publishers, belongs to the history of ideas rather than to social history – a monument to an optimistic faith that was shared by its patroness and its makers that '*Arts and Manufactures* contribute greatly to the *Wealth* and *power* of a Nation, and ... *Industry* and *Commerce* will soon improve, and People the most uncultivated Situation'.[49]

Michael Raeburn

G

By Imperial Command

Note: Items are grouped, as far as possible, according to the principal sources used for their decoration, and the sequence of these groups follows the general order in which these sources were first used by Bentley and his decorators in Chelsea.

All items from the Service are painted in purplish-black and green overglaze enamels on Queen's Ware. The number painted on the reverse of each piece corresponds to the Catalogue of the Service with a description (in French) of each view, compiled by Thomas Bentley for Catherine the Great, the only known copy of which is in the Wedgwood Archive (E32-5184).

Where three figures for measurement are given, height is given first, followed by length, then width.

BUCK'S ANTIQUITIES

G1 *Buck's Antiquities or Venerable Remains of above four hundred Castles, Monasteries, Palaces &c. &c. in England and Wales...* (Pl. 32)

Samuel and Nathaniel Buck
Published in London, 1774 (originally published 1726–42)
47 × 57 cm (open)

The *Antiquities* of Samuel Buck (1696–1779) and his brother Nathaniel (active 1727–53), published between 1726 and 1742 for all the counties of England and Wales, comprise 420 views of ruined abbeys and castles (see pp. 137–9). These reflected the antiquarian interest in Britain's ancient past and also stimulated the fashion for newly designed Gothic ruins. Since Catherine had asked that

ruins should be one of the subjects appearing on the Service, Wedgwood and Bentley were able to make an immediate start from these prints, and they appear to have used them for the decoration of over 80 flat plates before turning to prints of landscape gardens; later, they returned to them again and again. Although the Bucks' prints were rather old-fashioned, in the style of the 'Prospects' produced in the 17th century and early part of the 18th, they were the most frequently used source for the views on the Frog Service.

Victoria & Albert Museum. National Art Library (104.J.10)

G2 **Flat plate decorated with a view of Eynsham Abbey, Oxon.** *(Pl. 33)*

Mark: painted view number '10'
Diameter: 24.5 cm

The view is based on *The East View of the inside of Eynsham Abbey, near Oxford*, 1729, from *Buck's Antiquities*, V, 1730, pl. 1, and shows a façade which was pulled down in 1771. This plate is probably the first piece to have been decorated that was included in the Service (numbers 1–9 were reserved for views of gardens, which were not started until several weeks after the initial batch of antiquities).

State Hermitage Museum, St Petersburg (8902)
Lit: Raeburn, Voronikhina and Nurnberg 1995, cat. 204, view 676

G3 **Flat plate decorated with a view of Egremont Castle, Cumbria**

Mark: painted view number '18'
Diameter: 24.5 cm

The view is based based on *The South-West View of Egremont-Castle*, 1739, from *Buck's Antiquities*, XIV, 1739, pl. 7.

State Hermitage Museum, St Petersburg (8801)
Lit: Raeburn, Voronikhina and Nurnberg 1995, cat. 211, view 215

G4 **Flat plate decorated with a view of Bodiam Castle, E. Sussex**

Mark: painted view number '25'
Diameter: 24.5 cm

The view is based based on *The North East View of Bodiham Castle*, 1737, from *Buck's Antiquities*, XII, 1737, pl. 9.

State Hermitage Museum, St Petersburg (8929)
Lit: Raeburn, Voronikhina and Nurnberg 1995, cat. 218, view 912; Williamson 1909, facing p. 68

G5 **Flat plate decorated with a view of the Fort at Fowey, Cornwall**

Mark: painted view number '38'
Diameter: 25.3 cm

The view is based on *The South-East View of Fowey-Castle*, 1734, from *Buck's Antiquities*, X, 1735, pl. 10.

This plate was badly affected by 'spit out' during the firing and was not included in the Service. A new view (see Cat. G6), painted from the same model and given the same number, was done as a replacement.

Stoke-on-Trent City Museum and Art Gallery
Lit: Raeburn, Voronikhina and Nurnberg 1995, view A2

G 14

G6 Flat plate decorated with a view of the Fort at Fowey, Cornwall

Mark: painted view number '38'
Diameter: 24.5 cm

The view is based based on the same print as Cat. G5.

State Hermitage Museum, St Petersburg (8779)
Lit: Raeburn, Voronikhina and Nurnberg 1995, cat. 231, view 173

G7 Flat plate decorated with a view of Binham Priory, Norfolk

Mark: painted view number '51'
Diameter: 24.5 cm

The view is based on *The South West View of Binham Priory*, 1738, from *Buck's Antiquities*, XIII, 1738, pl. 7.

State Hermitage Museum, St Petersburg (8747)
Lit: Raeburn, Voronikhina and Nurnberg 1995, cat. 242, view 612

G8 Flat plate decorated with a view of Lindisfarne Castle on Holy Island, Northumbria

Mark: painted view number '55'
Diameter: 24.5 cm

The view is based on *The South View of Holy Island Monastery & Castle belonging to the Bishoprick of Durham*, 1728, from *Buck's Antiquities*, IV, 1729, pl. 1.

State Hermitage Museum, St Petersburg (8824)
Lit: Raeburn, Voronikhina and Nurnberg 1995, cat. 246, view 646; Williamson 1909, facing p. 90

G9 Flat plate decorated with a view of Bolton Priory, N. Yorks.

Mark: painted view number '73'
Diameter: 24.5 cm

The view is based on the left-hand part of *The South-East Prospect of the Ruins of Bolton Abbey, in the West Riding of Yorkshire*, 1720, from *Buck's Antiquities*, I, 1726, pl. 2.

State Hermitage Museum, St Petersburg (8752)
Lit: Raeburn, Voronikhina and Nurnberg 1995, cat. 263, view 980

G10 Flat plate decorated with a view of Tupholme Priory, Lincs.

Mark: painted view number '81'
Diameter: 24.5 cm

The view is based on the central section of *The South Prospect of Tupholme Priory, near Lincoln*, 1726, from *Buck's Antiquities*, II, 1727, pl. 11. This plate and Cat. G13 were omitted from the Service, not because of technical imperfections – they were not immediately replaced – but presumably because other views were preferred once the Service was completed (a number of additional items having been decorated). No items were included with these view numbers, which were omitted from the sequence in Bentley's Catalogue of the Service.

Trustees of the Wedgwood Museum, Barlaston, Staffordshire (1031)
Lit: Raeburn, Voronikhina and Nurnberg 1995, view A4

G11 Flat plate decorated with a view of Harlsey Castle, N. Yorks.

Mark: painted view number '87'
Diameter: 24.5 cm

The view is based on the left-hand side of *The South View of Harlsey-Castle near N:*

Allerton in York-shire, 1721, from *Buck's Antiquities*, I, 1726, pl. 8.

State Hermitage Museum, St Petersburg (8916)
Lit: Raeburn, Voronikhina and Nurnberg 1995, cat. 274, view 1009

G12 Flat plate decorated with a view of Harlsey Castle, N. Yorks.

Mark: painted view number '114'
Diameter: 24.5 cm

The view is based on the right-hand side of the same print as Cat. G11. Like Cat. G10 and 13, this plate was not included in the Service. Its number was reused at a late stage for an item in the dessert service.

Trustees of the National Galleries on Merseyside (Liverpool Museum)
Lit: Raeburn, Voronikhina and Nurnberg 1995, view A6

G13 Flat plate decorated with a view of Sandal Castle, W. Yorks.

Mark: painted view number '207'
Diameter: 24.5 cm

The view is based on *The South Prospect of the Ruins of Sandal Castle; and Town of Wakefield*, 1722, from *Buck's Antiquities*, I, 1726, pl. 20. See Cat. G10.

Victoria & Albert Museum (C.96-1932)
Lit: Raeburn, Voronikhina and Nurnberg 1995, view A12

G14 Flat plate decorated with a view of Kirkham Priory, N. Yorks.

Mark: painted view number '209'
Diameter: 24.5 cm

The view is based on the right-hand part of *The North View of Kirkham-Priory, near Malton in Yorkshire*, 1721, from *Buck's Antiquities*, I, 1726, pl. 9.

State Hermitage Museum, St Petersburg (8921)
Lit: Raeburn, Voronikhina and Nurnberg 1995, cat. 376, view 1016

G 137, G 33, G 316, G 31, G215. Sauce boat, spoons and sauce tureens from the dinner service.

G15 Flat plate decorated with a view of Scarborough Castle, N. Yorks.

Mark: painted view number '228'
Diameter: 24.5 cm

The view is based on the right-hand part of *The Castle & Town of Scarborough, as they appear a quarter of a mile from the Spaw, from a drawing in the possession of Jnᵒ: Bolter Esqʳ.*, from *Buck's Antiquities*, I, 1726, pl. 22.

State Hermitage Museum, St Petersburg (8884)
Lit: Raeburn, Voronikhina and Nurnberg 1995, cat. 393, view 1046

G16 Flat plate decorated with a view of Berkeley Castle, Glos.

Mark: painted view number '358'
Diameter: 24.5 cm

The view is based on *The South East View of Berkeley Castle*, 1732, from *Buck's Antiquities*, VIII, 1733, pl. 5.

State Hermitage Museum, St Petersburg (8919)
Lit: Raeburn, Voronikhina and Nurnberg 1995, cat. 421, view 326

G17 Soup plate decorated with a view of Dunstanburgh Castle, Northumbria

Mark: painted view number '267'
Diameter: 24.25 cm

The view is based on *The South-West View of Dunstanburgh Castle*, 1728, from *Buck's Antiquities*, IV, 1729, pl. 19.

State Hermitage Museum, St Petersburg (8958)
Lit: Raeburn, Voronikhina and Nurnberg 1995, cat. 495, view 644

G18 Soup plate decorated with a view of Amberley Castle, W. Sussex

Mark: painted view number '346'
Diameter: 24.25 cm

The view is based on *The South-West View of Amberley-Castle*, 1737, from *Buck's*

Antiquities, XII, 1737, pl. 10. This plate was omitted from the Service, possibly because of a confusion in the numbering: the plate described as no. 346 in Bentley's catalogue (a view of Carmarthen Castle) is, in fact, numbered '348' but was evidently preferred to this one.

Private collection
Lit: Raeburn, Voronikhina and Nurnberg 1995, view A15

G19 Soup plate decorated with a view of Brecon Castle, Powys

Mark: painted view number '351'
Diameter: 24.25 cm

The view is based on the right-hand part of *The South East-View of Brecknock Castle*, 1741, from *Buck's Antiquities*, *Wales* II, 1741, pl. 38.

State Hermitage Museum, St Petersburg (8969)
Lit: Raeburn, Voronikhina and Nurnberg 1995, cat. 534, view 1075

G20 Soup plate decorated with a view of Glastonbury Abbey, Somerset

Mark: painted view number '362'
Diameter: 24.25 cm

The view is based on the central and right-hand part of *The South View of Glastonbury Abby*, 1733, from *Buck's Antiquities*, IX, 1734, pl. 1.

State Hermitage Museum, St Petersburg (8936)
Lit: Raeburn, Voronikhina and Nurnberg 1995, cat. 537, view 718

G21 12-inch oval dish decorated with a view of Powderham Castle, Devon

Mark: painted view number '414'
31.5 × 24 cm

The view is based on *The East View of Powderham-Castle*, 1734, from *Buck's Antiquities*, X, 1735, pl. 21.

State Hermitage Museum, St Petersburg (8663)
Lit: Raeburn, Voronikhina and Nurnberg 1995, cat. 62, view 275; Williamson 1909, facing p. 30

G22 11-inch oval dish decorated with a view of 'John of Gaunt's Palace', Lincoln

Marks: 'WEDGWOOD' impressed; painted view number '521'
29 × 22 cm

The view is based on *The East Prospect of John of Gaunt's below the Hill in Lincoln*, 1726, from *Buck's Antiquities*, II, 1727, pl. 6.

State Hermitage Museum, St Petersburg (8672)
Lit: Raeburn, Voronikhina and Nurnberg 1995, cat. 72, view 488

G23 11-inch oval dish decorated with a view of Carlisle Castle, Cumbria

Marks: 'WEDGWOOD' impressed; painted view number '523'
29 × 22 cm

The view is based on *The North-West View of Carlisle Castle*, 1739, from *Buck's Antiquities*, XIV, 1739, pl. 12.

State Hermitage Museum, St Petersburg (8670)
Lit: Raeburn, Voronikhina and Nurnberg 1995, cat. 73, view 206

G24 13-inch round dish decorated with a view of Mount Grace Priory, N. Yorks.

Mark: painted view number '518'
Diameter: 33 cm

The view is based on *The West View of Mount-Grace near Osmotherley in Yorkshire*, 1722, from *Buck's Antiquities*, I, 1726, pl. 15.

State Hermitage Museum, St Petersburg (8702)
Lit: Raeburn, Voronikhina and Nurnberg 1995, cat. 97, view 1027

G25 12-inch round dish decorated with a view of Ashby de la Zouche Castle, Leics.

Mark: painted view number '463'
Diameter: 30.5 cm

The view is based on *The South View of Ashby-de-la-Zouch Castle*, 1730, from *Buck's Antiquities*, VI, 1731, pl. 22.

State Hermitage Museum, St Petersburg (8725)
Lit: Raeburn, Voronikhina and Nurnberg 1995, cat. 105, view 469

G26 12-inch round dish decorated with a view of Tattershall Castle, Lincs.

Mark: painted view number '464'
Diameter: 30.5 cm

G 26

G 28

The view is based on *The East Prospect of Tatershal-Castle near Boston*, 1726, from *Buck's Antiquities*, II, 1727, pl. 14.

State Hermitage Museum, St Petersburg (8723)
Lit: Raeburn, Voronikhina and Nurnberg 1995, cat. 106, view 496; Williamson 1909, facing p. 10

G27 12-inch round dish decorated with a view of Okehampton Castle, Devon

Mark: painted view number '467'
Diameter: 30.5 cm

The view is based on *The South View of Okehampton-Castle*, 1734, from *Buck's Antiquities*, X, 1735, pl. 20. Note the watermill on the River Okement at bottom right.

State Hermitage Museum, St Petersburg (8714)
Lit: Raeburn, Voronikhina and Nurnberg 1995, cat. 109, view 259; Williamson 1909, facing p. 96

G28 Triangular dish decorated with a view of Holdenby Hall, Northants.

Marks: 'WEDGWOOD' impressed; painted view number '642'
Length of each side: 28.5 cm

The view is based on *The South View of Holdenby-Palace*, 1729, from *Buck's Antiquities*, V, 1730, pl. 20.

State Hermitage Museum, St Petersburg (8504)
Lit: Raeburn, Voronikhina and Nurnberg 1995, cat. 142, view 627

G29 Triangular dish decorated with a view of St Michael's Mount, Cornwall

Marks: 'WEDGWOOD' impressed; painted view number '643'
Length of each side: 28.5 cm

The view is based on *The East View of St. Michael's Mount in the County of Cornwall*, 1734, from *Buck's Antiquities*, X, 1735, pl. 2.

State Hermitage Museum, St Petersburg (8502)
Lit: Raeburn, Voronikhina and Nurnberg 1995, cat. 143, view 189; Williamson 1909, facing p. 76

G30 Triangular dish decorated with a view of Dolwyddelan Castle, Gwynedd *(Pl. 22)*

Marks: 'WEDGWOOD' impressed; painted view number '645'
Length of each side: 28.5 cm

The view is based on *The East View of Dolwyddelan Castle, in the County of Caernarvon*, 1742, from *Buck's Antiquities, Wales* III, 1742, pl. 75.

State Hermitage Museum, St Petersburg (8575)
Lit: Raeburn, Voronikhina and Nurnberg 1995, cat. 145, view 1087

G31 Sauce tureen decorated with views of Pembroke Castle, Dyfed, and Aust Passage, Avon; lid decorated with views of Inverness Castle, Highland of Scotland, and Braemar Castle, Grampian, and features from Tattershall Castle, Lincs., and Kirkham Priory, N. Yorks.

Marks: 'WEDGWOOD' impressed; painted view numbers '563', '564'; lid: '583', '584', '585', '586'
Height: 11.75 cm; dimensions of lid: 16 × 12 cm

The views are based on details of *The North-West View of Pembroke Castle*, 1740, from *Buck's Antiquities, Wales* I, 1740, pl. 4; *A Ferry on the River Severn*, no. 3 of a set of engravings by J. Smith after Jean-Baptiste Pillement (around 1728–1808), 1773 (centre of print); *Inverness* and *Brae-mar Castle*, engravings by Peter Mazell (active 1760–1800) after paintings by William

Tomkins (around 1730–92), published in Thomas Pennant, *A Tour in Scotland MDCCLXIX*, 1771, pls 6 and 5 (see Cat. G237, 242, 46); *The East Prospect of Tatershal-Castle near Boston*, 1726, from *Buck's Antiquities*, II, 1727, pl. 14 (see Cat. G26); *The North View of Kirkham-Priory, near Malton in Yorkshire*, 1721, from *Buck's Antiquities*, I, 1726, pl. 9 (see Cat. G14).

State Hermitage Museum, St Petersburg (8491, 8491A)
Lit: Raeburn, Voronikhina and Nurnberg 1995, cat. 155, 156a; views 1151, 325, 1176, 1156, 498, 1017; Williamson 1909, facing p. 70

G32 Sauce tureen decorated with views of Llanstephan Castle, Dyfed, and Foots Cray House, Kent; lid decorated with views of Painshill, Surrey, and Oatlands, Surrey, and features from Caernarfon Castle, Gwynedd, and Dinefwr Castle, Dyfed

Marks: 'WEDGWOOD' impressed; painted view numbers '569', '570'; lid: '599', '600', '601', '602'
Height: 11.75 cm; dimensions of lid: 16 × 12 cm

The views are based on details of *The North-East View of Llanstephan-Castle, in the County of Caermathen*, 1740, from *Buck's Antiquities, Wales* I, 1740, pl. 20; *A View of Foots-Cray Place in Kent, the Seat of Bouchier Cleeve Esq*, designed and engraved by William Woollett (1735–85), 1760; *A View from the West Side of the Island in the Garden of the Hon. Charles Hamilton Esq*^{r}. *at Painshill near Cobham in Surry*, designed and engraved by Woollett, 1760 (see Cat. G108); *A View of Oatlands in Surry the Seat of the R*^{t}. *Hon*^{ble}. *the Earl of Lincoln*, designed and engraved by Luke Sullivan (1705–71), 1759 (see Cat. G97); *Caernarvon Castle*, engraving by William Byrne (1743–1805) after a painting by Richard Wilson (1713–82), 1766 (see Cat. G223); *The South View of Denefawr-Castle, in the County Caermarthen*, 1740, from *Buck's Antiquities, Wales* I, 1740, pl. 21.

State Hermitage Museum, St Petersburg (8493, 8483A)

Lit: Raeburn, Voronikhina and Nurnberg 1995, cat. 158, 160a; views 1099, 431, 877, 873, 1081, 1095; Williamson 1909, facing p. xviii; Reilly 1989 I, pl. 332

G33 Spoon for sauce tureen decorated with a view of Stainfield Hall and church, Lincs.

Mark: painted view number '612'
Length: 16.5 cm

The view is based on a detail from *The North West Prospect of Barlings Abbey, near Lincoln*, 1726, from *Buck's Antiquities*, II, 1727, pl. 10.

State Hermitage Museum, St Petersburg (8559B)
Lit: Raeburn, Voronikhina and Nurnberg 1995, cat. 670, view 493; Williamson 1909, facing p. xviii; Reilly 1989 I, pl. 332

G34 Spoon for sauce tureen decorated with a view of Carmarthen Castle, Dyfed

Mark: painted view number '1260'
Length: 15.5 cm

The view is based on a feature from the centre of *The South View of Caermarthen-Castle & town*, 1740, from *Buck's Antiquities, Wales* I, 1740, pl. 17.

State Hermitage Museum, St Petersburg (8556B)
Lit: Raeburn, Voronikhina and Nurnberg 1995, cat. 674, view 1093

G35 Dessert plate decorated with a view of Oakham Castle, Rutland

Mark: painted view number '893'
Diameter: 22 cm

The view is based on *The South-East View of Okeham-Castle*, 1730, from *Buck's Antiquities*, VI, 1731, pl. 24.

State Hermitage Museum, St Petersburg (9074)
Lit: Raeburn, Voronikhina and Nurnberg 1995, cat. 778, view 693

G36 Large compotier decorated with a view of Furness Abbey, Lancs.

Mark: painted view number '1270'
31.5 × 18 cm

The view is based on *The South View of Furness Abby*, 1727, from *Buck's Antiquities*, III, 1728, pl. 1.

State Hermitage Museum, St Petersburg (8481)
Lit: Raeburn, Voronikhina and Nurnberg 1995, cat. 900, view 461; Williamson 1909, facing p. 10

KING ALFRED'S HALL AND KEW GARDENS

G37 *The North East View of King Alfred's Hall*

Thomas Robins senior (1716–70)
Etching with engraving
Lettered with title, and 'Tho⁵. Robins delin 1763'
Dated 1763
Cut to 22.7 × 32.2 cm

The gardens of Cirencester Park were laid out in the early 18th century by Allen, 1st Lord Bathurst, on a very grand scale. Although the plan was quite formal, the most important of the garden buildings, 'King Alfred's Hall', built about 1721 (altered in 1732 to accommodate part of the neighbouring demolished manor house), was the earliest castellated garden ornament in England. The items from the Service with views based on Robins's print demonstrate the way many of the sources were used by the ceramic painters: one view on a flat plate (Cat. G39) was based on the left-hand part of the print, another (now lost) presumably on the central part and a third (Cat. G38) on the right-hand part, each being framed by trees to improve the composition; virtually the whole print was used for a view on an oval dish (Cat. G40); while a small detail from the background appeared as a feature on the end of a tureen lid (Cat. G41).

Trustees of the British Museum (BM 1955-4-25-45)

G38 Flat plate decorated with a view of King Alfred's Hall, Cirencester Park, Glos. *(Pl. 31)*

Mark: painted view number '86'
Diameter: 24.5 cm

See Cat. G37, on which the view is based.

State Hermitage Museum, St Petersburg (8917)
Lit: Raeburn, Voronikhina and Nurnberg 1995, cat. 273, view 334

G39 Flat plate decorated with a view of King Alfred's Hall *(Pl. 31)*

Mark: painted view number '222'
Diameter: 24.5 cm

See Cat. G37, on which the view is based.

State Hermitage Museum, St Petersburg (8791)
Lit: Raeburn, Voronikhina and Nurnberg 1995, cat. 388, view 335

G40 14-inch oval dish decorated with a view of King Alfred's Hall, Cirencester Park, Glos. *(Pl. 31)*

Mark: painted view number '509'
35.5 × 27 cm

See Cat. G37, on which the view is based.

State Hermitage Museum, St Petersburg (8650)
Lit: Raeburn, Voronikhina and Nurnberg 1995, cat. 48, view 336

G41 Lid for sauce tureen decorated with views of Lindisfarne Priory and Castle on Holy Island, Northumbria, and an English port, and features from King Alfred's Hall, Cirencester Park, Glos., and Kirkham Priory, N. Yorks. *(Pl. 31)*

Marks: painted view numbers '587', '588', '589', '590'
16 × 12 cm

See Cat. G37. The views are based on details of *The South View of Holy Island Monastery & Castle belonging to the Bishoprick of Durham*, 1728, from *Buck's Antiquities*, IV, 1729, pl. 1 (see Cat. G8); *An English Seaport*, no. 8 of a set of engravings

by J. Smith after Jean-Baptiste Pillement, 1773; *The North East View of King Alfreds Hall*, engraving after Robins, 1763; and *The North View of Kirkham-Priory, near Malton in Yorkshire*, 1721, from *Buck's Antiquities*, I, 1726, pl. 9 (see Cat. G14, 31).

State Hermitage Museum, St Petersburg (8556A)
Lit: Raeburn, Voronikhina and Nurnberg 1995, cat. 157a, views 647, 1203, 337, 1018

G42 *A View of the Lake and Island, with the Orangerie, The Temples of Eolus and Bellona, and the House of Confucius*

Thomas Major (1720–99) after William Marlow (1740–1813)
Etching with engraving
Lettered with title, and 'T. Marlow delinᵗ. T. Major Sculpᵗ.'
1763
Size of platemark: 32.8 × 48.5 cm

Plate 37 from *Plans, Elevations, Sections and Perspective Views of the Gardens and Buildings at Kew in Surrey... by William Chambers, London, 1763.*

William Chambers (1723–96) was employed from 1757 by Princess Augusta, the widow of Frederick Prince of Wales, to lay out her garden at Kew and design a series of garden buildings. These were described soon after their completion in this splendid book of engravings. The general pattern of the garden followed that of Stowe (see Cat. G117ff.), with each of the buildings signifying an allegorical or moral purpose, but there was greater stylistic variety at Kew, since Chambers was able to indulge his interest in Chinese architecture, and he also included buildings of Moorish character. At least five of the engravings were used as sources for the Frog Service, and most of these were used several times, the little temples and bridges being found very useful as features on small items and at the ends of lids.

The motifs from Kew on Cat. G43–52 are all based on plate 37. The House of Confucius (1757) was the earliest of the buildings, designed in fact by the scene-painter Joseph Goupy, though the bridge

G 42

G 44

See Cat. G42, on which the view is based. The buildings (left to right) are the Orangery, the Temple of Bellona, the Temple of Aeolus and the House of Confucius (behind the Chinese bridge).

State Hermitage Museum, St Petersburg (8658)
Lit: Raeburn, Voronikhina and Nurnberg 1995, cat. 51, view 837

G45 Cover for oblong dish decorated with views of Kew Gardens and features of an Entrance Pavilion at Stowe, Bucks., and a temple at Hagley, Hereford & Worcs.

Marks: painted view numbers '718', '719', '720', '721'
24 × 19.5 cm

See Cat. G42. The features at the ends are based on details from *A View over the Great Bason to the Entrance between the Pavillions*, pl. b from the collection of engravings of Stowe by George Bickham junior (d. around 1769) after Jean-Baptiste Claude Chatelain (1710–71) (see Cat. G117ff.); and *A View in Hagley Park...*, engraving by François Vivares (1709–80) after Thomas Smith (d. 1767), 1749 (see Cat. G69).

State Hermitage Museum, St Petersburg (8571A)
Lit: Raeburn, Voronikhina and Nurnberg 1995, cat. 132a, views 843, 57, 844, 975

G46 Cover for oblong dish decorated with views of Braemar Castle, Grampian, and Caernarfon Castle, Gwynedd, and features of Queen Caroline's Monument at Stowe and the Orangery at Kew Gardens

Marks: painted view numbers '722', '723', '724', '725'
24 × 19.5 cm

The views are based on *Brae-mar Castle*, engraving by Mazell after Tomkins, published in Pennant's *A Tour of Scotland MDCCLXIX*, 1771, pl. 5 (see Cat. G31); and *Caernarvon Castle*, engraving by Byrne after Wilson, 1766 (see Cat. G32); the feature of Stowe is based on *View of the Rotondo from the Queen's Theatre*, pl. h from the collection of engravings of Stowe

leading to it was designed by Chambers himself, as were the Orangery (1761), which still survives, the Temple of Aeolus, god of the winds, and the Temple of Bellona, goddess of war (both 1760, rebuilt in the 19th century).

Trustees of the British Museum (BM 1863-5-9-275)

G43 Flat plate decorated with a view of Kew Gardens

Mark: painted view number '93'
Diameter: 24.5 cm

See Cat. G42, on which the view is based. The Orangery is seen left and the Temple of Bellona right.

State Hermitage Museum, St Petersburg (8913)
Lit: Raeburn, Voronikhina and Nurnberg 1995, cat. 280, view 836

G44 13-inch oval dish decorated with a view of Kew Gardens

Mark: painted view number '401'
33 × 25 cm

by Bickham after Chatelain (see Cat. G117ff.); for the feature of Kew, see Cat. G42.

State Hermitage Museum, St Petersburg (8570A)
Lit: Raeburn, Voronikhina and Nurnberg 1995, cat. 133a, views 1157, 84, 1082, 845

G47 Cover for oblong dish decorated with views of Stirling Castle, Central Scotland, and the countryside around it and features of the Temples of Aeolus and Bellona in Kew Gardens

Marks: painted view numbers '730', '731', '732', '733'
24 × 19.5 cm

Both views are based on *Sterling Castle*, print by Mazell after Tomkins, published in Pennant's *A Tour of Scotland MDCCLXIX*, 1771, pl. 11 (see Cat. G237); for the features, see Cat. G42.

State Hermitage Museum, St Petersburg (8568A)
Lit: Raeburn, Voronikhina and Nurnberg 1995, cat. 135a, views 1198, 846, 1199, 847

G48 Stand for sauce boat decorated with a view of Kew Gardens

Marks: 'WEDGWOOD' impressed; painted view number '539'
20 × 16.5 cm

See Cat. G42. The view is based on the right-hand side of the engraving.

State Hermitage Museum, St Petersburg (8679)
Lit: Raeburn, Voronikhina and Nurnberg 1995, cat. 179, view 838

G49 Stand for sauce boat decorated with a view of Kew Gardens

Mark: painted view number '540'
20 × 16.5 cm

See Cat. G42. The view is based on the left-hand side of the engraving.

State Hermitage Museum, St Petersburg (8683)
Lit: Raeburn, Voronikhina and Nurnberg 1995, cat. 180, view 839

G50 Stand for sauce boat decorated with a view of Kew Gardens

Marks: 'WEDGWOOD' impressed; painted view number '541'
20 × 16.5 cm

See Cat. G42. The view is based on the central part of the engraving.

State Hermitage Museum, St Petersburg (8678)
Lit: Raeburn, Voronikhina and Nurnberg 1995, cat. 181, view 840

G51 Spoon for sauce tureen decorated with the feature of the Temple of Aeolus in Kew Gardens

Mark: painted view number '608'
Length: 16.5 cm

See Cat. G42

State Hermitage Museum, St Petersburg (8561B)
Lit: Raeburn, Voronikhina and Nurnberg 1995, cat. 666, view 841

G52 Spoon for sauce tureen decorated with the feature of the Temple of Bellona in Kew Gardens

Mark: painted view number '609'
Length: 16.5 cm

See Cat. G42.

State Hermitage Museum, St Petersburg (8558B)
Lit: Raeburn, Voronikhina and Nurnberg 1995, cat. 667, view 842

G53 Flat plate decorated with a view of Kew Gardens

Mark: painted view number '240'
Diameter: 24.5 cm

See Cat. G42. This view is based on the right-hand side of pl. 38 in Chambers' book: *A View of the Lake and Island at Kew, seen from the Lawn, with the Bridge, the Temples of Arethusa, and Victory, and the Great Pagoda*, engraved by Paul Sandby (1731–1809) after William Marlow. The Pagoda (1761) is the only one of the Chinese buildings at Kew that still survives.

State Hermitage Museum, St Petersburg (8822)
Lit: Raeburn, Voronikhina and Nurnberg 1995, cat. 405, view 850; Voronikhina 1988, p. 172

G54 15-inch oval dish decorated with a view of Kew Gardens

Mark: painted view number '291'
38.5 × 29 cm

See Cat. G42. This view is based on pl. 40 in Chambers' book: *A View of the Menagerie, and its Pavillion, at Kew*, engraving by Charles Grignion (1721–1810) after a drawing by Thomas Sandby (1723–98). The Chinese style of the Menagerie pavilion (1760) was appropriate for the oriental pheasants kept there; the building in the left background is the Temple of Bellona.

State Hermitage Museum, St Petersburg (8640)
Lit: Raeburn, Voronikhina and Nurnberg 1995, cat. 27, view 857

G55 Dessert plate decorated with a view of Kew Gardens

Mark: painted view number '840'
Diameter: 22 cm

See Cat. G54. This view is based on on the left-hand side of the print.

State Hermitage Museum, St Petersburg (9107)
Lit: Raeburn, Voronikhina and Nurnberg 1995, cat. 727, view 858

G 55

G56 14-inch oval dish decorated with a view of Kew Palace

Marks: 'WEDGWOOD' impressed; painted view number '534'
35.5 × 27 cm

See Cat. G42. This view (which was incorrectly numbered '534' – it should be '524') is based on pl. 36 in Chambers' book: *A View of the Palace at Kew from the Lawn*, engraving by William Woollett after a drawing by John Joshua Kirby (1716–74). The Palace, known as 'The White House', was rebuilt for Frederick Prince of Wales by William Kent around 1731–5. It was demolished, except for a surviving kitchen wing, in 1802 by George III.

State Hermitage Museum, St Petersburg (8651)
Lit: Raeburn, Voronikhina and Nurnberg 1995, cat. 49, view 833

G57 Stand for sauce boat decorated with a view of Kew Gardens

Marks: 'WEDGWOOD' impressed; painted view number '542'
20 × 16.5 cm

See Cat. G42. This view is based on the right-hand side of pl. 43 in Chambers' book: *A View of the Wilderness, with the Alhambra, the Pagoda and the Mosque*, engraving by Edward Rooker (around 1712–74) after a drawing by William Marlow. It features the Moorish Mosque, built in 1761 and since demolished.

State Hermitage Museum, St Petersburg (20859)
Lit: Raeburn, Voronikhina and Nurnberg 1995, cat. 182, view 849

THOMAS SMITH, GEORGE LAMBERT AND LANDSCAPE

G58 *A Prospect in the upper Part of Dove-Dale, five Miles north of Ashbourn*

James Roberts senior (1725–99) after a painting by Thomas Smith (d. 1767)
Engraving with etching

G 59

Lettered with title, publication line, and 'T Smith Pinx. Roberts sculp. J Boydell Execuᵗ.'
1769 (originally published 1743)
Size of platemark: 38.9 × 54.5 cm

Thomas Smith of Derby was probably the first landscape artist in Britain to paint not only gentlemen's estates but also views of wild and romantic scenery, in the Derbyshire Peak, in the Lake District and in Yorkshire. From 1743 until his death he himself issued prints after his paintings, often working with François Vivares (1709–80). Many of these were later reissued by other publishers in sets and were also copied in guidebooks to England published in the 1760s. His prints were one of the first sources chosen by Thomas Bentley for the decoration of the Frog Service, and almost all of Smith's large-scale engravings were eventually utilized.

His earliest set of engravings was the remarkable *Eight of the most extraordinary Prospects in the Mountainous parts of Derbyshire and Staffordshire commonly call'd the Peak and the Moorlands*, for which the title engraving is dated April 1743, although others in the series are dated between March and August. They are surely the earliest examples of 'sublime' landscapes painted in Britain, and their popularity is indicated by the fact that they were reprinted in 1757 and again in 1769, after Smith's death, by John Boydell (1719–1804), who kept them in his catalogue into the next century. This print is the second in the set.

Thomas Bentley, like Smith, was a native of Derbyshire, and his lyrical descriptions of these views in the Catalogue of the Service he made for the Empress stand out from the generally dry, matter-of-fact descriptions of other places.

Trustees of the British Museum (BM 1877-6-9-1919)

G59 16-inch oval dish decorated with a view of Dovedale, Derbys.

Marks: 'WEDGWOOD' impressed; painted view number '296'
41.5 × 32 cm

See Cat. G58, on which the view is based. The description in Bentley's catalogue reads: 'View of the upper part of Dove-Dale; This is one of the most charming and romantic of valleys, in the midst of which runs a fairly swift river, which meanders for several miles, between the slopes which form this valley.'

State Hermitage Museum, St Petersburg (8613)
Lit: Raeburn, Voronikhina and Nurnberg 1995, cat. 14, view 237; Williamson 1909, facing p. 52

G60 15-inch oval dish decorated with a view of Matlock Bath, Derbys.

Mark: painted view number '297'
38.5 × 29 cm

See Cat. G58. The view is based on the fourth of the *Eight of the most extraordinary Prospects...: A Prospect of Matlock-Bath &c. from the Lover's Walk*, engraving by François Vivares after a painting by Thomas Smith, 1743. The description in Bentley's catalogue reads: 'The watering-place of Matlock, seen from the Lovers' Walk, in the county of Derby. This view forms the most beautiful and enchanting spectacle; for here, on every side, the most charming and romantic landscapes appear. In summer it is the resort of many fashionable people, who take the waters and the baths and pass the time in very pleasant fashion. Lovers of nature experience special satisfaction in examining both the external beauties of the country, and the curious products of the neighbouring mines.'

State Hermitage Museum, St Petersburg (20852)
Lit: Raeburn, Voronikhina and Nurnberg 1995, cat. 32, view 249

G61 14-inch oval dish decorated with a view of Monsaldale, Derbys.

Mark: painted view number '504'
35.5 × 27 cm

See Cat. G58. The view is based on the sixth of *Eight of the most extraordinary Prospects...: Prospect of the River Wie, in Monsal-Dale, Two Miles North-West of*

Bakewell, engraving by François Vivares after a painting by Thomas Smith. The description in Bentley's catalogue reads: 'View on the river Wie, which flows through Monsal Valley, in the County of Derby. The banks of this river between Buxton and Beckwell present an infinite variety of rocks, woods and little valleys, out of which Nature has formed the most beautiful and varied landscapes.'

State Hermitage Museum, St Petersburg (8652)
Lit: Raeburn, Voronikhina and Nurnberg 1995, cat. 46, view 254

G62 13-inch round dish decorated with a view of Dovedale, Derbys.

Mark: painted view number '517'
Diameter: 33 cm

See Cat. G58. The view is based on the first of *Eight of the most extraordinary Prospects...: A Prospect in Dove-Dale, 3 Miles North of Ashbourne*, engraving by Antoine Benoist (1721–70) after a drawing and painting by Thomas Smith.

State Hermitage Museum, St Petersburg (8701)
Lit: Raeburn, Voronikhina and Nurnberg 1995, cat. 96, view 240; Williamson 1909, facing p. 68

G63 Flat plate decorated with a view of Haddon Hall, Derbys.

Mark: painted view number '106'
Diameter: 24.5 cm

See Cat. G58. Following his views of the Peak District, the other large engravings published by Thomas Smith in the 1740s were principally views of great estates: two Derbyshire houses, Chatsworth and Haddon, in 1744, Lyme Park in Cheshire in 1745, and four gardens in the Midlands – Belton, Hagley, Newstead and Exton – in 1749. However, he also published three on the River Trent in 1745 (see Cat. G70ff.), a view of Knaresborough in 1747 (see Cat. G73), and a set of abbeys (Fountains and Kirkstall) and castles (Kenilworth and Tynemouth) the same year (see Cat. G74–5). The view on the present plate is

based on a detail from the central part of *The North-West View of Haddon &c.*, engraving by François Vivares after Thomas Smith, 1744.

State Hermitage Museum, St Petersburg (8843)
Lit: Raeburn, Voronikhina and Nurnberg 1995, cat. 292, view 243

G64 11-inch round dish decorated with a view of Chatsworth, Derbys.

Enamelling of landscape attributed to Ralph Unwin
Mark: painted view number '662'
Diameter: 27.5 cm

See Cat. G63. The view is based on the right-hand part of *A South-West View of Chatsworth &c. a beautiful Seat of his Grace the Duke of Devonshire*, engraving by François Vivares after a painting by Thomas Smith, 1744. The view shows the formal garden laid out in the late 17th century with its famous waterworks, before it was remodelled by 'Capability' Brown in the 1760s. Unlike the other Thomas Smith prints, which appear to have been in Bentley's hands at the start of the work, the print of Chatsworth was purchased from John Pye on 7 February 1774. This piece is almost certainly one of the six 11-inch round dishes on Ralph Unwin's worksheet for 2 April 1774.

State Hermitage Museum, St Petersburg (8846)
Lit: Raeburn, Voronikhina and Nurnberg 1995, cat. 128, view 230; Williamson 1909, facing p. 94; Wedgwood MS E32-5253

G65 Flat plate decorated with a view of Exton Park, Rutland

Mark: painted view number '132'
Diameter: 24.5 cm

See Cat. G63. The view is based on the right-hand part of *A View in Exton Park belonging to the R.t Hon.ble the Earl of Gainsborough*, engraving by James Mason (1710–around 1780) after a painting by Thomas Smith, 1749. The gardens at Exton were also famous for their waterworks, which are reputed to have been planned by the great garden designer Stephen Switzer.

State Hermitage Museum, St Petersburg (8750)
Lit: Raeburn, Voronikhina and Nurnberg 1995, cat. 312, view 691

G66 13-inch oval dish decorated with a view of Newstead Abbey, Notts.

Marks: 'WEDGWOOD' impressed; painted view number '403'
33 × 25 cm

See Cat. G63. The view is based on the right-hand part of *A View in Newstead Park belonging to the R.ᵗ: Honᵇˡᵉ. the Lord Byron*, engraving by Mason after a painting by Thomas Smith, 1749. The house was built (16th–17th centuries) behind the façade of the 13th-century priory church, and the gardens were landscaped in the mid-18th century by 'Mad Jack' Byron.

State Hermitage Museum, St Petersburg (8654)
Lit: Raeburn, Voronikhina and Nurnberg 1995, cat. 53, view 665

G67 19-inch oval dishcover decorated with views of Belton House, Lincs., and Wimborne St Giles, Dorset

Marks: painted view numbers '746', '747'
43.5 × 33 cm

See Cat. G63. The views are based on *A View of the Waterworks &c at Belton in Lincolnshire, belonging to the R.ᵗ: Honᵇˡᵉ: the Lord Vis.ᵗ Tyrconnel*, engraving by François Vivares after a painting by Thomas Smith, October 1749; and *South East View of Wimborne St Giles, the Seat of Anthony Ashley Cooper Earl of Shaftesbury*, engraving by Thomas Vivares (1735–1808) in *The History and Antiquities of Dorset* by John Hutchins, vol.II, 1774 (see Cat. G235). Both gardens were remodelled in the 18th century. The two views demonstrate the remarkably imaginative way in which models were selected for paintings on the largest display pieces in the Service, although the poet William Shenstone commented on Smith's engraving

of Belton that it 'puts one in mind of a porridge-pot boiling over'.

State Hermitage Museum, St Petersburg (8508)
Lit: Raeburn, Voronikhina and Nurnberg 1995, cat. 604, views 482, 308

G68 Flat plate decorated with a view of the cascade at Belton House, Lincs.

Mark: painted view number '130'
Diameter: 24.5 cm

The view is based on the print by Vivares after Smith used for Cat. G67. The plate was omitted from the Service, presumably at a late stage, as the view number was not reused (see Cat. G10).

Trustees of the Wedgwood Museum, Barlaston, Staffordshire (5380)
Lit: Raeburn, Voronikhina and Nurnberg 1995, view A8

G69 15-inch oval dishcover decorated with views of Hagley Park, Hereford and Worcs.; and the grounds of Dalkeith Castle, Lothian

Marks: painted view numbers '1154', '1155'
34 × 24 cm

See Cat. G63. The views are based on *A View in Hagley Park belonging to S.ᵣ: Tho.ˢ: Littleton Bar.ᵗ*, engraving by François Vivares after a painting by Thomas Smith, 1749; and an untraced drawing, possibly from the painting exhibited by George Barret at the Royal Academy in 1770, *A view in his Grace the Duke of Buccleugh's Park, Dalkeith; with part of one of the wings of Dalkeith house* (see Cat. G290). The garden at Hagley, started by the first Lord Lyttleton in 1747, was one of the most celebrated in England, with an artificial ruin (on the left of the view) designed by Sanderson Miller, which was constructed at the time work began.

State Hermitage Museum, St Petersburg (8511)
Lit: Raeburn, Voronikhina and Nurnberg 1995, cat. 624, views 976, 1183; Williamson 1909, facing p. 36

G70 *A View of Anchor Church*

François Vivares after a painting by Thomas Smith
Etching with engraving
Lettered with title and publication line, and 'T. Smith Pinx. F. Vivares Scult.'
Dated 1765 (originally published 1745)
Size of platemark: 39 × 43.6 cm

See Cat. G63. This is one of the three views on the River Trent first published in 1745 and reissued 20 years later. Anchor Church was the name given to the caves overlooking the River Trent just north of Foremark, for reasons explained in the description in Bentley's catalogue of the first view based on this print: 'View on the river Trent, near Anchor Church, so called from an anchorite who made his dwelling there. This is a vast cavern opposite a fine rock situated on the banks of the river, in the county of Derby.'

Trustees of the British Museum (BM 1877-6-9-1936)

G71 16-inch oval dish decorated with a view of Anchor Church, Derbys.

Marks: 'WEDGWOOD' impressed; painted view number '278'
41.5 × 32 cm

See Cat. G70, on which the view is based. It was incorrectly numbered and corresponds to the description for no. 281 in Bentley's catalogue.

State Hermitage Museum, St Petersburg (8614)
Lit: Raeburn, Voronikhina and Nurnberg 1995, cat. 13, view 224

G72 16-inch oval dish decorated with a view of Donington Hills, Leics.

Marks: 'WEDGWOOD' impressed; painted view number '303'
41.5 × 32 cm

See Cat. G63. The view is based on *A View of Dunnington Cliff &c on the River Trent, (five Miles South East of Derby,) belonging to the Right Honourable the Earl of Huntingdon*, engraving by François Vivares after a painting by Thomas Smith, 1765, one of the three views on the River Trent first published in 1745. The view shows the river quay near King's Mills, which was probably the largest water-powered site in the country, with four mills, for iron-forging, flint- and gypsum-grinding and paper-making.

State Hermitage Museum, St Petersburg (8630)
Lit: Raeburn, Voronikhina and Nurnberg 1995, cat. 16, view 477; Williamson, facing p. 38

G73 13-inch round dish decorated with a view of the Petrifying Well, Knaresborough, N. Yorks.

Mark: painted view number '411'
Diameter: 33 cm

See Cat. G63. The view is based on the left-hand part of *A View of Petrifying Spring, commonly call'd the Dropping Well, &c at Knaresborough, in Yorkshire*, engraving by François Vivares after a painting by Thomas Smith, 1747.

State Hermitage Museum, St Petersburg (8711)
Lit: Raeburn, Voronikhina and Nurnberg 1995, cat. 83, view 1023; Williamson 1909, facing p. 16

G74 15-inch oval dish decorated with a view of Fountains Abbey, N. Yorks.

Marks: 'WEDGWOOD' impressed; painted view number '526'
38.5 × 29 cm

See Cat. G63. The view is based on *Fountains Abbey, from the South-East; Situate two Miles West of Rippon in Yorkshire*, undated engraving (1747) by François Vivares after a painting by Thomas Smith. One of the most majestic abbey ruins in England, Fountains was a popular subject for engravers, and three different prints were used as models for the Service, in addition to views of the gardens of Studley Park (see Cat. G146ff.), which were planned to focus on the abbey ruins as a viewpoint.

State Hermitage Museum, St Petersburg (8637)
Lit: Raeburn, Voronikhina and Nurnberg 1995, cat. 37, view 1000; Williamson 1909, facing p. 58

G75 Flat plate decorated with a view of Tynemouth Priory, Northumbria

Mark: painted view number '128'
Diameter: 24.5 cm

See Cat. G63. The view is based on the central part of *Tinmouth Castle, from the North; with a view of the Haven, &c.*, engraving by François Vivares after a painting by Thomas Smith, 1747.

State Hermitage Museum, St Petersburg (8763)
Lit: Raeburn, Voronikhina and Nurnberg 1995, cat. 310, view 654

G76 *The High Force*

James Mason after a painting by Thomas Smith
Etching with engraving
Lettered with title, and 'Tho: Smith Pinx. J. Mason Sculp.'
Dated 1751
Size of platemark: 38.7 × 54.5 cm

See Cat. G58. From 1750 onwards all Thomas Smith's large prints seem to have been devoted to landscape: four views in Derbyshire and Yorkshire (see Cat. G77ff) published in 1751, a view of St Vincent's Rocks near Bristol in 1756, two views of Colebrookdale (in collaboration with George Perry; see Cat. G82ff) in 1758, and four views in the Lake District (see Cat. G81) in 1767.

Trustees of the British Museum (BM 1866-11-14-455)

G77 Flat plate decorated with a view of High Force, N. Yorks.

Mark: painted view number '171'
Diameter: 24.5 cm

See Cat. G76. The view is based on the right-hand part of the engraving.

State Hermitage Museum, St Petersburg (8826)
Lit: Raeburn, Voronikhina and Nurnberg 1995, cat. 345, view 1012

G78 15-inch oval dish decorated with a view of High Force, N. Yorks.

Mark: painted view number '282'
38.5 × 29 cm

See Cat. G76. The view is based on the complete engraving.

State Hermitage Museum, St Petersburg (8624)
Lit: Raeburn, Voronikhina and Nurnberg 1995, cat. 19, view 1013

G79 16-inch oval dish decorated with a view of Thorpe Cloud, Derbys.

Marks: 'WEDGWOOD' impressed; painted view number '280'
41.5 × 32 cm

See Cat. G76. The view is based on *Thorpe Cloud &c.*, engraving by James Mason after a painting by Thomas Smith, 1751. Thorpe Cloud is a conical hill that stands at the entrance to Dovedale.

State Hermitage Museum, St Petersburg (8628)
Lit: Raeburn, Voronikhina and Nurnberg 1995, cat. 12, view 239

G80 15-inch oval dish decorated with a view of Matlock High Tor, Derbys.

Mark: painted view number '305'
38.5 × 29 cm

See Cat. G76. The view is based on *Matlock High-Torr &c.*, engraving by James Mason after a painting by Thomas Smith, 1751.

State Hermitage Museum, St Petersburg (8638)
Lit: Raeburn, Voronikhina and Nurnberg 1995, cat. 36, view 246; Voronikhina 1988, p. 168

G81 Flat plate decorated with a view of Lake Windermere, Cumbria

Mark: painted view number '246'
Diameter: 24.5 cm

See Cat. G76. The view is based on the central part of *A View of Windermeer*, painted, engraved and published by Thomas Smith, 1767.

State Hermitage Museum, St Petersburg (8731)
Lit: Raeburn, Voronikhina and Nurnberg 1995,
cat. 410, view 953

G82 *A View of the Upper Works at Coalbrook Dale, in the County of Salop*

Etched by François Vivares; designed and
published by George Perry (1719–71) and
Thomas Smith
Etching with engraving
Lettered with title, publication line, and
'F Vivares Sculp'
Dated 1758
Cut to 38.1 × 52.4 cm

Coalbrookdale, in the Severn valley, was
where Abraham Darby established his iron
works in 1708, developing a process for
smelting which used coke rather than
charcoal, and it became one of the key sites
of the early Industrial Revolution. The two
prints by Smith and Perry (an engineer who
established a foundry business in Liverpool
in 1758) are the earliest views of the site,
and they show some of the furnaces, a
cylinder made at the foundry, and Darby's
house, as well as cottages of the workmen.
The prints were published with an
accompanying text which celebrates the
development of the iron-working trade in
the most optimistic terms: 'The Face of the
Country shews the happy Effect of this
flourishing Trade, The lower Class of
People, who are very numerous here, are
enabled to live comfortably; their Cottages,
which almost cover some of the
neighbouring hills, are throng'd with
healthy Children, who soon are able to find
Employment and perhaps chearfulness and
contentment are not more visible in another
place. A pleasing Proof this, that *Arts* and
Manufactures contribute greatly to the
Wealth and *power* of a Nation, and the
Industry and *Commerce* will soon improve,
and People the most uncultivated
Situation.'

Trustees of the British Museum (BM 1871-8-12-
1601)

G83 Flat plate decorated with a view of Colebrookdale, Salop

Mark: painted view number '147'
Diameter: 24.5 cm

See Cat. G82. The view is based on the
right-hand part of the engraving.

State Hermitage Museum, St Petersburg (8866)
Lit: Raeburn, Voronikhina and Nurnberg 1995,
cat. 327, view 697

G84 Flat plate decorated with a view of Colebrookdale, Salop *(Pl. 35)*

Mark: painted view number '150'
Diameter: 24.5 cm

See Cat. G82. The view is based on the left-
hand part of the engraving. It shows the
furnaces and, 'near the fore-ground is
represented a large Cylinder on its Carriage,
supposed to be Seventy Inches Diameter, Ten
Feet Long, and weighing about Six Tons,
being the Real Dimensions of one lately cast
at this *Foundery*, and sent to *Cornwall*.'

State Hermitage Museum, St Petersburg (8783)
Lit: Raeburn, Voronikhina and Nurnberg 1995,
cat. 330, view 699

G85 14-inch oval dish decorated with a view of Colebrookdale, Salop

Marks: 'WEDGWOOD' impressed; painted
view number '508'
35.5 × 27 cm

See Cat. G82. The view is based on the
second of the engravings by Vivares after
Smith and Perry, *The South West Prospect of*
Colebrook-Dale, and the adjacent Country,
1758.

State Hermitage Museum, St Petersburg (8644)
Lit: Raeburn, Voronikhina and Nurnberg 1995,
cat. 47, view 702

G86 13-inch oval dish decorated with a view of Saltwood Castle, Kent

Marks: 'WEDGWOOD' impressed; painted
view number '507'
33 × 25 cm

The view is based on *A View of Saltwood-*
Castle at Hythe, engraving by James Mason,
published 20 February 1762, after a
drawing and painting by George Lambert
(1700–65). Lambert's painting with its
highly picturesque setting probably dates
from the 1740s (see p. 141).

Saltwood Castle had fallen into ruins as a
result of a violent earthquake in 1580 (it
was not rebuilt until the 1930s).

State Hermitage Museum, St Petersburg (8657)
Lit: Raeburn, Voronikhina and Nurnberg 1995,
cat. 57, view 449

G87 14-inch round dishcover decorated with views of Neath Abbey, West Glamorgan, and Longford Castle, Wilts. *(Pl. 37)*

Marks: painted view numbers '1131', '1132'
Diameter: 32 cm

The view of Neath Abbey, a house built out
of the abbey ruins, is based on an untraced
drawing by an unknown artist; the view of
Longford Castle is based on a privately
issued engraving after a painting by George
Lambert, 1743 (now in the Department of
the Environment Art Collection). Longford,
built around 1585–91 and altered during
the 18th century, is of special interest for
the Frog Service, since, as Peter Hayden has
shown, the Gothic Revival architecture of
the Kekerekeksinen Palace (1774–7), for
which the Service was destined, was
modelled by Yuri Felten on the triangular
plan of Longford.

State Hermitage Museum, St Petersburg (8459)
Lit: Raeburn, Voronikhina and Nurnberg 1995,
cat. 648, views 1124, 957; Williamson 1909, facing
p. 20; Hayden 1985 pp. 17ff and fig. 4

G88 12-inch round dish decorated with a view of Lake Windermere, Cumbria

Mark: painted view number '413'
Diameter: 30.5 cm

The view is based on *A View of Winander*
Meer near Ambleside, a Lake between
Lancashire & Westmoreland, engraving by
Jean-Baptiste Claude Chatelain (1710–71)

and Johann Sebastian Müller (around 1715–92) after a painting by William Bellers (active 1750–73), first published by Bellers 1 May 1753 and reissued 1774. Bellers' views in the Lake District precede those of Thomas Smith and are among the earliest to depict the scenery that was soon to fill visitors with such enthusiasm.

State Hermitage Museum, St Petersburg (8719) Lit: Raeburn, Voronikhina and Nurnberg 1995, cat. 104, view 955

G89 11-inch round dish decorated with a view of Ullswater, Cumbria

Enamelling of landscape attributed to Ralph Unwin
Mark: painted view number '659'
Diameter: 27.5 cm

The view is based on *A View of the head of Ulswater toward Patterdale*, engraving by Chatelain and James Mason after a painting by William Bellers, first published 18 April 1754 and reissued 1774. It is almost certainly one of the landscapes painted by Unwin just before 2 April 1774 (see Cat. G64).

State Hermitage Museum, St Petersburg (8854) Lit: Raeburn, Voronikhina and Nurnberg 1995, cat. 125, view 951; Wedgwood MS E32-5253

G90 Dessert plate decorated with a view of Netley Abbey, Hants.

Mark: painted view number '890'
Diameter: 22 cm

The view is based on the left-hand part of *South East View of Netley Abby Near Southampton*, engraving by William Henry Toms and James Mason after a painting by William Bellers, 1755. The picturesque ruins of Netley Abbey became a favourite goal for 18th-century tourists and were the subject of numerous paintings.

State Hermitage Museum, St Petersburg (9132) Lit: Raeburn, Voronikhina and Nurnberg 1995, cat. 775, view 354

G 89

G91 Flat plate decorated with a view of Aust Passage, Avon

Mark: painted view number '475'
Diameter: 24.5 cm

The view is based on the central part of *A Ferry on the River Severn*, engraving by J. Smith after Jean-Baptiste Pillement, 1773. It shows the inn and neighbouring buildings at Aust, the more northerly of the two crossing points over the Severn for travellers from London to South Wales, close to the site of the present road bridge.

State Hermitage Museum, St Petersburg (8737) Lit: Raeburn, Voronikhina and Nurnberg 1995, cat. 463, view 324

G92 Dessert plate decorated with a view of White Horse Hill, Berks.

Mark: painted view number '838'
Diameter: 22 cm

The view is based on an untraced print, prior to 1769. The White Horse of Uffington, which measures 109 metres from ear to tail, was believed to have been made by King Alfred to celebrate his victory over the Danes at Ashdown in 873. It is now thought to date from around 1000 BC – possibly a representation of the Celtic goddess Epona, the 'great mare'.

State Hermitage Museum, St Petersburg (9075) Lit: Raeburn, Voronikhina and Nurnberg 1995, cat. 725, view 15

LANDSCAPE GARDENS

G93 *The Lodge & Stables &c.* from *Eight Views of Windsor Great Park*

James Mason after Thomas Sandby (1723–98)
Etching with engraving
Lettered with title, and 'T. Sandby Delin Mason fecit'
1754
Cut to 33.3 × 55.6 cm

Windsor Great Park was landscaped from 1746 for the Duke of Cumberland. Thomas Sandby, who had been a military engineer on the Duke's campaigns in Scotland, planned the extensive developments, including the rebuilding of the Great Lodge (now known as Cumberland Lodge) and the construction of Virginia Water and its cascades. He also recorded the new layout in a series of watercolours, on which the set of *Eight Views*, executed by various engravers including his brother, Paul, was based.

Trustees of the British Museum (BM 1865-6-10-1873)

G94 Flat plate decorated with a view of the Great Lodge, Windsor Great Park, Berks.

Mark: painted view number '95'
Diameter: 24.5 cm

See Cat. G93. The view is based on the right-hand part of the engraving.

State Hermitage Museum, St Petersburg (8914) Lit: Raeburn, Voronikhina and Nurnberg 1995, cat. 281, view 19

G95 13-inch round dish decorated with a view of the Great Lodge, Windsor Great Park, Berks.

Mark: painted view number '460'
Diameter: 33 cm

See Cat. G93. The view is based on the left-hand part of the engraving.

State Hermitage Museum, St Petersburg (8710)

Lit: Raeburn, Voronikhina and Nurnberg 1995, cat. 85, view 21

G96 Flat plate decorated with a view of Virginia Water, Surrey

Mark: painted view number '134'
Diameter: 24.5 cm

See Cat. G93. The view is based on the left-hand part of *View from the North side of the Virginia River near the Manour Lodge*, engraved by Paul Sandby after Thomas Sandby, no. 4 of *Eight Views*.

State Hermitage Museum, St Petersburg (8788)
Lit: Raeburn, Voronikhina and Nurnberg 1995, cat. 314, view 22

G97 *A View of Esher in Surry the Seat of the Rt. Honble. Henry Pelham Esqr.*

Luke Sullivan (1705–71)
Etching with engraving
Lettered with title in English and French, with publication line, and 'Luke Sullivan delint & sculpt.'
Dated 1759
Size of platemark: 36.4 × 52 cm

Prints of the great English landscape gardens began to be published from the 1750s onwards, making it possible for Wedgwood and Bentley to include views showing many of the improvements made at the mid-century without having to have

G 99

drawings specially made. An outstanding group are the views of Oatlands, Esher Place, Woburn Farm, Wilton, Ditchley Park and Cliveden by Luke Sullivan, all published in 1759.

Both the house and gardens at Esher had been remodelled in the Gothic style by William Kent in the 1730s.

Trustees of the British Museum (BM 1867-12-14-755)

G98 Flat plate decorated with a view of Esher Place, Surrey

Mark: painted view number '4'
Diameter: 24.5 cm

See Cat. G97. The view is based on the extreme right-hand part of the engraving.

State Hermitage Museum, St Petersburg (8795)
Lit: Raeburn, Voronikhina and Nurnberg 1995, cat. 198, view 822

G99 17-inch oval dishcover decorated with views of Esher Place, Surrey, and Virginia Water, Surrey

Marks: painted view number '630', '631'
39 × 30 cm

See Cat. G97 and G93. The views are based on the complete print of Esher and on the right-hand part of *The Cascade and Grotto*, engraved by Paul Sandby and Edward Rooker after Thomas Sandby, no. 5 of *Eight Views of Windsor Great Park*.

State Hermitage Museum, St Petersburg (20837)
Lit: Raeburn, Voronikhina and Nurnberg 1995, cat. 606, views 824, 28

G100 Stand for sauce boat decorated with a view of Woburn Farm, Surrey

Mark: painted view number '543'
20 × 16.5 cm

See Cat. G97. The view is based on the central part of *A View of Woobourn in Surry the Seat of Philip Southcote Esqr.*, designed and engraved by Luke Sullivan. The gardens of Woburn, a 'ferme ornée', were laid out by Philip Southcote, who bought the estate in 1735. They were much admired and Woburn was, as Bentley says in his catalogue, 'one of the first places where modern taste was displayed in garden design'.

State Hermitage Museum, St Petersburg (8682)
Lit: Raeburn, Voronikhina and Nurnberg 1995, cat. 183, view 905

G 96

G101 Flat plate decorated with a view of the Thames from Cliveden House, Bucks.

Mark: painted view number '101'
Diameter: 24.5 cm

See Cat. G97. The view is based on the left-hand part of *A View of Cliveden in Buckinghamshire. The Seat of the R*^t*. Hon*^{ble}*. the Earl of Inchiquin*, designed and engraved by Luke Sullivan. The grounds were laid out in the early 18th century by the Earl of Orkney.

State Hermitage Museum, St Petersburg (8755)
Lit: Raeburn, Voronikhina and Nurnberg 1995, cat. 287, view 39

G102 14-inch oval dish decorated with a view of Cliveden House, Bucks.

Marks: 'WEDGWOOD' impressed; painted view number '405'
35.5 × 27 cm

See Cat. G101. The view is based on the whole engraving.

State Hermitage Museum, St Petersburg (8643)
Lit: Raeburn, Voronikhina and Nurnberg 1995, cat. 42, view 42

G103 Flat plate decorated with a view of Wilton House, Wilts.

Mark: painted view number '100'
Diameter: 24.5 cm

See Cat. G97. The view is based on the central part of *A view of Wilton in Wiltshire*, designed and engraved by Luke Sullivan. The 17th-century formal garden was landscaped by the 9th Earl of Pembroke, who collaborated with Roger Morris on the design of the Palladian bridge (1737) seen on the left of the view.

State Hermitage Museum, St Petersburg (8754)
Lit: Raeburn, Voronikhina and Nurnberg 1995, cat. 286, view 970

G104 *A View of the Canal and of the Gothic Tower in the Garden of His Grace of Argyl at Whitton*

William Woollett (1735–85)
Etching with engraving
Lettered with title in English and French, with publication line and 'W. Woollett del. et Sculp.'
Dated 1757
Size of platemark: 36.5 × 53.3 cm

William Woollett, like Luke Sullivan, contributed a group of fine engravings to the views of gardens published in the late 1750s, including Combe Bank, Foots Cray, Painshill, Hall Barn, Whitton and the gardens of Carlton House. He also engraved William Hannan's views of West Wycombe and a number of other views that were used on the Service.

The garden at Whitton was developed from 1722 by Archibald Campbell, 3rd Duke of Argyll, with his gardener, Daniel Crofts. The design of the triangular Gothic castle at the head of the canal has been attributed to James Gibbs.

Trustees of the British Museum (BM 1866-12-8-91)

G105 17-inch oval dish decorated with a view of Whitton Place, Greater London

Mark: painted view number '503'
44 × 34 cm

See Cat. G104, on which the view is based.

State Hermitage Museum, St Petersburg (20841)
Lit: Raeburn, Voronikhina and Nurnberg 1995, cat. 7, view 596

G106 Triangular dish decorated with a view of Whitton Place, Greater London

Marks: 'WEDGWOOD' impressed; painted view number '646'
Length of each side: 28.5 cm

See Cat. G104, on which the view is based.

State Hermitage Museum, St Petersburg (8501)
Lit: Raeburn, Voronikhina and Nurnberg 1995, cat. 146, view 597; Williamson 1909, facing p. 80; Voronikhina 1988, p. 170

G107 15-inch oval dish decorated with a view of Combe Bank, Kent

Marks: 'WEDGWOOD' impressed; painted view number '293'
38.5 × 29 cm

See Cat. G104. The view is based on *A View of Coombank near Sevenoaks in Kent, the seat of the Ho*^{ble} *Lieut. Gen*^l*. Campbell*, designed and engraved by William Woollett. The villa was built around 1726–7 by Roger Morris for John Campbell, later 4th Duke of Argyll.

State Hermitage Museum, St Petersburg (8616)
Lit: Raeburn, Voronikhina and Nurnberg 1995, cat. 29, view 405

G108 15-inch oval dish decorated with a view of Painshill, Surrey

Marks: 'WEDGWOOD' impressed; painted view number '304'
38.5 × 29 cm

See Cat. G104. The view is based on *A View from the West Side of the Island in the Garden of the Hon. Charles Hamilton Esq*^r*. at Painshill near Cobham in Surry*, designed and engraved by William Woollett. The landscape garden created at Painshill in the 1740s by Charles Hamilton was much admired by his contemporaries.

State Hermitage Museum, St Petersburg (8631)
Lit: Raeburn, Voronikhina and Nurnberg 1995, cat. 35, view 876

G109 *A View of the Cascade &c. in the Garden of S*^r*. Francis Dashwood Bar*^t*. & of the Parish Church &c at West Wycomb in the County of Bucks*

William Woollett after a painting by William Hannan (d. 1775)
Engraving with etching
Lettered with title in English and French, with publication line and 'W. Hannan pinx. W. Woollett sculp.'
1757
Cut to 35.8 × 52.2 cm

The gardens were laid out by Sir Francis

Dashwood from 1735 and included many of the standard features of the period – temples, bridges, cascades and a Turkish tent. Woollett did four views of the gardens, all based on paintings by the Scottish artist William Hannan, who also did ceiling paintings in the house.

Victoria & Albert Museum (29191.13)

G110 Flat plate decorated with a view of West Wycombe, Bucks.

Mark: painted view number '111'
Diameter: 24.5 cm

See Cat. G109. The view is based on a detail from the centre of the engraving. The tree from the left of the print has been brought in to balance the thick woods behind the tent.

State Hermitage Museum, St Petersburg (8765)
Lit: Raeburn, Voronikhina and Nurnberg 1995, cat. 297, view 115

G111 Flat plate decorated with a view of West Wycombe, Bucks.

Mark: painted view number '191'
Diameter: 24.5 cm

See Cat. G109. The view combines details from the left-hand background and centre foreground of the engraving.

State Hermitage Museum, St Petersburg (8738)
Lit: Raeburn, Voronikhina and Nurnberg 1995, cat. 363, view 116

G112 Flat plate decorated with a view of West Wycombe, Bucks.

Mark: painted view number '217'
Diameter: 24.5 cm

See Cat. G109. The view is based on a detail from the left-hand part of the engraving.

State Hermitage Museum, St Petersburg (8907)
Lit: Raeburn, Voronikhina and Nurnberg 1995, cat. 384, view 117

G 109

G 111

G113 15-inch oval dish decorated with a view of West Wycombe, Bucks.

Mark: painted view number '285'
38.5 × 29 cm

See Cat. G109. The view is based on the right-hand side of *A View of the Lake etc. taken from the Center Walk in the Garden of Sir Francis Dashwood Bart. in the County of Bucks*, engraved by William Woollett after a painting by William Hannan. This is the only piece omitted from the Service that was nevertheless included in Bentley's catalogue. Nineteen oval dishes of this size were decorated at an early stage, and two were added later, one with a view of

Fountains Abbey (Cat. G74), the other, when work was almost completed, with a view of Wedgwood's own house at Etruria (Cat. G289). Since the Service allowed for only 20 dishes of this size, the present one must have been omitted at the last minute, probably to accommodate the Etruria dish, without the catalogue entry being cancelled.

Victoria & Albert Museum (C.74-1931)
Lit: Raeburn, Voronikhina and Nurnberg 1995, view A13

G114 Sauce boat decorated with views of West Wycombe, Bucks., and Stowe, Bucks.

Marks: painted view numbers '547', '548'
6.5 × 20.5 × 9 cm

See Cat. G109. The view of West Wycombe is based on a detail from the extreme right-hand part of the print used for Cat. G113; the view of Stowe is based on *A View at the Queen's Statue*, pl. h from the book of engravings by George Bickham junior after Chatelain, 1753 (see Cat. G118).

State Hermitage Museum, St Petersburg (8566)
Lit: Raeburn, Voronikhina and Nurnberg 1995, cat. 171, views 108, 83

Chatelain del.   *According to Act of Parliam. Drawn from this Spot. 1753.* | *Vue dans les Champs Elisées prise de la Fontaine de l'Helicon.*   *G.Bickham Sculp.*

A View in the Elysian Fields from the Spring of Helicon.

G 117

G115 Flat plate decorated with a view of West Wycombe, Bucks.

Mark: painted view number '124'
Diameter: 24.5 cm

See Cat. G109. The view is based on a detail from the left-hand background of *A View of the Walton Bridge, Venus's Temple, &c. in the Garden of Sir Francis Dashwood Bart. at West Wycomb in the County of Bucks*, engraved by Woollett after a painting by Hannan.

State Hermitage Museum, St Petersburg (8764)
Lit: Raeburn, Voronikhina and Nurnberg 1995, cat. 306, view 111

G116 14-inch round dish decorated with a view of West Wycombe, Bucks.

Landscape enamelled by William Shuter
Mark: painted view number '990'
Diameter: 35 cm

See Cat. G109. The view is based on the left and centre of *A View of the House Park and Garden of Sir Francis Dashwood Bart. at West Wycomb in the County of Bucks*, engraved by Woollett after a painting by Hannan. According to his account of

19 April 1774, all eight round dishes of this size were decorated by Shuter.

State Hermitage Museum, St Petersburg (8707)
Lit: Raeburn, Voronikhina and Nurnberg 1995, cat. 77, view 119; Wedgwood MS E32-5269

G117 *Sixteen Perspective Views, together with a General Plan of the Magnificent Buildings and Gardens at Stow, in the County of Bucks, belonging to The Right Honourable Earl Temple, Viscount and Baron Cobham. Correctly drawn on the spot 1752, with His Lordship's permission and approbation*

George Bickham junior (d. around 1769) after drawings by Jean-Baptiste Claude Chatelain (1710–71)
Engravings with etching
George Bickham senior (publisher), London
All plates dated 1753
37.3 × 107 cm (open)

The gardens at Stowe were the most celebrated example of the English landscape garden, although the plethora of garden buildings, each with its own specific symbolism, were no longer in the modern

taste by the 1770s. Work was begun in 1713 by Sir Richard Temple, afterwards Viscount Cobham, according to the plan and under the supervision of Charles Bridgeman. The architects during the first phase were Sir John Vanbrugh and, after Vanbrugh's death in 1726, James Gibbs. There was still a strong element of formality in the layout, and this was progressively 'naturalized' by Bridgeman's successors, William Kent (from around 1730) and Lancelot Brown, who was head gardener at Stowe from 1741 to 1751. Lord Cobham died in 1749, and work was carried on by his nephew and heir, Richard Grenville, later Lord Temple, who employed Giovanni Battista Borra as his architect. The views on the Frog Service show the gardens in the early 1750s, but work was still continuing at the time the Service was made and the gardens were not completed until 1790. Several publications had been devoted to Stowe, but Bickham's engravings were the most modern ones available to Bentley.

Victoria & Albert Museum. National Art Library (86.J.21)

G118 Flat plate decorated with a view of Stowe, Bucks.

Mark: painted view number '213'
Diameter: 24.5 cm

See Cat. G117. The view is based on the central part of *A View at the Queen's Statue*, plate h in Bickham's book. The view shows Vanbrugh's Rotondo of 1721, which sheltered a gilded statue of Venus, patroness of gardens and gardeners.

State Hermitage Museum, St Petersburg (8873)
Lit: Raeburn, Voronikhina and Nurnberg 1995, cat. 380, view 81

G119 Flat plate decorated with a view of Stowe, Bucks.

Mark: painted view number '248'
Diameter: 24.5 cm

See Cat. G117. The view is based on the right-hand part of *A View from Nelson's*

Seat, plate e in Bickham's book. The print shows Rogers' Walk and Nelson's Walk (seen in this view), two diverging avenues laid out by Bridgeman and named after Lord Cobham's gardeners which lead to the Rotondo and to one of the Boycott Pavilions (see Cat. G121).

State Hermitage Museum, St Petersburg (8759)
Lit: Raeburn, Voronikhina and Nurnberg 1995, cat. 412, view 92

G120 13-inch oval dish decorated with a view of Stowe, Bucks.

Marks: 'WEDGWOOD' impressed; painted view number '506'
33 × 25 cm

See Cat. G117. The view, which is based on the same print as Cat. G119, shows both of the Walks.

State Hermitage Museum, St Petersburg (8661)
Lit: Raeburn, Voronikhina and Nurnberg 1995, cat. 56, view 93

G121 Spoon for sauce tureen decorated with a view of Stowe, Bucks.

Mark: painted view number '611'
Length: 16.5 cm

See Cat. G117. The feature is taken from the print used for Cat. G119. It shows one of the two Boycott Pavilions, so called from the hamlet that had formerly existed there. Their pyramidal roofs were replaced with domes by Borra in 1754.

State Hermitage Museum, St Petersburg (8560B)
Lit: Raeburn, Voronikhina and Nurnberg 1995, cat. 669, view 95

G122 15-inch oval dish decorated with a view of Stowe, Bucks.

Marks: 'WEDGWOOD' impressed; painted view number '284'
38.5 × 29 cm

See Cat. G117. The view is based on *A View to the Grotto of the Serpentine River in the Alder Grove*, plate l in Bickham's book.

The view shows the Grotto at the end of the water and the Cold Bath on the right, probably part of William Kent's designs in the 1730s.

State Hermitage Museum, St Petersburg (8633)
Lit: Raeburn, Voronikhina and Nurnberg 1995, cat. 21, view 78

G123 15-inch oval dish decorated with a view of Stowe, Bucks.

Mark: painted view number '288'
38.5 × 29 cm

See Cat. G117. The view is based on *A View at the Entrance between the Pavillions*, plate a in Bickham's book. The view shows the Guglio Fountain, a 70-foot obelisk, which was removed by Lord Temple, in the middle of the Octagonal Lake. Part of one of the pavilions designed by Vanbrugh before 1720 as the original entrance to the garden is seen on the right.

State Hermitage Museum, St Petersburg (8634)
Lit: Raeburn, Voronikhina and Nurnberg 1995, cat. 24, view 67

G124 15-inch oval dish decorated with a view of Stowe, Bucks.

Marks: 'WEDGWOOD' impressed; painted view number '289'
38.5 × 29 cm

See Cat. G117. The view is based on *A View of the Queen's Theatre from the Rotundo*, plate g in Bickham's book. The Queen's Theatre, planned by Bridgeman, was an amphitheatre of grassed terraces centred on Queen Caroline's Monument. For the Rotondo, see Cat. G118.

State Hermitage Museum, St Petersburg (8636)
Lit: Raeburn, Voronikhina and Nurnberg 1995, cat. 25, view 89

G125 15-inch oval dish decorated with a view of Stowe, Bucks.

Marks: 'WEDGWOOD' impressed; painted view number '295'
38.5 × 29 cm

See Cat. G117. The view is based on *A View from yᵉ Island Seat of yᵉ Lake of yᵉ Temple of Venus & Hermitage*, plate c in Bickham's book. The 11-acre lake was first laid out by Bridgeman in semi-formal style and later 'naturalized'. The Hermitage, seen across the Lake, was built by Kent before 1732.

State Hermitage Museum, St Petersburg (8617)
Lit: Raeburn, Voronikhina and Nurnberg 1995, cat. 31, view 74

G126 14-inch oval dish decorated with a view of Stowe, Bucks. *(Pl. 34)*

Marks: 'WEDGWOOD' impressed; painted view number '485'
35.5 × 27 cm

See Cat. G117. The view is based on *A View in the Elysian Fields from the Spring of Helicon*, plate m in Bickham's book. The Elysian Fields were laid out in the 1730s. In the background is the Temple of Friendship, built by Gibbs in 1739.

State Hermitage Museum, St Petersburg (8648)
Lit: Raeburn, Voronikhina and Nurnberg 1995, cat. 45, view 70

G127 14-inch oval dish decorated with a view of Stowe, Bucks.

Marks: 'WEDGWOOD' impressed; painted view number '529'
35.5 × 27 cm

See Cat. G117. The view is based on *A View of the Temple of Diana*, plate d in Bickham's book. The temple was erected around 1726 to designs by Gibbs. In the background can be seen the Hermitage, the Lake Walk and the Temple of Venus.

State Hermitage Museum, St Petersburg (8647)
Lit: Raeburn, Voronikhina and Nurnberg 1995, cat. 50, view 97

G128 12-inch oval dish decorated with a view of Stowe, Bucks.

Mark: painted view number '309'
31.5 × 24 cm

See Cat. G117. The view is based on *A View over the Great Bason to the Entrance between the Pavillions*, plate b in Bickham's book. It shows a view similar to that in Cat. G123, but from the other end of the Octagonal Lake, towards the Entrance Pavilions.

State Hermitage Museum, St Petersburg (8664)
Lit: Raeburn, Voronikhina and Nurnberg 1995, cat. 60, view 55

G129 14-inch round dish decorated with a view of Stowe, Bucks.

Landscape enamelled by William Shuter
Mark: painted view number '989'
Diameter: 35 cm

See Cat. G117. The view is based on *A View of the House from the Parterre. According to the plan proposed by Signor Borra. Extent 540 Feet exclusive of the Offices*, plate j in Bickham's book. This view is unique in the Service in that it shows a project that was not in fact ever carried out. It was copied at a fairly late stage in the decoration of the Service, when more houses – rather than their gardens – were included among the subjects for the views. Its decoration, like several others requiring special skill in rendering the architecture, was entrusted to Shuter (see Cat. G116).

State Hermitage Museum, St Petersburg (8698)
Lit: Raeburn, Voronikhina and Nurnberg 1995, cat. 76, view 100; Wedgwood MS E32-5269

G130 13-inch round dish decorated with a view of Stowe, Bucks.

Mark: painted view number '510'
Diameter: 33 cm

See Cat. G117. The view is based on the right-hand part of *A View from Capt. Grenvilles Monument, to the Grecian Temple*, plate n in Bickham's book. The Grenville Column (originally surmounted by the figure of Hercules seen here, who was later replaced by a figure symbolizing Heroic Poetry), was erected in 1747 in memory of Lord Cobham's nephew,

Captain Thomas Grenville, who died in action at sea. The Temple of Concord and Victory was built around the same time, probably to designs by Lord Temple.

State Hermitage Museum, St Petersburg (8700)
Lit: Raeburn, Voronikhina and Nurnberg 1995, cat. 90, view 91

G131 12-inch round dish decorated with a view of Stowe, Bucks.

Mark: painted view number '515'
Diameter: 30.5 cm

See Cat. G117. The view is based on *A View of the House from the Equestrian Statue in the Park*, plate q in Bickham's book. The view shows the north front of the house, remodelled in the 1720s, probably by Vanbrugh and Leoni. The equestrian statue of George I in Roman armour by John Nost was the earliest feature in the garden, erected around 1720.

State Hermitage Museum, St Petersburg (8726)
Lit: Raeburn, Voronikhina and Nurnberg 1995, cat. 113, view 65; Williamson 1909, facing p. 92

G132 Ice cup decorated with views of garden buildings at Stowe, Bucks.

Marks: painted view numbers '1121', '1122'
Height with cover: 7.5 cm; diameter: 6 cm

The views on this and the following item (which are incorrectly numbered; they correspond to nos 1117–20 in Bentley's catalogue) are based on a guide book to Stowe, *Stowe: A description of the Magnificent House and Gardens of Richard Earl Temple*, 1763, with engravings by G.L.Smith after Benton Seeley (1716–95). Seeley had published the first guide to the gardens in 1744 and, after this had proved highly successful, George Bickham produced a rival publication, *The Beauties of Stow*, in 1750. This led to what has been described by George Clarke as the 'battle of the guidebooks', in the course of which 'both publishers tried to outdo the other by adding extra features to each new edition. In the end it was Seeley who won. After the

appearance of the 1763 edition there was no reply from Bickham, who retired from the struggle.' The buildings shown here are one of the Entrance Pavilions (see Cat. G123) and the Hermitage (see Cat. G125).

State Hermitage Museum, St Petersburg (9168)
Lit: Raeburn, Voronikhina and Nurnberg 1995, cat. 924, views 101, 102; Clarke 1990, p. 174

G133 Ice cup decorated with views of garden buildings at Stowe, Bucks.

Marks: painted view numbers '1127', '1128'
Height with cover: 7.5 cm; diameter: 6 cm

See Cat. G132. The buildings shown here are Nelson's Seat, one of the pavilions designed by Vanbrugh, and the Cold Bath (see Cat. G122).

State Hermitage Museum, St Petersburg (9167)
Lit: Raeburn, Voronikhina and Nurnberg 1995, cat. 927, views 103, 104

G134 Flat plate decorated with a view of Mount Edgcumbe, Cornwall

Mark: painted view number '198'
Diameter: 24.5 cm

The view is based on *A View of Mount-Edgcumbe from the Block-house*, engraving by James Mason after a drawing by Coplestone Warre Bampfylde (1719–91) from a painting by George Lambert and Samuel Scott. Lambert (1700–65) and Scott (1710–72), who specialized in landscapes and seascapes respectively, collaborated on a number of paintings, including a set of five views at or near Mount Edgcumbe. This was one of the most visited gardens in the late 18th century and, while it was adorned with all the customary features, its special appeal came from the views over Plymouth Sound with the coastal defences and passing ships. This plate was omitted from the Service and replaced with another (now lost) with a view of the same place.

Private collection
Lit: Raeburn, Voronikhina and Nurnberg 1995, view A11

G135 Flat plate decorated with a view of Mount Edgcumbe, Cornwall

Mark: painted view number '242'
Diameter: 24.5 cm

The view is based on the left-hand part of the engraving used for Cat. G134.

State Hermitage Museum, St Petersburg (8893)
Lit: Raeburn, Voronikhina and Nurnberg 1995, cat. 407, view 262

G136 15-inch oval dish decorated with a distant view of Mount Edgcumbe, Cornwall

Mark: painted view number '299'
38.5 × 29 cm

The view is based on the central part of *A View of Mount Edgcumbe taken from S*^t*. Nicholas's Island*, engraving by Pierre Charles Canot (1710–77) after a drawing by Bampfylde from a painting by Lambert and Scott.

State Hermitage Museum, St Petersburg (8635)
Lit: Raeburn, Voronikhina and Nurnberg 1995, cat. 33, view 266

G137 Sauce boat decorated with views of Mount Edgcumbe, Cornwall

Marks: painted view numbers '549', '550'
6.5 × 20.5 × 9 cm

Both views are based on the engraving used for Cat. G136.

State Hermitage Museum, St Petersburg (8496)
Lit: Raeburn, Voronikhina and Nurnberg 1995, cat. 172, views 267, 268

G138 Flat plate decorated with a view of the gardens of Chiswick House, Greater London

Mark: painted view number '179'
Diameter: 24.5 cm

The view is based on the central and left-hand parts of *A Prospect of Lord Burlington's Orange Tree Garden at Chiswick*, anonymous engraving after a painting by Pieter Andreas Rysbrack

G 135

(1690–1748), around 1730. Rysbrack did a set of eight paintings of the gardens at Chiswick soon after they had been laid out by Lord Burlington. They surrounded the villa he had designed, attached to Chiswick House, to house his art collection. The original designs for the gardens were also by Burlington, although they were modified by William Kent, and they became one of the models for English landscape gardens.

State Hermitage Museum, St Petersburg (8834)
Lit: Raeburn, Voronikhina and Nurnberg 1995, cat. 352, view 519

G139 Flat plate decorated with a view of the gardens of Chiswick House, Greater London

Mark: painted view number '180'
Diameter: 24.5 cm

The view is based on the central and right-hand parts of the print that was used for Cat. G138.

State Hermitage Museum, St Petersburg (8900)
Lit: Raeburn, Voronikhina and Nurnberg 1995, cat. 353, view 520

G140 15-inch oval dish decorated with a view of the gardens of Chiswick House, Greater London

Marks: 'WEDGWOOD' impressed; painted view number '292'
38.5 × 29 cm

The view is based on *A Prospect of the Bridge upon ye Canal in Lord Burlington's Garden at Chiswick*, anonymous engraving after a painting by Pieter Andreas Rysbrack, around 1730. See Cat. G138.

State Hermitage Museum, St Petersburg (8619)
Lit: Raeburn, Voronikhina and Nurnberg 1995, cat. 28, view 522

G141 16-inch oval dish decorated with a view of Orleans House, Twickenham, Greater London

Marks: 'WEDGWOOD' impressed; painted view number '279'
41.5 × 32 cm

The view is based on *Governor Pitt's House (late Secretary Johnson's) at Twickenham*, engraving by James Mason after a drawing (1748) by Augustine Heckel (1690–1770), published 1749. The house was built in 1710 by John James, and the Octagon (the only part which still stands) was added by James Gibbs in 1720.

State Hermitage Museum, St Petersburg (8615)
Lit: Raeburn, Voronikhina and Nurnberg 1995, cat. 11, view 581

G142 14-inch round dish decorated with a view of Petersham Lodge, Greater London

Landscape enamelled by William Shuter
Mark: painted view number '988'
Diameter: 35 cm

The view is based on *A View of the Earl of Harrington's House towards the Garden at Petersham in Surry*, engraving by J. Steevens after a drawing by Heckel and was executed by Shuter (see Cat. G129). The house was built around 1733 to designs by Lord Burlington.

State Hermitage Museum, St Petersburg (8699)
Lit: Raeburn, Voronikhina and Nurnberg 1995, cat. 75, view 879; Wedgwood MS E32-5269

G143 13-inch round dish decorated with a view of Harleyford House, Bucks.

Mark: painted view number '511'
Diameter: 33 cm

The view is based on *The South East Prospect of Harleyford, The Seat of Sir William Clayton Esq'. near Great Marlow, Bucks*, engraving by Thomas Major after a painting (1760) by Francesco Zuccarelli (1702–88). The house was built in 1755 by Sir Robert Taylor. John Harris has pointed out that the view 'is no more than a capriccio, for although the house is sited correctly on the river the topography is completely idealised to conform to Zuccarelli's rococo style.'

State Hermitage Museum, St Petersburg (8706)
Lit: Raeburn, Voronikhina and Nurnberg 1995, cat. 91, view 52; Williamson 1909 facing p. 10; Harris 1979 p. 281

G144 14-inch oval dish decorated with a view of Kensington Palace, London

Marks: 'WEDGWOOD' impressed; painted view number '306'
35.5 × 27 cm

The view is based on *The South front of Kensington Palace, as seen from the Verges of the great Walk*, one of a set of engravings by John Tinney (d. 1761) after drawings by Anthony Highmore (1719–99). The gardens were replanned in the mid-1720s by Henry Wise, the royal gardener, and Charles Bridgeman, and the present Kensington Gardens still retain many features of Bridgeman's design, including the formal avenues and the sinuous artificial river known as the Serpentine.

State Hermitage Museum, St Petersburg (8642)
Lit: Raeburn, Voronikhina and Nurnberg 1995, cat. 39, view 563

G145 15-inch oval cover decorated with views of Prior Park, Bath, Avon, and Richmond Hill, Greater London

Marks: painted view numbers '676', '677'
34 × 24 cm

The views are based on *Prior Park the Seat of Ralph Allen, Esq'. near Bath. Drawn from Mr. Allen's Road in the Year 1750*, engraving by Anthony Walker (1726–65), 1752; and *A View of Richmond Hill up the River*, engraving by François Vivares after a painting by Antonio Joli (around 1700–77), 1749. Prior Park was built, from 1735 to around 1750, for Ralph Allen, a man of great wealth and culture who was the model for Squire Allworthy in Henry Fielding's *Tom Jones*. Richmond Hill, which rises steeply from the Thames, offers picturesque views over the curve of the river and the villas on its banks; it was a famous beauty spot, celebrated in James Thomson's *Seasons* and in views by many artists (see also Cat. G283).

State Hermitage Museum, St Petersburg (8444)
Lit: Raeburn, Voronikhina and Nurnberg 1995, cat. 613, views 725, 890

G146 13-inch oval dish decorated with a view of Studley Royal, N. Yorks.

Marks: 'WEDGWOOD' impressed; painted view number '502'
33 × 25 cm

The view is based on *A View of the Lake and Gardens from the Park at Studley, the Seat of William Aislabie Esq': in the West Riding of Yorkshire*, designed and engraved by Anthony Walker, 1758. The gardens of Studley Royal were begun by John Aislabie around 1720. The River Skell was expanded to form a straight canal and geometrically shaped pools, and a variety of picturesque vistas were created with the help of architectural adornments. In 1768 John's son, William Aislabie, bought the neighbouring estate, on which the ruins of Fountains Abbey stand, and these were incorporated into the garden as the focus of picturesque vistas.

State Hermitage Museum, St Petersburg (8659)
Lit: Raeburn, Voronikhina and Nurnberg 1995, cat. 55, view 1052

G147 11-inch round dish decorated with a view of Studley Royal, N. Yorks. *(Pl. 26)*

Enamelling of landscape attributed to Ralph Unwin
Mark: painted view number '663'
Diameter: 27.5 cm

The view is based on *A View of the Reservoir & Artificial Mount, in ye Gardens of Studley ye Seat of William Aislabie Esq'. with a fine View of Fountains Abby, in ye West Riding of Yorkshire*, designed and engraved by Walker, 1758 (see Cat. G146). It is almost certainly one of the landscapes painted by Unwin just before 2 April 1774 (see Cat. G64).

State Hermitage Museum, St Petersburg (8850)
Lit: Raeburn, Voronikhina and Nurnberg 1995, cat. 129, view 1054; Williamson 1909, facing p. 68; Wedgwood MS E32-5253

G148 Square compotier decorated with a view of Studley Royal, N. Yorks.

Mark: painted view number '967'
20 × 20 cm

The view appears to be based on one of a set of paintings of Studley Royal (see Cat. G146), made around the 1750s, possibly by Balthasar Nebot. The Chinese Building on the hill was built in 1745.

State Hermitage Museum, St Petersburg (8594)
Lit: Raeburn, Voronikhina and Nurnberg 1995, cat. 884, view 1055

G149 Round compotier decorated with a view of Studley Royal, N. Yorks.

Mark: painted view number '976'
Diameter: 21.5 cm

The view is based on an untraced drawing, perhaps from the same source as Cat. G148.

State Hermitage Museum, St Petersburg (8551)
Lit: Raeburn, Voronikhina and Nurnberg 1995, cat. 893, view 1062

G150 Oval compotier decorated with a view of Studley Royal, N. Yorks.

Marks: 'WEDGWOOD' impressed; painted view number '984'
28.5 × 21.5 cm

The view is based on an untraced drawing, perhaps from the same source as Cat. G148.

State Hermitage Museum, St Petersburg (8578)
Lit: Raeburn, Voronikhina and Nurnberg 1995, cat. 849, view 1063

G151 Square compotier decorated with a view of the gardens at Hackfall, N. Yorks.

Mark: painted view number '970'
20 × 20 cm

The view is based on an untraced drawing, possibly by Nicholas Dall (see Cat. G276), who is known to have made drawings at Hackfall in 1766. The gardens are close to Studley Royal and were an occasional retreat for the Aislabie family. The round pond was one of several features lying between the paths that lead down to the River Ure.

State Hermitage Museum, St Petersburg (8601)
Lit: Raeburn, Voronikhina and Nurnberg 1995, cat. 887, view 1004

G152 14-inch round dish decorated with a view of Castle Howard, N. Yorks.

Landscape enamelled by William Shuter
Mark: painted view number '991'
Diameter: 35 cm

The view is based on *A View of the Noble House and part of the Garden of Castle Howard, the Seat of the Right Hon*^{ble}. *the Earl of Carlisle near New-Malton in Yorkshire*, designed and engraved by Walker, 1758, and was executed by Shuter (see Cat. G129). The house was designed by Sir John Vanbrugh for the 3rd Earl of Carlisle and was begun in 1700, though it was still unfinished in 1726, when Vanbrugh died. The west wing was added in 1753–9 by Sir Thomas Robinson.

State Hermitage Museum, St Petersburg (8696)

G 151

Lit: Raeburn, Voronikhina and Nurnberg 1995, cat. 78, view 988; Williamson 1909, facing p. 72; Wedgwood MS E32-5269

SAMUEL STRINGER

G153 *Tabley Old Hall and Church across the Lake*

Samuel Stringer
Oil on canvas
1770
61.7 × 90 cm

Samuel Stringer (1750–84) was consulted by Wedgwood at the very outset of work on the Frog Service (see p. 137) and was commissioned to do a number of views in gardens in Staffordshire. He also made available some views he had done in the previous few years in his native Cheshire and possibly also some in Shropshire. A drawing for the present work (present whereabouts unknown) is signed 'S.S.' and dated 'Ju. 1770'. Stringer was a moderately competent draughtsman, but he never found it easy to use light and perspective to give volume to the buildings in his views. Nevertheless, their reproduction on the Frog Service does, in the majority of cases, provide a unique record of the gardens depicted. The medieval hall at Tabley, much

altered in the 17th century, became derelict after the New Hall was built for Sir Peter Leicester by John Carr in 1761–7.

University of Manchester (The Tabley House Collection)

G154 14-inch round cover decorated with views of Tabley, Cheshire, and Whitmore Hall, Staffs. *(Pl. 36)*

Marks: painted view numbers '780', '781'
Diameter: 32 cm

For the view of Tabley, see Cat. G153. Whitmore Hall was one of several houses just to the west and south of Stoke-on-Trent (Keele, Swynnerton, Butterton, Trentham were others) that were the subjects of drawings done by Samuel Stringer especially for the Frog Service. Whitmore, the seat of Edward Mainwaring, was a medieval house that had been remodelled by William Baker in 1756.

State Hermitage Museum, St Petersburg (8458)
Lit: Raeburn, Voronikhina and Nurnberg 1995, cat. 647, views 153, 803; Williamson 1909, facing p. 78

G155 Soup plate decorated with a view of Tabley, Cheshire

Mark: painted view number '325'
Diameter: 24.25 cm

See Cat. G153.

State Hermitage Museum, St Petersburg (9001)
Lit: Raeburn, Voronikhina and Nurnberg 1995, cat. 510, view 151

G156 Soup plate decorated with a view of Tabley, Cheshire

Mark: painted view number '332'
Diameter: 24.25 cm

See Cat. G153.

State Hermitage Museum, St Petersburg (8945)
Lit: Raeburn, Voronikhina and Nurnberg 1995, cat. 517, view 152

G157 11-inch round dish decorated with a view of Tabley, Cheshire

Mark: painted view number '651'
Diameter: 27.5 cm

The view is based on a second drawing of the church and Old Hall at Tabley, undoubtedly also by Samuel Stringer. See Cat. G153.

State Hermitage Museum, St Petersburg (8845)
Lit: Raeburn, Voronikhina and Nurnberg 1995, cat. 117, view 155

G158 Oval compotier decorated with a view of Tabley, Cheshire

Mark: painted view number '1017'
24 × 20 cm

The view is based on an untraced drawing of the lake at Tabley, probably also by Samuel Stringer. See Cat. G153.

State Hermitage Museum, St Petersburg (8684)
Lit: Raeburn, Voronikhina and Nurnberg 1995, cat. 861, view 156

G159 Oblong dish decorated with a view of Lymm church and rectory, Cheshire

Marks: 'WEDGWOOD' impressed; painted view number '538'
24 × 19.5 cm

The view is based on an untraced drawing, undoubtedly by Samuel Stringer. See Cat. G153. The church at Lymm (built in the 14th century but replaced in 1850) overlooks Lymm Dam.

State Hermitage Museum, St Petersburg (8569)
Lit: Raeburn, Voronikhina and Nurnberg 1995, cat. 138, view 147

G160 Sauce boat decorated with views of York and of Lymm rectory, Cheshire

Marks: painted view numbers '555', '556'
6.5 × 20.5 × 9 cm

The distant view of York (with the Minster quite radically reinterpreted) is from the background of *The North View of Sheriff*

Hutton-Castle near York, 1721, from *Buck's Antiquities*, I, 1726, pl. 23; for the view of Lymm, see Cat. G159.

State Hermitage Museum, St Petersburg (8495)
Lit: Raeburn, Voronikhina and Nurnberg 1995, cat. 175, views 1051, 148

G161 Dessert plate decorated with a view of Booth Hall, Cheshire

Mark: painted view number '899'
Diameter: 22 cm

The view is based on the left-hand part of an untraced drawing, undoubtedly by Samuel Stringer. See Cat. G153. Booth Hall, near Knutsford, was rebuilt around 1745 by Peter Legh, who employed Thomas Stringer, Samuel's father, as a servant in the early part of his life. The house was again rebuilt around 1850.

State Hermitage Museum, St Petersburg (9108)
Lit: Raeburn, Voronikhina and Nurnberg 1995, cat. 783, view 137

G162 16-inch oval dish decorated with a view of Barlaston Hall, Staffs.

Marks: 'WEDGWOOD' impressed; painted view number '996'
41.5 × 32 cm

The view is based on an untraced drawing, probably by Samuel Stringer. See Cat. G153 and G163. Barlaston Hall was [1756–8 for Thomas Mills, an at Leek, to designs firmly attribut Robert Taylor.

State Hermitage Museum, St Petersl (8629)
Lit: Raeburn, Voronikhina and Nurnberg 1995, cat. 17, view 731; Reilly 1989 I pl. 332

G163 19-inch oval dish decorated with a view of Trentham Hall, Staffs.

Mark: painted view number '31
49 × 38 cm

The view is based on one of a series of untraced drawings, undoubtedly by Samuel Stringer. See Cat. G153. On 4 November 1773 Wedgwood wrote to Bentley: 'We have two [views] from Trentham, finish'd, one in the rough sketch, one from Mr. Mills's [i.e., Barlaston – see Cat. G162], & one from Etruria [see Cat. G289] in the same situation... I am waiting upon Ld Gower with his sketches this morning, & to ask his farther advice...'

Trentham Hall was built around 1707–10 by William Smith for the 1st Lord Gower and was enlarged in the 1730s by Thomas Flitcroft and Francis Smith. The 2nd Earl Gower, a close associate of Wedgwood's on the Grand Trunk Canal project, engaged 'Capability' Brown to lay out the park in 1764 with the huge lake as its principal feature. This was altered by the creation of a formal terraced garden in the mid-19th century, and the house was demolished in 1910–12. Trentham is now a public park. The importance Wedgwood attached to Lord Gower's patronage is indicated by the fact that Trentham was featured on two of the six 19-inch dishes, the largest flat items in the Service (the second dish has not survived).

State Hermitage Museum, St Petersburg (20842)
Lit: Wedgwood MS E25-18495; Raeburn, Voronikhina and Nurnberg 1995, cat. 1, view 793

G 163

G 172, G 164, G 200. Soup plates and two tureens from the dinner service.

G164 Large oval tureen decorated with views of Trentham Hall, Staffs.; lid decorated with views of Winnington Bridge, Cheshire, and Windsor Great Park, Berks.

Marks: 'WEDGWOOD' impressed; painted view numbers '614', '615', '616', '617'
23 × 36 × 27 cm (with lid)

For the views of Trentham, see Cat. G163. It is likely that the view of Winnington Bridge is also based on an untraced drawing by Samuel Stringer; the house seen through the arch of the 18th-century bridge over the River Weaver was the seat of Richmond Pennant, later Lord Penrhyn. The view of Windsor is based on *The Great Lake, near the Lodge*, engraved by William Austin (1721–1820) after Thomas Sandby, no. 7 of *Eight Views of Windsor Great Park* (see Cat. G93).

State Hermitage Museum, St Petersburg (8469, 8535A)
Lit: Raeburn, Voronikhina and Nurnberg 1995,

cat. 187, views 795, 797, 162, 34; Williamson 1909, facing p. xx; Reilly 1989 I pl. 335

G165 Dessert plate decorated with a view of Trentham Hall, Staffs.

Mark: painted view number '901'
Diameter: 22 cm

The view is based on the left-hand part of one of the drawings used for Cat. G164.

State Hermitage Museum, St Petersburg (9105)
Lit: Raeburn, Voronikhina and Nurnberg 1995, cat. 785, view 798

G166 19-inch oval dish decorated with a view of Butterton Hall, Staffs.

Marks: 'WEDGWOOD' impressed; painted view number '489'
49 × 38 cm

The view is based on an untraced drawing, undoubtedly by Samuel Stringer. See Cat.

G153. Butterton Hall was the seat of Thomas Swinnerton, another of Wedgwood's neighbours, to whom he attached sufficient importance to place his house and park on this very large dish.

State Hermitage Museum, St Petersburg (8612)
Lit: Raeburn, Voronikhina and Nurnberg 1995, cat. 3, view 735

G167 14-inch oval cover decorated with views of Teddesley Hall, Staffs., and the Wrekin, Salop

Marks: painted view numbers '707', '708'
31 × 22.5 cm

The views are based on untraced drawings, the first undoubtedly by Samuel Stringer, the second quite possibly so. See Cat. G153. Teddesley Hall was built between 1757 and around 1765 for Sir Edward Littleton by William Baker, who also worked at Keele and Whitmore (see Cat.

G154). The view of the Wrekin is one of several views of Shropshire landscape that may well also have been based on Stringer's drawings.

State Hermitage Museum, St Petersburg (8452)
Lit: Raeburn, Voronikhina and Nurnberg 1995, cat. 629, views 791, 711

G168 12-inch round cover decorated with views of Swynnerton Hall, Staffs., and St Osyth Priory, Essex

Marks: painted view numbers '1149', '1150'
Diameter: 26 cm

The view of Swynnerton is based on an untraced drawing, undoubtedly by Samuel Stringer. See Cat. G153. The house was built in 1725–9 by Francis Smith for Thomas Fitzherbert (whose widow was to marry the Prince Regent); it was altered in the 19th and 20th centuries. The view of the 15th-century gatehouse of St Osyth Priory is based on *S^t. Osyth Priory the Seat of the Right Honble.the Earl of Rochford*, an undated engraving by J. Chapman after James Dunthorne senior (1730–1815).

State Hermitage Museum, St Petersburg (8532)
Lit: Raeburn, Voronikhina and Nurnberg 1995, cat. 662, views 788, 321; Williamson 1909, facing p. 20

G169 Oval compotier decorated with a view of Ingestre Park, Staffs.

Mark: painted view number '1008'
22 × 17 cm

The view is based on an untraced drawing, undoubtedly by Samuel Stringer. See Cat. G153. Wedgwood wrote to the owner, Mrs Talbot, in December 1773: 'We are now executing a comm^n. for the Empress of Russia. It is for a Table service consisting of near 2000 pieces upon each of which is to be a real view from English Gardens & pleasure grounds painted in Enamel. We are to n^o. each piece & send a Catalogue to the Empress, saying from whose seat each view is taken. May I beg the favour Mad^m., of enriching our collection with a few of these

views from your beautifull Park & Gardens. A Painter (Mr. Stringer of Knutsford) will wait upon you in a few days to ask this favor...'. Mrs Talbot was the daughter and heiress of the 2nd Viscount Chetwynd, who in 1756 had commissioned 'Capability' Brown to landscape the park – and she was also the cousin of Deborah Chetwynd (daughter of the 3rd Viscount), Wedgwood's go-between with Queen Charlotte.

State Hermitage Museum, St Petersburg (8487)
Lit: Wedgwood MS E25-18513; Raeburn, Voronikhina and Nurnberg 1995, cat. 876, view 764

ANTHONY DEVIS

G170 *Near Enuil, Staffordshire*

Anthony Thomas Devis (1729–1816)
Pencil on paper
Around 1770 (?)
22.5 × 31.4 cm

The park at Enville was landscaped by the Earl of Stamford, who, like Lord Gower (see Cat. G163), was associated with Wedgwood on the Grand Trunk Canal project. He started work around the middle of the century and was advised by the poet William Shenstone, whose own garden at the Leasowes, one of the most celebrated of all 18th-century gardens, was less than ten miles away, near Halesowen. Wedgwood had asked Lord Stamford if Samuel Stringer could do some drawings there, but Lord Stamford offered instead to lend Wedgwood drawings of Enville and of his estates in Leicestershire done by the London artist Anthony Devis.

The present drawing was not copied on to the Frog Service (none of the ones that were used have been traced), but it clearly belongs to the same series. The remarkable quality of this group of views on the Service, surely executed by James Bakewell, particularly in the rendering of subtleties of light and shade, make it virtually certain that all were based on drawings by Devis.

Harris Museum and Art Gallery, Preston

G171 11-inch oval dish decorated with a view of Enville, Staffs.

Mark: painted view number '310'
29 × 22 cm

The picture, a distant view of the Gothic gateway, is based on an untraced drawing by Anthony Devis: see Cat. G170.

State Hermitage Museum, St Petersburg (8671)
Lit: Raeburn, Voronikhina and Nurnberg 1995, cat. 67, view 738

G172 Soup plate decorated with a view of Enville, Staffs.

Mark: painted view number '327'
Diameter: 24.25 cm

The view, which shows a vase on the terrace, is based on an untraced drawing by Anthony Devis: see Cat. G170.

State Hermitage Museum, St Petersburg (8955)
Lit: Raeburn, Voronikhina and Nurnberg 1995, cat. 512, view 742

G173 12-inch round dish decorated with a view of Enville, Staffs.

Mark: painted view number '316'
Diameter: 30.5 cm

The view of the bottom of the meadow at Enville is based on an untraced drawing by Anthony Devis: see Cat. G170.

State Hermitage Museum, St Petersburg (8715)
Lit: Raeburn, Voronikhina and Nurnberg 1995, cat. 102, view 740

G174 12-inch round dish decorated with a view of Enville, Staffs.

Mark: painted view number '465'
Diameter: 30.5 cm

The view of the Shepherds' Bridge is based on an untraced drawing by Anthony Devis: see Cat. G170.

State Hermitage Museum, St Petersburg (8716)
Lit: Raeburn, Voronikhina and Nurnberg 1995, cat. 107, view 746

G175 Round salad dish decorated with a view of Enville, Staffs.

Marks: 'WEDGWOOD' impressed; painted view number '749'
Diameter: 24.5 cm; height: 7 cm

The view of the Cascade is based on an untraced drawing by Anthony Devis. See Cat. G170.

State Hermitage Museum, St Petersburg (8542)
Lit: Raeburn, Voronikhina and Nurnberg 1995, cat. 152, view 755

G176 15-inch oval cover decorated with views of Enville, Staffs., and the Thames at Chelsea, London

Marks: painted view numbers '683', '686'
34 × 24 cm

The view of the Sheep Walk at Enville is based on an untraced drawing by Anthony Devis: see Cat. G170. The view of Chelsea (based on an untraced drawing by an unknown artist) appears to show the waterworks which supplied much of Westminster with its water, and, behind it, one of the towers of Westminster Abbey.

State Hermitage Museum, St Petersburg (8446)
Lit: Raeburn, Voronikhina and Nurnberg 1995, cat. 616, views 748, 507

G177 14-inch oval cover decorated with views of Enville, Staffs., and Carclew House, Cornwall

Marks: painted view numbers '915', '916'
31 × 22.5 cm

The view of the Menagery at Enville is based on an untraced drawing by Anthony Devis: see Cat. G170. The view of Carclew House is based on *South View of Carclew House in the parish of Milor*, engraving by James Green after a drawing by William Borlase, pl. XI in Borlase's *Natural History of Cornwall*, 1758 (see Cat. G232). Carclew was built by Samuel Kempe in the 1720s and the wings, linked by colonnades to the body of the house, were added by Thomas Edwards in 1749 for the mine-owner

G 175

William Lemon. The house was gutted by fire in 1934.

State Hermitage Museum, St Petersburg (8453)
Lit: Raeburn, Voronikhina and Nurnberg 1995, cat. 632, views 758, 163

G178 Dessert plate decorated with a view of Enville, Staffs.

Mark: painted view number '874'
Diameter: 22 cm

The view of the Shepherds' Lodge is based on an untraced drawing by Anthony Devis: see Cat. G170.

State Hermitage Museum, St Petersburg (9063)
Lit: Raeburn, Voronikhina and Nurnberg 1995, cat. 760, view 757

G179 11-inch oval dish decorated with a view of Bradgate Park, Leics.

Marks: 'WEDGWOOD' impressed; painted view number '312'
29 × 22 cm

The view is based on an untraced drawing by Anthony Devis: see Cat. G170. Bradgate Park, built at the end of the 15th century, was the home of the Grey family and birthplace of Lady Jane Grey. It fell into ruins after the Earl of Stamford moved to Enville in 1739. The park was never landscaped and retained some of the character of a medieval hunting park.

State Hermitage Museum, St Petersburg (8675)
Lit: Raeburn, Voronikhina and Nurnberg 1995, cat. 68, view 470

G180 12-inch round dish decorated with a view of Bradgate Park, Leics.

Mark: painted view number '314'
Diameter: 30.5 cm

The view of the rocks in Bradgate Park is based on an untraced drawing by Anthony Devis: see Cat. G170 and G179.

State Hermitage Museum, St Petersburg (8721)
Lit: Raeburn, Voronikhina and Nurnberg 1995, cat. 100, view 472

G 180

G181 12-inch round dish decorated with a view of Bradgate Park, Leics.

Mark: painted view number '315'
Diameter: 30.5 cm

The view of the new village and Lord Stamford's park is based on an untraced drawing by Anthony Devis: see Cat. G170 and G179.

State Hermitage Museum, St Petersburg (8724)
Lit: Raeburn, Voronikhina and Nurnberg 1995, cat. 101, view 473; Williamson 1909, facing p. 72

G182 Dessert plate decorated with a view of Bradgate Park, Leics.

Mark: painted view number '875'
Diameter: 22 cm

The view of the ruined house is based on the same untraced drawing by Anthony Devis as Cat. G179.

State Hermitage Museum, St Petersburg (9081)
Lit: Raeburn, Voronikhina and Nurnberg 1995, cat. 761, view 471

G183 Soup plate decorated with a view of Bradgate Park, Leics.

Mark: painted view number '451'
Diameter: 24.25 cm

The view is based on an untraced drawing by Anthony Devis: see Cat. G170 and G179. Bentley's catalogue described this view as 'Grooby Park', and Groby is the village near Bradgate from which the Grey family originated. However, the position of the windmill, almost certainly on Markfield Hill, makes it virtually certain that this view, too, is of Bradgate.

State Hermitage Museum, St Petersburg (9028)
Lit: Raeburn, Voronikhina and Nurnberg 1995, cat. 571, view 475

FRANCIS GROSE

G184 *The Old Kitchen, Stanton Harcourt, Oxon.*

Francis Grose (1731–91) after an etching by Lord Nuneham (d. 1809)
Pen and ink and watercolour
About 1773
10.1 × 15.8 cm (excluding wash border)

This and Cat. G185–9 were drawings made by Grose for the engravers of his *Antiquities* (see p. 144), each one copied from an original drawings and redrawn to the size in which it was to appear in the book. He had made most of the original drawings himself, on journeys through England and Wales since 1759, but a number were done by other artists. Simon Harcourt, Viscount Nuneham, was the owner of Stanton Harcourt and executed the etching on which the present view is based under the supervision of Paul Sandby (see Cat. G190).

The Society of Antiquaries of London

G185 *Allington Castle, Kent*

Francis Grose
Pen and ink and watercolour
About 1772
11.1 × 15.3 cm (excluding wash border)

See Cat. G184. This view is based on Grose's own drawing, made in 1760 (see Cat. G197).

The Society of Antiquaries of London

G186 *The Chiding Stone, Kent*

Francis Grose
Pen and ink and watercolour
About 1772
9.7 × 14.8 cm (excluding wash border)

See Cat. G184. This view is based on Grose's own drawing, made in 1768 (see Cat. G201).

The Society of Antiquaries of London

G187 *Warwick Castle, Warwickshire*

Francis Grose after a drawing by Canaletto (1697–1768)
Pen and ink and watercolour
About 1772
10.5 × 15.3 cm (excluding wash border)

See Cat. G184. The Canaletto drawing that Grose copied was owned at the time by the Earl of Warwick.

The Society of Antiquaries of London

G188 *Aysgarth Bridge, Yorkshire*

Francis Grose
Pen and ink and watercolour
About 1774
10.7 × 15.3 cm (excluding wash border)

See Cat. G184. This view is based on Grose's own drawing, made in 1773. Although Bentley's artists generally worked from the finished engravings, Grose evidently made some of his drawings available before they were engraved. In this case the date of the engraving (11 July 1774) makes it certain that the drawing was used (see Cat. G210).

The Society of Antiquaries of London

G189 *Easby Abbey, Yorkshire*

Francis Grose
Pen and ink and watercolour
About 1774
10.1 × 15.2 cm (excluding wash border)

See Cat. G184. This view, probably based on Grose's own drawing (he was in North Yorkshire in 1773), was prepared for the *Antiquities* but never engraved. This drawing must, therefore, have served as the model for Bentley's painters (see Cat. G207).

The Society of Antiquaries of London

G190 14-inch oval dish decorated with a view of the Old Kitchen, Stanton Harcourt, Oxon.

Marks: 'WEDGWOOD' impressed; painted

view number '484'
35.5 × 27 cm

The view is based on *The Old Kitchen, at Stanton Harcourt*, engraving by Richard Bernard Godfrey (1728– after 1795) dated 7 August 1773 after an etching made by Lord Nuneham in 1760, published in vol. III of Grose's *Antiquities* (see Cat. G184).

State Hermitage Museum, St Petersburg (8649)
Lit: Raeburn, Voronikhina and Nurnberg 1995, cat. 44, view 685

G191 11-inch round dish decorated with a view of the Holy Sepulchre church, Northampton

Mark: painted view number '650'
Diameter 27.5 cm

The view is based on *Saint Sepulchre's Church, Northampton*, engraving by Godfrey dated 2 December 1773 after a drawing by Grose made in 1761, published in vol. II of his *Antiquities*.

State Hermitage Museum, St Petersburg (8856)
Lit: Raeburn, Voronikhina and Nurnberg 1995, cat. 116, view 628; Williamson 1909, facing p. 94

G192 11-inch round dish decorated with a view of the Bishop's Waltham palace, Hants.

Mark: painted view number '654'
Diameter 27.5 cm

The view is based on *The Bishop of Winchester's House, Waltham*, pl. II, engraving by Daniel Lerpinière (around 1745–85) dated 16 March 1773 after a drawing by Grose made in 1761, published in vol. II of his *Antiquities*.

State Hermitage Museum, St Petersburg (8852)
Lit: Raeburn, Voronikhina and Nurnberg 1995, cat. 120, view 348

G193 11-inch round dish decorated with a view of Tintern Abbey, Gwent

Mark: painted view number '657'
Diameter 27.5 cm

The view is based on *Tintern Abbey,*

G 194

Monmouthshire, engraving by S. Sparrow dated 12 August 1773 after a drawing by Edward Eyre junior made in 1773, published in vol. II of Grose's *Antiquities*.

State Hermitage Museum, St Petersburg (8847)
Lit: Raeburn, Voronikhina and Nurnberg 1995, cat. 123, view 608; Williamson 1909, facing p. 86

G194 Flat plate decorated with a view of the gatehouse of Erwarton Hall, Suffolk

Mark: painted view number '373'
Diameter 24.5 cm

The view is based on *The Gate at Arwerton-Hall, Suffolk*, engraving by Godfrey dated 1 January 1773 after a drawing by Grose made in 1769, published in vol. III of his *Antiquities*.

State Hermitage Museum, St Petersburg (8774)
Lit: Raeburn, Voronikhina and Nurnberg 1995, cat. 425, view 808

G195 Flat plate decorated with a view of the collegiate church of St Cybi, Holyhead, Gwynedd

Mark: painted view number '438'
Diameter 24.5 cm

The view is based on *The Collegiate Church of Holy Head*, engraving by Godfrey dated 1 June 1772 after a drawing by Grose made in 1769, published in vol. IV of his *Antiquities*.

G 196

State Hermitage Museum, St Petersburg (8749)
Lit: Raeburn, Voronikhina and Nurnberg 1995, cat. 449, view 1073

G196 Soup plate decorated with a view of Cowes Castle, Isle of Wight

Mark: painted view number '455'
Diameter 24.25 cm

The view is based on *West Cowes Castle, in the Isle of Wight*, engraving by William Ellis (1747– after 1800) dated 1 October 1772 after a drawing by Grose made in 1761, published in vol. II of his *Antiquities*.

State Hermitage Museum, St Petersburg (9017)
Lit: Raeburn, Voronikhina and Nurnberg 1995, cat. 575, view 370

G197 Round salad bowl decorated with a view of Allington Castle, Kent

Marks: 'WEDGWOOD' impressed; painted view number '751'
Diameter 24.5 cm; height: 7 cm

The view is based on *Allington Castle, Kent*, engraving by Sparrow dated 8 July 1772 after a drawing by Grose made in 1760, published in vol. II of his *Antiquities* (see Cat. G185).

State Hermitage Museum, St Petersburg (8543)
Lit: Raeburn, Voronikhina and Nurnberg 1995, cat. 154, view 392

G198 Stand for sauce boat decorated with a view of Halling House, Kent

Marks: 'WEDGWOOD' impressed; painted view number '546'
20 × 16.5 cm

The view is based on the left-hand part of *Halling House, Kent*, engraving by Godfrey dated 1 September 1772 after a drawing by Grose made in 1759, published in vol. II of his *Antiquities*.

State Hermitage Museum, St Petersburg (20858)
Lit: Raeburn, Voronikhina and Nurnberg 1995, cat. 186, view 433

G199 Large oval tureen decorated with views of St James's Hospital, Lewes, E. Sussex, and Walton Bridge, Surrey; lid decorated with views of Godstow Abbey, Oxon., and Carisbrooke Castle, Isle of Wight

Marks: 'WEDGWOOD' impressed; painted view numbers '776', '777'; lid: '778', '779'
23 × 36 × 27 cm

The views are based on *St James's Hospital, Lewes, Sussex*, engraving by James Peake dated 1 August 1772 after a drawing by Grose made in 1762, published in vol. III of his *Antiquities*; *A View of the Bridge over the Thames at Walton in Surry distance 20 miles from London*, undated engraving by Charles Grignion (1721–1810) after a drawing by Augustine Heckel; *Godstow Nunnery, Oxfordshire*, engraving by Godfrey dated 1 June 1772 after a drawing by Grose made in 1761, published in vol. III of his *Antiquities*; and *Carisbrook Castle, in the Isle of Wight*, engraving by Sparrow dated 1 September 1772 after a drawing by Grose made in 1772, published in vol. II of his *Antiquities*.

State Hermitage Museum, St Petersburg (8468, 8468A)
Lit: Raeburn, Voronikhina and Nurnberg 1995, cat. 190, views 923, 899, 678, 369

G 204

G200 Small oval tureen decorated with views of Bedford Bridge, Beds., and Bolton Priory, N. Yorks.; lid decorated with views of Enys House and Trewithen House, Cornwall

Marks: 'WEDGWOOD' impressed; painted view numbers '772', '773'; lid: '774', '775'
17.5 × 27.5 × 20 cm

The views are based on *Bedford Bridge*, engraving by Godfrey, dated 1 March 1772, after a drawing by Grose made in 1761, published in vol. I of his *Antiquities*; *Bolton Priory, in Craven, Yorkshire*, engraving by Godfrey dated 1 March 1773 after a drawing by Paul Sandby made in 1752, published in vol. IV of Grose's *Antiquities*; *View of Enys house in the parish of Gluvias*, plate VII in William Borlase's *Natural History of Cornwall*, 1758 (see Cat. G232);

and *South-east View of Trewithen, in the parish of Probus*, pl. XXIII in the same book.

State Hermitage Museum, St Petersburg (8537, 8471A)
Lit: Raeburn, Voronikhina and Nurnberg 1995, cat. 194, views 2, 982, 172, 197

G201 15-inch oval cover decorated with views of St Botolph's Priory, Colchester, Essex; and Chiddingstone, Kent

Marks: painted view numbers '667', '674'
34 × 24 cm

The views are based on *St. Botolph's Priory*, engraving by Godfrey dated 20 February 1772 after a drawing by Grose, published in vol. I of his *Antiquities*; and *The Chiding Stone, Kent*, engraving by Sparrow dated 2

June 1772 after a drawing by Grose made in 1768, published in vol. II of his *Antiquities* (see Cat. G186).

State Hermitage Museum, St Petersburg (8448)
Lit: Raeburn, Voronikhina and Nurnberg 1995, cat. 608, views 315, 401

G202 15-inch oval cover decorated with views of Warwick Castle; and Richmond Castle, N. Yorks.

Marks: painted view numbers '668', '675'
34 × 24 cm

The views (the first of which is incorrectly numbered; it corresponds to no. 669 in Bentley's catalogue) are based on *Warwick Castle, Warwickshire*, engraving by Godfrey dated 1 January 1773 after a drawing by Antonio Canaletto made in 1747, published in vol. IV of Grose's *Antiquities* (see Cat. G187); and *Richmond Castle, Yorkshire*, engraving by Lerpinière dated 1 August 1772 after a drawing by Paul Sandby made in 1763, published in vol. IV of Grose's *Antiquities*.

State Hermitage Museum, St Petersburg (8518)
Lit: Raeburn, Voronikhina and Nurnberg 1995, cat. 610, views 937, 1033

G203 12-inch round cover decorated with views of Farleigh Hungerford Castle, Somerset; and Lamphey Palace, Dyfed

Marks: painted view numbers '637', '638'
Diameter: 26 cm

The views are based on two preparatory drawings by Francis Grose, the first after a drawing by Edward Eyre junior made in 1774, engraved by Sparrow on 30 June 1774 and published as *Farley Castle, Somersetshire*, pl. I, in vol. III of his *Antiquities*; the second after a drawing by Paul Sandby made in 1770, engraved by Sparrow on 27 April 1774 and published as *Llanfeth, or Lantphey-Court, Pembrokeshire*, in vol. IV of his *Antiquities*.

State Hermitage Museum, St Petersburg (8529)
Lit: Raeburn, Voronikhina and Nurnberg 1995, cat. 649, views 715, 1145

G204 Dessert plate decorated with a view of Castle Acre Castle, Norfolk

Mark: painted view number '805'
Diameter: 22 cm

The view is based on *Castle-Acre Castle, Norfolk*, pl. II, engraving by William Ellis dated 18 December 1772 after a drawing by Thomas Hearne (1744–1813) made in 1771, published in vol. II of Grose's *Antiquities*. The sequence of numbers makes it clear that this was the first dessert plate to be decorated. However, it was painted with the oak-leaf border of the dinner service rather than the ivy-leaf of the dessert service and could not therefore be included in the Service.

Trustees of the Wedgwood Museum, Barlaston, Staffordshire (5379)
Lit: Raeburn, Voronikhina and Nurnberg 1995, view A18; Blake Roberts 1993, p. 32, fig. 7

G205 Dessert plate decorated with a view of Fountains Abbey, N. Yorks.

Mark: painted view number '806'
Diameter: 22 cm

The view is based on *Fountains Abby, Yorkshire*, pl. I, engraving by Sparrow dated 1 January 1773 after a drawing by Nicholas Dall (d. 1777) made in 1767, published in vol. IV of Grose's *Antiquities*. See also Cat. G74.

State Hermitage Museum, St Petersburg (9096)
Lit: Raeburn, Voronikhina and Nurnberg 1995, cat. 693, view 1001

G206 Dessert plate decorated with a view of the Abbot's Kitchen, Glastonbury, Somerset

Mark: painted view number '844'
Diameter: 22 cm

The view is based on *The Abbot's Kitchen, at Glastonbury, Somersetshire*, engraving by Sparrow dated 8 September 1773 after a drawing by John Inigo Richards (1731–1810) made in 1756, published in vol. III of Grose's *Antiquities*.

State Hermitage Museum, St Petersburg (9037)
Lit: Raeburn, Voronikhina and Nurnberg 1995, cat. 731, view 721; Williamson 1909, facing p. 98

G207 Cream bowl decorated with views of St Augustine's Monastery, Canterbury, Kent, and Coverham Abbey, N. Yorks.; lid decorated with views of Faversham Abbey, Kent, and Easby Abbey, N. Yorks.; stand decorated with a view of Stourhead, Wilts.

Marks: painted view numbers '1099', '1100', '1279', '1280', 1089
Height (with lid): 17.25 cm; diameter: 17.5 cm; diameter of stand: 22 cm

The views are based on *St Augustine's Monastery*, pl. II, engraving by Godfrey dated 2 May 1773 after a drawing by Grose made in 1759, published in vol. II of his *Antiquities*; Grose's preparatory drawing after his own drawing made in 1773, engraved by Godfrey on 3 May 1774 and published as *Coverham Abbey, Yorkshire*, pl. II, in vol. IV of his *Antiquities*; *Faversham Abbey, Kent*, pl. II, engraving by Benjamin Thomas Pouncy (d. 1799) dated 20 December 1772 after a drawing by Grose made in 1758, published in vol. II of his *Antiquities*; *Easby Abbey*, Grose's preparatory drawing probably after his own drawing prepared for publication in his *Antiquities* but not eventually included (see Cat. G189); and a feature from an untraced drawing of the gardens at Stourhead (see Cat. G311).

State Hermitage Museum, St Petersburg (8476, 20844)
Lit: Raeburn, Voronikhina and Nurnberg 1995, cat. 915, views 400, 995, 426, 998, 961

G208 Cream bowl decorated with views of Gatton Park, Surrey, and Farleigh Hungerford Castle, Somerset; lid decorated with views of Wimpole Hall, Cambs., and Shugborough Park, Staffs.; stand decorated with a view of Shugborough Park, Staffs.

Marks: painted view numbers '1101', '1102', '113', '114', 1088
Height (with lid): 17.25 cm; diameter: 17.5 cm; diameter of stand: 22 cm

The views are based on an untraced drawing of Gatton Park by an unknown artist (see Cat. G299); Grose's preparatory drawing after a drawing by Edward Eyre junior made in 1774, engraved by Sparrow on 10 July 1774 and published as *The Chapel, Fairley Castle, Somersetshire* in vol. III of his *Antiquities*; an untraced drawing by Lady Amabel Polwarth (1751–1833) of Wimpole Hall (see Cat. G314); a feature of the Chinese House at Shugborough from *The West Front of Shugborough...*, drawing by Dall, 1768 (see Cat. G281); and a feature of the Lanthorn of Demosthenes at Shugborough from *An extensive View of the Park and Monuments*, another drawing by Dall, 1768 (see Cat. G276).

State Hermitage Museum, St Petersburg (8477, 8690)
Lit: Raeburn, Voronikhina and Nurnberg 1995, cat. 916, views 828, 716, 128, 781, 778; Williamson 1909, facing p. 100

G209 Cream bowl decorated with views of Stourhead, Wilts., and Lympne Castle, Kent; lid decorated with views of Stourhead; stand decorated with a view of an unidentified garden temple *(Pl. 38)*

Marks: painted view numbers '1103', '1104', '1275', '1276', 1093'
Height (with lid): 17.25 cm; diameter: 17.5 cm; diameter of stand: 22 cm

The views are based on features from two untraced drawings of Stourhead (see Cat. G311); *Lyme Castle, Kent*, engraving by J. Morris after a drawing by Grose made in 1772, published in vol. II of his *Antiquities*; and an untraced print or drawing.

State Hermitage Museum, St Petersburg (8478, 8691)
Lit: Raeburn, Voronikhina and Nurnberg 1995, cat. 917, views 962, 440, 965, 966, 1217; Williamson 1909, facing p. 64

G210 Cream bowl decorated with views of Aysgarth Bridge, N. Yorks., and Weston Hall, Warwicks.; lid decorated with views of Tynemouth Priory, Northumbria, and Bamburgh Castle, Northumbria; stand decorated with a view of a temple (probably the Temple of Pan in Kew Gardens, Greater London)

Marks: painted view numbers '1109', '1110', '1273', '1274', '1091'
Height (with lid): 17.25 cm; diameter: 17.5 cm; diameter of stand: 22 cm

The views are based on Grose's preparatory drawing after his own drawing made in 1773, engraved by Sparrow on 11 July 1774 and published as *Aysgarth Bridge, Yorkshire*, in vol. IV of his *Antiquities* (see Cat. G188); an untraced drawing of Weston Hall, Warwicks., an Elizabethan house which was the seat of the Sheldon family, rebuilt in 1826–33 and demolished in 1932; Grose's preparatory drawing after his own drawing made in 1773, engraved by Godfrey on 12 March 1774 and published as *The Gate of Tynemouth Castle, Northumberland*, in vol. III of his *Antiquities*; Grose's preparatory drawing after his own drawing made in 1773, engraved by Lerpinière on 10 April 1774 and published as *Bamborough Castle*, pl. I, in vol. III of his *Antiquities*; and, probably, *The Temple of Pan*, engraving by Edward Rooker after William Chambers, pl. 13 in Chambers' *Plans, Elevations, Sections and Perspective Views of the Gardens and Buildings at Kew in Surrey...*, 1763 (see Cat. G42).

State Hermitage Museum, St Petersburg (8475, 8688)
Lit: Raeburn, Voronikhina and Nurnberg 1995, cat. 920, views 977, 939, 658, 633, 1216; Voronikhina 1988, p. 171

JEAN-BAPTISTE CLAUDE CHATELAIN AND LONDON VIEWS

G211 12-inch round dish decorated with a view of the Thames at Chiswick, Greater London

Mark: painted view number '412'
Diameter: 30.5 cm

The view is based on the left-hand part of *A View of the River Thames from Chiswick*, unsigned engraving by Jean-Baptiste Claude Chatelain (1710–71), no. 3 of a set of views published 2 May 1750.

Chatelain was a name adopted by the artist, whose real name was Philippe, and he may have been born in London of Huguenot parents. His hand is frequently seen on the Frog Service as either draughtsman or engraver: not only in his views of Stowe (see Cat. G117ff.), but in landscape views in the Lake District and elsewhere and in an extensive range of views around London, the majority done in 1745 and 1750.

State Hermitage Museum, St Petersburg (8717)
Lit: Raeburn, Voronikhina and Nurnberg 1995, cat. 103, view 514

G212 Dessert plate decorated with a view of the Thames at Chelsea, Greater London

Mark: painted view number '861'
Diameter: 22 cm

The view is based on the left-hand part of *Another View of the River at Chelsea*, unsigned engraving by Chatelain, no. 2 of a set of views published 2 May 1750. Bentley's painter, probably James Bakewell, replaced a group of houses along the river bank in Chatelain's print with the bottle-shaped kilns of the Chelsea pottery.

State Hermitage Museum, St Petersburg (9159)
Lit: Raeburn, Voronikhina and Nurnberg 1995, cat. 748, view 511

G213 *A View of ye Long Room at Hampsted from the Heath*

Jean-Baptiste Claude Chatelain
Engraving
Lettered with title in English and French, with publication line, and 'Chatelain Delin et Sculp'
Dated 1753 (originally published 1745)
Size of platemark: 18.6 × 27.7 cm

One of Chatelain's views of Hampstead, pl. 4 of the set of ten prints first issued in 1745 by William Henry Toms and republished in 1752 by Henry Overton and Robert Sayer as *Vues Diverses des Villages pres de Londres*. These views are a reminder of Hampstead's days as a fashionable spa in the early 18th century, when the Great Room (or Long Room) in Well Walk contained rooms for diversions of all kinds. Although a few of the prints were used more or less complete, in the main Bentley's painters used them for the sides of the small sauce tureens, copying only one or two buildings from the background of a print and setting them in an imaginary landscape.

London Borough of Camden. Local Studies & Archives Centre

G214 Sauce tureen with lid decorated with features from views of Hampstead, Greater London

Marks: 'WEDGWOOD' impressed; painted view numbers '492', '493', '622', '623'
11 × 13.5 × 10 cm

See Cat. G213. Both views on the sides of the tureen show features based on Chatelain's view of the Long Room; both views on the lid show features based on *A View of Hampstead from the Top of Pond Street*, pl. 2 of *Vues Diverses*; the garden buildings featured on the ends of the lid (not listed in Bentley's catalogue) are from untraced prints, perhaps from one of the many handbooks published with designs of ornamental garden structures.

State Hermitage Museum, St Petersburg (8559, 20848A)
Lit: Raeburn, Voronikhina and Nurnberg 1995, cat. 163, views 533, 534, 543, 544, 1205, 1206

G215 Sauce tureen with lid decorated with features from views of Hampstead and Highgate, Greater London

Marks: 'WEDGWOOD' impressed; painted view numbers '498', '499', '628', '629'
11 × 13.5 × 10 cm

See Cat. G213. The views on the sides of the tureen show features based on *A View of Hampstead from the Pond*, engraving by

G 217

Chatelain, pl. 5 of *Vues Diverses*, and *A View of Highgate from upper Holloway*, pl. 9 of *Vues Diverses*; both views on the lid show features based on *A View of Hampstead from ye corner of Mrs. Holford's Garden*, pl. 3 from the same set of prints; the garden buildings featured on the ends of the lid (not listed in Bentley's catalogue; see Cat. G214) are one of the Lake Pavilions and the Rotondo at Stowe, based on features from *A View over the Great Bason to the Entrance between the Pavilions* and *A View at the Queen's Statue*, plates b and h in Bickham's book of engravings of Stowe (see Cat. G117).

State Hermitage Museum, St Petersburg (8492, 8559A)
Lit: Raeburn, Voronikhina and Nurnberg 1995, cat. 166, views 541, 553, 548, 549, 58, 85

G216 14-inch oval cover decorated with views of St Marylebone Basin and Hampstead, Greater London

Marks: painted view numbers '948', '949'
31 × 22.5 cm

The views are based on *A View of St. Mary le Bone*, engraving after a pencil drawing by Chatelain made in 1761; and Chatelain's view of the Long Room at Hampstead (see Cat. G213).

State Hermitage Museum, St Petersburg (8513)
Lit: Raeburn, Voronikhina and Nurnberg 1995, cat. 633, views 569, 537; Williamson 1909, facing p. 44

G217 11-inch round dish decorated with a view of the Mall, St James's Park, London

Enamelling of landscape attributed to Ralph Unwin
Mark: painted view number '664'
Diameter: 27.5 cm

The view is based on the right-hand part of *A View of the Mall in St James's Park*, engraving by William Henry Toms (1712–50) after a drawing by Chatelain, before 1750. It is almost certainly one of the landscapes painted by Unwin just before 2 April 1774 (see Cat. G64).

State Hermitage Museum, St Petersburg (8851)
Lit: Raeburn, Voronikhina and Nurnberg 1995, cat. 130, view 582; Williamson 1909, facing p. 84; Wedgwood MS E32-5253

G218 Dessert plate decorated with a view of Old London Bridge

Mark: painted view number '864'
Diameter: 22 cm

The view is based on the left-hand part of *A View of London Bridge with the Ruins of ye Temporary bridge. Drawn the day after the Dreadful Fire April the 11th 1758*, designed and engraved by Anthony Walker, published 28 June 1758. The rows of shops and houses which lined the sides of the 12th-century bridge had several times been destroyed by fire, but they were finally removed in 1758 during the remodelling carried out to plans by George Dance senior and Sir Robert Taylor. Several houses are still visible in Walker's view.

State Hermitage Museum, St Petersburg (9019)
Lit: Raeburn, Voronikhina and Nurnberg 1995, cat. 751, view 567

G219 Oval compotier decorated with a view of Horseguards Parade, London

Marks: 'WEDGWOOD' impressed; painted view number '1011'
25 × 19.5 cm

The view is based on an untraced drawing by an unknown artist showing the Horse

G 223 (top) G 47 (below)

Guards building (1750–59) designed by William Kent. The Canal in the foreground was part of Charles II's layout of St James's Park in the formal French style in the 17th century.

State Hermitage Museum, St Petersburg (8584)
Lit: Raeburn, Voronikhina and Nurnberg 1995, cat. 855, view 586

RICHARD WILSON AND WALES

G220 *The Summit of Cader-Idris Mountain, in North Wales*

Edward Rooker (around 1712–74) and
Michael Angelo Rooker (1747–1801) after
Richard Wilson (1713–82)
Etching with engraving
Lettered with title in English and French
and 'Rich^d. pinx^t. E. & M. Rooker
Sculpse^rt.'
Around 1767
Cut to: 39.5 × 52.8cm

Richard Wilson's six Welsh views issued as prints on subscription in 1767 show the influence of the years he had spent in Italy: the landscapes are far more open and carefully composed than the less sophisticated views by Thomas Smith. They were published at a time of growing interest in the Celtic origins of the 'Ancient Britons' (see Sam Smiles 1994), and Bentley included them despite Wedgwood's concern that they contained not 'the least Pleasure ground' (see p. 140). The painters in Chelsea responded to the quality of the pictures and produced some of the finest decorations on the Service from them.

The painting on which the engraving is based is now in the Tate Gallery, London.

Trustees of the British Museum (BM 1863-7-25-663)

G221 14-inch round dish decorated with a view of Cadair Idris, Gwynedd

Landscape enamelled by William Shuter
Mark: painted view number '994'
Diameter: 35 cm

See Cat. G220, on which the view is based, and for Shuter Cat. G116.

State Hermitage Museum, St Petersburg (8697)
Lit: Raeburn, Voronikhina and Nurnberg 1995, cat. 81, view 1136; Wedgwood MS E32-5269

G222 Oblong dish decorated with a view of Pembroke Castle, Dyfed

Marks: 'WEDGWOOD' impressed; painted view number '531'
24 × 19.5 cm

The view is based on *Pembroke Town and Castle in South Wales*, engraving by James Mason after a painting by Richard Wilson, around 1767.

State Hermitage Museum, St Petersburg (8571)
Lit: Raeburn, Voronikhina and Nurnberg 1995, cat. 131, view 1152; Williamson 1909, facing p. 74

G223 Oblong dish decorated with a view of Caernarfon Castle, Gwynedd

Marks: 'WEDGWOOD' impressed; painted view number '534'
24 × 19.5 cm

The view is based on *Caernarvon Castle*, engraving by William Byrne (1743–1805) after a painting by Richard Wilson, 1766. Although the set of engravings was not issued until the following year, some of the plates, including this and the one used for Cat. G225, were exhibited in 1766 at the Society of Artists.

State Hermitage Museum, St Petersburg (8489)
Lit: Raeburn, Voronikhina and Nurnberg 1995, cat. 134, view 1080; Williamson 1909, facing p. 82

G224 Oval salad bowl decorated with a view of Snowdon, Gwynedd

Marks: 'WEDGWOOD' impressed; painted view number '613'
7.5 × 31.5 × 22.5 cm

The view is based on *Snowdon Hill and the adjacent Country in North Wales*, engraving by William Woollett after a painting by Richard Wilson (now in the Walker Art Gallery, Liverpool), around 1767. Thomas Pennant described Wilson's painting, which shows Snowdon from the west across Llyn Nantlle Uchaf, as 'as magnificent as it is faithful'.

State Hermitage Museum, St Petersburg (8548)
Lit: Raeburn, Voronikhina and Nurnberg 1995, cat. 149, view 1089; Williamson 1909, facing p. 74

G225 19-inch oval cover decorated with views of Keele Hall, Staffs., and Pont-y-prydd, Mid Glamorgan

Enamelling of landscapes attributed to Ralph Unwin
Marks: painted view numbers '618', '619'
43.5 × 33 cm

The views are based on a drawing of Keele Hall, almost certainly made by Samuel Stringer in 1773 (see Cat. G153); and *The Great Bridge over the Taaffe in South Wales*,

24

25

G226 Square compotier decorated with a view of Pistill Rhaeadr, Llanrhaeadr-ym-Mochnant, Clwyd

Mark: painted view number '961'
20 × 20 cm

A number of prints of this spectacular waterfall on the Disgynfa River were published around 1750, but the one that was copied for this view has not been identified.

State Hermitage Museum, St Petersburg (8597)
Lit: Raeburn, Voronikhina and Nurnberg 1995, cat. 878, view 1104

G227 12-inch round cover decorated with views of Haverfordwest, Dyfed, and Kidwelly Castle, Dyfed

Marks: painted view numbers '921', '922'
Diameter: 26 cm

The views are both based on untraced drawings by unknown artists. The view of Haverfordwest shows the medieval bridge over the Western Cleddau, with the ruins of the castle above it and the old priory in the middle distance. On the left of the view of Kidwelly Castle can be seen the gatehouse built in 1399–1401 for John of Gaunt or his son Henry IV.

State Hermitage Museum, St Petersburg (8462)
Lit: Raeburn, Voronikhina and Nurnberg 1995, cat. 655, views 1144, 1097

WILLIAM BORLASE AND
JOHN HUTCHINS

G228 *Observations on the Antiquities Historical and Monumental, of the County of Cornwall* (Pl. 24)

William Borlase
Published in Oxford, 1754
36 × 49.5 cm (open)

The Revd. William Borlase (1695–1772) was rector of Ludgvan in the south of Cornwall and was a passionate antiquary (see p. 145). His three books on Cornwall and the

engraving by Pierre Charles Canot after a painting by Richard Wilson, around 1766. Keele Hall was the home of Ralph Sneyd, an acquaintance of Wedgwood's, who lent him the set of prints after Richard Wilson to use on the Service. Pont-y-prydd ('the bridge of the earthen hut') was built by a local farmer and self-taught mason, William Edwards, and completed in 1756 after two failed attempts. Edwards subsequently built many other bridges in South Wales and his fame reached Catherine the Great, who invited him to her court, but he refused to leave Wales. This cover is almost certainly the one that appears on Unwin's worksheet for 26 March 1774.

State Hermitage Museum, St Petersburg (8443)
Lit: Raeburn, Voronikhina and Nurnberg 1995, cat. 603, views 769, 1133; Wedgwood MS E32-5254

Scillies were all used by Bentley, but this one, his first (the present copy of which bears the bookplate of Horace Walpole), was particularly useful, in that it contained illustrations of Celtic antiquities, which were otherwise completely unavailable, since neither the Bucks nor Grose (who omitted Cornwall altogether from his *Antiquities*) showed any real interest in such primitive monuments.

Victoria & Albert Museum. National Art Library (222.G.2)

G229 Soup plate decorated with a view of a dolmen near Constantine, Cornwall

Mark: painted view number '260'
Diameter: 24.25 cm

The view is based on *Tolmen in Constantine Parish in Cornwall*, engraving by James Green (d. about 1757) after a drawing by Borlase, pl. XI in Borlase's *Observations* (see Cat. G228). The monument consisted of a large pitted granite rock supported on two stones leaving a passageway large enough for a man to crawl through. Bentley's artists reduced the size of the figures to exaggerate the scale of the rock.

State Hermitage Museum, St Petersburg (8931)
Lit: Raeburn, Voronikhina and Nurnberg 1995, cat. 488, view 171

G230 Dessert plate decorated with a view of Zennor Quoit, Cornwall

Mark: painted view number '826'
Diameter: 22 cm

The view is based on *Zenor Cromleh*, pl. XVIII, fig. 3 in Borlase's *Observations* (see Cat. G228). This is a late neolithic chambered tomb covered by a capstone, which today rests with one end on the ground. It would originally have been covered by a round barrow.

State Hermitage Museum, St Petersburg (9058)
Lit: Raeburn, Voronikhina and Nurnberg 1995, cat. 713, view 199

G231 Dessert plate decorated with a view of Lanyon Quoit, Cornwall *(Pl. 23)*

Mark: painted view number '829'
Diameter: 22 cm

The view is based on *Lanyon Cromlech*, pl. XVIII, fig. 1 in Borlase's *Observations* (see Cat. G228). Another neolithic tomb, near Morvah, it fell in 1815, and although it was re-erected some of the stones were broken and its height was reduced.

State Hermitage Museum, St Petersburg (9153)
Lit: Raeburn, Voronikhina and Nurnberg 1995, cat. 716, view 176

G232 14-inch oval cover decorated with views of Pendarves House, Camborne, Cornwall, and Westenhanger House, Kent

Marks: painted view numbers '697', '698'
31 × 22.5 cm

The views are based on *Western View of Pendarves House in the Parish of Camborn, Cornwall*, pl. XIV in the *Natural History of Cornwall*, published in Oxford in 1758, the last of William Borlase's books on the Duchy (see Cat. G228); and Grose's preparatory drawing after his own drawing made in 1773, engraved by J. Morris on 11

January 1774 and published as *Ostenhanger House*, pl. II in vol. II of his *Antiquities*. Pendarves House still survives, though both house and garden were altered in the 19th century. Westenhanger Castle, near Stanford, was a fortified mansion built in the 14th century, which, according to legend, was the residence of 'Fair Rosamund', the mistress of Henry II.

State Hermitage Museum, St Petersburg (8506)
Lit: Raeburn, Voronikhina and Nurnberg 1995, cat. 628, views 185, 454

G233 Dessert plate decorated with a view of Looe, Cornwall

Mark: painted view number '822'
Diameter: 22 cm

The view is based on the left-hand part of *View of the Port and part of the Boroughs of East and West Loo*, pl. II in Borlase's *Natural History of Cornwall* (see Cat. G232) and shows West Looe. The stone bridge across the Looe estuary was built in 1411–18; it was demolished in 1853.

State Hermitage Museum, St Petersburg (9053)
Lit: Raeburn, Voronikhina and Nurnberg 1995, cat. 709, view 182

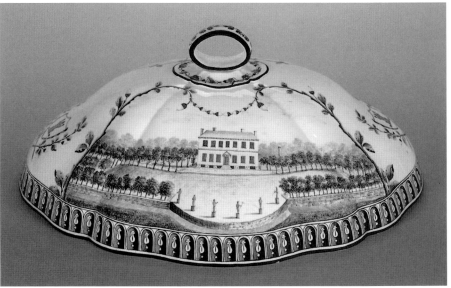

G

36

added to the south front in the remodelling undertaken by Humphrey Sturt after 1765.

State Hermitage Museum, St Petersburg (8586)
Lit: Raeburn, Voronikhina and Nurnberg 1995, cat. 860, view 290; Williamson 1909, facing p. 42

THOMAS PENNANT

G237 *Eu a no Fin or Fingalls Cave on the island of Staffa*

James Miller (active 1772–91)
Inscribed with title
1772
37 × 53 cm
From an album of drawings done on Sir Joseph Banks's voyage to the Hebrides and Iceland

Miller's drawing and others done on Banks's expedition would have come to Bentley through Thomas Pennant (1726–98), who included engravings of several of them in the second of his two books on Scotland, published in 1774. Pennant was a traveller and naturalist whose interest in antiquities was stimulated by a visit to William Borlase in 1746–7. He made two tours of Scotland, in 1769 and 1772, and the illustrations prepared for his books about these furnished virtually the only available Scottish material for the Frog Service – and most had not yet been engraved until the Service was nearly completed. Pennant asked his printer to make available all the as yet unpublished engravings, based not only on the original views drawn by his servant Moses Griffiths (1747–1819), who had accompanied him, but also on other views he had collected, including those from Banks's expedition (see p. 000).

Despite the popularity of James Macpherson's *Ossian* poems, very few landscape artists had ventured into Scotland and hardly any views of the country had been published. Boswell and Johnson covered some of the same ground as Pennant in their own tour of Scotland in 1773, and while Boswell stated that 'from a

G234 Dessert plate decorated with a view of Looe, Cornwall

Mark: painted view number '834'
Diameter: 22 cm

The view is based on the right-hand part of the print used for Cat. G233 and shows East Looe.

State Hermitage Museum, St Petersburg (9141)
Lit: Raeburn, Voronikhina and Nurnberg 1995, cat. 721, view 183

G235 Oval compotier decorated with a view of Upwey Manor, Dorset

Marks: 'WEDGWOOD' impressed; painted view number '987'
28.5 × 21.5 cm

The view is based on *Upway-House in Dorsetshire A seat of George Gould Esq*, engraving by Bayly after a drawing by Benjamin Pryce, in *The History and Antiquities of Dorset* by John Hutchins, vol. I, 1774. Apart from William Borlase's books

on Cornwall (see Cat. G228), Hutchins' two-volume work was the only county history with engraved plates that Bentley was able to use for the Service. The majority of views show quite recent houses set in their parkland (see also Cat. G67). Upwey Manor was built in 1639.

State Hermitage Museum, St Petersburg (8581)
Lit: Raeburn, Voronikhina and Nurnberg 1995, cat. 852, view 306

G236 Oval compotier decorated with a view of Crichel House, Dorset

Marks: 'WEDGWOOD' impressed; painted view number '1016'
25 × 19.5 cm

The view is based on *South East View of Critchill House the Seat of Humphrey Sturt Esq'.*, unsigned engraving in *The History and Antiquities of Dorset* by John Hutchins, vol. II, 1774. The present Crichel House was built after an earlier house was destroyed by fire in 1742. The portico was

G 238

desire of ingratiating himself with the Scotch, [Pennant] has flattered the people of North Briton so inordinately and with so little discrimination, that the judicious and candid amongst them must be digusted...', Johnson said: 'He's a <u>whig</u>, Sir, a <u>sad dog</u>, but he's the best traveller I ever read; he observes more things than anyone else does.'

Pennant's *A Tour in Scotland MDCCLXIX* was first published in 1771, and a third edition with additional illustrations was published in June 1774 together with the first edition of *A Tour in Scotland and Voyage to the Hebrides 1772*.

British Library (Add. MS 15510 fol. 42)

G238 Soup plate decorated with a view of Ailsa Craig, Strathclyde

Mark: painted view number '1048'
Diameter: 24.25 cm

The view is based on *Crag of Aisla*, drawing by Moses Griffiths, 1772, engraved by Peter Mazell (active 1760–1800) as pl. 14 in Pennant's second *Tour*, 1774 (see Cat. G237). Ailsa Craig is a granite rock some ten miles off Girvan on the west coast of Scotland.

State Hermitage Museum, St Petersburg (9005)
Lit: Raeburn, Voronikhina and Nurnberg 1995, cat. 583, view 1168

G239 Soup plate decorated with a view of Dupplin Castle, Tayside

Mark: painted view number '1050'
Diameter: 24.25 cm

The view is based on *Dupplin House*, drawing by Griffiths, engraved by Mazell as pl. 7 in the 1774 edition of Pennant's first *Tour* (see Cat. G237). Dupplin was the seat of the Earls of Kinnoul. It was destroyed by fire in 1827 and rebuilt in the Jacobean style.

State Hermitage Museum, St Petersburg (8970)
Lit: Raeburn, Voronikhina and Nurnberg 1995, cat. 585, view 1192

G240 Soup plate decorated with a view of the abbey on Iona, Strathclyde

Mark: painted view number '1052'
Diameter: 24.25 cm

The view is based on *General View of Jona*, anonymous drawing (probably by Griffiths), 1772 (?), engraved by Canot as pl. 21 in Pennant's second *Tour*, 1774 (see Cat. G237). Iona became one of the centres of Irish Christianity with the arrival of St Columba soon after 563. The abbey in the view was a Benedictine foundation of around 1200.

State Hermitage Museum, St Petersburg (8992)
Lit: Raeburn, Voronikhina and Nurnberg 1995, cat. 587, view 1164

G241 Soup plate decorated with a view of Duntulm Castle, Skye, Highland of Scotland

Mark: painted view number '1053'
Diameter: 24.25 cm

The view is based on *Duntulme Castle*, drawing by Griffiths, 1772, engraved by Pierre Charles Canot as pl. 38 in Pennant's second *Tour*, 1774 (see Cat. G237). Duntulm, at the extreme north of the island of Skye, was once the principal residence of the Macdonald family.

State Hermitage Museum, St Petersburg (8940)
Lit: Raeburn, Voronikhina and Nurnberg 1995, cat. 588, view 1179

G242 Oblong dish with cover decorated with a view of Inverness, Highland of Scotland; lid decorated with views of Blair Castle, Tayside, and Freswick Castle, Highland of Scotland, and features of the temple of Arethusa in Kew Gardens, Greater London, and the octagonal temple at Woburn Farm, Surrey

Marks: 'WEDGWOOD' impressed; painted view numbers '533', '714', '715', '716', '717'
8.5 × 24 × 19.5 cm

The view on the dish is based on *Inverness*, engraving by Mazell after a painting by William Tomkins (1730–92), pl. 6 in the 1771 edition of Pennant's first *Tour* (see Cat. G237); the views on the lid are based on *View near Blair*, engraving by Mazell after a drawing by Paul Sandby, pl. 15 in the same volume, and *Freshwick Castle*, engraving by Mazell after his own painting, pl. 7 in the same volume. The features at the ends are based on details from *A View of the Lake and Island at Kew, seen from the Lawn, with the Bridge, the Temples of Arethusa, and Victory, and the Great Pagoda*, engraving by Paul Sandby after William Marlow, pl. 38 in Chambers' book (see Cat. G42), and *A View of Woobourn in Surry the*

G

Seat of Philip Southcote Esqr., designed and engraved by Luke Sullivan, 1759 (see Cat. G100).

Inverness was the principal town of the Scottish Highlands, and the castle in the foreground of the view was a reminder of the recent '45 rebellion: it was blown up by the troops of Bonnie Prince Charlie in 1746 (Culloden Moor, where the Highlanders were finally defeated that year by the English under the 'Butcher' Duke of Cumberland, lies five miles to the east). The old bridge was washed away by floods in 1849.

State Hermitage Museum, St Petersburg (8568, 20849A)
Lit: Raeburn, Voronikhina and Nurnberg 1995, cat. 133, 131a, views 1175, 1188, 856, 1170, 908; Williamson 1909, facing p. 82

G243 Oval salad bowl decorated with a view near Blair Castle, Tayside

Marks: 'WEDGWOOD' impressed; painted view number '491'
7.5 × 31.5 × 22.5 cm

The view is based on an untraced drawing similar to a marginal illustration signed by Peter Mazell as engraver on a map of Perth and Clackmannanshire; it might be based on a drawing done for Pennant but not included in any of the editions of his books (see Cat. G237). The castle, remodelled in 1747–58 by James Winter for the 2nd Duke of Atholl, appears in the left background of the view.

State Hermitage Museum, St Petersburg (8479)
Lit: Raeburn, Voronikhina and Nurnberg 1995, cat. 148, view 1186

G244 Dessert plate decorated with a view of cottages on the Island of Jura, Strathclyde

Mark: painted view number '1043'
Diameter: 22 cm

The view is based on *Sheelins in Jura and a distant View of the Paps*, drawing by James Miller, 1772, engraved as pl. 15 in Pennant's second *Tour*, 1774 (see Cat. G237). The

G 244

G 246

hills known as the Paps of Jura are in the southern part of the island. The beehive or shieling huts of the Hebridean summer pastures were, according to Pennant, built of sticks, sods and clay; stone versions were in use as late as the end of the 19th century.

State Hermitage Museum, St Petersburg (9055)
Lit: Raeburn, Voronikhina and Nurnberg 1995, cat. 810, view 1166; Williamson 1909, facing p. 34

G245 Dessert plate decorated with a view of a cottage on the Island of Islay, Strathclyde

Mark: painted view number '1044'
Diameter: 22 cm

The view is based on *Back front of the Weaver's House near Bomore on the Island of Ila*, drawing by James Miller, 1772,

engraved as pl. 31 in Pennant's second *Tour*, 1774 (see Cat. G237). The view shows an example of the more permanent Hebridean dwellings, described by Pennant as being built of turf and hardened earth. The weights hanging over the roofs to keep them secure can clearly be seen.

State Hermitage Museum, St Petersburg (9156)
Lit: Raeburn, Voronikhina and Nurnberg 1995, cat. 811, view 1165; Williamson 1909, facing p. 18

G246 Ice pail decorated with views of Old Inveraray Castle, Strathclyde, and Edinburgh Castle, Lothian

Marks: painted view numbers '1033', '1034'
Height: 16.5 cm; diameter: 16.5 cm

The views are based on *Old Inveraray*, anonymous drawing engraved by Mazell as pl. 17 in the 1774 edition of Pennant's first *Tour* (see Cat. G237); and *Edinbrugh Castle from Grey Friars churchyard*, drawing by Griffiths, engraved by Mazell as pl. 4 in the same volume. The engraving of Inveraray must be based on an old drawing, as this building was demolished soon after 1745. A new castle in the Gothick style was built in 1746–58 for Archibald Campbell, 3rd Duke of Argyll, to designs by Roger Morris with William Adam as his clerk of works. Edinburgh Castle is an ancient medieval foundation, although the major fortifications date from the 16th century.

State Hermitage Museum, St Petersburg (20836)
Lit: Raeburn, Voronikhina and Nurnberg 1995, cat. 689, views 1161, 1184

G247 Ice pail decorated with views of Rothesay Castle, Island of Bute, Strathclyde, and the cascade at Cotton Hall, Staffs.

Marks: painted view numbers '1037', '1038'
Height: 16.5 cm; diameter: 16.5 cm

The views are based on *Rothesay Castle*, drawing by Griffiths, 1772, engraved by Mazell as pl. 12 in Pennant's second *Tour* (see Cat. G237); and an untraced drawing, perhaps by Stringer, of the cascade at Cotton Hall, the seat of Thomas Gilbert,

MP for Newcastle-under-Lyme. Rothesay castle on the isle of Bute, rebuilt in the 13th century, passed into the hands of the Stuarts and became a fortress for the king against the Hebrides. The great gateway is largely the work of James IV in the 1500s. It was ruined during the Civil War in the 17th century.

State Hermitage Museum, St Petersburg (8474)
Lit: Raeburn, Voronikhina and Nurnberg 1995, cat. 691, views 1169, 736; Williamson 1909, facing p. 70

G248 Oval compotier decorated with a view of Fingal's Cave, Island of Staffa, Strathclyde

Landscape enamelled by James Bakewell
Mark: painted view number '1027'
32 × 22.5 cm

The view is based on James Miller's drawing (Cat. G237), engraved by [Thomas?] Major as pl. 28 in Pennant's second *Tour*, 1774. Ossian was the great heroic poet of the Gael, the son of the celebrated hero Fionn MacCumhail (or Fingal), who lived in the 3rd century AD Although some medieval ballads survive, Ossian's fame throughout Europe in the later 18th century was due to a series of epics published by James Macpherson, starting with *Fingal* (1761), which pretended to be translations from the original Gaelic but were in fact almost entirely original compositions. Nevertheless, they contributed enormously to promoting the cult of ancient Celtic and British heroism.

Fingal's Cave appears to have been the traditional name for the most dramatic of the remarkable caves on Staffa, which was rediscovered on Banks's expedition and first depicted and described in Pennant's book. The painting on the Frog Service was put on display virtually the same day that Pennant's book was published. It was executed by James Bakewell, whose worksheet for 20 May 1774 includes '1 [Compt.] with Fingal's Cave 1 Day ½ Work', for which he charged six shillings.

G 237

G 248

State Hermitage Museum, St Petersburg (8609)
Lit: Raeburn, Voronikhina and Nurnberg 1995, cat. 839, view 1160; Williamson 1909, facing p. 54; Voronikhina 1988, p. 172; Wedgwood MS E32-5264

G249 Oval compotier decorated with a view of the abbey on Iona, Strathclyde

Marks: 'WEDGWOOD' impressed; painted view number '1013'
25 × 19.5 cm

The view is based on *Cathedral in Jona*, drawing by Griffiths, 1772, engraved by Mazell as pl. 22 in Pennant's second *Tour*. See Cat. G240.

State Hermitage Museum, St Petersburg (8583)
Lit: Raeburn, Voronikhina and Nurnberg 1995, cat. 857, view 1163; Williamson 1909, facing p. 74

G250 Oval compotier decorated with a view of Buachaille, Island of Staffa, Strathclyde

Mark: painted view number '1019'
24 × 20 cm

The view is based on a drawing by John Cleveley junior (1747–86) done on Banks's expedition to the Hebrides, 1772, engraved as pl. 31 in Pennant's second *Tour* (see Cat. G237). The description in Bentley's catalogue describes this as a 'View of the Island of Boo-sha-la, and of the pliant basalt columns near Staffa of which Mr. Pennant has given a description in his Journeys in the Hebrides'.

State Hermitage Museum, St Petersburg (8686)
Lit: Raeburn, Voronikhina and Nurnberg 1995, cat. 863, view 1158; Williamson 1909, facing p. 102

G251 Round compotier decorated with a view of the Fall of Foyers, Highland of Scotland

Mark: painted view number '977'
Diameter: 21.5 cm

The view is based on *Upper Fall of Fyres*, engraving by Mazell after a painting by Tomkins, pl. 10 in the 1771 edition of Pennant's first *Tour* (see Cat. G237). This waterfall is situated near the point where the River Foyers enters Loch Ness. Dr Johnson and Boswell visited it in 1773, noting the 'black piles of stone, by which

the stream is obstructed and broken, till it comes to a very steep descent of such a dreadful depth that we were naturally inclined to turn aside our eyes' (Johnson).

State Hermitage Museum, St Petersburg (8545)
Lit: Raeburn, Voronikhina and Nurnberg 1995, cat. 894, view 1174

G252 Ice cup decorated with views of Downing House, Clwyd, and Milton Abbas, Dorset

Marks: painted view numbers '1123', '1124'
Height (with cover): 7.5 cm; diameter: 6 cm

The views are based on details from a drawing by Griffiths engraved by Mazell as the frontispiece to the 1774 edition of Pennant's first *Tour* (see Cat. G237); and *The North West View of Milton Abby the Seat of the R^t. Honble. Joseph Lord Milton*, engraving by Edward Rooker in vol. II of Hutchins' *History and Antiquities of Dorset*, 1774 (see Cat. G235). Bentley's catalogue description of the main view of Downing, a 17th-century house, reads: 'View of Dawning, Flintshire, country seat of the celebrated naturalist, Mr. Pennant, who has devoted all his powers to the perfecting of this work.'

State Hermitage Museum, St Petersburg (9171)
Lit: Raeburn, Voronikhina and Nurnberg 1995, cat. 925, views 1109, 298

INDUSTRIAL VIEWS

See also Cat. G27, 72, 82–5, 212

G253 Lid of small oval tureen decorated with views of Prescot glass works, Merseyside

Marks: painted view numbers '766', '767'
27.5 × 20 cm

The views are based on the central and right-hand parts of *South Prospect of Prescot in Lancaster*, engraving by Toms after a drawing by William Winstanley, 1744. South-west Lancashire was a centre for

glassmaking from at least the 17th century – as St Helens still is today. The works at Prescot produced green glass, but it was not a major factory, and in 1751 it was stated that it was to be closed.

State Hermitage Museum, St Petersburg (8537A)
Lit: Raeburn, Voronikhina and Nurnberg 1995, cat. 192a, views 464, 465

G254 Lid of small oval tureen decorated with views of Kensington Palace, London, and Prescot glass works, Merseyside

Marks: painted view numbers '770', '771'
27.5 × 20 cm

The view of Kensington is based on *A distant View of Kensington Palace, with part of the Garden, & the Queen's Temple, as seen from the side of the Serpentine River*, engraving by John Tinney after a drawing by Anthony Highmore (see Cat. G144), and that of Prescot on the left-hand part of the print used for Cat. G253.

State Hermitage Museum, St Petersburg (8470A)
Lit: Raeburn, Voronikhina and Nurnberg 1995, cat. 193a, views 564, 466

G255 *Vuë du Canal du Duc de Bridgewater près du pont de Worsley*

Peter Perez Burdett (d. 1793)
Etching and aquatint
Inscribed with title in French and 'Par J.J Rousseau', and inscribed in ink 'From a private plate in the possession of M^r. Ford Manchester' and signed 'P. Burdett fecit'
Around 1770
Cut to 25.3 × 33 cm

This is one of two prints of the Bridgewater Canal by Burdett which were used for the Service (the other, with a view of the Barton Aqueduct, was copied on to a 13-inch round dish which has not survived). The text on the prints themselves states that Jean-Jacques Rousseau was the author of the drawings, but this seems unlikely. Although Rousseau did botanical drawings, no comparable views by him are known, and although he was staying in Derbyshire

G 255

G 256

in 1767, there is no mention of any visit to the canal in his exhaustive correspondence. Burdett might well have been the author of the drawings himself, and a false attribution to Rousseau seems quite consistent with his character. Wedgwood wrote to Bentley on 12 December 1774, having tried to collaborate with Burdett on printing on pottery with a process derived from making aquatints: 'Your Burd^{ts} & Sm——s & all such flighty, unsolid Genius's are very dangerous people to have any sort of connection with – They are absolutely mad themselves, & yet, in their own conciet, are too wise to be guided by anybody else.'

The canal built by James Brindley for the Duke of Bridgewater in 1759–61, to transport coal from his estates at Worsley to Manchester, formed the nucleus from which the entire inland waterway system of Britain grew, its most spectacular engineering achievement being the stone Barton Aqueduct, which took it over the River Irwell. Five years later the consortium for which Wedgwood was treasurer (see Cat. G163) was empowered to build the Trent & Mersey Canal, designed to link the Trent near Burton with the Mersey in Lancashire (joining the Bridgewater Canal at Preston Brook), opening navigation between the east and west coasts from Hull to Liverpool.

Manchester Public Libraries (Local Studies Unit)
Ref: Wedgwood MS E25-18573

G256 16-inch oval dish decorated with a view of Worsley Bridge on the Bridgewater Canal, Greater Manchester

Marks: 'WEDGWOOD' impressed; painted view number '1130'
41.5 × 32 cm

The view is based on Burdett's print (Cat. G255).

State Hermitage Museum, St Petersburg (8627)
Lit: Raeburn, Voronikhina and Nurnberg 1995, cat. 18, view 460; Williamson 1909, facing p. 52

G257 12-inch round cover decorated with views of a charcoal burner's hut in the Forest of Dean, Glos., and Hollingclose Hall, N. Yorks.

Marks: painted view numbers '768', '769'
Diameter: 26 cm

The views are based on two untraced drawings by unknown artists. Charcoal-burning was an important activity in the Forest of Dean, often associated with the smelting of iron ore. The building shown in the view may represent the furnace and casting-house at Flaxley, which was first worked by Cistercian monks in 1154 and had been in the hands of the Crawley-Boevey family since 1726. Hollingclose Hall, the seat of Richard Wood, was situated two miles south of Ripon.

State Hermitage Museum, St Petersburg (8534)
Lit: Raeburn, Voronikhina and Nurnberg 1995, cat. 652, views 339, 1014

G 258

G258 Dessert plate decorated with a view of a colliery at Kingswood, Avon

Mark: painted view number '1205'
Diameter: 22 cm

The view is based on an untraced drawing. According to John Cornwall, there is a strong possibility that it represents Lower Soundwell Colliery. Not only does the geography of the view tally, but that pit had two shafts, and the derelict, or half-built,

wooden horse gin in front of the stone tower indicates that this was also the case here. The red sandstone engine house, known locally as 'the old red engine house', was built around 1750 and stood for about one hundred years.

State Hermitage Museum, St Petersburg (9085)
Lit: Raeburn, Voronikhina and Nurnberg 1995, cat. 830, view 341

JOHN BOYDELL

G259 *Collection of 100 Views*

John Boydell (1719–1804)
Published in London, 1770
52 × 77.5 cm (open)

John Boydell was the son of a Derbyshire surveyor, who walked to London and became the apprentice of William Henry Toms, for whom he worked from 1741 to 1750. After Toms' death that year, he continued to work as an artist and engraver until the mid-1760s, when he turned exclusively to publishing, becoming the most successful print-publisher in London. He became an alderman of the City of London in 1782 and was Lord Mayor in 1790. His most famous project was the publication of his Shakespeare Gallery, a vast repertory of illustrations to the plays, but he also published a large range of topographical views, many of which were reprints from plates which he had acquired from their original engravers or publishers. His *Collection of 100 Views*, first published in 1770, contains many prints of his own design, most dating from the early 1750s. These have been criticised as being the pedestrian views of a surveyor, but the scenes on the river Thames provided many details that Bentley's artists were able to turn into very attractive views.

Guildhall Library, City of London

G260 Oblong dish with cover decorated with a view of Sheriff Hutton Castle, N. Yorks.; cover decorated with views on the Thames near London and features of the parish church at Woodstock, Oxon., and St Mary's church, Oxford

Marks: 'WEDGWOOD' impressed; painted view numbers '535', '742', '743', '744', '745'
8.5 × 24 × 19.5 cm

The view on the dish is based on *The North View of Sheriff Hutton-Castle near York*, 1721, from *Buck's Antiquities*, I, pl. 23 (see Cat. G160); the views on the cover are based on the right-hand part of *A view of Erith, looking up the Thames*, designed and engraved by Boydell, 1750, pl. 9 of his *100 Views* (see Cat. G259), and the central part of *A View of Sion House and the Parts adjacent, Taken from the Road next to the Royal Garden, at Richmond*, engraving by Peter Paul Benazech after a drawing by Peter Brookes, 1750, pl. 28 of Boydell's *100 Views*; the features are based on *North West View of Blenheim House and Park in the County of Oxford, with Woodstock in the Distance*, designed and engraved by Boydell, 1752, pl. 53 of his *100 Views*, and *An East Prospect of the City of Oxford*, designed and engraved by Boydell, 1751, pl. 50 of his *100 Views*.

State Hermitage Museum, St Petersburg (8570, 8569A)
Lit: Raeburn, Voronikhina and Nurnberg 1995, cat. 135, 138a, views 1049, 423, 859, 687, 679

G261 Cover of oblong dish decorated with views on the Thames at Chelsea and Chiswick, Greater London, and features of monuments at Shugborough Park

Marks: painted view numbers '738', '739', '740', '741'
24 × 19.5 cm

The views are based on the right-hand part of *A View of Chelsea Water Works*, designed and engraved by Boydell, 1752, no.5 of his *100 Views* (see Cat. G259), and the right-hand side of *A View of … the Earl of Burlington's House*, engraving by Ignace Fougeron after a

G 269

drawing by Peter Brookes, 1750, no.27 of Boydell's *100 Views*; the features are based on one of the drawings of Shugborough Park by Nicholas Dall (see Cat. G276).

The view of Chelsea shows Westminster Abbey (right) and the dome of St Paul's Cathedral (centre) behind the old mill tower, while the view of Chiswick shows the parish church and the western part of Chiswick Mall. The two monuments at Shugborough are the Triumphal Arch and the Lanthorn of Demosthenes.

State Hermitage Museum, St Petersburg (8490A)
Lit: Raeburn, Voronikhina and Nurnberg 1995,
cat. 137a, views 584, 515, 772, 773

G262 Dessert plate decorated with a view of a house on the Thames at Isleworth, Greater London

Mark: painted view number '930'
Diameter: 22 cm

The view is based on a detail of the background of *A view up the Thames between Richmond and Isleworth*, designed and engraved by Boydell, around 1752, pl. 1 of his *100 Views* (see Cat. G259). The house shown in the view was demolished in the 1820s.

State Hermitage Museum, St Petersburg (9163)
Lit: Raeburn, Voronikhina and Nurnberg 1995,
cat. 793, view 561

G263 Dessert plate decorated with a view of a house on the Thames at Isleworth, Greater London

Mark: painted view number '932'
Diameter: 22 cm

The view is based on a detail of the central part of the print used for Cat. G262. The house shown in the view was pulled down soon after the engraving was made, to be replaced by one built in 1759 for the impresario James Lacy. This dessert plate was omitted from the Service.

Trustees of the Wedgwood Museum, Barlaston, Staffordshire (5381)
Lit: Raeburn, Voronikhina and Nurnberg 1995, view A20; Blake Roberts 1986 I, p. 83, fig. 11

G264 Dessert plate decorated with a view of Purfleet, Essex

Mark: painted view number '936'
Diameter: 22 cm

The view is based on the left-hand part of *A View of Purfleet in the County of Essex*, designed and engraved by Boydell, 1752, pl. 18 of his *100 Views* (see Cat. G259).

State Hermitage Museum, St Petersburg (9148)
Lit: Raeburn, Voronikhina and Nurnberg 1995,
cat. 798, view 319

G265 Dessert plate decorated with a view of Conway Castle, Gwynedd

Mark: painted view number '939'
Diameter: 22 cm

The view is based on *West Prospect of Conway Castle in Caernarvon Shire*, designed and engraved by Boydell, 1749, pl. 70 of his *100 Views* (see Cat. G259).

State Hermitage Museum, St Petersburg (9139)
Lit: Raeburn, Voronikhina and Nurnberg 1995,
cat. 801, view 1085

G266 Dessert plate decorated with a view of Elizabeth Castle, Jersey

Mark: painted view number '941'
Diameter: 22 cm

The view is based on *A View of Elizabeth Castle in the Island of Jersey*, engraving by

Le Comte after a painting by Charles Brooking (1723–59), pl. 61 of Boydell's *100 Views* (see Cat. G259). The Elizabethan castle was famous for withstanding a siege of eight years (1643–51) during the Civil War, when it was held for the King by Sir George Carteret. He was rewarded by Charles II at the Restoration with a grant of land in America, which he named New Jersey.

State Hermitage Museum, St Petersburg (9076)
Lit: Raeburn, Voronikhina and Nurnberg 1995,
cat. 803, view 1069

G267 Dessert plate decorated with a view of Chester Castle, Cheshire

Mark: painted view number '942'
Diameter: 22 cm

The view is based on *A South Prospect of the City of Chester*, designed and engraved by Boydell, 1749, pl. 67 of his *100 Views* (see Cat. G259).

State Hermitage Museum, St Petersburg (9073)
Lit: Raeburn, Voronikhina and Nurnberg 1995,
cat. 804, view 142

G268 Oval compotier decorated with a view of Oxford from the Meadows

Mark: painted view number '1021'
24 × 20 cm

The view is based on the right-hand part of *A South Prospect of the City of Oxford*, designed and engraved by Boydell, 1751, pl. 51 of his *100 Views* (see Cat. G259).

State Hermitage Museum, St Petersburg (8687)
Lit: Raeburn, Voronikhina and Nurnberg 1995,
cat. 865, view 683; Voronikhina 1988, p. 167

G269 Square compotier decorated with a view of Chiswick House, Greater London

Mark: painted view number '966'
20 × 20 cm

The view is based on the left-hand part of *A View of ... the Earl of Burlington's House*, engraving by Ignace Fougeron after a

G 319, G132, G274, G271. Twig baskets and ice cups from the dessert service.

drawing by Peter Brookes, 1750, pl. 27 of Boydell's *100 Views* (see Cat. G261).

State Hermitage Museum, St Petersburg (20850)
Lit: Raeburn, Voronikhina and Nurnberg 1995, cat. 883, view 524

G270 Square compotier decorated with a view of Blenheim Palace, Oxon.

Landscape enamelled by James Bakewell
Mark: painted view number '971'
20 × 20 cm

The view is based on the central part of

A North View of Blenheim House & Park, in the County of Oxford, one of the Seats of the Duke of Marlborough, wth. ye Monument which was erected in memory of the late Duke, designed and engraved by Boydell, 1752, pl. 52 of his *100 Views* (see Cat. G259). John Churchill received the manor and a sum of money to build a house as a reward from Queen Anne for his victory at the Battle of Blenheim in Bavaria (1704). The architect was Sir John Vanbrugh, although the house was not completed (by Nicholas Hawksmoor) until after the Duke's death in 1722. The Column of

Victory, designed by the Earl of Pembroke in 1727–30, supports a statue of Marlborough with Roman eagles at his feet. The view was executed by James Bakewell, whose worksheet for 20 May 1774 includes '1 Compt. with Blenheim House 9 hours', for which he charged three shillings and sixpence.

State Hermitage Museum, St Petersburg (8598)
Lit: Raeburn, Voronikhina and Nurnberg 1995, cat. 888, view 673; Voronikhina 1988, p. 173; Wedgwood MS E32-5264

G271 Ice cup decorated with views on the Thames near London

Marks: painted view numbers '1221', '1222'
Height (with cover): 7.5 cm; diameter: 6 cm

The views are based on a feature from the central background of the print used for Cat. G269 and a detail from the extreme left of *Mortlake up the Thames*, designed and engraved by Boydell, 1753, pl. 25 of his *100 Views* (see Cat. G259).

State Hermitage Museum, St Petersburg (9169)
Lit: Raeburn, Voronikhina and Nurnberg 1995, cat. 928, views 517, 864

G272 Ice cup decorated with views of the bridge at Rhuddlan Castle, Clwyd, and Caernarfon Castle, Gwynedd

Marks: painted view numbers '1233', '1234'
Height (with cover): 7.5 cm; diameter: 6 cm

The views are based on a feature from the left-hand part of *A North West View of Rhuddlan Castle, in Flintshire*, designed and engraved by Boydell, 1749, pl. 71 of his *100 Views* (see Cat. G259); and a detail of the extreme right-hand part of *The South East View of Caernarvon Castle*, 1742, from *Buck's Antiquities*, Wales III, 1742, pl. 74.

State Hermitage Museum, St Petersburg (9166)
Lit: Raeburn, Voronikhina and Nurnberg 1995, cat. 933, views 1117, 1083

G273 Ice cup decorated with views of Lamphey Palace, Dyfed, and the Thames at Kew, Greater London

Marks: painted view numbers '1241', '1242'
Height (with cover): 7.5 cm; diameter: 6 cm

The views (which are incorrectly numbered; they correspond to nos 1235–6 in Bentley's catalogue) are based on the right-hand part of *Llanfeth, or Lantphey-Court, Pembroke-shire*, preparatory drawing by Francis Grose after a drawing made in 1770 by Paul Sandby (see Cat. G203); and a detail of *A View of Sion House and the Parts adjacent, Taken from the Road next to the Royal Garden, at Richmond*, engraving by

Benazech after a drawing by Brookes, pl. 28 of Boydell's *100 Views* (see Cat. G260).

State Hermitage Museum, St Petersburg (20860)
Lit: Raeburn, Voronikhina and Nurnberg 1995, cat. 937, views 1146, 860

G274 Ice cup decorated with views on the Thames near London

Marks: painted view numbers '1245', '1246'
Height (with cover): 7.5 cm; diameter: 6 cm

The views are based on a detail of the background of *A View of Sunbury, up the River Thames*, designed and engraved by Boydell, about 1752, pl. 2 of his *100 Views* (see Cat. G259); and a detail of *A view up the Thames between Richmond and Isleworth*, pl. 1 of Boydell's *100 Views* (see Cat. G262).

State Hermitage Museum, St Petersburg (9174)
Lit: Raeburn, Voronikhina and Nurnberg 1995, cat. 939, views 576, 562

G275 Ice cup decorated with views of Denbigh Castle, Clwyd

Marks: painted view numbers '1255', '1256'
Height (with cover): 7.5 cm; diameter: 6 cm

The views are based on two details of *A North View of Denbigh Castle, in North Wales*, designed and engraved by Boydell, 1750, pl. 72 of his *100 Views* (see Cat. G259).

State Hermitage Museum, St Petersburg (9170)
Lit: Raeburn, Voronikhina and Nurnberg 1995, cat. 944, view 1101, 1102

NICHOLAS DALL

G276 *An extensive View of the Park and Monuments*

Nicholas Thomas Dall (d. 1777)
Oil on canvas
Signed
Dated 1768
113 × 169 cm

This is one of three views of Shugborough Park, Staffs., for which both drawings and

oil paintings exist by Nicholas Dall. Dall, a Scandinavian theatrical scene-painter, who settled in London before 1760, made a significant contribution to the Frog Service (see p. 145). He was brought to Wedgwood's attention by Thomas Anson, for whom he had done the views of Shugborough, and he was able to supply Bentley with a number of further drawings to have copied. Only two of these (Cat. G283 and G285) have been traced, although it seems likely that quite a number of Yorkshire views, as well as some others in the Midlands and around London, were based on his work.

Thomas Anson, aided by his younger brother Admiral George Anson, began the development of the garden at Shugborough in the late 1740s. The earliest of the ornamental buildings was the Chinese House, 1747, designed by Sir Percy Brett, one of Admiral Anson's officers, and soon after this the Ruins were built to designs by Thomas Wright. The pagoda was under construction in 1752, and during the 1760s James 'Athenian' Stuart was employed to carry out alterations to the house and erect a group of classical monuments in the Park. These included the Triumphal Arch, the Tower of the Winds and the Lanthorn of Demosthenes, all based on models Stuart had drawn in Athens. He also designed the Orangery in 1764 to house Anson's art collection. Several of these features had already been pulled down by the early 19th century, but with the exception of the Orangery (demolished around 1855) most of the others survive in the care of the National Trust.

The monuments in the southern part of the Park shown in the painting (east to west) are: the Tower of the Winds, the Cascade and Palladian Bridge, the Obelisk, the Triumphal Arch, the Pagoda and the Lanthorn of Demosthenes. The second painting (see Cat. G281–2) shows the west front of the house with the Ruins, Orangery and Chinese House, while the third (see Cat. G287) is a closer view of the Ruins with a distant view of the Park.

Photograph exhibited by courtesy of Shugborough Park, National Trust (Lichfield Collection)

G 282

G277 Oval compotier decorated with a view of the Tower of the Winds at Shugborough Park, Staffs.

Marks: 'WEDGWOOD' impressed; painted view number '1005'
22 × 17 cm

The view is based on the extreme left-hand part of Dall's drawing of the Park and Monuments (see Cat. G276).

State Hermitage Museum, St Petersburg (8590)
Lit: Raeburn, Voronikhina and Nurnberg 1995, cat. 873, view 774

G278 Oval compotier decorated with a view of the Pagoda and Lanthorn of Demosthenes at Shugborough Park, Staffs.

Marks: 'WEDGWOOD' impressed; painted view number '1014'
25 × 19.5 cm

The view is based on the right-hand part of Dall's drawing of the Park and Monuments (see Cat. G276).

State Hermitage Museum, St Petersburg (8585)
Lit: Raeburn, Voronikhina and Nurnberg 1995, cat. 858, view 775

G279 Oval compotier decorated with a view of the Obelisk and Triumphal Arch at Shugborough Park, Staffs.

Marks: 'WEDGWOOD' impressed; painted view number '1015'
25 × 19.5 cm

The view is based on the central part of Dall's drawing of the Park and Monuments (see Cat. G276).

State Hermitage Museum, St Petersburg (8582)
Lit: Raeburn, Voronikhina and Nurnberg 1995, cat. 859, view 776

G280 Oval compotier decorated with a view of the Cascade and Palladian Bridge at Shugborough Park, Staffs.

Mark: painted view number '1026'
32 × 22.5 cm

The view is based on the centre background of Dall's drawing of the Park and Monuments (see Cat. G276).

State Hermitage Museum, St Petersburg (8603)
Lit: Raeburn, Voronikhina and Nurnberg 1995, cat. 838, view 777

G281 Round compotier decorated with a view of the Chinese House at Shugborough Park, Staffs.

Mark: painted view number '979'
Diameter: 21.5 cm

The view is based on the left-hand part of Dall's second drawing, *The West Front of Shugborough, with the Ruins, Orangery and Chinese House* (see Cat. G276).

State Hermitage Museum, St Petersburg (8546)
Lit: Raeburn, Voronikhina and Nurnberg 1995, cat. 896, view 779

G282 Oval compotier decorated with a view of the Ruins and Orangery at Shugborough Park, Staffs.

Mark: painted view number '1030'
32 × 22.5 cm

The view is based on the central part of Dall's second drawing (see Cat. G281).

State Hermitage Museum, St Petersburg (8606)
Lit: Raeburn, Voronikhina and Nurnberg 1995, cat. 842, view 780

G283 *Richmond Hill up the River*

Nicholas Thomas Dall
Grey wash over preparatory pencil
Inscribed with title and 'N8.' and signed
'N. T Dall'
Dated 1774
Cut to 20.5 × 46 cm

See Cat. G276. For another view of
Richmond Hill, see Cat. G145.

Trustees of the British Museum (BM 1962-7-14-28)

**G284 Oval compotier decorated with a
view of the Thames at Richmond, Greater
London**

Mark: painted view number '1032'
32 × 22.5 cm

The view is based on Dall's drawing (Cat.
G283).

State Hermitage Museum, St Petersburg (8607)
*Lit: Raeburn, Voronikhina and Nurnberg 1995,
cat. 844, view 895*

G285 *Lord Patchett's House in Budesert in
Staffordshire*

Nicholas Thomas Dall
Watercolour and ink, squared up for
enlargement
Inscribed with title and 'N^r.11' and signed
'N.T.Dall: delin'
Dated 1770
21 × 50 cm

See Cat. G276. Beaudesert was built by
Thomas Lord Paget in 1574–5 on the site of
the medieval palace of the Bishops of
Lichfield in Cannock Chase. Howard
Colvin has pointed out that Dall's drawing
shows the house just before extensive
alterations were undertaken in 1771–2
(while another view, used to decorate a
cream bowl, based on a drawing lent to
Bentley by Major Rooks, shows it after
these alterations). The house was
demolished in 1932.

Trustees of the William Salt Library, Stafford

**G286 Glacier decorated with views of Moor
Park, Herts., and Beaudesert, Staffs.; liner
decorated with feature of the Rotunda at
Enville, Staffs.; lid decorated with features
from Booth Hall, Cheshire, Came House,
Dorset, and, possibly, Sedbury Park,
N. Yorks.**

Marks: 'WEDGWOOD' impressed; painted
view numbers '1065', '1066', '1074', '1075',
'1076', '1077'
Height: 34.5 cm; diameter: 23.5 cm

The glaciers were the most elaborate pieces
in the Service and were designed especially
for it. The main pail (with views on either
side) contained ice, on top of which was
placed the liner (with a view on the inside),
in which the frozen dessert was placed. An
inner lid (with both borders but no views),
which also contained ice, was placed above
this and then covered with the outer lid.
This was decorated with three small views
and an elaborate finial moulded with
figures of three Sibyls, supposed to
represent Ice, Cold and Winter and
designed by Wedgwood after a print by
Stefano della Bella (see Cat. E15).
   The view of Moor Park is based on a
drawing quite possibly by Dall, who made
drawings there in 1770; the view of
Beaudesert is based on Dall's drawing (Cat.
G285). Moor Park was acquired around
1750 by Admiral George Anson (see Cat.
G276), who employed Matthew
Brettingham to make alterations to the
house (1751–4) and 'Capability' Brown to
lay out the park (around 1755–60). The
estate was bought by Sir Lawrence Dundas
on Anson's death in 1762.
   The rotunda at Enville was probably
copied from one of Devis's drawings (see
Cat. G170). The island in the lake at Booth
Hall is from one of Samuel Stringer's
Cheshire drawings (see Cat. G161), while
the view at Came is from the right-hand
edge of *East View of...Came in Dorsetshire*,
from vol. I of Hutchins' *History and
Antiquities of Dorset*, 1774 (see. Cat. G235).
The third feature on the lid is described in
Bentley's Catalogue as 'View of the statue of
the Medici Venus on Mr Hilliard's island',

which may refer to Robert D'Arcy
Hildyard, who lived at Sedbury Park, near
Richmond. Venus was the goddess of
gardens, and copies of the Medici Venus
featured in several 18th-century gardens.

*State Hermitage Museum, St Petersburg (8473,
8472B)*
*Lit: Raeburn, Voronikhina and Nurnberg 1995,
cat. 686a, 686b, 687d, views 387, 732, 754, 1047,
135, 283; Williamson 1909, frontispiece; Reilly
1989 I pl. 329*

**G287 Glacier decorated with views of
Fountains Abbey and Harewood House,
N. Yorks.; liner decorated with feature of
Fishers Hall at Hackfall, N. Yorks.; lid
decorated with features from Shugborough
Park, Staffs.** *(Pl. 25)*

Marks: 'WEDGWOOD' impressed; painted
view numbers '1063', '1064', '1073', '1078',
'1079', '1080'
Height: 34.5 cm; diameter: 23.5 cm

All the views and features on this piece may
be from drawings by Dall, who is known to
have made several paintings of Fountains
Abbey, as well as working at Harewood and
Hackfall, although none of them have been
traced – with the exception of the drawing
of the Ruins at Shugborough (see Cat.
G276), from which the features on the lid
are taken. For Fountains Abbey see Cat.
G74. For Hackfall see Cat. G151; the little
octagonal pavilion known as Fishers Hall,
built in 1750, was a viewpoint for the rapids
in the River Ure. Harewood House was
built for Edwin Lascelles by John Carr of
York in 1759–71.

*State Hermitage Museum, St Petersburg (8539,
8539B)*
*Lit: Raeburn, Voronikhina and Nurnberg 1995,
cat. 685, views 1002, 1008, 1007, 784, 785, 786;
Williamson 1909, facing p. 46*

**G288 Glacier decorated with views of
Richmond Castle, N. Yorks., and Milton
Abbas, Dorset; liner decorated with feature
of houses at Stratford-upon-Avon,
Warwicks.; lid decorated with features from**

Milborne St Andrew, Dorset, and Kirkstead Abbey, Lincs.

Marks: 'WEDGWOOD' impressed; painted view numbers '1067', '1068', '1072', '1084', '1085'
Height: 34.5 cm; diameter: 23.5 cm

The view of Richmond Castle may again be from a drawing by Dall. It shows the great Norman castle from the east, with a garden pavilion overlooking the River Swale. The drawing was probably made before 1771, when the bridge was damaged by floods (and eventually replaced). The view of Milton Abbas is based on *The North West View of Milton Abby the Seat of the R*t*. Hon*ble*. Joseph Lord Milton*, engraving by Edward Rooker published in vol. II of Hutchins' *History and Antiquities of Dorset*, 1774 (see Cat. G252). The engraving is undated but the view must date from 1773 or 1774, since the mansion built in the Gothic style to replace the old monastic buildings was not begun by William Chambers until 1771. For the past several years, starting in 1763, the gardens had been landscaped by 'Capability' Brown, and he returned later when further developments by James Wyatt entailed demolishing the old market town and moving the inhabitants to a new village – created by Brown – three quarters of a mile away. The feature from a view of Stratford-upon-Avon (which was also depicted on the side of a cream bowl) may also be from a drawing by Dall, who exhibited *A view of Stratford upon Avon, as it appeared at the late Jubilee in honour of Shakespeare* at the Free Society of Artists in 1770. The features of the 17th-century house at Milborne St Andrew are taken from *Milbourn St. Andrew, the Seat of Edm*d*. Morton Pleydell Esq.*, engraving by Peter Mazell after a painting by William Tomkins in vol. I of Hutchins' book. The feature of Kirkstead Abbey is a detail from *The East Prospect of Kirksted Abbey near Horncastle*, 1726, from *Buck's Antiquities*, II, pl. 17, 1727.

State Hermitage Museum, St Petersburg (8472, 20834A, 20834B)
Lit: Raeburn, Voronikhina and Nurnberg 1995,

cat. 687a, 688b, 688d, views 1034, 297, 933, 295, 296, 485; Williamson 1909, facing pp. xviii, 46; Reilly 1989 I, pl. 332

G289 15-inch oval dish decorated with a view of Etruria Hall, Staffs. *(Pl. 16)*

Marks: 'WEDGWOOD' impressed; painted view number '1129'
38.5 × 29 cm

The view is based on an untraced drawing, evidently the same one that was used for the ceramic plaque attributed to James Bakewell (Cat. D4), who was probably also the painter of this dish. Samuel Stringer certainly did a view of Etruria in the autumn of 1773 (see Cat. G163), but it seems doubtful (though not impossible) that it served as a model for this piece. The other drawings he did at that time were all used quite quickly, and this dish was not decorated until around May 1774. Furthermore, this view appears to be based on a drawing by a more accomplished artist. There is a very similar composition by Dall of Oakedge (on the Shugborough estate) with a barge passing in front, which exists in several versions, and he is perhaps more likely to be the author of the original.

Etruria Hall was built for Josiah Wedgwood by Joseph Pickford in 1767–9 (at the same time as he was building Bank House for Thomas Bentley nearby).

State Hermitage Museum, St Petersburg (8641)
Lit: Raeburn, Voronikhina and Nurnberg 1995, cat. 38, view 760; Williamson 1909, facing p. 8; Reilly 1989 I pl. 330

GEORGE BARRET

G290 *Melrose Abbey, east front*

George Barret senior (1728/32–84)
Oil on canvas
76 × 120 cm

One of a pair of paintings by the Irish artist George Barret, who worked in England from 1762 and was later one of the

founders of the Royal Academy. His principal patrons were the Duke of Portland and the Duke of Buccleuch, for whom the views of Melrose were painted. Barret and Nicholas Dall were singled out for acknowledgement in the preface to Bentley's catalogue of the Frog Service, but Barret's contribution is not easy to determine. He seems to have appeared on the scene at a late stage and furnished Bentley with drawings from which he had executed paintings. If he himself supplied original drawings of the Melrose views, that would account for the item in Wedgwood's memorandum to Bentley of 20 June 1774 (Wedgwood MS E25-18539) that 'A note sho*d*. be sent to the Duke of Buccleughs, to acquaint his G—— why we do not send to copy his Pictures.' On the same sheet is another item – 'L*d*. Rockingham's House – from Mr. Barrat', referring to the view of Wentworth Woodhouse (Cat. G297). Apart from these, other views that might readily be attributed to Barret are those of Dalkeith (Cat. G69) and of Terrace Gardens, Richmond (Cat. G294–5). However, given the number of unattributable source drawings that we believe were used and the fact that Barret's work is not well documented, it is quite possible that other views were also based on drawings he made available to Bentley. After the completion of the Service, Bentley suggested that Barret, who had chronic financial problems, should be retained to instruct the painters at Chelsea. Wedgwood doubted 'whether we shall have sufficient encouragement in Landskip painting upon usefull ware to enable us to pay M*r*. Barrat any great matter for that purpose, but I think we should have a good handsome Dessert service painted in that stile & kept to show, & I have no objection to paying M*r*. Barrat for some instruction to our People. – I suppose they will be the best bestow'd upon Ralph [Unwin].' (Wedgwood MS E25-18552, Wedgwood to Bentley, 14 August 1774). The production of the polychrome pieces (Cat. G320ff) may, therefore, be partly due to Barret's presence in Chelsea.

The imposing ruins of Melrose Abbey

stood on the estates of the Duke of Buccleuch, a few miles from their residence at Bowhill.

Duke of Buccleuch Collection, Bowhill, Selkirk

G291 *Melrose Abbey, south front*

George Barret senior
Oil on canvas
76 × 120 cm

See Cat. G290.

Duke of Buccleuch Collection, Bowhill, Selkirk

G292 12-inch round cover decorated with views of Melrose Abbey, Borders, and Guisborough Priory, N. Yorks.

Marks: painted view numbers '1137', '1138'
Diameter: 26 cm

The view of Melrose is based on *Melrose Abbey, east front* by Barret (Cat. G290). That of Guisborough Priory is based on an untraced drawing by an unknown artist.

State Hermitage Museum, St Petersburg (8467)
Lit: Raeburn, Voronikhina and Nurnberg 1995, cat. 660, views 1196, 1003

G293 Monteith decorated with views of Melrose Abbey, Borders, and Audley End, Essex

Landscapes enamelled by James Bakewell
Marks: painted view numbers '1271', '1272'
Inscription on base: 'This Table and Dessert Service, consisting of 952 Pieces, and ornamented, in Enamel, with (above) 1244 real Views of Great-Britain, was made at Etruria in Staffordshire and Chelsea in Middlesex, in the years 1773 & 1774, at the Command of that illustrious Patroness of the Arts Catherine II, Empress of All the Russias, by Wedgwood & Bentley.'
14 × 33 × 22 cm

The view of Melrose is based on *Melrose Abbey, south front* by Barret (Cat. G291). The view of Audley End is based on an untraced drawing by an unknown artist. The house was begun in 1603 by Thomas

G

G

Howard, Earl of Suffolk, and belonged for a time to King Charles II. It was reduced to less than half its size in alterations made by Vanbrugh around 1721, and in the 1760s Sir John Griffin employed 'Capability' Brown to landscape the grounds. The earliest of the garden ornaments was the bridge over the River Cam built in 1764 by

Robert Adam. The view was executed by James Bakewell, whose worksheet for 16 July 1774 includes '1 Monteith with a Abby of the Duke of Buccleuch', for which he charged six shillings.

State Hermitage Museum, St Petersburg (20832)
Lit: Raeburn, Voronikhina and Nurnberg 1995, cat. 684, views 1197, 313

G294 17-inch oval dish decorated with a view of Terrace Gardens, Richmond, Greater London

Marks: 'WEDGWOOD' impressed; painted view number '527'
44 × 34 cm

The view is based on an untraced drawing. The visitors are landing at Terrace Gardens, part of the grounds of Buccleuch House, built for the Duke of Montagu, who developed the gardens from the 1760s onwards. A passage under the Petersham Road connected the upper grounds with the lawns sloping down the Thames. The house was demolished in 1937. The drawing may well have been one provided by George Barret (see Cat. G290).

State Hermitage Museum, St Petersburg (8623)
Lit: Raeburn, Voronikhina and Nurnberg 1995, cat. 10, view 888

G 294

G295 12-inch oval cover decorated with views of St Just, Cornwall, and the Thames at Richmond, Greater London

Marks: painted view numbers '701', '702'
26.5 × 19.5 cm

The views are based on *Pornavon Cove in the Parish of S^t. Just*, pl. XIX, fig. 4 in Borlase's *Natural History of Cornwall* (see Cat. G232); and on the right-hand part of the drawing of the Thames at Terrace Gardens, Richmond (see Cat. G294).

State Hermitage Museum, St Petersburg (8454)
Lit: Raeburn, Voronikhina and Nurnberg 1995, cat. 644, views 187, 889

VIEWS MADE AVAILABLE BY PATRONS

G296 *Sandwell*

Unknown artist
Ink and wash
Inscribed 'D. 1770'
20.5 × 33 cm

This drawing of Sandwell Park, seat of the Earl of Dartmouth, has traditionally been

ascribed to T. Carter, but there is no evidence to support this attribution. It is unlikely to be by Stringer, Dall or Devis, all of whom supplied views of Staffordshire to be reproduced on the Service, but could well have been an amateur's drawing loaned by Lord Dartmouth. The house had been rebuilt in 1705–11 for the 1st Earl by William Smith. It was demolished in 1928.

Trustees of the William Salt Library, Stafford

G297 15-inch oval cover decorated with views of Wentworth Woodhouse, S. Yorks., and Sandwell Park, Staffs.

Marks: painted view numbers '1147', '1148'
34 × 24 cm

The views are based on an untraced drawing of Wentworth Woodhouse by Barret (see Cat. G290) and the anonymous drawing of Sandwell (Cat. G296). The east front of Wentworth Woodhouse, designed by Henry Flitcroft (from around 1735), extends for 180 metres, the longest façade of any English country house. The view is curiously inaccurate, for the ends of the

central block were never stepped forward, and the whole façade as built lacks depth, as it had to incorporate an earlier house (built around 1725).

State Hermitage Museum, St Petersburg (8449)
Lit: Raeburn, Voronikhina and Nurnberg 1995, cat. 623, views 1065, 771; Williamson 1909, facing p. 32; Wedgwood MS E25-18539

G298 15-inch oval cover decorated with views of Stoke Gifford Park, Glos., and Richmond, N. Yorks.

Marks: painted view numbers '1153', '1154'
34 × 24 cm

The views (which are omitted from Bentley's catalogue) are based on untraced drawings by unknown artists. The 16th-century house at Stoke Gifford was replaced in the mid-18th century with a building in the castellated style designed for Norborne Berkeley, Lord Botetourt, by Thomas Wright, who also landscaped the grounds. The view of Richmond is from part of a drawing (perhaps by Dall, see Cat. G276) with the castle in the distance on the

G 247, G 286, G 299. Ice pail, glacier and monteith from the dessert service.

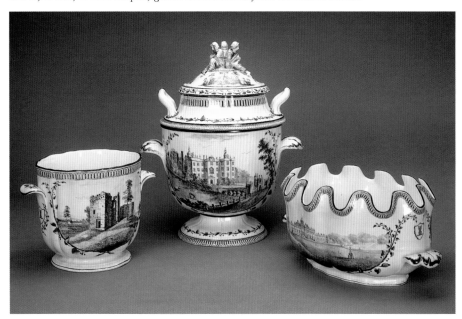

left. The fullest extent of the drawing can be seen around the polychrome cup (Cat. G330).

State Hermitage Museum, St Petersburg (8466)
Lit: Raeburn, Voronikhina and Nurnberg 1995, cat. 664, views 343, 1037

G299 Monteith decorated with views of Gatton Park, Surrey, and Castle Howard, N. Yorks.

Marks: painted view numbers '1159', '1160'
14 × 33 × 22 cm

The view of Gatton is based on one of a group of untraced drawings by an unknown artist. The house was built in the mid-18th century by Sir James Colebrooke, who turned much of the glebe into a great lake. His brother, Sir George Colebrooke, who succeeded him, engaged 'Capability' Brown to landscape the park, and work continued from 1762 to 1768 at a cost of over £3,000, the plans including a 'great water menagerie'. The estate was bought in January 1774 by Sir William Mayne, whom Bentley's catalogue names as the owner. The house was demolished in 1808, though parts of the garden survive.

The view of Castle Howard is based on one of four paintings by William Marlow commissioned by Lord Carlisle in 1772 and exhibited at the Free Society of Artists the same year. It shows the principal façade, begun by Vanbrugh and completed by Sir Thomas Robinson in the 1750s.

State Hermitage Museum, St Petersburg (20833)
Lit: Raeburn, Voronikhina and Nurnberg 1995, cat. 682, views 828, 989

G300 Oval compotier decorated with a view of Windsor Castle, Berks.

Mark: painted view number '1031'
32 × 22.5 cm

The view, based on an untraced drawing by an unknown artist, shows the south-east corner of the upper ward, which contained the apartments for the royal family, as it was remodelled for Charles II by Hugh May between 1675 and 1680. May's work was extensively altered by Wyatville after 1820.

State Hermitage Museum, St Petersburg (8605)
Lit: Raeburn, Voronikhina and Nurnberg 1995, cat. 843, view 16; Williamson 1909, facing p. 20; Reilly 1989 I, pl. 335

G301 Flat plate decorated with a view of the ruined arch at Painshill, Surrey

Mark: painted view number '435'
Diameter: 24.5 cm

The view is based on an anonymous painting at Painshill. For Charles Hamilton's landscape garden at Painshill, see Cat. G108.

State Hermitage Museum, St Petersburg (8746)
Lit: Raeburn, Voronikhina and Nurnberg 1995, cat. 446, view 878

G302 19-inch oval dish decorated with a view of Syon House, Greater London

Mark: painted view number '647'
49 × 38 cm

The view is based on an untraced drawing probably made available to Bentley by the Duke of Northumberland (see Cat. G303ff.). Two of the six dishes of this size – the largest in the Service – were devoted to views of Syon (the other does not survive), suggesting the high value Wedgwood and Bentley placed on the Duke's patronage. The house was formed out of the old nunnery buildings in the 16th century, and when Robert Adam remodelled it for the 1st Duke in 1761 the exterior was largely unchanged. The gardens were landscaped by 'Capability' Brown at the same period.

State Hermitage Museum, St Petersburg (8611)
Lit: Raeburn, Voronikhina and Nurnberg 1995, cat. 4, view 577; Williamson 1909, facing p. 40

G303 *A view from the Hermitage near Warkworth, taken from one of the Cells*

William Beilby (1740–1819)
Watercolour
Inscribed with title and signed 'W. Beilby'
Dated 25 October 1773
8.5 × 12.5 cm

The album of drawings – *A Series of Sketches. Views in Great Britain, The Continent and America, 1772–1778* – by William Beilby, done for the Duke of Northumberland, was evidently lent to Bentley, probably with other views of the

Alnwick estate (see Cat. G305) and of Syon (see Cat. G302). Warkworth Castle was the principal seat of the Percy family until 1750, when they moved to Alnwick, six miles away. The Hermitage consisted of three rooms and a chapel, dating from the early 14th and early 15th centuries, hewn in the rock in the valley of the River Coquet, providing relatively spacious and comfortable accommodation for the hermit.

Duke of Northumberland, Alnwick Castle

G304 Oval compotier decorated with a view of Warkworth Hermitage, Northumbria

Marks: 'WEDGWOOD' impressed; painted view number '1001'
22 × 17 cm

The view is based on Beilby's drawing (Cat. G303).

State Hermitage Museum, St Petersburg (8592)
Lit: Raeburn, Voronikhina and Nurnberg 1995, cat. 869, view 662

G305 Oval compotier decorated with a view of the 'Nine Year Auld Hole', Hulne Park, Northumbria

Marks: 'WEDGWOOD' impressed; painted view number '1002'
22 × 17 cm

The view is surely based on a drawing lent to Wedgwood and Bentley by the Duke of Northumberland, very likely also by William Beilby (see Cat. G303). The Hole, described in Bentley's catalogue as 'A Druid's Cavern', was developed as a grotto by the 1st Duke. Colin Shrimpton has provided the information that the figure of a friar at the entrance of the grotto was installed in 1765, while another figure, of an Egyptian mummy, was placed inside. They were carved by Matthew Mills, one of the principal masons employed on the restoration of Alnwick Castle, who embellished the site of Hulne Priory with similar figures.

State Hermitage Museum, St Petersburg (8593)
Lit: Raeburn, Voronikhina and Nurnberg 1995, cat. 870, view 648

G306 Oval compotier decorated with a view of Durham

Marks: 'WEDGWOOD' impressed; painted view number '1004'
22 × 17 cm

The view is based on another of the drawings in the album by William Beilby (see Cat. G303). It shows the cathedral and castle situated on a tongue of land on a loop in the River Wear.

State Hermitage Museum, St Petersburg (8591)

Lit: Raeburn, Voronikhina and Nurnberg 1995, cat. 872, view 310

G307 15-inch oval cover decorated with views of Bolsover Castle, Derbys., and Shobdon Court, Hereford and Worcs.

Marks: painted view numbers '1141', '1142'
34 × 24 cm

The view of Bolsover is based on an untraced drawing by an unknown artist. The view of Shobdon Court is based on one of a series of drawings by Mary Gardiner (active 1762–70). Bolsover was a sumptuous mansion built in the 17th century in the fortified style on the site of a Norman fortress, but by the early 18th century it was no longer inhabited. Shobdon Court was built in the early 18th century, but the original formal garden was transformed into the landscape garden seen in the views by John, 2nd Viscount Bateman. He was certainly assisted by his uncle, Richard 'Dicky' Bateman, a friend of Horace Walpole's who had a celebrated garden at Windsor – and the Chinese house in the garden at Shobdon (see Cat. G309) was known as 'Little Windsor'. One of the principal features was Shobdon Arches (see Cat. G308), made up of the chancel arch and two doorways from the old Norman church, which were preserved and erected

06

G 308

on a nearby hillside when the church was demolished in 1751. Mary Gardiner's drawings, which are a unique record of the garden at this time (apart from the copies on the Service), were in an album which was sold at auction in 1976, but the purchaser broke up the album, and the drawings are now apparently dispersed and cannot be traced.

State Hermitage Museum, St Petersburg (8507)
Lit: Raeburn, Voronikhina and Nurnberg 1995, cat. 620, views 225, 378

G308 15-inch oval cover decorated with views of Shobdon Court, Hereford and Worcs.

Marks: painted view numbers '1143', '1144'
34 × 24 cm

The views are based on two more of the drawings in Mary Gardiner's album (see Cat. G307).

State Hermitage Museum, St Petersburg (8509)
Lit: Raeburn, Voronikhina and Nurnberg 1995, cat. 621, views 379, 380

G309 15-inch oval cover decorated with views of Shobdon Court, Hereford and Worcs.

Marks: painted view numbers '1145', '1146'
34 × 24 cm

The views are based on two more of the drawings in Mary Gardiner's album (see Cat. G307).

State Hermitage Museum, St Petersburg (8520)
Lit: Raeburn, Voronikhina and Nurnberg 1995, cat. 622, views 381, 382

G310 12-inch round cover decorated with views of Purbrook House, Hants., and St Donat's Castle, S. Glamorgan

Marks: painted view numbers '925', '805'
Diameter: 26 cm

The views are both based on untraced drawings or paintings. The view described in Bentley's catalogue as 'Mr. Taylor's Park'

is surely Purbrook House on Portsdown Hill, built for Peter Taylor, MP for Portsmouth, in 1770 to the designs of Sir Robert Taylor. The house was demolished in 1829.

State Hermitage Museum, St Petersburg (8465)
Lit: Raeburn, Voronikhina and Nurnberg 1995, cat. 657, views 360, 1130

FINAL PIECES IN THE SERVICE

G311 15-inch oval cover decorated with views of Westminster Bridge, London, and Stourhead, Wilts.

Marks: painted view numbers '1163', '1165'
34 × 24 cm

The views are based on *A View of Westminster Bridge*, designed and engraved by Boydell, 1753, pl. 23 of his *100 Views* (see Cat. G259); and an untraced drawing of the gardens at Stourhead. Bentley's description of the bridge reads: 'View of Westminster Bridge, with part of London. This beautiful bridge is 1,220 ft. in length; it is divided into 15 arches, the centre one of which is 76 ft. diameter; its width is 44 ft., and the two sides are 7 each. It took twelve years to build and cost £218,000 sterling.' The bridge was built between 1738 and 1750 to designs by Charles Labelye, whom his enemies described as an 'unsolvent, ignorant arrogating Swiss'. It was replaced in the mid-19th century by the present bridge.

The gardens at Stourhead, despite the Victorian planting of rhododendrons, are probably the best preserved of all the great Georgian gardens in England, with the full range of garden buildings essentially unaltered. They were begun by Henry Hoare in 1743, and he created what Horace Walpole described in 1762 as 'one of the most picturesque scenes in the world'. The buildings were designed by Henry Flitcroft, and those seen in the present view include the Turkish Tent made of painted canvas (removed in 1792), the Grotto, the stone bridge, the village church and the Temple

of Apollo. Unaccountably, the Bristol High Cross, erected near the bridge in 1765 (before the Temple of Apollo was built), is omitted, although this view and its companion (used for one of the views on the lid of Cat. G209) were probably recent when copied on to the Service. Their authorship is unknown, but the viewpoints are very similar to two drawings done around 1775 by Coplestone Warre Bampfylde (see Cat. G134ff.), which are still in the house at Stourhead.

State Hermitage Museum, St Petersburg (8445)
Lit: Raeburn, Voronikhina and Nurnberg 1995, cat. 626, views 588, 963; Williamson 1909, facing p. 58; Voronikhina 1988, p. 169; Reilly 1989 I, pl. 331

G312 Dessert plate decorated with a view in Somerset

Mark: painted view number '1193'
Diameter: 22 cm

Described in Bentley's catalogue as a 'View of a path through a wood in Somersetshire', this is one of a small group of purely landscape views, somewhat in the manner of Gainsborough, that were among the last pieces of the Service to be decorated. The sources for them remain untraced.

State Hermitage Museum, St Petersburg (9047)
Lit: Raeburn, Voronikhina and Nurnberg 1995, cat. 818, view 728

G313 Dessert plate decorated with a view of Wilton Castle, Hereford and Worcs.

Mark: painted view number '1195'
Diameter: 22 cm

The view is based on an unknown drawing. The Elizabethan house built on to the south-west range of the medieval castle belonged at one time to Thomas Guy, who bequeathed it to the London Hospital that bears his name.

State Hermitage Museum, St Petersburg (9069)
Lit: Raeburn, Voronikhina and Nurnberg 1995, cat. 820, view 386

11

18

Prospect House (dated by David Watkin to 1775–7) must already have been completed. The garden had been landscaped for Lord Hardwicke by 'Capability' Brown, who completed his work there in 1773.

State Hermitage Museum, St Petersburg (9045)
Lit: Raeburn, Voronikhina and Nurnberg 1995, cat. 825, view 124

G315 Soup plate decorated with a view of Somerset House, London

Mark: painted view number '1179'
Diameter: 24.25 cm

The view is based on *Somerset House*, engraving by Edward Rooker after a drawing by Samuel Wale (about 1721–86) in vol. VI of *London and its Environs Described*, published by R. and J. Dodsley, 1761. It shows the house as remodelled in the 17th century by Inigo Jones and, probably, John Webb, which was demolished in 1776 and replaced by the building by Sir William Chambers. Several views of public buildings in London were added to the Service at a late stage, all being based on the engravings after Wale that were done for the Dodsleys' guidebook to London (or on later versions of these prints).

State Hermitage Museum, St Petersburg (9016)
Lit: Raeburn, Voronikhina and Nurnberg 1995, cat. 596, view 589

G316 Spoon for sauce tureen decorated with feature of the gatehouse of Lambeth Palace, London

Mark: painted view number '1261'
Length: 15.5 cm

The view is based on a detail of *Lambeth Palace*, engraving by Ignace Fougeron after a drawing by Samuel Wale in vol. III of *London and its Environs Described*, published by R. and J. Dodsley, 1761 (see Cat. G315).

State Hermitage Museum, St Petersburg (8491B)
Lit: Raeburn, Voronikhina and Nurnberg 1995, cat. 675, view 863

G314 Dessert plate decorated with a view of the Prospect House at Wimpole Hall, Cambs.

Mark: painted view number '1200'
Diameter: 22 cm

The drawing on which this view is based was undoubtedly lent to Bentley by the Countess of Hardwicke, who had seen the exhibition of the Green Frog Service at the London showroom, but it seems much more accomplished than those by her daughter, Lady Amabel Polwarth, of the family's estates (see p. 147 and Cat. G208). It is almost certainly from a drawing by James 'Athenian' Stuart (1713–88), who was the architect of the Prospect House (his last garden building). It was engraved by Daniel Lerpinière in 1777, but the drawing cannot be later than mid-1774, indicating that the

G317 Large compotier decorated with a view of Westminster Hall, London

Marks: 'WEDGWOOD' impressed; painted view number '1267'

31.5 × 18 cm

The view is based on *Westminster Hall*, engraving by James Green after a drawing by Samuel Wale in vol. VI of *London and its Environs Described*, published by R. and J. Dodsley, 1761 (see Cat. G315). Westminster Hall was part of the medieval Palace of Westminster and housed the courts of King's Bench and Chancery. The four 'large compotiers' were late additions to the Service and, apart from a few lids for cream bowls, were the last items to be decorated.

State Hermitage Museum, St Petersburg (8554)
Lit: Raeburn, Voronikhina and Nurnberg 1995, cat. 897, view 590; Williamson 1909, facing p. 24

G318 Large compotier decorated with a view of the Royal Exchange, London

Marks: 'WEDGWOOD' impressed; painted view number '1269'

31.5 × 18 cm

The view is based on *Front of the Royal Exchange*, engraving by James Green after a drawing by Samuel Wale in vol. V of *London and its Environs Described*, published by R. and J. Dodsley, 1761 (see Cat. G315), probably using the altered version of the print that appeared in *A New History of London* by John Noorthouck, 1773. The Royal Exchange, symbol of Britain's trading supremacy, had been established by Sir Thomas Gresham in 1566–7 but was destroyed a century later in the Great Fire. The building in the view, designed by Edward Jerman, was built in 1671. This, too, burned down in 1838 and was replaced by the building that stands today.

State Hermitage Museum, St Petersburg (8482)
Lit: Raeburn, Voronikhina and Nurnberg 1995, cat. 899, view 568; Williamson 1909, facing p. 10

G319 Three twig baskets

Unmarked

25 × 21.5; 27.5 × 24.5; diameter: 24 cm

These baskets for fruit formed part of the dessert service. Although space was found for the frog, it was impossible to decorate them with any views.

State Hermitage Museum, St Petersburg (8498, 8500, 8573)
Lit: Raeburn, Voronikhina and Nurnberg 1995, cat. 905, 902, 909

POLYCHROME PIECES

G320 Dessert plate decorated with a polychrome view of Aysgarth Bridge, N. Yorks.

Unmarked
Inscribed: 'Aysgarth Bridge, Yorkshire.'
Diameter: 22 cm

After the Service had been completed, Wedgwood and Bentley again addressed the question as to how to make the most of the great effort that had been expended. They needed to find new projects to which the painters in Chelsea could devote their experience, and they wanted to exploit the prestige of the Frog Service with patrons in the home market. It seems likely that the monochrome decoration was found too dull. Lady Hardwicke wrote: 'The whole [Service] together does not make a Shew nor strike you at first with beauty, being only painted with the Black Colour heightend with a Purplish Cast, but each Piece is separ[at]ely extremely pretty & generally very well executed.' A decision was made to decorate a number of dessert items in polychrome enamels (one cup and saucer also survives), with the title lettered below the view, and of course without the frog.

A letter to Wedgwood of 5 November 1774 from Benjamin Mather in Chelsea (quoted in Cat. D4) recommends that they should undertake a small dessert service with polychrome enamel decoration, and it could be that the 21 surviving pieces that have been traced are the remains of this. (Wedgwood had made the same suggestion himself a few weeks earlier; see Cat. G290.) However, the fact that the pieces seem to have such a varied provenance suggests that individual items were sold or given away separately. All these pieces have views that had been used on the Frog Service, and it seems significant that several are based on drawings by Francis Grose, who had given Bentley so much help, while almost all the others have views based on drawings that were very probably made available by the owners of the estates depicted – including the Dukes of Richmond, Beaufort and Portland, Viscount Bateman, Sir William Mains, Sir Lawrence Dundas, William Aislabie, Henry Hoare and Thomas Anson – or by the artists with their owners' permission. We know that an oval plaque was decorated in colours and given to Thomas Pennant (see p. 146 & note 41), and some, at least, of the polychrome dessert pieces may have been gifts to acknowledge help that had been given.

What is certain is that Wedgwood saw no long-term commercial possibilities in this kind of decoration – both because of the cost and the necessity of creating unique pieces. After the dessert pieces had been finished, no doubt at the end of 1774, no more appear to have been done (see also Raeburn 1992).

The view on the present piece is based on the drawing by Grose which appears on Cat. G188 and was also used for Cat. G210. Of the eleven polychrome dessert plates that are known, five are based on drawings done for Grose's *Antiquities*, all, almost certainly, copied from the drawings Grose had made for his engravers.

Trustees of the Wedgwood Museum, Barlaston, Staffordshire (No. 4931)
Lit: Letter from Jemima Marchioness Grey to Lady Amabel Polwarth, 19 June 1774 (Bedfordshire Record Office L30/11/122/60, quoted by permission of the Lady Lucas of Dingwall); Wedgwood MS 6-42333; Raeburn, Voronikhina and Nurnberg 1995, view B3

G321 Dessert plate decorated with a polychrome view of Coverham Abbey, N. Yorks.

Unmarked
Inscribed: 'Coverham Abbey, Yorkshire.'
Diameter: 22 cm

The view is based on the drawing by Francis Grose used for Cat. G207.

Trustees of the Wedgwood Museum, Barlaston, Staffordshire (4872)
Lit: Raeburn, Voronikhina and Nurnberg 1995, view B4

G 327

G 323

G322 Dessert plate decorated with a polychrome view of Welbeck Abbey, Notts.

Unmarked
Inscribed: 'Welbeck, in Nottinghamshire.'
Diameter: 22 cm

The view is based on an untraced drawing previously used to decorate one of the cream bowls in the Service. Henrietta Countess of Oxford had employed John James to remodel the house in the 1740s and Francis Richardson created the Great Lake at the same period.

Trustees of the Wedgwood Museum, Barlaston, Staffordshire (No. 4871)
Lit: Raeburn, Voronikhina and Nurnberg 1995, view B9

G 320

G323 Dessert plate decorated with a polychrome view of Moor Park, Herts.

Unmarked
Inscribed: 'Moore Park.'
Diameter: 22 cm

The view is based on the drawing, possibly by Nicholas Dall, that was used for Cat. G286.

Trustees of the Wedgwood Museum, Barlaston, Staffordshire (No. 4875)
Lit: Raeburn, Voronikhina and Nurnberg 1995, view B10

G324 Dessert plate decorated with a polychrome view of Shobdon Court, Hereford and Worcs.

Unmarked
Inscribed: 'Shobden Court, in Herefordshire.'
Diameter: 22 cm

The view is based on the drawing by Mary Gardiner that was used for Cat. G307.

Private collection
Lit: Raeburn, Voronikhina and Nurnberg 1995, view B8

G325 Oval compotier decorated with a polychrome view of Stourhead, Wilts.

Unmarked
Inscribed: 'Stour head, Glocestershire.'
22 × 29 cm

The view is based on one of the two drawings used for Cat. G209 (see also Cat. G311).

Private collection
Lit: Raeburn, Voronikhina and Nurnberg 1995, view B12

G326 Oval compotier decorated with a polychrome view of Wentworth Woodhouse, S. Yorks.

Unmarked
Inscribed: 'Wentworth House, Yorkshire.'
22 × 29 cm

The view is based on the drawing by Barret used for Cat. G297.

Private collection
Lit: Raeburn, Voronikhina and Nurnberg 1995, view B13

G327 Dessert plate decorated with a polychrome view of the gardens at Hackfall, N. Yorks.

Unmarked
Inscribed: 'A view, at Hackfall, in Yorkshire.'
Diameter 22 cm

The view is based on a drawing, possibly by Nicholas Dall.

Trustees of the Wedgwood Museum, Barlaston, Staffordshire (No. 4874)
Lit: Raeburn, Voronikhina and Nurnberg 1995, view B11

G328 Square compotier decorated with a polychrome view of Stoke Gifford, Glos.

Unmarked
Inscribed 'Stoke Gilford, in Glocestershire.'
20 × 20 cm

The view is based on the drawing used for Cat. G298.

Trustees of the Wedgwood Museum, Barlaston, Staffordshire (No. 4873)
Lit: Raeburn, Voronikhina and Nurnberg 1995, view B14

G329 Cream bowl (without stand) decorated with polychrome views of Shugborough Park, Staffs., and Richmond, N. Yorks.; lid decorated with views of Ludlow Castle, Salop

Unmarked
Inscriptions: 'near Richmond Castle, Yorkshire.', 'Shugborough Park, Staffordshire', and 'near Ludlow Castle, Shropshire.'
Height (with lid): 17.25 cm; diameter: 17.5 cm

The views are based on those used for the

following pieces in the Service: Cat. G287, Cat. G288 and a stand for a cream bowl with a view based on *Ludlow Castle*, drawing by Francis Grose after a drawing by Paul Sandby made in 1774 for vol. III of his *Antiquities*.

Shugborough Park. National Trust (Lichfield Collection)
Lit: Raeburn, Voronikhina and Nurnberg 1995, views B15, B16, B17, B18; Reilly 1989 I, pl. 337

G330 Cup and saucer decorated with polychrome views of Richmond Castle, N. Yorks (around cup), Castle Howard, N. Yorks. (inside cup), and Stoke Gifford, Glos. (on saucer)

Marks: 'C' incised (cup); 'O' impressed (saucer)
Height (cup): 5.1 cm; diameter (saucer): 11.8 cm

The views are based on those used for the following pieces in the Service: Cat. G298; the cover of a cream bowl with a view based on an untraced drawing of a temple at Castle Howard by an unknown artist; and a stand for a cream bowl with a view of Ludlow Castle (see Cat. G329).

Trustees of the National Galleries on Merseyside (Walker Art Gallery, Liverpool)
Lit: Raeburn, Voronikhina and Nurnberg 1995, views B19, B20, B21; Williamson 1909, facing p. 26; Reilly 1989 I, pl. 336

THE FROG SERVICE IN RUSSIA

The social anthropologist and traveller I. G. Georgi, who compiled an account of the palaces and objects of note in St Petersburg and its environs in 1794,[1] referred to the palace for which Wedgwood made the celebrated Frog Service as a 'pleasure palace'. The building owed its original name, the 'Kekerekeksinensky Palace', to its swampy location, 'Kekerekesinen' being the Finnish for 'Frog marsh'; and it was in allusion to this that each piece of Wedgwood's Service was painted with the amusing device of a frog on a heraldic shield.

The palace, designed in Gothic style by the architect Yuri Felten, was built between 1774 and 1777 in a deserted spot overgrown with woods and shrubbery, where it created the effect of a medieval castle. On a triangular plan, with turrets at each corner and lancet windows, it was very similar in plan to Longford Castle, Wiltshire, which was built by Sir Thomas Gorges and completed in 1591 (Cat. G87). An earthen ramp and a moat encircled the building, the latter being both attractive and practical in function, as it served to drain the swampy plot of land. The fashion for reviving medieval and Gothic architecture came to Russia from England, where Gothic styles had never wholly died out in spite of the prevailing taste for Classicism. The Kekerekeksinensky Palace was one of the first and most significant of the Gothic buildings to be built near St Petersburg; and perhaps it was intended that the commissioned service, painted with views of British castles and estates would harmonize with the architectural style of this 'castle-palace' for which it was made. Drawing on Josiah Wedgwood's

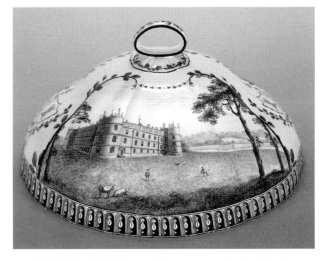

Pl. 37 (Cat. G87) Round dishcover from the Frog Service decorated with a view of Longford Castle, Wilts.

surviving letters to Thomas Bentley dealing with the decoration of the Frog Service, Peter Hayden concluded that the Empress's order might have expressly stipulated that all the buildings represented should be Gothic in style. But the range of views included was also influenced by Catherine's passion for English landscape gardening.[2] Russian interest in English garden design was growing, and from the late 1770s landscaped parks based on English models began to be created in Russia, the most celebrated of these being the so-called 'English Park' at Peterhof near St Petersburg.

During the first few years of the palace's existence the Empress paid periodic visits, most of these being brief stops made en route from St Petersburg to her summer residence at Tsarskoe Selo. These visits gave the Empress an opportunity to relax and to pass her time, not so much with entertainments as with diversions of a more intellectual kind. Just as the ancestral home of a European aristocrat would include a portrait gallery containing pictures establishing his lineage, so Kekerekeksinensky Palace contained portrait medallions in low relief of all the Russian grand princes, princesses and tsars, from Rurikh to Elizabeth I; but in addition Catherine also displayed here painted portraits of all the European monarchs ruling in 1775, together with their families (including the English royal family, in room no. 2),[3] as a political demonstration of her allegiances and status within this powerful circle.

Writing to his father on 3 June 1777, the English ambassador to Russia, James Harris, the future Earl of Malmesbury, stated:

I have the good fortune to have made myself not disagreeable to the Empress. She notices me much more than any of my colleagues; more, indeed, I believe, than any stranger is used to. She admits me to all her parties of cards, and a few days ago carried me with only two of her courtiers to a country palace, where she has placed the portraits of all the crowned heads of Europe. We discoursed much of their several merits; and still more on the great demerits of the modern portrait-painters ... she calls this place la Grenoilliere; and it was for it that Wedgwood made, some years ago, a very remarkable service of his ware, on which a green frog was painted. It represented the different country-houses and gardens in England. This also, we were shown; and this led us to a conversation on English gardening, in which the Empress is a great adept.[4]

From the 'Kamer-fouriersky' ceremonial register – which recorded the day-to-day life of the Empress and the imperial court and listed all those attending events at court – it can be established that Harris's visit to Kekerekeksinensky Palace took place on 20 May 1779.[5] As usual, Catherine the Great had stopped at the palace en route to Tsarskoe Selo. The 'Kamer-fourier' register includes the following note: 'On arrival at the aforementioned palace she deigned to drink coffee with both the gathered retinue and accompanying persons, and the duration of her visit to the palace was over an hour'. This entry indicates that the Frog Service was then regarded as a 'cabinet' service, intended not so much for use as for display. Clearly the coffee must have been drunk from some other set, as there are no coffee cups or drinking vessels in the Frog Service.

It is worth noting that James Harris was correct about his favourable impression on the Empress: he was frequently favoured with 'private audiences', and on 10 March 1779 he was given a 'sword with a gold hilt studded with cut diamonds'.[6] During the spring and summer of this year, Catherine the Great called at Kekerekeksinensky Palace particularly frequently, usually taking coffee while she was there.

In later years Catherine continued to visit this romantic castle. A woman of some imagination and literary talent, she started to write about it under the title: 'Chesme Palace. The Conversation between the Portraits and the Medallions', using the new name given to the palace in 1780. The piece, which unfortunately was never finished, continued: 'While an old sentry was making his rounds of Chesme Palace, he suddenly heard a noise. He pricked up his ears and to his great surprise realized that the portraits and medallions that were housed in the palace were exchanging remarks with one another'.[7] Catherine noted that a line of commentary to the text was the work of 'the Chesme Palace translator', which suggests that a translator may have been employed there to interpret for visiting foreign travellers.

Kekerekeksinensky Palace was not, however, just used for Catherine the Great's brief halts, and the Frog Service

Pl. 38 (Cat. G209,G207) Two cream bowls and stands from the dessert service.

became more than a mere conversation-piece. Soon after the building work had been completed the palace became the setting for magnificent ceremonies, crowned with banquets at which the tables were set with the Frog Service. The 'Kamer-fourier' register reports this fact briefly but clearly. On 6 June 1777 Catherine set out from Tsarskoe Selo for the recently finished Kekerekeksinensky Palace to lay the foundations of a church dedicated to St John the Baptist.[8] The King of Sweden, Gustav III, visiting St Petersburg as the Count of Gotland, arrived from the city with his escort. After the consecration of the site for the church, a ceremonial service began. Then the guests retired to the palace, where 'all the rooms had been sprinkled with holy water' and a banquet had been laid for 36 people: 'The table was set with a glazed earthenware service [the Frog Service was the only dinner service kept in the palace]. The dessert service was new and gilded. The crystal ware was standard'.

Three years later, on 24 June 1780, St John the Baptist's day, the church – which was built to designs also by Felten – was consecrated. Those attending the ceremony were: the Russian Empress, the heir to the throne, Tsarevich Paul, his wife the Grand Duchess Maria, and the Austrian Emperor, Josef II, visiting St Petersburg under the name of Count Falkenstein.[9] After the service, an artillery salute was fired. Those present returned to the palace and spent some time in conversation 'in the Prussian portrait room', where they were then served with a ceremonial luncheon 'laid out for 56 persons, woodwind music being played throughout. Six tables were set with the palace's glazed earthenware service and the place-settings were also from the same service ...

Engraved Hermitage crystal-ware was used'. The same day Catherine the Great gave the palace its new name, the 'Chesmensky' or simply Chesme Palace, in honour of the victory by the Russian fleet over the Turks on 24–26 June 1770 in the bay of Chesme in the Aegean Sea. This triumph, in which a Russian squadron of 11 vessels had defeated the Turkish fleet of 70 battleships, had determined the successful outcome of the Russo-Turkish war of 1768–74. On this day of celebration, it was reported that the Empress 'deigned to dress in a long naval uniform'. From 1780 onwards on 24 June, the anniversary of the Battle of Chesme, fairs were regularly organized in front of the palace, 'where for the occasion an arcade had been built together with other shops for the sale of small wares'.

The following year, 1781, Catherine the Great again held a banquet in Chesme Palace after the service commemorating the victory.[10] Again six tables (on this occasion they were round) were arranged in the palace's round hall and laid for 53 people. As before, woodwind instruments played music to accompany the meal, while the 'aforementioned tables were served in two shifts with a glazed earthenware service'. On 24 June of both 1782 and 1783 Catherine also stopped off at Chesme Palace, but only briefly; no banquets were given, and after the service in the church of St John the Baptist she had a short rest before returning to Tsarskoe Selo. From 1784 the ceremonial service marking the victory over the Turkish fleet was usually held in the church at the Tsarskoe Selo Palace. Meanwhile, the Duma of the Knights of the Order of St George, established by Catherine in 1783, began to hold their meetings at Chesme Palace; but this belongs to a completely new and separate phase of the palace's history.

Following the loss of its briefly held status as a site for official Russian court activities, the palace was used again as a 'pleasure palace'. On 18 February 1791 a 'sleigh procession'[11] was held at Chesme Palace for Shrove-tide. Four tables, in four rooms, were laid with 105 place-settings. In attendance at the luncheon were the Empress, the heir to the throne, Tsarevich Paul, with his wife, the Grand Duchess Maria, and their children, the Grand Dukes Alexander and Konstantin, and 'The tables were laid with the Chesme glazed earthenware service'. After the meal, at about 4 o'clock in the afternoon, the nobles returned to St Petersburg. It was in this year, 1791, that the 'Kamer-fourier' register for the first time referred to the Frog Service as the 'Chesme Service', in accordance with the palace's new name.

An even more magnificent procession was held on 10 February 1795.[12] Setting out in large town sleighs, and then switching to 'small hand sleds', Catherine the Great, accompanied by her grandchildren (the Grand Duke Alexander with his wife, the Grand Duchess Elizabeth, the Grand Duke Konstantin and the Grand Duchesses Alexandra, Elena and Maria), and a large retinue, arrived at Chesme Palace. Dining tables in various rooms were arranged with 112 place-settings, and they 'were laid with the Chesme glazed earthenware service'. Following the meal, their Imperial Highnesses and their guests departed in sleighs for St Petersburg.

The number of people attending these banquets at Chesme Palace is astonishing, given that the Frog Service was made to serve only 50 diners. A recently discovered document may help to clarify this discrepancy, for it appears from this list that additional pieces for the Service were manufactured by the Imperial Porcelain Works in St Petersburg. To judge from the document these extra pieces were not exact copies of those by Wedgwood; while they were fashioned in the style of the Frog Service they differed from the originals in certain crucial respects. The list of 'how many various glazed porcelain [or china] wares were delivered from the porcelain factory to the chambers of Your Imperial

Majesty from the 1st January though to the 1st May, 1793' mentions '37 pieces of the Chesme service, smooth plates figuring views of English gardens, with decorated gilt edges, at a total cost of 592 roubles'.[13] The reference to gilding means that these cannot have been from Wedgwood's Service, which had no gilding and was made of creamware, whereas the Russian additions were made of porcelain. There are, however, a number of pieces of Russian porcelain made in Catherine the Great's period that are decorated with monochrome views and have gilt edges, and it is clear that the Frog Service had a marked influence on their design.[14] While there is still some uncertainty as to whether any of these pieces could have been the additions made to Wedgwood's Service, it is nevertheless of great interest that Wedgwood ware exerted such a noticeable influence on the design of Russian ceramics.

The later history of the Service in Russia had some rather less fortunate episodes. The *St Petersburg Gazette* announced on 31 October 1777 that 'eighty-five shallow plates, two small fretted baskets, eight ice-cream pots with lids, each item bearing the image of a green-coloured frog and belonging to the decorated, pale yellow glazed earthenware service housed at the Kekerekeksinensky country retreat, were stolen last week'.[15] It is impossible to determine now whether all these items were recovered by the police, but it seems that most of the pieces were in fact returned to the palace.

After Catherine the Great's death in 1796 the Chesme Service attracted less and less attention, and the palace itself gradually fell into decline. The deposed Polish king, Stanislas Augustus Poniatowski, who had been invited to St Petersburg by the Emperor Paul I in 1797, was one of the last of the distinguished travellers to visit the palace after the death of the Empress Catherine. He apparently found it rather 'strange', and although he wrote about the Chesme Service in considerable detail

(noting, incidentally, that it was then kept on the lower floor of the two-storeyed palace), he did not express any opinions on it as a work of art.[16]

There was still some interest in the Service at the beginning of the 19th century. While travelling in England, the Grand Duke Michael placed an order at Robert Chamberlain's factory in Worcester for a service to be decorated with English views, and it is quite clear that he was familiar with the Service that Wedgwood had made for his grandmother.

While visits by the Russian Court to the Chesme Palace virtually ceased with the death of Catherine the Great, exceptions were made in the summers of 1827 and 1828, when the young wards of the Elizabeth Institute were accommodated at the palace while the Institute's own building underwent reconstruction. During this period the Emperor Nicholas I, the Empress Alexandra and Nicholas I's mother, the Dowager Empress Maria, all made frequent visits. Two years later, on 21 April 1830, the Emperor Nicholas I decreed that the building should be reconstituted as a home for disabled soldiers. On 25 April he ordered 'two chandeliers, the dining service, and the portraits of sovereigns from the halls of the palace to be sent to Major-General Eikhen at Peterhof, with directions that the service and portraits should be accommodated in the English Palace'.[17] Chesme Palace's register for the service storeroom indicates that, in 1830, 825 pieces of the Service were kept in three cupboards. However, on examination of the pieces after their arrival in Peterhof ' ... as against the list there proved to be: ...one broken plate that remained undelivered, whilst received over and above the list were: 8 lids for small "shkaliks" [cream-pots], 2 fruit baskets without plates, and a round salad-dish.'[18] From this date and until 1912 the majority of the pieces remained at the English Palace.

In 1879 the Tsarevich Alexander, the future Emperor Alexander III, selected a representative group of items from the Service, picking out one example of each type for his own personal collection in the Cottage Palace at Peterhof. This had been built in 1829 in the then popular Gothic style by the architect A. Menelaws, the traditional English manorial estate serving as a model. Thus, on the Tsarevich Alexander's initiative, the Frog Service (or rather, a part of it) was again housed under an 'English' roof. In addition to taking a selection from the Frog Service, he also took a number of items from the Husk Service, which Wedgwood had made for Catherine the Great in 1770 (Cat. D59)[19] and a number of rare and early works produced by the Imperial Porcelain Works in St Petersburg, making up a total of about 100 pieces. He had a passion for ceramics, and in selecting what china and glazed earthenware he wanted for the Cottage he displayed considerable knowledge of the subject. A document in the State Historical Archive states that 'His Imperial Majesty proposes to house these articles in one of the rooms in the Cottage Palace on shelves especially constructed for them, and until that time he has deigned to command that they be kept in the storeroom together with the rest of the crockery belonging to the Cottage Palace'.[20]

By the end of the 19th century the Frog Service was paid little attention. Nevertheless, it was neither spurned nor forgotten. A 'List of objects of principal artistic significance', compiled by V. D. Grigorovich and published in 1855, described objects of note in the palaces at Peterhof. This contained a small but informative article on the Service 'with the green frog', together with a list of all the pieces that it then comprised,[21] excluding, of course, those pieces selected by the then Tsarevich Alexander for his own private collection.

In 1899 the Ministry of the Imperial Court's office received a letter from a trustee of the Bernet Goldney Museum in Canterbury asking whether the Service had been preserved and if it was still in Russia. On 6 July of that year the Directorate of the Court Marshal's department in St Petersburg wrote officially that 'at the command of his Highness the Marshal of the Imperial Court, Count Benkendorf, the directorate has the honour to inform you of the fact that the dinner service of the name "Grenouilliere" is kept in the storeroom of the English Palace at Peterhof, while a part of it is also housed ... in the Cottage. Although this service is not a work of any particular artistic significance, its importance as a historical rarity is indubitable ...'[22]

It was only in 1909 that the Frog Service again began to attract public notice, this time in connection with the preparations for a jubilee exhibition of Wedgwood ceramics in London. This was to celebrate the 150th anniversary of Wedgwood's first independent activities as a potter, and a number of pieces from the Service were sent to England for inclusion. Three years later, in 1912, the Service was one of the chief exhibits of an exhibition of Wedgwood ceramics held in the St Petersburg Academy of Arts. It was directly after this exhibition that the largest part of the Frog Service, which had been housed in the English Palace, was handed over to the Imperial Hermitage. In the instructions for the transfer of the Service to the Hermitage it was specifically stipulated that 'certain articles from the aforementioned service are housed ... in the Cottage, where Her Majesty the Sovereign Empress Maria [the wife of Alexander III and mother of the then ruling Emperor Nicholas II] deigns to reside during the summer months; these articles cannot be given to the Imperial Hermitage'.[23] In 1921 those pieces that had remained at Peterhof were finally acquired by the State Hermitage Collection; and from this date this unique work and masterpiece of English ceramics entered a new phase of its history.

Lydia Liackhova
(Translation by Christina Raeburn)

Josiah Wedgwood's Trade with Russia

Josiah Wedgwood's export trade with Russia was an integral and important part of his commercial activities. From 1768 onwards it encompassed both utilitarian creamware and the most elaborate ornamental pieces. At a time when communications were neither easy nor fast – with letters and orders being carried by mail coaches, and, until the opening of the canal system, with the finished pottery being transported on strings of pack horses known as 'pot waggons' – the size and success of Wedgwood's trade with Russia was a remarkable achievement. Wedgwood's introduction to the Russian court through ambassadorial channels was to ensure his acceptance.

On 24 March 1768 Josiah had an interview in London with Lord Cathcart, 'Our Embassador to Russia', an event that was of the utmost importance for the future trading connection. Lord and Lady Cathcart took a particular interest in Wedgwood's products; Jane Cathcart (1726–71) was the sister of Sir William Hamilton, himself an admirer of Wedgwood's pottery and a friend of both the potter and Thomas Bentley. After this meeting Josiah commented: 'I have spent several hours with Ld Cathcart ... & we are to do great things for each other'.[1] A few days earlier, on 19 March, Wedgwood had written from Charles Street, London, to Boulton & Fothergill in Birmingham:

I have waited upon Lord Cathcart, the Ambassador appointed for Russia, to bring about the plan we settled of introducing my Manufacture at the Court of Russia, I laid before him the great advantages which would arise from such an introduction to a manufacture which might be much more important than it had hitherto been thought capable of attaining to. The Ambassador, but particularly his Lady, came into measures with the utmost readiness, and I am to get a Plate done by way of specimen, with the Russian Arms, and an edging round the Plate, both in gold burnt in, and this I must get done in town. His Lordship has ordered a large Service, plain, to take out with him.[2]

Part of this order is confirmed in a surviving document dated in July 1768, which reads: 'A copy of Lord Cathcarts dessert and other articles from London Warehouse 15 July 1768 viz pierced, silver pattern'. The order includes centrepieces, compotiers of various shapes, oval baskets, sugar dishes of two different forms and five dozen plates. Other objects purchased included salad bowls, '4 double sels [sic] & ladles', sauceboats and eight dozen dinner plates and three dozen soups.[3]

Charles Cathcart (1721–76) was the Russian Ambassador from 1768 to 1771 and, once he and Jane were settled in St Petersburg, Wedgwood took advantage of their offer to sponsor his products. The first shipment of goods was mentioned in a letter of 20 September 1769, in which Wedgwood wrote to Bentley:

Pl. 39 Jasper portrait medallion of Catherine the Great (1729–1796), about 1785. Made after a model of 1782 by Maria Feodorowna. Glass paste versions of the portrait were made by James Tassie, who described them as 'the present Empress in the Character of Minerva'.

I hope the inclosed will not come too late to go along with the goods to St Petersburg; indeed, I should have wrote sooner, but I have had so much business upon my hands, and hate writing to great folks, that both together have prevented me till just now. You'll see you are to write with the Vases. There seems to be a difficulty now to deliver these Vases to Lady Cathcart. They must not be presented, and we must not pretend to charge them, so that they must neither be given nor sold – but we must borrow a pair of her Ladyship's chimney pieces to shew them upon.[4]

Lady Cathcart's reply from St Petersburg early in 1770 was written over several days:

I sho^d sooner have acknowledged the receipt of your letter & obliging attention in Sending us two Sets of your new Vases in the Etruscan Stile or rather exact Model of some of those in my Bro's. Collection: (We hope the rest of that publication will be further useful to you) but that there has been so unlucky a delay in receiving them that I could say nothing to you upon them. We have indeed just received the Vases within these very few days and shown them to some people, but, whether they will take in this County I can't as yet say, but I rather am inclined to think their taste this way is very confined & that the useful, is all they will ever commission, unless it is one or two of the very highest Names here, who have not yet had an opportunity of seeing them, but we shall certainly do every thing in our Power to do the justice & Credit to the point of the Undertakers & undertaking Wch. we think very highly of, & am Sir with best wishes for continuance of success to your self & Partner.[5]

The question of how to indicate the cost of the vases was obviously overcome by Thomas Bentley, as the postscript to Lady Cathcart's letter implies: 'You are per-

fectly right in mark^g. the Price on the Vases without which I could have been of no use towards the Sale of any such'. The subsequent correspondence from Lady Cathcart illustrates the reaction of the Russian court to Wedgwood's vases. Writing on 5 October 1770 she was effusive in her praises:

I give you the trouble of this letter by post without waiting for other opportunities, because, I can give you the pleasure of knowing that your Commissions of this year have been extremely successful, Every thing received safe, & Mr Weltden tells me that her Imperial Majesty is vastly pleased with what was executed by her Command, wch. he will I suppose tell you at more length. I saw some pieces, & thought them wonderfully well executed in all respects: Mr Weltden will also tell you that her Im: Majesty has kept all the Vases & the Dejeuné you sent to me, as samples, & that they were much liked. I flatter myself you will have large demands in Every Branch of y^r Manufacture from this Country the admiration of it, has travell'd as far as Mosco' as you will find, by orders from thence. It will always give my Lord who desires his Complim^ts. to you, & me very particular pleasure either to hear of, or to assist when we can in the Encouragem^t. of a Manufacture Carried on with so much Skill & Industry & at so reasonable a charge which I hope will always Continue & which really does hon^r to our Country.[6]

The ambassadorial introduction had the desired effect, and Wedgwood and Bentley were soon able to approach influential merchants in the Russian capital with specific proposals for the sale of their 'Ornamental Wares'. Soon after the Empress Catherine II had shown her approval, Josiah wrote to Messrs James Jackson & Co. in a letter dated 22 March 1771:

Mr Jackson will probably inform you of some Articles

Pl. 40 (Cat. C19) Portrait of Charles, 9th Baron Cathcart, British Ambassador at St Petersburg, by Sir Joshua Reynolds, 1753–5.

of our Manufacture altogether in the Ornamented way, Viz Vases Urns & Bas-reliefs after Etruscan, Greek & Roman Models, a small specimen of which was sent to Lady Cathcart & by her presented to her Imperial Majesty, which her Ladyship has had the Goodness to inform us was highly approved of – we should therefore hope that these ornamentals so happily introduced may become a Valuable article of demand amongst the Nobility in Russia & as these high finished goods are necessarily pretty high priced they will therefore be better worth your attention ...[7]

The interest in their products occurred, as Josiah commented to Bentley, at a time when the general trade was 'going to ruin on the Gallop .... This Russian trade comes very opportunely for the useful ware, and may prevent me lowering the prices here ... even though we should be obliged to run some considerable risque in the adventure, and you know my sentiments as well as I do myself respecting the conditions with Jackson & Company, so do the best you can with them, and we must leave the rest to time and Chance'.[8]

Many documents referring to the trade with the far north contain anxious requests for details of the last sailing of boats to St Petersburg, the River Neva on which the port is situated being frozen and inaccessible by boat for over half the year. A typical answer to such a request was sent to Peter Swift at Etruria from John Wood in London: 'I am not able to inform you by this post when the last vessel will sail for St. Petersburg, tho I have sent purposely into the City'.[9] The next letter, dated a day later, provided the sad answer: 'I waited today on the Russia Consul, who informed me that all the vessels which intended sailing from hence were gone: that the last went yesterday down the River'.[10] Even six days later, enquiries for ships were still being made, but to no avail: 'I have made further enquiries for a ship to Russia this Season & have received the same answer as the Consul's that the last Vessel is certainly sailed –'.[11]

Other manuscripts refer to the urgency of certain orders. An undated document by a Williamson Esq., from Hull, on behalf of 'Mr. Wedgwood', reads 'I have several crates to send you for the St. Petersburg Ship ... to travel night and day till they arrive at Gainborough – I have written to Mr. Maullin to have a vessel in readyness ... proceed immediately with them'.[12]

There are numerous references to, and surviving bills of loading for trade with Russia. Wedgwood also employed an agent at Hull, Isaac Broadley, to act on his behalf whenever necessary. Much of the ware sent through Broadley was forwarded to Otto Edvald Settler in St Petersburg. A further indication of the time required for shipping goods to Russia is given in a note from Falcon-bridge & Husband of Birmingham: they commented on 16 August 1777 that 'Orders intended for Russia, must be in Hull early in September'.[13] Many of the orders from Russian merchants stress that goods should be well packed, complaining that items arrived damaged or broken. One such adds: 'We are desirous of having them dispatched immediately fearful that the beginning of next month they may be no more ships this season from Hull'.[14] Edmund Radcliffe wrote about this problem in a letter to Wedgwood in September 1774:

I have received a letter from Mr. John Stephenson of Hull dated 27th inst. whereby he informs me that the Cask Earthenware of which you gave me Invoice the 6th inst. & which was to be shipped for St. Petersburg was not yet arrived, & that the last vessel for that Port this season was already sailed. Be pleased therefore to give him the needful orders whether to send it back to you or keep it in Warehouse at Hull till next Spring: mean while I shall write to my Friend to know if he will agree to have the Goods sent him next Spring. A little more Diligence in the execution of this order & sending would have prevented this disappointment.[15]

Once despatched, the goods would not necessarily have had an easy passage to Russia, as is indicated in Lady Cathcart's letter from St Petersburg early in 1770:

The ship that brought me y^r Letter, & Mr Bentley's met with an accid^t. just as it was coming into port and lay in a manner a wreck for I believe too months. Since the frost has been hard enough to get at it the things have been taking out & are still but in miserable confusion & loss of the perishable commodities beside that which no body from the Petersb^g side could get at it, some pirates from islands near at hand have Plunder'd many things w^h. most people say will not be recover'd.

I believe we have lost a Box with Plate ...'

They did receive something:

I inclose to you a list of the condition in which we have received it, oweing no doubt to the mistake in packing, for had the whole been in boxes (as was desired) instead of hampers in w^h. they were sent 'tis probable they wo^d. have come as safe as the vases, w^h. were more difficult to pack & yet being in a box are not broke, one top of a thick gilt one only is missing. Count Golowkin, Mon^s. Rio, Mon^s Le Chevalier Lanconi are all very impatient to receive their services and expect what is broke is to be deducted or repaired I beg to hear from you upon the subject as they have not seen the contents I hear nothing but complaint & disappoint^{mt}.[16]

A further reference to Count Galowkin's order is made in an undated manuscript inscribed only 'Mar' for March, but which probably dates from 1770, as it refers to the placing of their order. After listing the items ordered, the memorandum continues: 'NB all the above are likewise wanted to warehouse & the round dishes all sizes in particular. I expect they had known here everything about the services sent to Russia, viz Monsr Lascoves, Monsr Rio – Count Rectorin, & Countess Gallowkin, viz. which of them had p^d & to whom, but I find they know nothing at all about it so desire Mr. Swift will send us the best acc^t he can from Lady Cathcart's last letter but one ...'[17]

The cold winter sometimes lessened the problems of moving pieces within Russia, as is noted in a letter from John Tamesz & Co. of Moscow: 'The Goods must remain at St Petersburg till the next winter, when carriage is much cheaper than in summer & more proper (by means of sledges) to transport such brittle ware hither'.[18]

Despite difficulties, a vast quantity of pottery was being exported by the end of the 18th century, as is indicated in a sworn statement made before the Mayor, B. Coombe, and a Justice of the Peace in Stafford on 3 August 1789:

Josiah Wedgwood & Byerley of Etruria, Potters to Her Maj.ᵗʸ. the Queen of Great Britain, & Their Royˡ. Highnesses the Duke of York & Albany, & The Duke of Clarence, who made Oath and depose, that Two Casks marked K&R No 1 & 2 & Fifty One Casks marked HSW No 1 to 51 which were sent off from Etruria the 14th Ulᵗᵐ. July, for the port of Hull by the said Josiah Wedgwood & Byerley, do contain together, Eighteen Thousand = Four Hundred and Forty Nine Pieces of Earthenware ... and are directed to be shipped at the above Port of Hull for the Port of St Petersburg in Russia.[19]

The duty payable on all ceramic items entering Russia and constantly changing regulations added to the burden of the shippers, Tamesz of Moscow complaining at having to pay 40 per cent. There were, however, unscrupulous agents who would run the risk of contravening the regulations. Charles Hampeln, in his accounts from St Petersburg, states: 'Duty I paid here the regulation for this commodity being 40 per cent, but I run the hazard of declaring the full value, & in consequence paid but 28 per cent'.[20] Similarly, the 'Act of Customs' in Russia of 1 January 1783 insisted that Russian boats must have native crews with an English Pilot, and if this was complied with, they paid proportionally less duty in Russia than any other vessel. Even in the early years of the 19th century Thomas Byerley was writing to Josiah Wedgwood II saying: 'The duty in Russia on Earthenware imports is so high as to amount to a prohibition – I understand you are not likely to receive many orders from hence 'till that is removed – I understand a small plate pays as much as one shilling the piece ... This accounts for so few orders coming from Russia – they

wish I understand, to encourage their infant potteries established during the war'.[21]

From the surviving manuscripts it is evident that Wedgwood was prepared to adapt his normal production of Queen's Ware, his cream-coloured earthenware, to suit the Russian taste and market. He commented to Bentley in 1772: 'A second plan is to make it yellower than it is at present, but not of the dull brownish yellow you see in the shops; I would aim at as bright a <u>Straw Colour</u> as possible – This would be just the thing the Russians and some of the Germans want'.[22] His action was possibly prompted by orders specifically referring to the shade required, such as one placed by Alexander Baxter (later the Russian Consul in London), on 15 August 1769, in which he requested '4 Sets of Queens Ware', 290 items in each set, to be packed in separate casks. This bears the additional note: 'We have no doubt from your character but you will take care that the quality is of the best & at the lowest prices with the usual allowances for Discount & Breakage for money which you may draw for when you dispatch them to Hull: Should they give Satisfaction depend of receiving very considerable orders annualy from our friends in Russia. They desire that the colour may not be of <u>too light a yellow</u>'.[23] A few years later, in 1775, in another order, there was again specific reference to the tone of creamware: 'design'd for one of the first Ministers of the Empress of Russia. A compleat Service Earthenware for 18 persons, to be of a higher yellow than the former send & quite even in the very newest & neatest Taste, quite plain, without any gold on or pictures'.[24]

Even when Russian officials were abroad, their passion for Wedgwood's wares persisted. In a letter from London to Peter Swift at Etruria of July 1787, Wedgwood asks: 'I must beg also that you will on no account delay the coffee cans for the Russian Ambassador made after the China one sent down sometime since'.[25]

The orders from both St Petersburg and Moscow, as well as others, such as that from Mr Graves at Archangel, show that every form of 'Useful' and 'Ornamental' wares was being exported, for example: 'I shall be obliged to you to send me a table set neat Earthenware as soon as you can & about 20 or 30 shillings worth of the small medals with a catalogue of them'.[26] On 3 July 1784 Thomas Byerley listed in his 'Particular Orders': 'Mons' J' Saphouin for Russia with a large order and the last time of Shipping draws near –

1 large Epergne Pine Apple top PWGS
1 do -- -- -- -- PWBS.

I shall be glad to have them by the next 4 days waggon'.[27]

It is also evident from the orders that plain- and feather-pattern edges were amongst the most popular, although on one occasion the substitution of the 'Royal' Pattern was not well received by Otto Edvald Settler of St Petersburg, as Wedgwood's reply to him in August 1773 makes clear:

The Queens Ware Plates are of a superior Quality to those you had from Messrs Freeze, Falconbridge & Co. which I thought might suit you better but am sorry to find the patt[n] is not agreeable to you, to which I can only say that I sent it to you for the best it is our newest pattern was modeled purposely for his Majesty, for which reason we call it Royal Pattern and it is now in general demand being thought the most Elegant and being quite plain is easily kept clean which is no small recommendation to anything intended for the use of y[e] table.[28]

Other orders of 1777 specifically request Plain 'Royal' Pattern, implying that the objections raised by the Russian patrons were overcome.

Another interesting reference to specific designs occurs in a memorandum dated 10 February 1782,

written in London by Thomas Byerley – Wedgwood's nephew and London manager – in which he requested for 'The Count Ostermann, Chancellor of Russia: 10 doz large desert plates black birds and gilt feather edge'.[29] The order almost certainly refers to the design commonly called 'Liverpool Birds', transfer-printed by Sadler & Green. Earlier, in August 1781, Byerley was complaining to Peter Swift in Staffordshire: 'we cannot make up a blue Antique table service for Mr Hampeln, St Petersburg because you will not send us the covers we have so long ordered'.[30]

The individual orders for Queen's Ware were enormous, often in excess of '350 dozen plates together with five complete services', and '25 dozen beer jugs', and many individual objects.[31] Other orders give more detailed specifications of the patterns required: one reads: 'Table Service of Fine English Earthen ware with painted black flowers. The Desert plates and other articles belonging to the Desert with pierced Rims'; after listing all the items required for a complete dinner and dessert service Byerley's note continues: 'it is for Russia and is wanted in May about the middle of the month'.[32] It is probable that the service would have been painted in enamels with black and yellow flowers – examples of which exist – as no floral decoration painted entirely in black is known.

Requests for ware, ultimately destined for Russia, were also arriving at the factory through other agents, as is indicated in a letter from Trout & Bourgeoi of Birmingham: 'Application having been made to us for a cat. of y[r]. Q' wares & also of intaglios & & our friend resides in Russia where, he tells us, y[r] articles are much prized. You likewise send boxes of samples perhaps you may think it worth y[r]. while to let us have one to send to the above mentioned friend'.[33]

Given the quantity of Queen's Ware being ordered it is not surprising that confusion arose occasionally about what exactly was wanted. A surviving memorandum of 1789 indicates some of the problems: 'The order from Petersburg – Some parts of it I must beg you to get me a little further explanation of, for the explanation already given is not quite satisfactory nor indeed altogether consistent – I understand the 5 divisions as follows:

1) Plain with blue border, the same as the sample sent – that is plain with blue enamel[d] broad & fine line

2) Same as the preceding, without the blue border.

3) The same sort as usually sent, which was Royal pattern – but in the order itself it is called <u>Plain</u> – and in the explanation it is said "he wants <u>all plain round edge</u>, without feather edge, except the <u>last</u> order, which is expressly ordered to be <u>with</u> feather edge", – Now the fourth as well as the last is ordered in the confirmation to be <u>with</u> feather edge, so there is plainly an error somewhere; and if this 3rd division be meant as an exception to the <u>plain round edge</u>, as well as the 4th & 5th, the <u>all</u> can have reference only to two of the divisions, an the <u>exception</u> to three

4) With feather edge
   I have little or no doubt that the <u>Feather edge</u> is meant <u>shelled</u> because we make the latter with blue border, but not the former – & a large qu[ty] of shell edge & blue border has been sent before but none of what we call feather edge.

5) With feather edge and blue border.'[34]

Language difficulties also caused problems, but it is interesting to note that Mr Ohm, one of Wedgwood's regular correspondents in Russia, informed him in 1783 that 'Already rep. for a Mr Clay speaks of merchants representing Businesses from B'ham & Sheffield being

taught in Russia'.[35] Some assistance was also provided by English merchants, such as Peter Capper, who settled in St Petersburg, where orders could be translated. Nevertheless, Wedgwood continued to receive 'Orders of great Consequence NB some from Russia'. Undoubtedly the two most prestigious commissions were from the Empress Catherine II, for the dinner and dessert Husk Service painted in pink enamels and made in 1770; and the dinner and dessert service known as the Frog Service and made in 1773–4.

That Josiah Wedgwood's Jasper Ware and its range of colours on which Wedgwood himself had experimented from 1771, was admired in Russia is evident from sur-

Pl. 41 (Cat. B57) Jasper water ewer ('Sacred to Neptune'), about 1790. 'Neptune and Bacchus' vases are among the orders from Russia of 1786.

viving manuscripts referring to the trade in St Petersburg. Benjamin Hawksford, a merchant in St Petersburg, commented on 11 July 1786: 'The 3 prs of Vases I have sold to Prince Potempkin (tho-by the bye I have not yet reced a [Ro?? (Rouble) for 'em] they as well as the other things having pleased extremely. The Dejeuner in Blue I sold to her Imperial Highness the Grand Duchess; and am well persuaded there is yet a good deal to be done in your line'. At the bottom of the letter in red ink is a description of the vases, which were all priced at 10 guineas, 'Neptune and Bacchus', 'Muses' and 'Snake handle'. In a memorandum attached to the letter, Hawksford indicated the range of pieces he required, which gives a clear idea of the prevailing taste in 1786. The list includes '2 prs Flower Pots in Blue Jasper square Altar Forms & Covers, 2 prs chased Tripod candlesticks Blue Jasper, Ornamental Vases' and cane coloured tea ware, dejeuner sets and ewers and basins and '3 or 4 setts sorted Portraits in Fames', to which is added the note in red: 'Cook Banks & Solander called a set, pairs Emperor & Empress' together with seals unmounted and set in gold. Included in the order is the statement: 'I have also a commission from [a] Gent for one of your Pyrometer or metallic thermometers'.[36]

The decoration of a room in Catherine the Great's palace at Tsarskoe Selo (now called Pushkin), designed by the Scottish-born architect Charles Cameron, must have made a tremendous impact on the court and increased the demand for Wedgwood's Jasper. The first reference to this project occurs in a letter from Benjamin Hawksford dated 25 July 1786, in which he writes: 'I am at present endeavouring to introduce some of the bas-reliefs for a new Room filling up at Tarsco & I hope I shall succeed in it'.[37] Whether it was Hawksford or Peter Capper who was ultimately responsible for the ordering of the plaques for Tsarskoe Selo is unclear at present although they were certainly installed in the late 1780s.

Orders from Peter Capper for large quantities of relief plaques have survived, many of these being specifically requested for 'an Artist employed at Court and so Earnestly does he wish to have them that I have a good security for the value of £100 wh is to be paid down at the shipping of the goods'.[38] Commissions for orders for Jasper plaques often contain the name or description of the subject-matter, as well as specific detail relating to the size required. One order carried the footnote: 'All the above are things known at Mr. Wedgwood's they are of a particular composition made by him. The ground of which is blue representing Lapis Lazuli & the figures are White'.[39] To a letter and commission from St Petersburg in June 1786, is added the comment: 'A small assortment of Mr. Wedgwood's own taste and choice of such Basso Relievos taken from the History of Mythology of the ancients either oval or round, he may send of them to the value £30. The ground may be different from the above, if there is any variety. The whole should be well finished and repaired without defect. They being for an artist who is judge and may in the future have occasion for many more if he is satisfied with the work and the prices. This is in the way of being a trial.'[40] The receipt of another large order, which came in April 1787 from Peter Capper, is headed 'To be executed as soon as possible', and includes some plaques identical to those actually used in Catherine the Great's bedroom. Amongst others it specifically itemised: 'The Birth of Bacchus from Mr. Angus' cabinet, 27"x12". Triumph of Cupid (same measurements); Offering to Cupid 25 ins x 10½ ins; Bacchus and Ariadne 26 ins x 10¾ ins.' There then follows a considerable list of smaller plaques including: 'Judgement of Paris 5½ ins x 6: Offering to Hymen 3 ins x 3¼: And to match Cupid and Psyche'.[41] Orders for such plaques continued, although occasionally the goods failed to arrive on schedule: 'I don't expect to receive the money in less than 12 months but this I entirely submit to your own determinations – and you will remember they did not get to Russia till more than twelve months after they were promised'.[42]

An indication of the range of wares being marketed in Russia by 1786 is provided in an 'Account of Goods belonging to Mr. J. Wedgwood of London found in the Warehouse of the late J. Ohm'.[43] The list includes: library busts of Lord Chatham, Cicero and Gemanicus, a tripod candlestick and a triton candelabra, lamps on pedestals in imitation of agate and a pair of griffin candelabra, a range of vases in imitation of granite, together with Jasper tablets of the *Sacrifice to Bacchus* and *Apollo and the Nine Muses*. Other items listed include three encaustic-painted tablets – 'Offering to Flora', 'Supplicating Province' and 'Hercules & Amphiale' – a plaque depicting 'Lion & Horse', or 'The Frightened Horse' as it is better known, and a frame of gems. The total value of the remaining stock was £135 1s 0d.

The fame of Wedgwood's manufactory at Etruria had spread through Russia, and the model factory became one of the sights to be taken in by members of the Russian nobility when travelling in England. Several references are made to prospective visits. In 1774 Edmund Radcliffe wrote from Manchester on 9 January: 'Some Gentlemen from Petersburg are gone from my House, Northward – I shall return with them next Month as far as Birmingham when I hope to see my Friends and Etruria'.[44] Some years later in 1785 Thomas Byerley in London informed Peter Swift at Etruria: 'If the Russian Prince Poutiatin shall call & give you his name pray shew him the Works & pay him every respect – pray hang up his name that it may not be forgotten as it is of some consequence'.[45] Another interesting visitor is indicated in part of a manuscript cut from the main body of a letter from Byerley, which was probably written in the 1790s: 'His Highness Prince Gallitzin, a Russian Prince of great distinction, proposes to visit Etruria, and I have assured

him here he will meet the most respectful attention which I have no doubt he will for his own sake and for ours – for it is of very considerable consequence to keep well with the Russian Foreigners of Distinction who travel –'.[46] Unfortunately, it is impossible to verify whether or not these distinguished Russians ever called on Josiah Wedgwood, but through the years he continued to receive 'Orders of great Consequence'.

The market in Russia that Wedgwood's pottery enjoyed during the 18th century was extensive and prestigious, embracing the nobility, the court and the Empress herself. Josiah regarded it highly; as he commented to Bentley on 22 August 1777: 'The sale of our manufacture had been greatly extended of late in Germany and Russia and our business continued good notwithstanding so many prohibitions and high duties laid upon it abroad, and I believe the demand for it at foreign markets, under all these disadvantages, was owing to its being the best and cheapest pottery ware in Europe'.[47] Wedgwood was justly proud of his ware and of his patronage from Russia. Even with his later successes, he remembered with pride the service he had made for Catherine the Great 'the first Empress in the World'.[48] Writing to John Tamesz & Co. of Moscow on 18 October 1788, he commented: 'I had the honour of Serving the Empress some years ago, it is the most superb service I ever sent to the Continent'.[49]

Pl. 42 (Cat. C23) Black Basalt Griffin candlestick, first produced 1771. Griffin candelabra are among the orders from Russia of 1786.

Gaye Blake Roberts, FMA, FRSA

BIBLIOGRAPHY AND WORKS CITED

Details are given below of a small number of general books on Wedgwood, together with full details of all works cited in the catalogue and essays.

Adams 1992
Elizabeth Bryding Adams, *The Dwight and Lucille Beeson Wedgwood Collection at the Birmingham Museum of Art*, Birmingham Museum of Art, Birmingham, AL, 1992

Agnew 1993
Jean-Christophe Agnew, 'Consumer Culture in Historical Perspective', in John Brewer and Roy Porter (eds), *Consumption and the World of Goods*, Routledge, London and New York, 1993

Alexander and Godfrey 1980
David Alexander and Richard T. Godfrey, *Painters and Engraving: The Reproductive Print from Hogarth to Wilkie*, exhibition catalogue, Yale Center for British Art, New Haven, 1980

Alexandrenko 1897
V. M. Alexandrenko, *Russkie diplomatskie agenty ...*, Warsaw, 1897

Allan and Abbot 1992
D. G. C. Allan and J. L. Abbot (eds), *The Virtuoso Tribe of Arts and Sciences – Studies in the Eighteenth-Century Work and Membership of the London Society of Arts*, Athens, GI, and London, 1992

Allen 1962
Harold Allen, 'Egyptian Influences in Wedgwood Designs', *7th Wedgwood International Seminar*, Chicago, IL, 1962, pp. 75–7

Allen 1991
Brian Allen, 'The Society of Arts and the First Exhibition of Contemporary Art in 1760', *Royal Society of Art Journal*, Vol. CXXXIX, 1991, pp. 265–9

Altick 1978
Richard D. Altick, *The Shows of London: A Panoramic History of Exhibitions, 1600–1862*, Harvard University Press, 1978

Andrews 1989
Malcolm Andrews, *The Search for the Picturesque*, Scolar Press, Aldershot, 1989

Ars Ceramica 1994
'Wedgwood & Bentley – the Art of Deception', *Ars Ceramica: The Journal of the Wedgwood Society of New York*, No. 11, 1994

Arts Council 1972
The Arts Council of Great Britain, *The Age of Neo-classicism*, exhibition catalogue, Royal Academy and Victoria & Albert Museum, London, 1972

Barker 1991
David Barker, *William Greatbatch, a Staffordshire Potter*, Jonathan Horne Publications, London, 1991

Barrell 1990
John Barrell, 'The Public Prospect and the Private View: the Politics of taste in Eighteenth-century Britain', in Simon Pugh (ed.), *Reading Landscape: Country – City – Capital*, Manchester, 1990

Bennett 1978
Mary Bennett, *Merseyside Painters, People & Places*, Catalogue of Oil Paintings, Walker Art Gallery, Liverpool, 1978

Bermingham 1986
Ann Bermingham, *Landscape and Ideology. The English Rustic Tradition, 1740–1860*, London, 1986

Bermingham 1992
Ann Bermingham, 'The Origins of Painting and the Ends of Art: Wright of Derby's "Corinthian Maid"' in John Barrell (ed.), *Painting and the Politics of Culture*, Oxford University Press, 1992

Bindman 1979
David Bindman (ed.), *John Flaxman*, exhibition catalogue, Royal Academy of Arts, Thames & Hudson, London, 1979

Bindman 1989
David Bindman, *The Shadow of the Guillotine: Britain and the French Revolution*, British Museum Publications, London, 1989

Bindman and Baker 1995
David Bindman and Malcolm Baker, *Roubilliac and the Eighteenth-century Monument. Sculpture as Theatre*, Yale University Press, New Haven and London, 1995

de Bolla 1994
Peter de Bolla, 'The Charm'd Eye', in Veronica Kelly and Dorothea Mücke (eds) *Body and Text in the Eighteenth Century*, Stanford University Press, 1994, pp. 89–111

Blake Roberts 1986 I
Gaye Blake Roberts, 'Wedgwood in Russia', No. IV, *Ceramics*, July/August 1986, pp. 77–85

Blake Roberts 1986 II
Gaye Blake Roberts, 'The Wedgwood School in Rome', *Proceedings of the Wedgwood Society*, No. 12, 1986, pp. 216–27

Blake Roberts 1993
Gaye Blake Roberts, 'Ceramics Unsung Hero – Thomas Bentley', *Transactions of the English Ceramic Circle*, Vol. 15, Part 1, 1993, pp. 24–36

Bond 1990
William H. Bond, *Thomas Hollis of Lincoln's Inn: A Whig & His Books*, Cambridge University Press, 1990

Brewer and Porter 1993
John Brewer and Roy Porter (eds), *Consumption and the World of Goods*, Routledge, London and New York, 1993

Buten 1980
David Buten, *18th-Century Wedgwood: A Guide for Collectors & Connoisseurs*, Methuen, New York, 1980

Chellis 1962
Mrs Robert D. Chellis, 'Wedgwood and Bentley Source Books', *The 7th Wedgwood International Seminar*, Chicago, IL, 1962, pp. 60–64

Christie's 1986
Matthew Boulton and Family Library Sale, Christie's, London, 12 December 1986

Clarke 1990
G. B. Clarke (ed.), *Descriptions of Lord Cobham's Gardens at Stowe (1700–1750)*, Buckinghamshire Record Society, 1990

Clarkson 1808
T. Clarkson, *History of ... the Abolition of the African Slave Trade*, 2 vols, London, 1808

Clifford 1974
Timothy Clifford, 'Ormolu by Boulton' [review of Goodison 1974, below], *Burlington Magazine*, Vol. CXVI, No. 861, December 1974, pp. 673–5

Clifford 1978
Timothy Clifford, 'Some English Vases and their Sources, Part I', *Transactions of the English Ceramic Circle*, Vol. 10, Part 3, 1978, pp. 159–73

Clifford 1985
Timothy Clifford, 'John Bacon and the Manufacturers', *Apollo*, Vol. CXXII, No. 284, October 1985, pp. 288–304

Clifford 1990
Timothy Clifford, 'Vulliamy Clocks and British Sculpture', *Apollo*, Vol. CXXXII, No. 344, October 1990, pp. 226–37

Clifford 1992
Timothy Clifford, 'The Plaster Shops of the Rococo and Neo-classical Era in Britain', *Journal of the History Collections*, 4, No. 1, 1992, pp. 39–65

Conner 1983
Patrick Conner, *The Inspiration of Egypt*, exhibition catalogue, Brighton Borough Council Publications, 1983

Constable 1927
William G. Constable, *John Flaxman, 1755–1826*, University of London Press, 1927

le Corbeiller 1970
Clare le Corbeiller, 'James Cox: A Biographical Review', *Burlington Magazine*, Vol. CXII, No. 807, June 1970, pp. 351–8

Cross 1980
A. G. Cross, *By the Banks of the Thames: Russians in Eighteenth-Century Britain*, Newtonville, MA, 1980

Cross 1985
A. G. Cross, '"The Great Patroness of the North": Catherine II's Role in Fostering Anglo-Russian Cultural Contacts', *Oxford Slavonic Papers*, n.s., Vol. 18, 1985

Dawson 1984
Aileen Dawson, *Masterpieces of Wedgwood in the British Museum*, British Museum Publications, London, 1984

Deutsch 1943
O. E. Deutsch, 'Sir William Hamilton's Picture Gallery', *Burlington Magazine*, Vol. LXXXII, No. 478, February 1943, pp. 36–41

Drakard 1992
David Drakard, *Printed English Pottery*, Jonathan Horne Publications, London, 1992

Eatwell 1983
Ann Eatwell, 'The Wedgwood Copies of the Portland Vase', *Victoria and Albert Museum Masterpieces*, Sheet 26, 1983

Eaves 1992
Morris Eaves, *The Counter-Arts Conspiracy. Art and Industry in the Age of Blake*, Cornell University Press, Ithaca and London, 1992

Edwards 1994
Diana Edwards, *Black Basalt: Wedgwood and Contemporary Manufacturers*, Antique Collectors' Club, Woodbridge, 1994

Farrer 1903–06
Katherine Euphemia, Lady Farrar (ed.), *Letters of Josiah Wedgwood*, 3 vols, privately printed, 1903–06, facsimile edition published by E. J. Morton, Manchester, in association with the Wedgwood Museum, Barlaston, 1973

Forty 1986
Adrian Forty, *Objects of Desire: Design and Society, 1750–1980*, Thames & Hudson, London, 1986

Georgi 1794
I. G. Georgi, *Description of the Russian Imperial Capital St Petersburg and the Sights of Note in its Environs*, St Petersburg, 1794

Goodison 1974
Nicholas Goodison, *Ormolu: The Work of Matthew Boulton*, Phaidon Press, London and New York, 1974

Goodison 1977
Nicholas Goodison, 'Matthew Boulton's Bacchanalian Vase', *Connoisseur*, Vol. 195, No. 785, July 1977, pp. 182–7

Goryainov 1908
S. Goryainov, 'King Stanislav-August's Artistic Impressions on his visit to St. Petersburg in 1797', *Starye Gody*, October 1908, pp. 602–603

Harris 1845
Diaries and Correspondence of James Harris, First Earl of Malmesbury, London, 1845

Harris 1970
John Harris, *Sir William Chambers*, A. Zwemmer Ltd, London, 1970

Harris 1979
John Harris, *The Artist and the Country House: a History of Country House and Garden View Painting in Britain, 1540–1870*, Sotheby Parke Bernet, London, 1979

Harris 1986
John Harris, 'The Guide in the Hand', *Country Life*, 1 May 1986, pp. 1200–1203

Hawes 1965
Lloyd E. Hawes, 'Herculaneum Wall Paintings', *The American Wedgwoodian*, December 1965, pp. 17–27

Hawes and Schneidemantel 1969
Lloyd E. Hawes and Vivian J. Schneidemantel, 'Shugborough', *The American Wedgwoodian*, February 1969, pp. 29–34

Hayden 1909
Arthur Hayden, 'The Wedgwood Exhibition. The Record of 150 Years' Work', *Connoisseur*, Vol. XXV, No. 99, November 1909, pp. 1–16

Hayden 1985
Peter Hayden, 'British Seats on Imperial Russian Tables', *Garden History*, Vol. 13, No. 1, 1985, pp. 17–32

Holloway 1986
James Holloway, *James Tassie*, Trustees of the National Galleries of Scotland, Edinburgh, 1986

Honey 1948
W. B. Honey, *Wedgwood Ware*, Faber & Faber, London, 1948

Humbert 1994
Jean-Marcel Humbert (ed.), *Egyptomania: L'Égypte dans l'art occidental, 1730–1930*, Musée du Louvre, Réunion des Musées Nationaux, Paris, 1994

Hurlbutt (n.d.)
Frank Hurlbutt, 'A Wedgwood Plaque', typescript, Victoria & Albert Museum, Ceramics and Glass Collection, Lit. Mat. No. 29 (n.d.)

Hyde 1994
Ralph Hyde, *A Prospect of Britain: The Town Panoramas of Samuel and Nathaniel Buck*, Thames & Hudson, London, 1994

Irwin 1979
David Irwin, *John Flaxman 1755–1826, Sculptor, Illustrator, Designer*, Studio Vista/Christie's, London, 1979

Iveagh Bequest 1985
John Joseph Merlin – The Ingenious Mechanick, exhibition catalogue, Iveagh Bequest, Kenwood House, Greater London Council, 1985

Jordan 1985
Marc Jordan, 'Edme Bouchardon: A Sculptor, a Draughtsman, and his Reputation in Eighteenth-Century France', *Apollo*, Vol. CXXI, No. 280, 1985, pp. 388–94

Kudriatseva 1994
T. Kudriatseva, 'Russisches Porzellan' in *Zur Tafel im Winterpalast. Russische und westeuropäische Porzellan – und Fayencearbeiten aus der Zweiten Hälfte des 18. Jahrbunderts, Leihgaben aus den Sammlungen der Ermitage in St Petersburg*, Kolding, 1994

Leeuwarden and The Hague 1982
Leeuwarden and The Hague, *Wedgwood en Nederland in de*

18de Eeuw, exhibition catalogue, Gemeentelijk Museum het Princesseho, and Haags Gemeentemuseum, 's-Gravenhage, 1982

Lewis, Smith, Lam and Martz 1967
W. S. Lewis, Warren Hunting Smith and George L. Lam with the assistance of Edwine M. Martz (eds), *Horace Walpole's Correspondence with Sir Horace Mann*, Oxford University Press, London and New Haven, 1967

Luxmore 1924
Charles Luxmore, *English Salt-Glazed Earthenware*, The Holland Press, Exeter, 1924

Macht 1957
Carol Macht, *Classical Wedgwood Designs*, M. Barrows and Co., New York, 1957

McKendrick 1963
Neil McKendrick, 'Josiah Wedgwood and Factory Discipline', *Proceedings of the Wedgwood Society*, No. 5, 1963, pp. 1–29

McKendrick 1964
Neil McKendrick, 'Creamware for Cottage and Castle', *9th International Wedgwood Seminar, Metropolitan Museum of Art*, New York, 1964, pp. 35–61

McKendrick 1982
Neil McKendrick, 'Josiah Wedgwood and the Commercialization of the Potteries' in Neil McKendrick, John Brewer, J. H. Plumb, *The Birth of a Consumer Society: The Commercialization of Eighteenth-century England*, Europa Publications, London, 1982, pp. 100–145

McKendrick, Brewer and Plumb 1982
Neil McKendrick, John Brewer, J. H. Plumb, *The Birth of a Consumer Society: The Commercialization of Eighteenth-century England*, Europa Publications, London, 1982

Mallet 1975
J. V. G. Mallet, 'Wedgwood and the Rococo', *Proceedings of the Wedgwood Society*, No. 9, 1975, pp. 36–61

Manchester 1983
Manchester City Art Galleries, *A Century of Collecting, 1882-1982*, 1983

Mankowitz 1952
W. Mankowitz, *The Portland Vase*, Andre Deutsch, London, 1952

Martin, forthcoming
Ann Smart Martin, '"Fashionable Sugar Dishes, Latest Fashion Ware": The Creamware Revolution in the Eighteenth-Century Chesapeake', forthcoming in Paul Shakel and Barbara J. Little (eds), *The Historic Chesapeake: Archaeological Contributions*, Smithsonian University Press, forthcoming

Meteyard 1865–6
Eliza Meteyard, *The Life of Josiah Wedgwood* (2 vols), Hurst & Blackett, London, 1865–6

Miller 1981
Michael Miller, *The Bon Marché; Bourgeois Culture and the Department Store, 1869–1920*, George Allen & Unwin, London, 1981

Montagu 1954
Jennifer Montagu, 'A Renaissance Work Copied by Wedgwood', *Journal of the Warburg and Courtauld Institute*, Vol. XVII, Nos 3–4, 1954, pp. 380–81

Morton and Wess 1993
Alan Q. Morton and Jane A. Wess, *Public & Private Science: The King George III Collection*, Oxford University Press in association with the Science Museum, Oxford, 1993

Nibblet 1984
Kathy Nibblet, 'A Useful Partner – Thomas Wedgwood 1734–1788', *Northern Ceramic Society Journal*, Vol. 5, 1984, pp. 1–22

Nottingham 1975
Mr. Wedgwood, exhibition catalogue, Nottingham Castle Museum, 1975

Painter and Whitehouse 1990 I
Kenneth Painter and David Whitehouse, 'The History of the Portland Vase', *Journal of Glass Studies*, Corning Museum of Glass, Vol. 32, 1990, pp. 24–84

Painter and Whitehouse 1990 II
Kenneth Painter and David Whitehouse, 'Style, Date, and Place of Manufacture [of the Portland Vase]', *Journal of Glass Studies*, Corning Museum of Glass, Vol. 32, 1990, pp. 122–5

Pears 1988
Iain Pears, *The Discovery of Painting*, Yale University Press, New Haven and London, 1988

Penny 1986
Nicholas Penny (ed.), *Sir Joshua Reynolds*, exhibition catalogue, Royal Academy of Arts published in association with Weidenfeld & Nicolson, London, 1986

Peterhof 1885
Peterhof, *A List of Objects of Principal Artistic Significance*, St Petersburg, 1885

Pollard 1970
J. Graham Pollard, 'Matthew Boulton and Conrad Heinrich Küchler', *Numismatic Chronicle*, 7th Series, Vol. X, 1970, pp. 273–85

Poniatowski 1914
Mémoires du roi Stanislas-Auguste Poniatowski, St Petersburg, 1914

Poole 1986
Julia Poole, *Plagiarism Personified?*, exhibition catalogue, Fitzwilliam Museum, Cambridge, 1986

Poulet and Scherf 1992
Anne L. Poulet and Guilhem Scherf, *Clodion, 1738–1814*, exhibition catalogue, Musée du Louvre, Réunion des Musées Nationaux, Paris, 1992

Pressly 1984
William L. Pressly (ed.), 'Facts and Recollections of the XVIIIth Century in a Memoir of John Francis Rigaud Esq., R.A. by Stephen Dutilh Rigaud', *Walpole Society*, Vol. L, 1984, pp. 1–165

Raeburn 1990
Michael Raeburn, 'Land of the Free: The Views on the Green Frog Service', *35th Annual Wedgwood International Seminar*, Birmingham, 1990, pp. 21–39

Raeburn 1992
Michael Raeburn, 'Wedgwood and Bentley's Green Frog Service outside Russia', *Antiques*, Vol. CXLI, March 1992, pp. 450–59

Raeburn, Voronikhina and Nurnberg 1995
Michael Raeburn, L. N. Voronikhina and Andrew Nurnberg (eds), *The Green Frog Service*, Cacklegoose Press, London, 1995

Ramage 1990
Nancy Ramage, 'The Artists ... Wedgwood and Sir William Hamilton: Their Personal and Artistic Relationship', *35th Annual Wedgwood International Seminar*, Birmingham, 1990, pp. 71–89

Raspe 1791
R. E. Raspe, *A Descriptive Catalogue of a General Collection of Ancient and Modern Engraved Gems, Cameos as well as Intaglios ... cast by James Tassie*, London, 1791

Ray 1973
Anthony Ray, 'Liverpool Printed Tiles', *Transactions of the English Ceramic Circle*, Vol. 9, Part 1, 1973, pp. 36–66

Reddaway 1931
W. F. Reddaway (ed.), *Documents of Catherine the Great*, Cambridge, 1931

Reilly 1972
Robin Reilly, *Wedgwood Jasper*, Charles Letts & Co. Ltd, London, 1972

Reilly 1989
Robin Reilly, *Wedgwood* (2 vols), Macmillan Ltd, London, and Stockton Press, New York, 1989

Reilly 1990
Robin Reilly, 'The Connoisseurs ... Wedgwood and Bentley, Vase Makers', *35th Annual Wedgwood International Seminar*, Birmingham AL, 1990, pp. 155–92

Reilly 1992
Robin Reilly, *Josiah Wedgwood, 1730–1795*, Macmillan, London, 1992

Reilly 1994
Robin Reilly, *Wedgwood Jasper*, Thames & Hudson, London and New York, 1994

Reilly and Savage 1973
Robin Reilly and George Savage, *Wedgwood: The Portrait Medallions*, Barrie & Jenkins, London, 1973

Reilly and Savage 1980
Robin Reilly and George Savage, *The Dictionary of Wedgwood*, Antique Collectors' Club, Woodbridge, 1980

Rhead 1906
G. W. and F. A. Rhead, *Staffordshire Pots and Potters*, Hutchinson & Co, London, 1906

Rowan 1988
Alistair Rowan, *Robert Adam: Catalogue of Architectural Drawings in the Victoria & Albert Museum*, Victoria & Albert Museum, London, 1988

Science Museum 1978
Josiah Wedgwood: the Arts and Sciences United, exhibition catalogue, Science Museum, London, 1978

Smiles 1994
Sam Smiles, *The Image of Antiquity*, Yale University Press, London and New Haven, 1994

Smith 1828
J. T. Smith, *Nollekens and his Times*, London, 1828

Snodin 1987
Michael Snodin, 'Matthew Boulton's Sheffield Plate Catalogues', *Apollo*, Vol. CXXVI, No. 35, July 1987, pp. 25–32

Solkin 1993
David H. Solkin, *Painting for Money: the Visual Arts and the Public Sphere in 18th Century England*, Yale University Press, New Haven and London, 1993

Stretton 1994
Norman Stretton, 'Fable Subjects on English Pottery', *Transactions of the English Ceramic Circle*, Vol. 15, Part 2, 1994, pp. 205–209

Styles 1993
John Styles, 'Manufacturing, Consumption and Design in Eighteenth-Century England', in John Brewer and Roy Porter (eds) *Consumption and the World of Goods*, Routledge, London and New York, 1993

Svetlov 1782
M. Svetlov, *The Sights of Note at Chesme Palace, Situated on the Moscow Road, 7 versts from St Petersburg*, St Petersburg, 1782

Tate Gallery 1974
Bruce Tattersall, *Stubbs and Wedgwood: Unique Alliance Between Artist and Potter*, exhibition catalogue, Tate Gallery, London, 1974

Thomas 1971
John Thomas, *The Rise of the Staffordshire Potteries*, Adams & Dart, Bath, 1971

Toppin 1959
A. J. Toppin, 'William Hopkins Craft, Enamel Painter (1730?–1810)', *Transactions of the English Ceramic Circle*, Vol. 4, Part 4, 1959, pp. 14–18

Towner 1963
Donald Towner, 'William Greatbatch and the Early Wedgwood Wares', *Transactions of the English Ceramic Circle*, Vol. 5, Part 4, 1963, pp. 180–93

Towner 1978
Donald Towner, *Creamware*, Faber & Faber, London, 1978

Treuherz and Figueiredo 1988
Julian Treuherz and Peter Figueiredo, *Cheshire Country Houses*, Phillimore, Chichester, 1988

Victoria & Albert Museum 1959
Victoria & Albert Museum, *Wedgwood Bicentenary Exhibition, 1759–1959*, exhibition catalogue, Victoria & Albert Museum, London, 1959

Victoria & Albert Museum 1984
Victoria & Albert Museum, *Rococo: Art and Design in Hogarth's England*, Michael Snodin (ed.), exhibition catalogue, London, Trefoil Books, 1984

Voronikina 1988
L. N. Voronikina, 'O Paisazhakh 'Serviza s zelenoi lyagushkoi', *Muzeu*, 1988, N.9

de Vries 1993
Jan de Vries, 'Between Purchasing Power and the World of Goods ...', in John Brewer and Roy Porter (eds), *Consumption and the World of Goods*, Routledge, London and New York, 1993, pp. 85–132

Walsh 1993
Claire Walsh, *Shop Design and the Display of Goods in the Eigteenth Century*, V&A/RCA MA Thesis, 1993

Warrilow 1971
E. J. D. Warrilow, *The History of Etruria*, Hanley, 1953

Weatherill 1971
Lorna Weatherill, *The Pottery Trade and North Staffordshire, 1660–1760*, Manchester University Press, Manchester, 1971

Weatherill 1986
Lorna Weatherill, 'The Business of Middleman in the English Pottery Trade before 1780', *Business History*, Vol. 28, Part II, 1986, pp. 51–76

Wedgwood 1973
Wedgwood at Woburn, exhibition catalogue, Woburn Abbey, Josiah Wedgwood and Sons Ltd, 1973

Wedgwood 1984
Wedgwood in London: 225th Anniversary Exhibition 1759–1984, Josiah Wedgwood & Sons Ltd, 1984

Whitley 1928
William T. Whitley, *Artists and their Friends in England* (2 vols), Medici Society, London and Boston, 1928

Williams 1973
Raymond Williams, *The Country and the City*, Chatto & Windus, London, 1973

Williamson 1909
Dr George C. Williamson, *The Imperial Russian Dinner Service*, George Bell & Sons, London, 1909

Williamson and Bellamy 1987
Tom Williamson and Liz Bellamy, *Property and Landscape. A Social History of Land Ownership and the English Countryside*, George Philip, London, 1987

Wills 1980
Geoffrey Wills, *Wedgwood*, Country Life Books, London, 1980

Wills 1982
Geoffrey Wills, 'A Riddle of a Sphinx', *Proceedings of the Wedgwood Society*, No. 11, 1982, pp. 149–52

Young 1987
Hilary Young, 'Sir William Chambers and the Duke of Marlborough's Silver', *Apollo*, Vol. CXXV, No. 304, June 1987, pp. 396–400

Zeitlin 1968
Charlotte Zeitlin, 'Wedgwood Copies of a Vase in the Hamilton Collection', *Proceedings of the Wedgwood Society*, No. 7, 1968, pp. 147–51

Notes

INTRODUCTION

1. Wedgwood MS E25-18392, Wedgwood to Bentley, 23 August 1772; see p. 12 below.

2. The underlying causes lie outside the scope of this essay, but they include poulation shifts, increased female and child employment, technological and agricultural change, colonial imports and foreign trade.

3. See Weatherill 1971 p. 15 and passim.

4. Weatherill 1966 p. 90.

5. Weatherill 1971 p. 83.

6. McKendrick 1982 p. 21.

7. Weatherill 1986 pp. 55 and 62.

8. Notably Lorna Weatherill. See Weatherill 1971 and Weatherill 1986, works that have been drawn on heavily for the picture of Staffordshire pottery trade outlined here. See also Thomas 1971.

9. Nor were Wedgwood's wares mass-produced in the sense that the term is understood today; see Styles 1993 pp. 529–35.

10. See Weatherill 1986 p. 61 for a corrective to McKendrick's essay of 1982, which attributes as innovations to Wedgwood many practices that were common in the Staffordshire pottery and English porcelain trade. On this see also Styles 1993 pp. 543–4, and Weatherill 1971 (which responds to McKendrick's earlier essays on Wedgwood).

11. Wedgwood MS (LHP MS), Wedgwood to Bentley, 2 September 1771, see McKendrick 1982. However, for Wedgwood's marketing, see also Reilly 1992 pp. 202–225.

12. Matthew Boulton to Mrs Montagu in 1772, see Goodison 1974 p. 47.

13. Forty 1986 pp. 13–16.

14. Raeburn 1990 p. 27 and passim., and *The Frog Service and its Sources*, pp. 134–48 below.

15. See Reilly 1990.

16. The pioneering work on this subject was Clifford 1978, an article that has been drawn on extensively for the `Vase Maker General' section of the current exhibition. See also Reilly 1989

I pp. 346–63 and Reilly 1990.

17. Chellis 1962 p. 60.

18. Wedgwood MS E26-18898, Wedgwood to Bentley, 19 June 1779, see McKendrick 1982 p. 100 and Reilly 1992 p. 206.

19. Wedgwood MS E25-18167, Wedgwood to Bentley, n.d., about 15 September 1767, see McKendrick 1982 p. 108 and Reilly 1989 I p. 201.

20. See Reilly 1992 pp. 125–6.

21. Wedgwood MS E25-18498, Wedgwood to Bentley, 14 November 1773, see Mckendrick p. 121.

22. Wedgwood MS E25-18335, Wedgwood to Bentley 24 and 25 December 1770, see McKendrick 1982 p. 115

23. McKendrick 1982 p. 106.

24. Wedgwood MS E25-18392, Wedgwood to Bentley, 23 August 1772, see Reilly 1989 I p. 361.

25. Travelling salesmen and sample books had already been introduced in the textile industry. Possibly other promotional techniques employed by Wedgwood reflect practices elsewhere.

26. See Reilly 1992 p. 216. A Wedgwood & Bentley bill head in the British Museum dated 30 June 1770 (Heal 98.11) already advertises carriage-free delivery.

27. See McKendrick 1982 p. 126 and Reilly 1992 p. 216.

28. Wedgwood MS E25-18149, Wedgwood to Bentley, 31 May 1767, see Wedgwood 1984 pp. 8–9.

29. Miller 1981 p. 24.

30. See Walsh 1993.

31. Agnew 1993 p. 25.

32. See McKendrick 1982 p. 135 and Reilly 1992 p. 217.

33. Thomas 1971 p. 120.

34. See McKendrick 1982 p. 130.

35. See Leeuwarden and The Hague 1982, and Gaye Blake Roberts' essay, *Josiah Wedgwood's Trade with Russia*, pp. 213–221 below, respectively. Martin (forthcoming) analyses the chronology and use of creamware in colonial America.

36. See McKendrick, Brewer and Plumb 1982. However, see also Agnew 1993 pp. 24–5, Porter 1993 pp. 65–6, de Vries 1993 p. 117, and Styles 1993 pp. 535–42, all published in Brewer and Porter 1993.

A LIFETIME OF ACHIEVEMENT

1. Wedgwood MS W/M 402, Godfrey Wedgwood to Eliza Meteyard, 18 October 1862.

2. See Reilly 1992, p. 1.

3. Ibid., n.1.

4. Ibid., n.2.

5. Mayer MSS quoted in Meteyard 1865–6, I, p. 193, n.1.

6. This story, first published by Meteyard (op.cit., I, p. 208, n.1), was related to her by Blunt's grandson.

7. See Reilly, op.cit., p. 4.

8. Wedgwood MS 29-19121.

9. See Reilly 1989 I, pp. 18–19.

10. Wedgwood MS 29-19121.

11. Wedgwood MS 27-19281, 30 December 1758.

12. See Reilly 1989 I, pp. 42,44 and 699 n. 16; also Nibblet 1984 p. 3 for a different dating of this move.

13. Wedgwood MS E25-18073, Wedgwood to John Wedgwood (brother), 17 June 1765.

14. Wedgwood MS E25-18324, Wedgwood to Bentley, 3 September 1770.

15. Wedgwood MS E25-18167, Wedgwood to Bentley, n.d. (about 15 September) 1767.

16. Wedgwood Manuscript W/M, 'Basis of the Agreement between W&B Novr 15 1767'.

17. See Reilly 1992, pp. 34, 36–7, 58–9, 168–9.

18. The spy was Louis-Victor Gerverot. See Reilly 1992 pp. 146–7.

19. *Ibid.*, p. 69.

20. Wedgwood MS E25-18080, 6 July 1765.

21. Wedgwood MS E25-18392, Wedgwood to Bentley, 23 August 1772.

22. Caylus, Anne-Claude-Philippe de Thubières, Comte de, *Receuil d'Antiquités Egyptiennes, Etrusques, Grecques et Romaines*, 7 vols, Paris, 1752–67; Hamilton, Sir William, and d'Hancarville, P. H., *Antiquités Etrusques, Grecques et Romaines*, 4 vols, Naples, 1766–76.

23. Wedgwood MS E25-18240, Wedgwood to Bentley, 1 May 1769.

24. Wedgwood MS E25-18432, Wedgwood to Bentley, 31 December 1772.

25. Wedgwood MS E25-18443, Wedgwood to Bentley, 6 February 1773.

26. Wedgwood MS E25-18521, Wedgwood to Bentley, 7 March 1774.

27. Wedgwood MS E25-18555, Wedgwood to Bentley, 30 August 1774.

28. See Reilly 1989 I, pp. 97–8.

29. Wedgwood MS E25-18642, Wedgwood to Bentley, 14 January 1776.

30. Wedgwood MS E25-18673, Wedgwood to Bentley, 6 June 1776.

31. Ibid.

32. Wedgwood MS E25-18790, Wedgwood to Bentley, 3 November 1777.

33. Wedgwood MS E25-18803, Wedgwood to Bentley, 17 December 1777; and see Reilly 1994, pp. 86–7.

34. See Reilly 1989 I, pp. 534–7.

35. Wedgwood MS E25-18256, Wedgwood to Bentley, 16 September 1769.

36. Wedgwood MS E25-18486, Wedgwood to Bentley, 12 August 1773.

37. See Reilly 1989 I, pp. 663–84.

38. Ibid., pp. 583–5.

39. See Reilly 1992, pp. 304–07.

40. Clarkson, 1808, pp. 191–2; and see Reilly 1989 I, pp. 284–9.

41. Wedgwood to Matthew Boulton, 23rd February 1787, Soho MSS, quoted by Meteyard, op.cit., II, p. 562.

42. See Reilly 1989 I, pp. 190–1.

43. The statement, published in 1980, that Josiah Wedgwood committed suicide is without foundation. See Reilly 1989 I, pp. 141–3.

44. Quoted in Rhead 1906, p. 223.

45. Wedgwood MS E25-18264, Wedgwood to Bentley, 1 October 1769.

LONDON DECORATING STUDIO

1. Wedgwood MS E25-18196, 24 March 1768.

2. Undated newspaper cutting in Wedgwood archives, repr. pl. 7, above.

3. Wedgwood MS E25-18692, 12 September 1776.

4. Wedgwood MS E25-18452, Wedgwood to Bentley, 29 March 1773.

5. Wedgwood MS 39-28408, Josiah Wedgwood's 'Common Place Book I', August 1784.

6. Wedgewood MS E1-623.

7. Wedgwood MS E25-18238, 14 April 1769.

8. Wedgwood MS 10-31080, 6 December 1770.

9. Wedgwood MS E96-17663, Wedgwood to William Cox, 30 June 1768.

10. Wedgwood MS E25-18285, Wedgwood to Bentley, 22 January 1770.

11. Wedgwood MS E25-18328, Wedgwood to Bentley, 25 October 1770.

12. Wedgwood MS E25-18285, Wedgwood to Bentley.

13. Wedgwood MS E25-18301, 19 May 1770.

14. Wedgwood MS E25-18300, Wedgwood to Bentley, 19 May 1770.

15. Wedgwood MS E25-18299, Wedgwood to Bentley, 12 May 1770.

16. Wedgwood MS E25-18299, Wedgwood to Bentley, 12 May 1770.

17. Wedgwood MS E25-18302, 23 May 1770.

18. Wedgwood MS E25-18301, Wedgwood to Bentley, 19 May 1770.

19. Wedgwood MS E25-18245, Wedgwood to Bentley, 25 June 1769.

20. Ibid.

21. Wedgwood MS E25-18255, 17 September 1769.

22. Wedgwood MS E25-18296, Wedgwood to Bentley.

23. Wedgwood MS E25-18297, 29 April 1770.

24. Wedgwood MS E25-18294.

25. Wedgwood MS E25-32851.

26. Wedgwood MS E25-18311, Wedgwood to Bentley, 19 June 1770.

27. Wedgwood MS E25-18294, Wedgwood to Bentley, 23 April 1770.

28. Wedgwood MS E9-7449.

29. Wedgwood MS E25-18455, Wedgwood to Bentley.

30. Wedgwood MS E25-18450.

31. Wedgwood MS E25-18452, Wedgwood to Bentley, 29 March 1773.

32. Wedgwood MS E32-24188, 1768–74.

33. Wedgwood MS E32-24197, n.d.

34. Wedgwood MS E32-24194/95, dated 1774.

35. Wedgwood MS E32-24191.

36. Wedgwood MS E32-24192, n.d.

37. Wedgwood MS E32-24197, n.d.

38. Wedgwood MS E32-24198, n.d.

39. Wedgwood MS E32-24197[A].

40. Wedgwood MS E32-24198, n.d.

41. Wedgwood MS E32-24188, 1768–74.

42. Wedgwood MS E 25-18536, Wedgwood to Richard Wedgwood, 31 May 1774.

43. Wedgwood MS E25-18547, July 15–16 1774.

44. Wedgwood MS E31-24189.

45. Wedgwood MS E25-18540, Wedgwood to Bentley, 20th June 1774.

46. Wedgwood MS E25-18540.

47. Wedgwood MS E25-18297, Wedgwood to Bentley, 29 April 1770.

48. See Wedgwood 1984 p. 26.

A RAGE FOR EXHIBITIONS

1. Walpole to Horace Mann 6 May 1770, for which see Lewis, Smith, Lam and Martz 1967 p. 211.

2. For the notion of the 'public sphere' in discussions of visual culture in England see Solkin 1993 and Bindman and Baker 1995.

3. The rich and fundamental study of this subject is Altick 1978; surprisingly, however, Wedgwood's exhibitions are not mentioned here.

4. The details quoted here are taken from a broadsheet in the Sarah Banks Collection at the British Museum (J9.530).

5. Allan and Abbot 1992; Allen 1991; Pears 1988; Solkin 1993.

6. Solkin 1993 p. 273.

7. Burney Collection, British Library.

8. Wedgwood MS E25-18427, Wedgwood to Bentley, 7 December 1772, quoted in McKendrick 1982 p. 124.

9. Further quotations from this letter (Wedgwood MS E25-18149, Wedgwood to Bentley, n.d. late May or early June 1967) are given below.

10. For Merlin see Iveagh Bequest 1985.

11. Iveagh Bequest 1985; le Corbeiller 1970 p. 351.

12. Wedgwood MS E25-18365, Wedgwood to Bentley 11 April 1772, cited in Mallet 1975 p. 55.

13. I have here relied on the passages from the correspondence quoted in Goodison 1974 pp. 87–9.

14. Goodison 1974 p. 88.

15. For an analysis of the evidence for the 18th-century shop fittings see Walsh 1993.

16. Was the service of plate exhibited by the goldsmiths Green & Ward in February 1793 shown in a similar way? This display, documented through an annotated private view ticket in the

Sarah Banks Collection (C2-711), suggests that others followed Wedgwood's example.

17. For an important discussion of Wedgwood see Bermingham 1992 pp. 135–64. The way in which Wedgwood marketed his ceramic production 'as if it were of artistic significance' has been stressed recently by Eaves 1992 pp. 38–41, where the connection is made between Wedgwood's display strategies and contemporary exhibitions.

18. Solkin 1993.

19. An engraving of the earrings is pasted into the Victoria & Albert Museum's copy of the 1772 edition of the catalogue to Cox's Museum (Cat. F9).

20. Morton and Wess 1993; papers on public lectures and demonstrations of science and technology will be published in the forthcoming *British Journal of the History of Science*, 28, 1995.

21. Raeburn 1992 p. 458.

22. For the relationship between the Frog Service exhibition and later topographical prints see Andrews 1989 p. 35. This relationship is, however, perhaps more complex than is suggested here.

23. Quoted in Raeburn 1992 p. 458.

24. de Bolla 1994 pp. 89–111.

25. H. Walpole, 'The History of the modern taste in Gardening', quoted in de Bolla 1994 p.92. The political meanings of the scenes are discussed in Raeburn 1990. The images of landscape on the Service need to be seen in relation to the discussion of the organization of estates in Williamson and Bellamy 1987, and the analysis of representations of landscape in Bermingham 1986.

26. Recent discussions of this topic owe much to Williams 1973.

27. This is discussed in de Bolla 1994, where recent literature on 18th-century tourism is cited. For the development of the guidebook see the brief but informative article Harris 1986. The way in which the landscapes on the Frog Service were viewed might also be considered in terms of the viewing of different types of landscape by different classes of people, as discussed in Barrell 1990.

28. Wedgwood wrote to Bentley on 31 May 1767 that 'such services are absolutely necessary to be shewn, in order to do the needful with the Ladys in the neatest, genteelest and best method' (Wedgwood MS E25-18149).

29. Wedgwood to Bentley, 31 May 1767, Wedgwood MS E25-18149.

THE FROG SERVICE

The catalogue entries for the Frog Service are based on the list of views compiled by Michael Raeburn and L. N. Voronikhina in Raeburn, Voronikhina and Nurnberg 1995.

1. Alexandrenko 1897 Vol. 2 p. 166.

2. See Blake Roberts 1986 I.

3. Wedgwood MS E25-18450.

4. Wedgwood MS E25-18452.

5. Artists working on trials in the weeks of 3 and 10 April (both Saturdays) included James Bakewell and Sarah Wilcox (landscapes), Nathaniel Cooper and Ralph Wilcox (inner borders) and Joseph Lin(d)ley (outer borders). Work on trials continued until the end of May, the artists named being joined by Ralph Unwin (also painting landscapes) at the beginning of that month. Wedgwood MS E32-5274.

6. Jemima Marchioness Grey writing to her daughter Lady Amabel Polwarth on 19 June 1774. (Bedfordshire Record Office L30/11/122/60, quoted by permission of the Lady Lucas of Dingwall.)

7. Bentley had reported this in a (lost) letter of 30 March and Wedgwood replied on 5 April (MS E25-18454) that it could be done for that price, but 'not fit for an Empress's Table, or to do us any Credit, at double that sum.'

8. Wedgwood MS E25-18484.

9. Wedgwood MS E25-18450, Wedgwood to Bentley, 23 March 1773.

10. Wedgwood MS E25-18453, Wedgwood to Bentley, 3 April 1773.

11. There has been some confusion in Wedgwood literature about the Stringers. Samuel Stringer (1750–84), who did drawings for the Frog Service and his brother Daniel (1754–1808) were both artists, the sons of Thomas Stringer (1722–90), who had originally been a servant of Peter Legh of Booth Hall, near Knutsford. Thomas quarrelled with his master and became a painter, principally of horses and other animals, although at least one country house view by him is known – a quite primitive depiction of Poynton Old Hall (reproduced in Treuherz and de Figueireido 1988). He may possibly have been a kinsman of Josiah's mother (born Mary Stringer), but appears to have been unrelated to Edward Stringer, a Lichfield artist whose name has often been cited, erroneously, in connection with the Service. Mrs Marjorie Carney, who has done extensive research on the Knutsford Stringers (proving, among other things, that Samuel committed suicide), thinks it likely that it was Thomas whom Wedgwood went to consult in April 1773, but since Samuel had recently done a number of views of local houses and gardens, he seems to me – despite his youth – to be

perhaps the likelier source for the advice given on this occasion.

12. Letter of 9 April 1773 cited above at note 5.

13. Wedgwood MS E25-18487, Wedgwood to Bentley, 14 August 1773.

14. Most of the drawings for the first issue had been designed in 1720 and 1721 (a few in 1722, 1723 and 1725). The next 24, published in 1727, covered Lincolnshire and Nottinghamshire and are all dated 1726. Thereafter, a new issue devoted to one or more counties came out every year, with all the prints generally bearing the date of the previous year. For information on the Bucks, see Hyde 1994.

15. Around 190 of the 420 plates were used from the 17 parts, and some 250 views were based on these. The average of 10 pictures from each 24-plate part is close to what was actually used, although the count for the first two volumes was higher – 20 from part 1, Yorkshire; and 15 from part 2, Lincolnshire and Nottinghamshire – and only 4 views were used from part 11, Kent.

16. Poniatowski 1914 Vol. 1 p. 120.

17. Letter sent from Peterhof and dated 25 June (o.s.); in Reddaway 1931.

18. See Cross 1980 pp. 219 ff.

19. E. Karabaeva, quoted in Hayden 1985 p. 29 n. 18.

20. This is how the prints of Wilton and West Wycombe appear in Sayer's 1775 catalogue (reprinted 1970 by the Holland Press, London). This also contains Sullivan's views of Oatlands, Esher, Cliveden, Ditchley Park, Wilton and Woburn Farm; Walker's views of Castle Howard and Studley Park; etc. etc.

21. *Arkhiv vneshnei politiki Rossii*, Moscow, *delo* 261, f. 69, cited in Cross 1985.

22. Wedgwood MS E25-18507, Wedgwood to Bentley, 10 December 1773.

23. 47 views were eventually based on the 16 prints.

24. There are more than 20 of these items known which were not finally included in the Service. They are discussed in Raeburn 1992 pp. 450–59.

25. Wedgwood MS E25-18487, Wedgwood to Bentley, 14 August 1773.

26. Wedgwood MS E25-18495.

27. Wedgwood MS E25-18498, Wedgwood to Bentley, 14 November 1773.

28. Wedgwood MS E25-18502, Wedgwood to Bentley, 27 November 1773.

29. A dish decorated with a view of Conway Castle might possibly also be based on a Devis drawing, and a few others may have been borrowed later from a collector. It could be that Devis wanted to charge more than Wedgwood and Bentley felt they could afford for the use of his drawings: see note 36.

30. An analysis of the list indicates, as one might expect, that the normal method of working was to have a batch of similar items – flat plates, round or oval dishes of various sizes, covers, compotiers etc. etc. – decorated using prints or drawings from only one or two groups of sources. As a result, when an item of a different kind or one decorated from a quite different source makes an unexpected appearance in a batch, it is likely that it was done later and given a 'free' number. Working from the evidence provided by the catalogue, it has been possible to prepare a reasonably accurate list of the order in which the Service was decorated. However, it is not always ascertainable whether a particular view or group of views comes in its natural place or has been interpolated and in some cases batches of numbers may have been assigned in advance, so that a detailed sequence cannot always be reconstructed. Running catalogues were kept in the Decorating Shop in both numerical and alphabetical order, and it was from these that Bentley's final catalogue was prepared, although this itself contains a number of errors. There is also a considerable amount of documentation in the Wedgwood Archive at Keele University of payments to painters at Chelsea in 1773 and 1774, including a number of detailed worksheets for painters who were paid wholly or partly on a piecework basis rather than at a daily rate. It is, however, frustratingly incomplete and often difficult to relate to individual pieces, so that it tends to obscure rather than clarify the detailed chronology, but in a few cases it does establish which painters were responsible for certain views, and in the entries which follow a few pieces are assigned to James Bakewell, Ralph Unwin and William Shuter. On the basis of this evidence, it should be possible to attribute a large number of the views to individual painters, since there are several clearly recognizable characteristics in each of their styles, but this would require a more detailed first-hand examination of all the surviving pieces in the Service, which has not yet been undertaken.

31. 'Hogarth's Act' passed in May 1735 allowed artists to claim copyright in their prints as long as they bore the date of issue, so that the great majority of prints of this period can be accurately dated. It is often necessary, however, to determine which edition of an engraving Bentley used, as so many were reissues.

32. Roughly 220 of these were included when the Service was eventually shipped.

33. Grose planned for his work to appear in 4 volumes, but the prints appeared in quite haphazard batches, which the purchaser was expected to have bound up once the work was completed. It is not clear how many prints were included in each issue, but those purchased at this time appear to have included all that had been issued up to 20 January 1774.

34. The majority of these are preserved in the library of the Society of Antiquaries, London.

35. Wedgwood MSS 32-5267-73, accounts from William Shuter, 5 February–13 July 1774.

36. From the outset Wedgwood had urged Bentley to try and find drawings in London, but in a letter of 1 December 1773 he wrote: 'A Guinea & half is too much per View, we can have some hundreds cheaper – but do not break off with the Gent[n]. – tell him if you please that I am coming to Town &c.' (Wedgwood MS E25-18503). The artist in question may well have been Anthony Devis: see note 26. A 'Volume of Views' purchased for 3 guineas on 7 February 1774 together with three prints from the engraver John Pye, then working on the new Wedgwood Queen's Ware catalogue, may have included some drawings, but it seems more likely that it refers to the copy of Boydell's *Collection of Views*.

37. Wedgwood MS E25-18508, 13 December 1773.

38. Apart from the Shugborough drawings (which are still in the house), drawings by Dall have been located that were used for a view of Beau Desert, Staffordshire, and a view of the Thames at Richmond. In addition, it seems likely that several of his Yorkshire views were used as well as views of Moor Park, Herts., and a view of Stratford-upon-Avon, and possibly others too.

39. See announcement in the *Public Advertiser* no.3038 of 1 June 1774, which Hilary Young kindly brought to my attention.

40. 'M[r] Pennants compliments attend Messr[s] Wedgwood & Bentley & begs they would accept the remainder of the Prints. He having sent the list to M[r] Hixon copperplate Printer in Russel Court who will deliver to either those wanted. Lichfield May 6th 1774' Wedgwood MS E59-10556.

41. Frank Hurlbutt reported having seen an oval creamware plaque with a polychrome view of Fingal's Cave and an inscription in Pennant's hand on the reverse: 'The gift of Mr. Wedgwood in return for some small services I had done him.' It had apparently been included in the sale of the effects of the Earl of Denbigh at Downing House. See Hurlbutt (n.d.).

42. The sixth of these 19-inch oval dishes (which has not survived) probably had a view of Christ Church, Oxford, based on an unknown source.

43. Letter of 1 December 1773, cited above in note 36.

44. Wedgwood MS E25-18498, Wedgwood to Bentley, 14 November 1773.

45. Letter of 19 June 1774, cited above, see note 6.

46. Wedgwood MS E6-4236A, cited in McKendrick 1964 p. 50.

47. See Lydia Liakhova's essay, Chapter 6.

48. From Gunning's diplomatic letter-books preserved in the British Library (Egerton MSS 2701-3). These provide a fascinatingly detailed account of Catherine's court and of Anglo-Russian relations during the period 1772–7 (see Raeburn, Voronikhina and Nurnberg 1995). The first extract quoted is from a letter dated 10/21 August (old and new style), the second 7/18 September 1772.

49. From the subscription sheet accompanying the prints of Colebrookdale engraved by François Vivares after Thomas Smith and George Perry, 1758.

THE FROG SERVICE IN RUSSIA

1. Georgi 1794 p. 682.

2. Hayden 1985 pp. 17–20.

3. Svetlov 1782 p. 7.

4. Harris 1845 pp. 198–199.

5. Kamer-fourier ceremonial register for 1779, 1 January to 1 July, St Petersburg, 1883, pp. 226–8.

6. Ibid. p.103.

7. Catherine the Great on her royal predecessors and contemporary sovereigns. Chesme Palace (The Conversation between the Portraits and the Medallions), Russian archive, 1907, Vol II, p. 516.

8. Kamer-fourier ceremonial register for 1777, St Petersburg, 1880, pp. 398–402.

9. Kamer-fourier ceremonial register for 1780, St Petersburg, 1888, pp. 469–77.

10. Kamer-fourier ceremonial register for 1781, St Petersburg, 1890, pp. 348–51.

11. Kamer-fourier ceremonial register for 1791, St Petersburg, 1890, pp. 146–55.

12. Kamer-fourier ceremonial register for 1795, St Petersburg, 1894, pp. 163–175.

13. Russian State Historical Archive (RGIA), F.468, op. 37, d.I, l.5.

14. Kudriavtseva 1994.

15. St Petersburg Gazette [Sankt-Peterburgskie Vedomosti], 1777, No. 87.

16. Goryainov 1908 pp. 602–3.

17. Russian State Historical Archive, F.470, op. 2 (106/540), d.44, l.9.

18. Ibid., l.65.

19. Russian State Historical Archive, F.469, op.13, d.471, ll.5ob.-20.

20. Russian State Historical Archive, F.469, op.9, d.2608, l.6.

21. Peterhof 1885 pp. 179-180.

22. Russian State Historical Archive, F.472, op.43 (472/2421), d.145, l.11.

23. Russian State Historical Archive, F.472, op.49, d.1146, l.5.

WEDGWOOD'S TRADE WITH RUSSIA

1. Wedgwood MS E25-18196, Wedgwood to Bentley, 24 March 1768.

2. Boulton Papers, Birmingham Central Library, Wedgwood to Boulton & Fothergill, 19 March 1768.

3. Wedgwood MS E30-22506, 15 July 1768.

4. Wedgwood MS E25-18258.

5. Wedgwood MS E30-32848, Lady Cathcart to Wedgwood 28 January and 8 February 1770.

6. Wedgwood MS E30-32849, Lady Cathcart to Wedgwood.

7. Wedgwood MS WM1444.

8. Wedgwood MS LHP, Wedgwood to Bentley, dated 21 and 22 April 1771.

9. Wedgwood MS E5-3792, John Wood to Peter Swift, dated 28 September 1774.

10. Wedgwood MS E5-3793, John Wood to Peter Swift, 29 September 1774.

11. Wedgwood MS E5-3794, John Wood to Peter Swift, 5 October 1774.

12. Wedgwood MS 14-13204A, from Williamson Esq. no surviving address, undated.

13. Wedgwood MS 11-9220, Falconbridge & Husband of Birmingham to Wedgwood.

14. Wedgwood MS E31-23273, Alexander Baxter to Wedgwood, 15 August 1769.

15. Wedgwood MS E2-1140, Edmund Radcliffe to Wedgwood, 30 September 1774.

16. Wedgwood MS E30-22508, Lady Cathcart to Wedgwood, 28 January and 8 February 1770.

17. Wedgwood MS 30-22510, factory memorandum, undated.

18. Wedgwood MS E8-6911, John Tamesz & Co. of Moscow to Wedgwood, 14 June 1787.

19. Wedgwood MS E10-7986, sworn statement signed by Hamlet Wood.

20. Wedgwood MS E8-6855, Charles Hampeln to Wedgwood, undated.

21. Wedgwood MS 13-11923, Thomas Byerley to Wedgwood, 20 February 1813.

22. Wedgwood MS E25-18373, 18 April 1772.

23. Wedgwood MS E31-23273, Alexander Baxter to Wedgwood.

24. Wedgwood MS E2-1148, P. Paulet for Edmund Radcliffe to Wedgwood, 22 July 1775.

25. Wedgwood MS 12-10384, Wedgwood to Peter Swift, 19 July 1787.

26. Wedgwood MS 30968, Mr Graves to Wedgwood, 1789.

27. Wedgwood MS 12-10221, Thomas Byerley to Wedgwood.

28. Wedgwood MS E7-30360, Wedgwood to Otto Edvald Settler, 26 August 1773.

29. Wedgwood MS 13-12465, Thomas Byerley to Wedgwood.

30. Wedgwood MS 13-12451.

31. Wedgwood MS 11-90220, Falconbridge & Husband to Wedgwood, 16 August 1777.

32. Wedgwood MS 12-10205, Thomas Byerley to Etruria, undated.

33. Wedgwood MS 12-10984, Trout & Bourgeoi of Birmingham to Wedgwood, 8 October 1777.

34. Wedgwood MS 12-10496, Etruria memorandum, 19 March 1789.

35. Wedgwood MS 107-20192, Mr Ohm to Wedgwood, 1783.

36. Wedgwood MS E120-23307, Benjamin Hawksford to Wedgwood.

37. Wedgwood MS E120-23308, Benjamin Hawksford to Wedgwood.

38. Wedgwood MS E12-11370, Peter Capper for Wedgwood, 12 June 1786.

39. Wedgwood MS E12-32853, from St Petersburg to Wedgwood, 12 June 1786.

40. Wedgwood MS 12-32853, from St Petersburg to Wedgwood, 12 June 1787.

41. Wedgwood MS 12-11371, Peter Capper to Wedgwood.

42. Wedgwood MS E53-10586, Peter Capper to Wedgwood, 9 January 1789.

43. Wedgwood MS 120-23309, written by Benjamin Hawksford from St Petersburg, 1786.

44. Wedgwood MS 2-1130, Edmund Radcliffe to Wedgwood, 9 January 1774.

45. Wedgwood MS 12-10267, Thomas Byerley to Peter Swift, 29 March 1785.

46. Wedgwood MS 12-10904, Thomas Byerley to Peter Swift.

47. Wedgwood MS E25-18650.

48. Wedgwood MS E25-18455, Wedgwood to Bentley, 9 April 1773.

49. Wedgwood MS E84-14951.

INDEX

PHOTOGRAPHIC ACKNOWLEDGEMENTS

Pls 16, 22, 23, 25, 26, 31, 33, 34, 35, 36, 37, 38 and catalogue
illustrations G14, G26, G28, G31, G33, G44, G47, G55, G59,
G89, G96, G99, G111, G132, G137, G215, G316, G135,
G151, G163, G164, G172, G175, G180, G194, G196, G200,
G217, G223, G224, G225, G232, G236, G238, G242, G244,
G246, G247, G248, G255, G258, G269, G271, G274, G281,
G282, G286, G292, G293, G294, G299, G306, G308, G311,
G318, G319 © 1995 State Hermitage, St Petersburg
    Pl. 29 and catalogue illustration G237 © The British Library
    Pls 27, 28 and catalogue illustrations C7, C16, F19 ©
Trustees of the British Museum
    Pl. 40 © Manchester City Art Galleries
    Catalogue illustration G255 © Manchester Public Libraries
(Local Studies Unit)
    Pls 12, 41 and catalogue illustrations C22, D22, D41 ©
Trustees of the National Museums and Galleries on Merseyside
    Catalogue illustrations C12, D34, D37, D64 © Nottingham
City Museums
    Catalogue illustration E30 © Russell-Cotes Art Gallery and
Museum, Bournemouth
    Pl. 9 © City of Stoke-on-Trent Museum and Art Gallery
    Pls 1, 2, 3, 5, 6, 8, 11, 17, 21, 24, 30, 32, 42 and catalogue
illustrations A7, A13, B4, B5, B6, B10, B18, B20, B23, B30,
B31, B39, B53, B55, B56, C5, C6, C9, C10, C18, C20, C24,
C27, C29, C30, C34, D21, D29, D30, D32, D33, D36, D38,
D40, D43, D46, D47, D57, E1, E8, E9, E14, E19, E23, E26,
E27, E29, E33, E39, F8, F10, F12, F15, G42, G109, G117 ©
Trustees of the Victoria and Albert Museum
    Pls 4, 7, 10, 13, 14, 15, 18, 19, 20, 39 and catalogue
illustrations B8, B9, B15, B25, B26, B46, B52, B60, B62, C26,
C28, D2, D4, D18, D28, D55, D56, D69, E5, E6, E7, E11, E17,
E20, E22, E31, E32, F18, G204, G320, G323, G327 © Trustees
of the Wedgwood Museum
    Cover illustrations © as indicated above and in the
catalogue.